Between One and Many
The Art and Science of Public Speaking

Second Edition

Steven R. Brydon
Michael D. Scott
California State University, Chico

Mayfield Publishing Company
Mountain View, California
London ▪ Toronto

To our students, who have taught us well

Library of Congress Cataloging-in-Publication Data
Brydon, Steven R.
  Between one and many : the art and science of public speaking / Steven R.
Brydon, Michael D. Scott.—2nd ed.
    p. cm.
  Includes bibliographical references and index.
  ISBN 1-55934-589-6
  1. Public speaking. I. Scott, Michael D. II. Title.
  808.5'1—dc20   96-15053
                                                                                  CIP

International Standard Book Number information:
Text only   1-55934-589-6
Text with videotape and video guide   1-55934-776-7
Videotape and video guide   1-55934-758-9

Manufactured in the United States of America
10 9 8 7 6 5 4 3 2

Mayfield Publishing Company
1280 Villa Street
Mountain View, CA 94041

Sponsoring editor, Holly J. Allen; developmental editors, Jane Townsend and
Kathleen Engelberg; production editor, Julianna Scott Fein; manuscript editor,
Margaret Moore; art director, Jeanne M. Schreiber; text and cover designer,
Nancy Benedict; art manager, Jean Mailander; illustrator, Joan Carol; photo re-
searcher, Brian Pecko; manufacturing manager, Amy Folden; cover art, Lauren
Uram. The text was set in 9.5/12 Stone Serif by York Graphic Services and
printed on acid-free 45# Mead Publisher's Matte by Quebecor Printing Book
Group.

Preface

Public speaking is a dynamic transaction between speaker and audience, one in which the meaning of the message emerges from the relationship between the one who is speaking and the many who are listening. Because of the transactional nature of public speaking, no speaker can succeed without knowing his or her audience, and no audience member can benefit by just passively receiving a message. Both speaker and audience—and the transaction between them—are essential to successful public speaking. As teachers and as authors, we emphasize the transactional nature of public speaking as a crucial characteristic of this complex undertaking.

We also emphasize the fact that public speaking is an art, a science, and a skill—one that can be learned, improved, and finely honed. We encourage students to think of public speaking as a learning process—they don't have to be perfect at the outset!—and we offer them the tools to become the speakers they want to be. Public speakers can draw from a vast body of information on this art and science, ranging from the rhetorical theories to empirical communication research. In this book, we emphasize both traditional topics, such as logos, ethos, and pathos, and current approaches, such as thinking of public speaking as an opportunity to become an opinion leader—an influential figure in the lives of audience members.

Today's students of public speaking will face many different rhetorical situations in their lives, and they will face audiences of increasing cultural, demographic, and individual diversity. Throughout this book, we focus on ways to adapt to audiences in order to have the best chance of being heard and understood. We stress the responsibilities and ethical issues involved in being a good public speaker. And we discuss how to be a good audience member: one who knows how to listen, to behave ethically, and to critically evaluate the message being presented.

In sum, we attempt to provide students with a broad understanding of the nature of public speaking as well as the specific skills they need to become successful, effective public speakers, both as college students and throughout their lives.

FEATURES OF THE BOOK

Integrated Text and Video *Between One and Many* provides an *integrated* package of text and videotape for the students (and was the first book to do so in 1994). This twelve part videotape brings to life the theories and skills discussed in the text. Rather than simply reading examples of speeches and perhaps seeing them in class, students can view and study speeches and delivery styles on their own time and at their own pace. Text and video are coordinated so that students see examples of the type of speech they are studying throughout the course, along with a commentary and critique. This technique allows us to reinforce our points through modeling, which research has shown to be an excellent way to learn skills like public speaking.

Instructors can, of course, use *Between One and Many* without adopting the videotape for student use. The concepts and skills required for effective public speaking are fully described and illustrated in the text. Annotated outlines and the full texts of student speeches are included to show students how to apply the principles discussed in the book to actual speech situations.

Emphasis on Critical Thinking   Central to effective and ethical communication are the abilities to critically evaluate evidence, to present sound reasoning in one's speeches, and to detect fallacious reasoning in the speeches of others. *Between One and Many* has a strong critical thinking component, based on Toulmin's model of argument. Also included is an extensive discussion of the most common fallacies of reasoning.

Help for Speech Anxiety   We recognize that most students come to a public speaking class with considerable trepidation. We devote a full chapter early in the text to speech anxiety, as well as a segment of the videotape. The text and video package offers many specific, concrete techniques that students can use to manage and even benefit from anxiety.

Focus on Opinion Leadership   Beginning in the first chapter and continuing throughout the book, we focus on opinion leadership. We want students to understand the opportunities for leadership that will come to them in their personal, professional, and public lives if they become effective public speakers.

Integrated Pedagogy   Throughout the text, boxes are used to focus attention on subjects of special interest. Four different types of boxes appear: profiles of individuals who have used public speaking to enrich their lives, self-assessment instruments, speech excerpts illustrating principles discussed in the chapter, and discussions of skills-related issues.

HIGHLIGHTS OF THE SECOND EDITION

Based on the feedback from many instructors who used the first edition, we have incorporated a number of changes into this edition that we believe strengthen the book.

Stronger Emphasis on Audience This edition places a stronger emphasis on the audience. Each of the skills chapters now begins with an explicit discussion of how the skill presented can be guided by the speaker's analysis of the audience and the situation.

Expanded Treatment of Audience Diversity We give more attention to audience diversity in this edition. We base our discussion, in part, on Geert Hofstede's work on understanding cultural diversity. Using Hofstede's dimensions of collectivism and individualism, power and distance, uncertainty avoidance, masculinity and femininity, and long-term versus short-term orientation, we offer ideas on how to analyze and adapt to audience diversity.

New Chapter on Ethics This edition includes a full chapter on ethics. Working from basic ethical principles, we provide ethical guidelines for both public speakers and audience members.

Streamlined Organization For this edition we have streamlined the organization of the book. Students move more quickly through the necessary background material and get to the "nuts and bolts" of speechmaking earlier. Important topics have not been sacrificed; rather, we have consolidated material that was distributed among several different chapters in the first edition.

Skills Lists Throughout the book, speechmaking skills are highlighted in special Skills Lists. These lists make it easy for the student to apply practical suggestions to their own speeches.

Use of Computer Technology Extensive coverage of online library research is now included in the book. We discuss the use of both the Internet and the World Wide Web.

Updated Material Examples have been updated throughout the book, and new student speeches have been included both in the text and on the videotape.

ORGANIZATION OF THE TEXT

Between One and Many is organized to allow students to get up and speak early in the semester. As they learn more about the art and science of public speaking, they are also preparing for more demanding speaking assignments. We hope that our organizational scheme will suit the needs of most instructors, but we also know that different instructors have different preferences for how material is sequenced. Therefore, we have designed each chapter to stand alone. Instructors can assign them in the order that best matches their own course plan. Additionally, instructors may choose to use a segment of the videotape in lieu of assigning a chapter in the text. For example, the video segment on visual aids could be used early in the semester if visual aids were required for an early speech; the text chapter could be assigned later.

Part One deals with the foundations of the art and science of public speaking. In Chapter 1 we discuss the personal, professional, and public reasons for becoming a good public speaker. We also introduce basic theories of communication. The topic of opinion leadership is introduced in this chapter and continued in later ones. Chapter 2 provides an overview of the skills needed by public speakers and allows instructors to assign speeches early on without having to assign chapters out of order. Chapter 3 provides students with the tools they need to cope with the nearly universal experience of speech anxiety. Chapter 4 presents an expanded treatment of listening, a topic that we believe must be introduced early.

Part Two deals directly with adapting to the audience. We make explicit what was implicit in the first edition—that the key to success in public speaking is focusing on the audience. Chapter 5 weaves together topics that were distributed throughout several chapters in the first edition. We continue to use Bitzer's concept of the rhetorical situation as an organizing principle, but we now focus more on adapting to diverse audiences. We also introduce a new scheme for analyzing cultural diversity. Chapter 6 opens up the topic of ethical communication behavior, both by speakers and by audience members.

Part Three is about putting theory into practice. Chapter 7 covers invention; the chapter includes new sections on focusing on the audience and using the Internet. Chapter 8 treats organization from an audience-focused perspective. We include a variety of organizational patterns, including Monroe's Motivated Sequence, the Extended Narrative, and a Problem-Solution format based on a stock issues perspective. Chapter 9 addresses language use, with particular attention to adapting language to diverse audiences. We suggest ways to choose language that is inclusive rather than exclusive, nonsexist rather than sexist, and thoughtful rather than stereotypic. Chapter 10 deals with delivery skills, again focusing on audience adaptation. The chapter provides both a strong theoretical foundation based in nonverbal communication research and solid, practical advice for the public speaker. Chapter 11 presents a comprehensive discussion of visual, audio, and audiovisual materials that can be adapted to the audience and occasion to enhance most public speeches.

Part Four addresses the most common contexts for public speaking that students are likely to face in the classroom and in their lives after college. Chapter 12 treats informative speaking as an important part of the opinion leadership process. In this chapter we again stress audience adaptation, particularly in terms of diverse learning styles. Practical applications of learning principles are shown for speeches that explain, instruct, demonstrate, and describe. Chapter 13 introduces persuasive speaking with an audience focus. This chapter integrates the traditional Aristotelian principles of speaking with modern models of the persuasive process, such as the Elaboration Likelihood Model and Toulmin's model of reasoning. The principles of persuasion are illustrated with annotated texts of persuasive messages from both a student and a public figure. Chapter 14 provides a detailed treatment of critical thinking, with a special focus on recognizing and responding to fallacies of reasoning. Principles of critical thinking are illustrated by the annotated text of a persuasive message by a public figure. Chapters 13 and 14 are closely related; together, they provide students with a solid foundation in the use of sound reasoning in persuasion. Finally, Chapter 15 provides a discussion of speaking in everyday life. It includes helpful guidelines for impromptu speaking; speeches of acceptance, introduction, recognition, and commemoration; speeches to entertain; and speaking on television.

TEACHING SUPPORT PACKAGE

The textbook is part of a comprehensive package designed to help you solve teaching problems in your public speaking course.

Instructor's Manual   Written by the authors and updated with the assistance of Susan Christensen, an experienced college instructor, the instructor's manual includes suggested in-class teaching activities, sample semester and quarter syllabi, sample evaluation forms and numerous teaching suggestions based on the authors' collective four decades of experience. Many of the activities and materials in the manual have been class-tested with thousands of students enrolled in the basic public speaking course at California State University, Chico.

Printed and Computerized Test Items   Approximately 750 test questions, including multiple choice, true-false, and essay questions, are printed in the instructor's manual. Computerized versions of these test questions for both IBM and Macintosh platforms are available at no charge from the publisher, subject to minimum adoption requirements. As with other items in the instructional packet, many of these test questions have been class-tested.

Transparencies   Overhead color transparencies are available free of charge to adopting instructors. The transparencies illustrate and review major concepts from the text.

Teaching Assistant Materials   Programs employing graduate teaching assistants or other first-time instructors will receive two additional package components, free upon request, subject to minimum adoption requirements. One is a book, *Between Teachers and Students: A Primer for Teaching Assistants and First-Time Instructors*. The other is a videotape, *Agents of Change: Graduate Teaching Assistants in the Basic Course*. The guidebook and videotape answer many of the practical questions asked by first-time teachers—everything from what to do the first day of class to how to handle office-hour meetings with students.

Videotape   The videotape that accompanies this book is available at minimal cost to students when the book and tape are adopted together. The videotape for the second edition has been expanded to include topics not on the first tape, including sample introductions and conclusions. In addition, sample student speeches have been chosen from our best students in introductory speech classes, rather than from forensics competitors.

The two-hour video begins with a brief motivational introduction. It continues with segments in which students:

- are introduced to a model of communication
- view a sample speech
- learn how to manage their speech anxiety
- explore the issues of rhetorical sensitivity in a diverse society
- see effective speech delivery techniques in action
- see examples of effective introductions and conclusions
- view a demonstration of how to use visual aids
- watch sample informative and persuasive speeches followed by critiques
- see reasoning in action

Additional speeches are included at the end of the tape for students to evaluate on their own.

The videotape allows us to show what most texts only talk about. It also frees up valuable class time for the instructor and the student to use in other productive ways. Each segment can be viewed independently of the others and is coordinated with a specific chapter in the text. "Video File" boxes in the margin of the book indicate where a particular video segment would be appropriate. The video not only reinforces the text but also previews material to be covered later in the class in more depth.

We have found that over 70% of students currently own VCRs; those who do not can normally obtain access to them either through friends or campus libraries and study centers. When the text is ordered without the video, instructors may still request a copy to show during class time.

Accompanying each student's copy of the videotape is the *Video Guide*, a study guide designed to assist the student in getting maximum benefit from the videotape. It is available at no extra charge to the student.

ACKNOWLEDGMENTS

We gratefully acknowledge the support and assistance of many people at Mayfield Publishing Co. who played a role in this book, including Holly Allen, our sponsoring editor; Jane Townsend and Kate Engelberg, our developmental editors; Margaret Moore, our copyeditor, Julianna Scott Fein, our production editor, and Brian Pecko, our photo researcher.

We are especially grateful to George Rogers, of Chico State, who produced the videotape that accompanies this text, and Michele Hunkele, who narrated it. We thank the numerous students who consented to be videotaped for this project. Special thanks go to the speakers who shared their talents in providing sample speeches: Sally Garber, Kelli Wells, Ryland G. Hill, Jr., David A. Sanders, Jonathan Studebaker, Jennie Rees, and Diedra Dukes.

We also would like to thank the individuals profiled in this book for generously consenting to contribute to our effort: Keith Hawkins, Jonathan Studebaker, Enrique "Rick" Rigsby, Russ Woody, and Madeline Keaveney. They are friends, colleagues, former students, and role models; they have all enriched our book and our lives.

A grateful thank you for the reviews and counsel of our peers in the classroom who graciously prepared careful critiques of our manuscript and videotape in various stages of development: Cecile S. Blanche, Villanova University; R. B. Bookwalter, Marshall University; Barbara L. Breaden, Lane Community College; Denys J. Gary, Lock Haven University; Angela Grupas, St. Louis Community College, Meramec; Lynn O'Neal Heberling, University of Akron; Rachel L. Holloway, Virginia Tech; Susan Stathas Houlihan, Santa Rosa Junior College; Diana K. Ivy, Texas A&M University, Corpus Christi; James A. Jaksa, Western Michigan University; Cynthia K. Matthews, New Mexico State University; Joyce N. Ngoh, Marist College; Sharon Porter, Northern Arizona University; Michael E. Scott, Shelby State Community College; Elayne J. Shapiro, University of Portland; Bill Snider, Valencia Community College; Jessica Stowell, Tulsa Junior College; Philip K. Taylor, University of Central Florida; Glenda J. Treadaway, Appalachian State University; and David Warne, Saint Cloud State University. We appreciate the help of all these individuals in preparing this book but we are, of course, ultimately responsible for its content. Any errors or omissions are solely our own.

And last, but certainly not least, we wish to thank our families, Pamela, Robert, Julie, Randi, and Colin, who not only showed great patience as we worked on this project but often provided assistance in more ways than we can possibly list.

Contents

PART TWO   Adapting to the Audience   115

CHAPTER 5   Audience-Focused Speaking: Mastering the Rhetorical Situation   117

CHAPTER 6   Ethical Speaking   155

PART THREE   Putting Theory into Practice   183

CHAPTER 7   Inventing Your Message   185

CHAPTER 8   Organizing Your Message   221

CHAPTER 9   Language: Making Verbal Sense of Your Message   257

CHAPTER 13   Persuasive Speaking   373

CHAPTER 14   Thinking and Speaking Critically   411

CHAPTER 15   Public Speaking in Everyday Life   449

PART ONE | Foundations

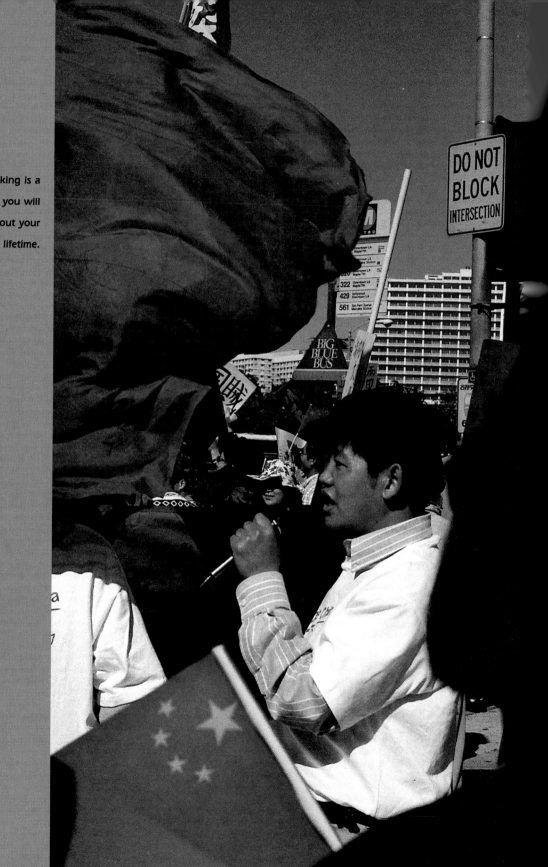

Public speaking is a skill that you will use throughout your lifetime.

1

An Invitation to Speak

If all my talents and powers were to be taken from me . . . and I had my choice of keeping but one, I would unhesitatingly ask to be allowed to keep the Power of Speaking, for through it, I would quickly recover all the rest.

—Daniel Webster

OBJECTIVES

After reading this chapter, you should be able to:

- Describe the relationship between personal needs and the ability to speak publicly.
- Discuss ways public speakers can be potential opinion leaders.
- Discuss the role public speaking plays in the professional promotion of self.
- Describe the public reasons for developing skill in public speaking.
- Demonstrate an understanding of the transactional and symbolic nature of public speaking.

KEY CONCEPTS

In each chapter we will introduce you to some key terms you need to know. We place these at the beginning of each chapter to alert you to important concepts you will encounter. In this chapter look for the following terms:

channel
content [of messages]
decoding
deficiency needs
encoding
feedback
growth needs

interaction
linear
opinion leader
relational component [of messages]
symbol
transaction

Martin Luther King, Jr., stirred the conscience of America when he proclaimed "I have a dream . . ."

How many times have you delivered a public speech in the past 10 years? Who are the people who commonly come to mind when you think about public speaking, and what are the circumstances in which you imagine these people speaking?

If you're like most students, you've given very few speeches in the past 10 years. And, when you think of people who do give speeches, you probably think of public figures. You may remember Hillary Rodham Clinton addressing the 1995 United Nations conference on women in Beijing, China. You may think of Martin Luther King, Jr.'s, "I Have a Dream" speech, delivered in 1963 to hundreds of thousands assembled before the Lincoln Memorial in Washington, D.C. Or you may picture Newt Gingrich speaking before a cheering crowd of conservative activists.

These highly publicized speaking events bear little relationship to the speaking situations most people face in their everyday lives. As you will see in this chapter, public speaking is a very important skill to cultivate. But as you will also see, it is not an utterly foreign activity undertaken only by highly prominent public figures. Instead, it is an extension and refinement of your everyday communication encounters. Our goal, then, is to show you the importance of public speaking to your life and how it fits in with your other communication experiences. This will include discussion of (1) *personal* reasons for becoming a skilled speaker; (2) *professional* reasons for developing speaking skills, including becoming an opinion leader;

(3) *public reasons* for developing speaking skills, including becoming an agent of change in a democratic society; and (4) the process of *public speaking as a transaction.*

PERSONAL REASONS FOR DEVELOPING SPEAKING SKILLS

Although we may not consciously realize it, human communication is a need as basic to our well-being as the food we eat, water we drink, and air we breathe. Both clinical and case studies compellingly show that when we are deprived of this need, we are affected both physically and psychologically. Human communication is also the primary medium through which we *satisfy* our needs and help others satisfy theirs. If it were not for this unique ability to articulate our needs, it is doubtful we would have survived as a species. An immediate benefit of learning to become a better speaker, consequently, is the ease with which you'll be able to communicate your needs and help others communicate theirs. See the box "Accepting the Challenge: Keith Hawkins" for the story of one person who turned his life around by developing speaking skills.

Satisfying Your Personal Needs

Abraham Maslow wrote that we experience two sets of personal needs: deficiency needs and growth needs.[1] **Deficiency needs** are basic human needs, which must be satisfied before higher-order needs can be met. **Growth needs** are higher-order human needs, which can be satisfied only after deficiency needs have been met. Maslow arranged these two sets of needs in the form of a hierarchy, with deficiency needs at the base and growth needs at the top. This arrangement was meant to show that our deficiency needs must be satisfied routinely before our growth needs will become important to us.

As Figure 1.1 indicates, there are four sets of deficiency needs: (1) *biological needs,* such as food, water, and air; (2) *safety needs,* such as protection from physical harm; (3) *belongingness and love needs,* such as those experienced by a child for the love of a parent; and (4) *self- and social-esteem needs,* which involve believing in our self-worth and finding confirmation from others of that belief.

Growth needs are not as straightforward as deficiency needs. They include self-actualization, knowledge and understanding, and aesthetic needs. According to Maslow, *self-actualization* is the process of fully realizing one's potential. Self-actualized people not only understand themselves but also accept themselves for who they are and what they have achieved.

The ability to present skillfully our thoughts and feelings publicly is increasingly important to the satisfaction of both our deficiency needs and

VIDEO FILE

If you have access to the videotape that accompanies this book, view segment 1, which includes statements from students who have found a course in public speaking challenging and fulfilling.

Accepting the Challenge: Keith Hawkins

Keith Hawkins's life reads like a scene out of a movie about inner-city life. Born to a teenage mother in South Central Los Angeles, abandoned by his father, and forced to live in a one-room shack in rural Florida by his mother's crack-addicted boyfriend, Keith was never in one school for more than 6 months until he was 13 years old. Passed from one grade to the next, even though he needed to be held back, he lacked basic skills in reading, writing, and math.

In the 10th grade, Keith had a life-changing experience. His best friend and football teammate was murdered. After the funeral, Keith's coach handed him his friend's jersey and issued him a challenge—to do something his friend had never done, despite being a star athlete: Stay out of trouble and make something of his life.

Not only did Keith accept the challenge, but his football coach became his mentor. In the process he became a better student, held office in his statewide student government association, and discovered a talent other than sports.

Specifically, Keith learned not only that he enjoyed speaking before groups, but that he was pretty good at it. As a result, he took classes in speaking and received advanced training while he was serving as president of the California Association of Student Governments. He also began speaking to groups of kids with backgrounds similar to his own.

Today, Keith is a college sophomore majoring in communication, a football player, and a paid public speaker. He has traveled throughout the United States speaking to youth groups, schools, and even an assembly of the United Nations. Articles about Keith have appeared in the *New York Times* and *Time* magazine. Keith's long-term goal is to become a professional speaker. He says this about his still young life, "I feel you need three things in life: Something to do, something to hope for, and someone to love. Speaking gives me something to do, and the kids who come up to me afterwards to talk give me something to hope for, and someone to love."

our growth needs. Just how important public speaking can be to our survival is exemplified by the fact that through public speaking, leaders from throughout the world influence others about ways to protect the environment, including the very air we breathe.

Public speaking is equally relevant to the satisfaction of psychological deficiency needs. Self-esteem is one such need all of us experience. Satisfaction of that need has been linked to success in life. Rare is the person who doesn't admire and value people who can "stand and deliver" publicly. In fact, we admire and value such people so much, we are willing to

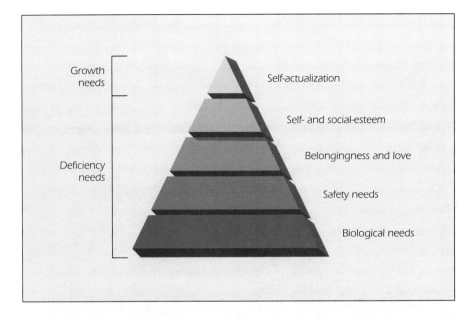

FIGURE 1.1
Maslow's hierarchy of needs. (Based on Abraham Maslow, *Motivation and Personality,* 2nd ed. [New York: Harper & Row, 1970]. Adapted with permission from Michael D. Scott and William G. Powers, *Interpersonal Communication: A Question of Needs* [Boston: Houghton Mifflin, 1978], 10.)

pay to listen to them or to hire them to speak for us. For example, there are between 400 and 500 professional speakers in this country whose annual incomes are in the range of $100,000 and above. In addition, there are thousands of unpaid speakers who draw large audiences around the country—from college campuses to county fairs. It seems reasonable to suggest that their own satisfaction of self-esteem needs stems at least in part from their public speaking skills. As you become increasingly skilled as a speaker, the reinforcement you can expect from others will tell you that they value you and that you have every right to value yourself.

Meeting the Personal Needs of Others

Your skill as a speaker also can empower others to satisfy their own deficiency and growth needs. Often people need someone who can bring their needs into better focus and enable them to act to meet those needs. Actor/activist Edward James Olmos, star of *Stand and Deliver* and *Miami Vice,* spoke at the authors' campus on the topic "We Are All the Same Gang."[2] Having succeeded in meeting his personal and professional needs as a critically acclaimed actor, Olmos is now using his talents to speak out for the needs of others. He targets his message to those who are tempted to join gangs. His speeches promote peace, racial harmony, and the need for children to be vaccinated against violence. As he pointed out, "No child comes out of his mother's womb with a pistol."[3]

Despite his fame, actor and director Edward James Olmos continues to be a visible opinion leader in the Latino community. In this photo he is shown helping in the cleanup of South Central Los Angeles after the riots of 1992.

PROFESSIONAL REASONS FOR DEVELOPING SPEAKING SKILLS

Becoming an Opinion Leader

Because people generally resist changing their ways of thinking and behaving, they generally resist changing their opinions as well. This is true even when people are confronted with clear evidence that such change is warranted. Surgeons, for example, initially resisted the idea that they should operate under antiseptic conditions even when there was clear evidence to suggest that doing so would save lives. Military leaders resisted the idea that the armed forces should be racially integrated until after World War II. And today, some people continue to resist the idea that women should be given equal opportunity in business and the professions.

Opinions don't "just change." They have to come under the influence of some agent capable of convincing people that change is "the right thing to do." We call these agents of change opinion leaders. An **opinion leader** is a person who influences others to adopt innovative ideas, products, or processes.[4]

Regardless of the situation, opinion leaders seem to share a number of characteristics.[5] Some of these are: more formal education than the average person, greater openness to innovation, heightened empathic abilities, and

Opinion Leadership and the Story of the Post-it Note

Have you ever wondered how those sticky little yellow notes called Post-its ever came into being? They were invented by a scientist at 3M by the name of Arthur Fry. According to the video *In Search of Excellence* (based on the book of the same name by Thomas J. Peters and Robert H. Waterman, Jr.), Fry became frustrated when the papers he used to mark his place in his church hymnal kept falling out. So he used a weak adhesive, the kind 3M normally would reject, to create something that would temporarily stick to the page but could be removed without damaging the page. He made up samples and had his secretary distribute them to his bosses' secretaries. Once the secretaries were addicted to the handy notes, he stopped distributing them. Of course his bosses were intrigued and immediately saw the potential for sales. But how did 3M convince other companies to buy the sticky yellow notes?

3M CEO Lewis Lehr had his secretary distribute them to the executive secretaries of the nation's top 500 CEOs (the so-called *Fortune* 500). The same thing happened as had occurred when they were distributed internally at 3M. Soon 3M was getting calls for more of the notes—the idea had caught on. As of 1985, 3M was doing $200 million a year in the sales of Post-it notes. Today, virtually every office in America has them.

Notice that the key opinion leaders in this process were the secretaries. By virtue of their central role in the communication pattern of their organization, they were able to spread the use of the innovative sticky yellow notes.

SOURCE: *In Search of Excellence* [videorecording]. (Boston: Nathan/Tyler Productions, 1985.)

a high degree of social involvement. These characteristics increase a person's chances of becoming an effective public speaker. Education broadens a person's knowledge and perspective; greater openness to innovation is essential to becoming an agent of change. Empathic abilities are important to public speakers in analyzing and adapting to their audiences. And social involvement means that a person has experience interacting and communicating with others. One case of successful innovation is described in the box "Opinion Leadership and the Story of the Post-it Note."

The process of opinion leadership begins with two steps closely related to public speaking: knowledge and persuasion.

Knowledge   One of your early assignments is likely to be an informative speech. Your goal, like that of the opinion leader, should be to present audience members with information that is potentially valuable to them.

Consider the case of a new computer program, such as Windows 95. Although Bill Gates, founder and chairman of Microsoft Corporation, initiated the development of this new operating system for IBM-compatible computers, awareness of the program has been created by those who establish a connection between the software developers and the public. An example is computer columnist Steve Levy, who writes regularly for *Newsweek* and *Macworld,* discussing the latest developments in the computer world. He cuts through the hype about the latest software, providing reliable information to his readers. As an opinion leader he links the developer of new software and the average consumer by explaining the latest innovations.

Persuasion   Another class assignment you are likely to face is a persuasive speech. The goal of a persuasive speech is to modify, change, and sometimes reinforce what audience members think. While it's one thing to present an audience with information that should make it more knowledgeable, it's another to convince the audience to *act* on the basis of this newly acquired knowledge. Besides informing audiences about the latest innovations in computers, such as Microsoft's Windows 95, opinion leaders like Levy are often instrumental in persuading them to adopt the innovations.

Promoting Your Professional Self

As a potential opinion leader, you will have the opportunity to enhance your professional credibility. Some time ago the authors of this text were treated to a presentation by Dr. Bonnie Johnson. She spoke about work she had done for Intel, the world's largest manufacturer of silicon chips. As someone trained in organizational communication, she was given permission by Intel to study how well personnel were adapting to technological change in the workplace—for example, electronic work stations. At the conclusion of her study, Intel offered her a position with the corporation.

Following her presentation, Dr. Johnson welcomed questions from the audience. One undergraduate asked her why she thought Intel hired her. "Do you want to know candidly?" she asked. "Because initially they were more impressed with the public presentation I made to top management on the results of my study than the study itself. They hired me because I not only knew my subject but could effectively speak about it and its implications for Intel."

As exemplified by Dr. Johnson's anecdote about her experience with Intel, communication skills in general and public speaking skills specifically are both desired and rewarded in the workplace. Surveys of personnel managers consistently demonstrate that they look for college graduates who not only can communicate interpersonally and in writing but who also can deliver a speech well. Ask just about anyone who has climbed the corporate ladder, and you will learn that public speaking skills helped tremendously along the way.

Presenting Ideas to Decision Makers

Another reason organizations put such a high premium on speaking skills concerns the effective communication of ideas. Your success depends not only on your ideas but also on how well you can present those ideas to people whose decisions will affect your career. When you think about it, every occupation and profession involves selling ideas to other people. For example, the life insurance salesperson who must persuade a client to increase coverage is unlikely to close the deal by simply dropping a brochure in the mail. On a larger scale, most corporations require managers to present reports or briefings describing their accomplishments and future plans and goals. Those individuals who seek to move beyond entry-level positions need to be able to convince others of the wisdom of their ideas. Thus, being able to speak to decision makers with confidence and authority is an indispensable tool for corporate success.

For example, Dave Davies, a developer of laser disks who worked for 3M, had to present his case orally—a request for $20 million in investment in a new product—to an executive operations committee of the company, including the CEO and the heads of major divisions. His whole future with the company and that of his division were riding on his presentation that day. Although Davies was a scientist, his future and that of his product depended on his ability to speak in public.[6] His success in obtaining the investment money was attributable not only to his product but to his ability to convince the executives that it would be a profitable enterprise for 3M.

Creating Change in the Workplace

One of the most important tasks for any supervisor or manager is to be able to convince subordinates that proposed changes are desirable. To remain competitive, companies must implement new technologies and procedures. Yet many employees fear change. Often the best way to implement change is to sell employees on new ideas rather than to give them orders. A willing and enthusiastic work force is far more likely to accept change in the workplace than is a reluctant and suspicious one.

In addition, change need not always be initiated from the top. Many of the best ideas in industry come from employees who convince their managers that change is necessary. Consider the example of America's most successful retail store, Wal-Mart, whose founder, Sam Walton, believed in listening to his employees. He claimed: "Our best ideas come from clerks and stockboys."[7] He once rode 100 miles in a Wal-Mart truck just to talk to the driver.

Lest you believe that this approach is unique, companies as diverse as Delta Airlines and Hewlett-Packard also listen to their employees. For example, "Delta spends a lot of time and money . . . checking out the employee's side of the story. Often the result is a substantial policy change," according to management consultants Tom Peters and Robert Waterman.[8] They report that senior management at Delta meet in an "open forum" at least once a year. Those in the lowest ranks of the organization have the opportunity to directly communicate with those at the highest levels. And Hewlett-Packard has an "open lab stock" policy that allows workers to take equipment home for their personal use, in the hope that they might come up with an innovation.[9] Successful organizations don't just talk to their employees, they listen to them as well.

Becoming a Functioning Force in Meetings

Although small group communication is not the principal focus of this book, many of the skills we discuss—ranging from active listening to critical thinking to making impromptu presentations—are directly applicable to functioning in group meetings. As Communication Professor Ronald Adler reports, the average business executive spends about 45 minutes out of every hour communicating, much of this time in meetings.[10] Further, surveys show that executives spend a large amount of their time in meetings: about 700 hours per year according to one study, 46 percent of their time according to another.[11] Your ability to speak effectively in meetings will be indispensable to success in the workplace.

Developing Active Listening Skills

It is not enough to know how to present your ideas to others. You need to listen to the needs of others and to what they say in response to your ideas. On the average we spend up to 55 percent of our day in situations that involve the potential to listen.[12] Seldom, however, do we take full advantage of this potential. Active listening, which we discuss at length in Chapter 4, is essential to your development as a speaker. First, you won't have anything important to say unless you have listened actively to those around you. Second, listening will make you more effective in working with people. Study after study demonstrates that people who actually hear what is being communicated to them are much more responsive to others than those who listen with "only one ear." Responsiveness, moreover, is one of the distinguishing characteristics of the effective communicator.

Public speaking skills will help your development as a listener. For example, learning to give an effective speech requires the ability to organize your thoughts and highlight key points for listeners. As you learn to do this for your speeches, you will also learn how to organize the information you receive from speakers, separating the important ideas from the unimportant. Speakers have to learn how to research and support their ideas. As a listener, you will need to evaluate the research and support speakers provide to you. In fact, almost every public speaking skill we will discuss has a parallel skill for the listener.

PUBLIC REASONS FOR DEVELOPING SPEAKING SKILLS

Opinion leaders serve as agents of change not only in the workplace but in the larger world as well. Were it not for those who spoke out publicly, the voting age would still be 21 and only men would be able to vote. All the progress of the past century has resulted from opinion leaders coming up with new and sometimes controversial ideas and persuading others of the wisdom of adopting them.

Becoming a Critical Thinker

As we discuss at length in Chapter 14, the ability to think critically about your own messages and those of others is essential to reaching sound conclusions about the issues of the day. Not only should speakers strive to base their persuasive efforts on sound reasoning, listeners need to take the responsibility to detect fallacious reasoning. Some arguments that seem valid actually contain flaws that render them invalid. Becoming a critical thinker will make you less susceptible to phony arguments and less prone to engage in them yourself.

Functioning as an Informed Citizen

Our nation is a democratic republic based on the premise that for our country to thrive there must be a free exchange of ideas. Thus, it is no accident that the First Amendment to the Constitution guarantees freedom of speech, as well as freedom of the press, religion, and peaceable assembly. The fundamental premise of our constitution is that the people must have the information necessary to make informed decisions. Even if you never have occasion to speak on an issue of public policy, you will be the consumer of countless speeches on every issue imaginable. The ability to forcefully and publicly present your thoughts to others—whether as a speaker or as an audience member questioning the speaker—is more than a desirable skill. It is also a responsibility.

Preserving Freedom of Speech

For some people, the way to deal with unpopular ideas is to invoke a quick fix—censorship. One of our goals in this book is to give you an apprecia-

VIDEO FILE

If you have access to the videotape that accompanies this book, view segment 2, which provides a brief introduction to the public speaking transaction.

tion for the importance of free speech in a democratic society. As more and more citizens are empowered to express their own views publicly, this should lead to vigorous debate about those ideas. Those who have confidence in the truth of their own view should welcome the opportunity to debate opposing views rather than suppress those views.

Raising the Level of Public Discourse

Regrettably, much of the public discourse of recent years has degenerated into name-calling and emotional appeals in response to controversial issues. While one can debate the substance of these issues—from abortion to Zionism—the tendency to polarize and attack on a personal level those who disagree has been pronounced in the recent past. Learning to focus one's public speaking skills on the substance of a controversy rather than the personality of an opponent is an important step in raising the level of public discourse. As more Americans learn how to make their views known rationally, and learn the critical thinking skills necessary to evaluate public discourse, the overall level of debate about issues in contemporary society is likely to improve.

THE PROCESS OF PUBLIC SPEAKING

Although this book deals with public speaking specifically, we recognize that public speaking is but one of many modes of human communication. We communicate one-on-one, in small groups, and through the mass media, as well as in public. Although each context in which we communicate has its own distinguishing features, certain principles of communication apply to all of them. Whether you focus on an intimate conversation between lovers or an informative speech before your class or a speech at a political rally, the process of communication is always transactional. A **transaction** is a simultaneous exchange of messages between two or more people. The **speech transaction** is the simultaneous exchange that occurs between public speakers and their audience. In this section and the next, we discuss the public speaking process as a form of communication that is both transactional and symbolic.

The Public Speaking Transaction

It may seem at first glance that public speaking is a one-way process, dominated by the speaker who conveys his or her ideas to audience members who simply listen and comply. Such a view of public speaking assumes the process is **linear,** moving in one direction, from cause to effect. But, in public speaking, as in other forms of communication, the process is not one-directional, moving from speaker to audience. It is not as if a speaker simply says the right words and the audience does what the speaker requests.

Clearly the audience has at least the potential to respond to the speaker. When audience members respond, both verbally and nonverbally to a speaker, this is known as **feedback.** Adding the concept of feedback as a kind of loop goes beyond a simple one-way model of public speaking. This perspective treats public speaking as an **interaction,** an exchange of messages between two or more people that has clear-cut steps with a beginning and an end. This is somewhat like a tennis match, where the speaker serves up a message and then waits for the audience to return it.

A *transactional* model of public speaking suggests the process is far more complex.[13] Rather than a linear interaction, public speaking is a simultaneous exchange between the *one* speaker and the *many* who form an audience. The basic components of the speech transaction include *source/receiver, encoding and decoding, message, channel, context,* and *perception.* These components occur *simultaneously* and are *interdependent.* This model is illustrated in Figure 1.2, and each of the components is discussed below.

Source/Receiver   A linear model treats the speaker as the sole source of communication in public speaking. From a transactional perspective, however, the speaker is primarily responsible for the spoken words of a speech, but the audience also produces numerous messages. These may be verbal, as in spoken questions or even heckling. They may also be nonverbal, as in applause, facial reactions, posture, and the like. The point is that *both* speakers and audience members are at the same time **sources and receivers** of messages. Unlike in the interaction model, with its added feedback loop, the audience does not wait for the speaker to complete a message. As soon as speaker and audience meet, the exchange of messages begins.

Encoding and Decoding   When someone seeks to convey ideas to other people, unless he or she is a practitioner of ESP, there is no way to directly communicate ideas. They must be converted into words or other codes that can be translated by those receiving the message. Thus, the process of communication requires **encoding** by the source, that is, translating ideas into a code that can be understood by receivers. **Decoding** is the process by which a code is translated back into ideas. If receivers and sources do not share common codes, the likelihood of effective communication is very low. Even those who speak the same language often have different interpretations of the same words. When the codes of communication become nonverbal, such as gestures, it becomes even more difficult to understand one another.

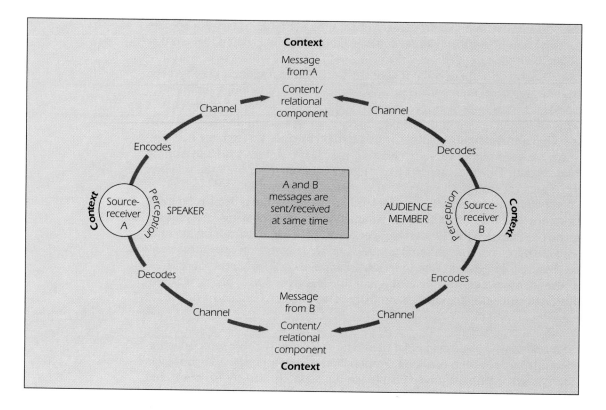

Context

Message
from A

Content/
relational
component

Channel   Channel

Encodes   Decodes

Context

Source-
receiver
A

Perception

SPEAKER

A and B
messages are
sent/received
at same time

AUDIENCE
MEMBER

Perception

Source-
receiver
B

Context

Decodes   Encodes

Channel   Channel

Message
from B

Content/
relational
component

Context

FIGURE 1.2

Public speaking as a transaction. In this model, messages are simultaneously conveyed between speakers and listeners, with both parties functioning as sources and receivers. Communication is bound by the context, and each person's perceptions are significant in interpreting the content and relational components of messages.

Message   The **message** is the meaning produced by communicators. In the transactional model, the message and the medium through which it travels are intentionally blurred. This is because the two are *interdependent*— not independent. What we would like to say to our audience is significantly affected by the manner in which we say it, and the way we convey the message is affected by what we want to say. This reciprocal process has a tremendous impact on how our message is perceived by our audience.

All messages are composed of two parts. The first part of the message is its **content,** the essential meaning, the gist or substance, of what a speaker wants to convey. For example, you might wish to convey your affection for another with the three words "I love you." The second part of the message, called its **relational component,** involves the collective impact of the verbal and nonverbal components of a message as it is conveyed. Consider how you might use your voice, face, and eyes to alter the impact of the words "I love you." You could make these three words an expression of sincere endearment, a plea, or even a statement of wanton desire.

Meaning is derived from both the content and the relational components. Moreover, neither component is subordinate to the other in its contribution to meaning. They are roughly proportional in this regard.

Channel   The **channel** is the physical medium through which communication occurs. The transmission of the light and sound waves that make up the picture you see on your TV set requires a channel through which they can be signaled and received. Picture and audio are encoded into electronic impulses which must be decoded by your television receiver. In human communication, we use our senses as channels for the messages we send and receive. We use our voice, eyes, and body, for example, to channel our speeches, conversations, and group discussions. On occasion, we also use our sense of touch, sense of smell, and even our sense of taste as channels of communication.

Context   In the transactional model, the boundaries of the public speaking system define the **context** in which communication occurs (see Figure 1.2). For example, the physical surroundings in which we speak have an impact on what we say and how we say it. How large or small, warm or cool, comfortable or uncomfortable a room is directly affects our overall communication behavior. So too do the seating arrangement, windows, wall decorations, lighting, and the purpose for which the room originally was intended.

Of course, context involves more than just the physical setting. There can be situational factors that affect context. Though a sermon, eulogy, and wedding can all take place in the physical setting of a place of worship, the situational context makes each a very different occasion. The historical setting is another contextual factor. For an example of a speech with an especially complex context, see the box "Ronald Reagan at Bergen-Belsen Concentration Camp."

Perception   Our transactional perspective demands that we both understand and appreciate the role of perception in public speaking. **Perception** is the process by which we give meaning to our experiences. It also is a highly selective process, as you are about to see.

Take a close look at the accompanying drawing by M. C. Escher. Though it appears at first glance that the water is running downhill, a more careful examination will tell you that this is impossible, since the water is flowing continuously. Escher was able to create "impossible illusions" by taking advantage of our perceptual predispositions. We assume that the perspective in this drawing is an accurate representation of reality, when, of course, it cannot be so. When people look at an ambiguous stimulus such as this picture, they automatically look for something familiar . . . something for which they have preexisting meaning. This helps fool the eye, in this case, into seeing something that cannot exist.

This tendency to perceive the familiar is both good and bad from the standpoint of public speaking. It is good because it enables us to establish a reference point quickly from which we can plan our own speaking

Ronald Reagan at Bergen-Belsen Concentration Camp

President Ronald Reagan delivered one of his most eloquent and moving speeches on May 6, 1985, at the Bergen-Belsen concentration camp, where some 60,000 persons, including Anne Frank, died at the hands of Nazis during World War II. As you read this excerpt, ask yourself what effect the historical context of a concentration camp had on the speech.

Everywhere here are memories—pulling us, touching us, making us understand that they can never be erased. Such memories take us where God intended His children to go—toward learning, toward healing, and above all, toward redemption. They beckon us through the endless stretches of our heart to the knowing commitment that the life of each individual can change the world and make it better.

We're all witnesses; we share the glistening hope that rests in every human soul. Hope leads us, if we're prepared to trust it, toward what our President Lincoln called the better angels of our nature. And then, rising above all this cruelty, out of this tragic and nightmarish time, beyond

the anguish, the pain, the suffering for all time, we can and must pledge: Never again.[1]

Public reaction to the speech was also affected by Reagan's visit earlier that day to the Bitburg military cemetery, where 49 members of the dreaded Nazi SS were buried. The context of Reagan's speech at the concentration camp included the fact that he had earlier visited the cemetery, despite widespread criticism from people like Nobel Peace Prize winner Elie Wiesel. The physical setting of a concentration camp, the historical setting of the Holocaust, and the immediate past action of visiting a cemetery where those who persecuted the Jews were buried influenced not only Reagan's speech but how it was perceived by different audiences.[2]

---

[1] Reprinted from *Weekly Compilation of Presidential Documents*, Vol. 21, No. 17, 29 April 1985, p. 587.

[2] Lou Cannon, *President Reagan: The Role of a Lifetime* (New York: Simon & Schuster, 1991).

behavior as well as interpret that of others. It's bad, on the other hand, because it can perceptually blind us to other data that may be even more important to how we behave and interpret the behavior of others.

Consider a cross-cultural example. Direct eye contact is perceived as a sign of attention and respect in most of North America. Thus, when giving a speech we use this knowledge to gauge how our audience is reacting to our message and delivery. This North American norm, however, is not universal. Direct eye contact in some cultures, such as certain Asian societies, is perceived as an aggressive sign of disdain and disrespect.

It's common, then, for unaware North Americans who speak in one of these cultures to walk away from the experience with their confidence se-

This print by
M. C. Escher creates
an "impossible illu-
sion" by taking
advantage of
our perceptual
predispositions.

verely shaken. They mistakenly perceive their audience's lack of eye contact with them as a sign of disapproval. This mistaken perception, in turn, usually has a negative influence on their entire speaking performance.

As a public speaker, therefore, you should never assume that your perceptions of people, places, and things are foolproof. Just because someone, some place, or some circumstance strikes you as familiar, that doesn't necessarily make it so.

Simultaneity As we noted earlier, in this model of public speaking, we are simultaneously sources and receivers—not one and then the other. Thus, **simultaneity,** the quality of occurring at the same time, is an important aspect of the communication transaction. Whereas this may be obvious in a face-to-face encounter with one other person, it may be less so when you think about one person communicating to many. You may be very conscious of the fact that as you talk with one person you are at the same time receiving a tremendous amount of information from the person nonverbally. Although you may be less conscious of it, the same is true when you speak in public. When we speak publicly we receive messages from people in our audience through their facial expressions and posture. Thus, as we speak, we are both sending messages through multiple channels and receiving messages through multiple channels from the audience by way of their feedback.

Yet, important as it is to recognize these messages, it is what we do with that feedback that really counts. Put simply, the feedback we receive as we speak can impact both the content of our message and the manner in which we deliver it. For example, speakers who sense they are losing their audience may behave much differently from those who sense they are "on a roll." They may make a transition to another part of their speech sooner than planned, speed up their delivery, and increase the volume of their voice. What's more, they may do all three with little conscious thought.

The best speakers both know and appreciate the power that is inherent in such feedback. As a result, they consciously monitor and adapt their presentations to it, rather than letting it "get to them." You already do this in your interpersonal communication encounters. For instance, when the person seated across from you looks puzzled or agitated because of what you are saying, you probably modify your message in recognition of the feedback. With coaching from your public speaking instructor, you will learn to generalize this kind of interpersonal sensitivity to the public arena.

Interdependence   As you can see, when viewed from a transactional perspective, public speaking is not a series of independent steps but a system of interdependent components. Again, these components act in concert. As a result, a change in one component will produce changes in all the others. And this is why no two public speaking events are ever exactly alike.

THE SYMBOLIC NATURE OF PUBLIC SPEAKING

Public speaking, like other forms of communication, is symbolic.[14] A **symbol** is something that stands for or suggests something else by reason of relationship or association. This means that the verbal and nonverbal behaviors with which we express ourselves are representations of "other things," for example, objects, emotional states, and abstract thoughts. For instance, the word "gas" or "gasoline" refers to the fuel we commonly use in our automobiles in the United States. In Great Britain, the same fuel is called "petrol." These are simply culturally agreed upon symbols for the object in question. For more examples of the divergence between American and British words, see the box "Words as Symbols."

On a less concrete level, the word "joy" is a symbolic label for an emotional state. The word "democracy" is a symbolic label for abstract thoughts

SPEAKING OF . . .

Words as Symbols

The following are examples of words and terms that describe the same things in the United States and Great Britain, illustrating that language is symbolic. As Henry Higgins points out in *My Fair Lady*, English (as the British know it) has not been spoken in America for years!

United States	Great Britain	United States	Great Britain
car trunk	boot	sausage	banger
pharmacist	chemist	washcloth	flannel
rude	cheeky	vacation	holiday
gasoline	petrol	french fries	chips
truck	lorry	chips	crisps
period (punctuation)	full stop	crackers	biscuits
worn out	knackered	subway	tube
elevator	lift	lawyer	barrister

about a system of government. Thus, just as the words "gasoline" and "petrol" are not really the fuel placed in our cars, the words "joy" and "democracy" are not the things themselves but symbolic representations of them. Similarly, the American flag, though a powerful symbol of the United States, is not the country itself. Yet, as the controversy over burning the flag has demonstrated, confusing a symbol and what it represents can unleash powerful emotions.

Although we deal with the symbolic nature of public speaking at length in Chapter 9, we mention it here because you need to understand this concept as you prepare for your initial presentations. Specifically, the meaning you attach to the symbolic representations you use to express yourself and the meaning your audience may attach to them are not necessarily the same. Many words are what we call *relative terms*. Their meaning depends on some standard on which people can agree. Words such as "hot" and "cold," "beautiful" and "ugly" are relative terms. Consider Jim and Nanci. Jim's from Anchorage, Alaska. Nanci's from Phoenix, Arizona. There's little chance that the meanings they attach to hot and cold weather are even remotely similar. Their standards for making judgments about what is hot versus what is cold are based on radically different geographic and climatic experience.

The point, then, is simple. When we speak, we should not assume that the meaning we attach to the symbols we use will be identical to the meaning others attach to those symbols. As your communication competence grows, moreover, this fact will become increasingly useful to you.

SUMMARY

There are good reasons to study and practice public speaking. A personal reason for developing public speaking skills is to satisfy your own needs. *Deficiency needs* are basic human needs, which must be satisfied before higher-order needs can be met. They include needs for food, water, air, physical safety, belongingness and love, and self-esteem and social-esteem. *Growth needs* are higher-order human needs, which can be satisfied only after deficiency needs have been met. They include self-actualization (the process of fully realizing one's potential), knowledge and understanding, and aesthetic needs. Public speaking can also help meet the needs of others by empowering them to satisfy their own deficiency and growth needs.

Professional reasons for developing public speaking skills include becoming an opinion leader, promoting your professional self, being able to present ideas to decision makers, creating change in the workplace, becoming a functioning force in meetings, and developing active listening skills. Public reasons for developing your public speaking skills include becoming a critical thinker, functioning as an informed citizen, preserving freedom of speech, and raising the level of public discourse.

While some might view public speaking as a *linear process,* the addition of *feedback* creates an *interactive* model. In contrast, *transactional* models of public speaking view it as a system of interdependent components, all of which are capable of affecting one another simultaneously. The basic components of the speech transaction include *source/receiver, encoding* and *decoding, message, channel, context,* and *perception.* These components occur *simultaneously* and are *interdependent.* Public speaking is *symbolic* in nature. In preparing or presenting a speech, it's important to realize that the meanings people attach to various symbolic representations may differ greatly.

Check Your Understanding: Exercises and Activities

1. This chapter introduces you to Maslow's hierarchy of needs. How can public speaking skills help you fulfill each of these needs? Write a short paper or give a brief speech explaining your answer and giving examples.

2. Do you own a personal computer, a compact disc player, a VCR, a video camera, or a pocket calculator? If so, how did you decide to acquire it? How did you first become aware of the product (gain knowledge of it)? Who or what finally persuaded you to acquire it? Was

there someone who functioned as an opinion leader for you with respect to any of these products? If so, how? Be specific.

3. How important are public speaking skills in the profession for which you are preparing by attending college? If possible, interview either a practitioner of the profession or a professor in the appropriate department about the ways public speaking might be applicable in your field. Give a brief (one- to two-minute) presentation to your classmates or write a short paper about your findings.

4. Attend a meeting of a local governmental agency, such as a city council, planning commission, or board of supervisors, or attend a student government meeting on your campus. Chances are you will see several speakers present their views in a public forum. Write a short paper about one of the speakers. What impressed you most about the speaker, and what impressed you least? How did the ability to speak help this person achieve his or her goals?

Notes

1. Abraham H. Maslow, *Motivation and Personality*, 2nd ed. (New York: Harper & Row, 1970).

2. Elaine Gray, "Actor/Activist Brings His Message of Peace to a Packed Laxson," *Chico Enterprise Record*, 16 September 1995, 1A.

3. Gray, "Actor/Activist Brings His Message," 8A.

4. Everett M. Rogers, *Diffusion of Innovations*, 3rd ed. (New York: Free Press, 1983).

5. James C. McCroskey, *An Introduction to Rhetorical Communication*, 5th ed. (Englewood Cliffs, N.J.: Prentice-Hall, 1986).

6. *In Search of Excellence* [videorecording]. (Boston: Nathan/Tyler Productions, 1985.)

7. Thomas J. Peters and Robert H. Waterman, Jr., *In Search of Excellence: Lessons from America's Best Run Corporations* (New York: Harper & Row, 1982), 247.

8. Peters and Waterman, *In Search of Excellence*, 253.

9. Peters and Waterman, *In Search of Excellence*, 245.

10. Ronald B. Adler, *Communicating at Work: Principles and Practices for Business and the Professions*, 3rd ed. (New York: Random House, 1989), 4.

11. Adler, *Communicating at Work*, 216.

12. Anthony P. Carnevale, Leila J. Gainer, and Ann S. Meltzer, *Workplace Basics: The Skills Employers Want* (Washington, D.C.: U.S. Government Printing Office, 1988), 11.

13. Dean C. Barnlund, "Toward a Meaning-Centered Philosophy of Communication," *Journal of Communication* 12 (1962): 197–211; P. S. Watzlawick, J. H. Beavin, and D. J. Jackson, *Pragmatics of Communication: A Study of Interactional Patterns, Pathologies and Paradoxes* (New York: Norton, 1967).

14. W. Barnett Pearce and Vernon E. Cronen, *Communication, Action and Meaning: The Creation of Social Realities* (New York: Praeger, 1980).

Practice helps ensure an effective public speech.

2

Your First Speech

A journey of a
thousand miles
begins with a
first step.
—Chinese proverb

OBJECTIVES

After reading this chapter, you should be able to:

- Analyze the basic features of the speech situation as it applies to your first speech.
- Identify the general purposes associated with public speaking.
- Select an appropriate topic for your first speech.
- Construct a specific purpose for your first speech.
- Invent your first speech, utilizing appropriate sources for information.
- Organize your speech so that it (1) opens with impact, (2) focuses on your thesis statement, (3) connects with your audience, (4) organizes your ideas with up to three main points, (5) summarizes your main points, and (6) closes with impact.
- Present your speech in a conversational, extemporaneous manner.

KEY CONCEPTS

brainstorming

credibility

extemporaneous delivery

general purpose

impromptu delivery

invention

manuscript delivery

memorized delivery

preview

signposts

specific purpose

thesis statement

The wisdom of the proverb "A journey of a thousand miles begins with a first step," rings true for anyone who has ever given a speech. Often the toughest part of a speaking assignment is deciding where to begin. For example, you may have a general idea about what you'd like to speak about but have no clue about where to begin your research. Or you may be like many students, uncertain about a topic that you find interesting. Will your audience also find it interesting? Is it appropriate for the classroom?

This chapter overviews the individual steps you will need to master in order to develop and deliver your first speech. This is not a substitute for the content to follow in later chapters, but a detailed preview. It's designed to assist you in developing an overall sense of what effective public speaking involves, starting with choosing the right topic and ending with a style of delivery that best suits the situation. The steps we will discuss are: (1) analyzing the situation with which you are faced; (2) deciding on a purpose; (3) choosing a topic that is suitable to both the situation and the purpose chosen; (4) inventing the substance of your speech; (5) organizing your speech; and (6) presenting your speech effectively.

ANALYZING THE SITUATION

One of your first speech assignments may be to introduce a classmate or yourself, to share a brief story with the class, to prove a controversial point, or to illustrate your pet peeve. Whatever the assignment, you need to understand completely the situation in which you find yourself and the expectations that come with the situation. This is essential in order to effectively develop a speech that fits the situation and addresses those expectations.

For starters, you need to know who your audience is. **Audience** refers to the individuals who share and listen to a public speech. Typically, you will be speaking to your classmates, some of whom you may already have come to know in the first few days of class. But even if you have not, you can make certain assumptions about them based on their attendance at your university or college. Do you attend a small, rural, liberal arts college or a large, urban university? What are the common majors emphasized in your institution? Beyond these general facts, you can also observe your classmates in the effort to discover things about them. Are most of them the same age as you, older, or younger? People of the same age tend to share many of the same experiences. For example, the authors of this text grew up in the '50s and '60s. For us, the assassination of President John F. Kennedy was a defining experience. Yet for most of today's younger college students, Kennedy is but a distant historical figure. Although Kennedy's death is still important in a historical sense, Operation Desert Storm, the O. J. Simpson trial, or the death of Kurt Cobain or even Jerry Garcia may seem like defining experiences for you and your classmates.

Today's public speakers need to adapt to increasingly diverse audiences.

Knowing the common experiences you share with your audience allows you to predict what topics are likely to elicit a favorable response. Factors such as age, sex, and social status of the people with whom you speak may also help you predict audience response. Depending on who they are and what experiences they share, audience members come to any speech situation with a variety of expectations. For example, your classmates probably expect you to speak to them as a peer. If you violate that expectation, taking on an air of superiority, for example, you may not get the response you desire. Regardless, only after you thoroughly understand your speech situation, your audience, and their expectations, should you begin to consider the purpose for your speech.

DECIDING ON A PURPOSE

One of the first decisions a speaker faces is to decide on the **general purpose**—the primary function—of the speech. The three commonly agreed upon general purposes are to inform, to persuade, and to entertain. The most common types of speeches seek to *inform* others about things they do not already know or to *persuade* others to believe or behave in certain ways. Persuasive speeches not only seek change, they also may seek to reinforce social values, as when someone gives a Fourth of July speech or a sermon.

Other speeches seek to *entertain* by sharing an enjoyable experience. Obviously, these general purposes are not mutually exclusive. A persuasive speech will also inform the audience, and an informative speech should be interesting enough that it persuades the audience to listen. Nevertheless, the general purpose you either have been assigned or have decided on yourself should tell you something about the topic you ultimately choose. Simply put, some topics may be inappropriate or only marginally appropriate to your purpose. Though controversial topics, for example, lend themselves to a persuasive speech, they are less well suited to an informative speech.

You may be assigned a general purpose—to inform, to persuade, or to entertain—for your early speeches. But you will not be assigned a specific purpose. The **specific purpose** is the goal or objective you hope to achieve in speaking to a particular audience. What you want to accomplish specifically with your audience rests with you. For example, assume you are asked to introduce yourself to the rest of the class. What do you want your classmates to think and feel about you? Do you want them to like, respect, and admire you? Then your specific purpose might be "to have the class develop a favorable opinion of me." Clearly this is a persuasive effort. You are creating attitudes about yourself where none existed before. Thus, even in early speech assignments, you should try to articulate a specific purpose for your speech.

CHOOSING A TOPIC

Once you've clearly identified the response you hope to achieve from your audience, you face one of the hardest things for beginning speakers, the selection of your topic. Sometimes your instructor will do this for you, but just as likely you'll have to decide on a topic yourself. (For one student's thoughts on topic selection, see the box "Speaking with Passion: Jonathan Studebaker.") To help you in this process, we offer the following criteria for what makes an appropriate speech topic.

Six Criteria for an Appropriate Speech Topic

1. *The topic should be interesting to you.* **If you don't care about the topic, how can you expect your audience to care?**
2. *It should be interesting to your audience* **or at least be capable of being made interesting to them. This is why it is crucial to know as much as possible about your audience.**
3. *It should be appropriate to the situation.* **If your instructor has asked you to speak on your pet peeve, she or he probably is thinking of topics like "dorm food," "roommates," or "people**

VIDEO FILE

If you have access to the videotape that accompanies this book, view segment 12, which shows a speech by Jonathan Studebaker.

Speaking with Passion: Jonathan Studebaker

Born with osteogenesis imperfecta, or brittle bones, Jonathan Studebaker has conquered his disability while leading a full and productive life. From 1983 to 1992, he was the honorary head coach at the East-West Shrine Football Classic. He was the kicking coach for the Chico State football team for three years. After graduating from Chico State, he founded Project Speak Out as a forum to educate people on the challenges of having a disability while encouraging others to reach for the stars. Jonathan speaks to audiences ranging from service organizations to church, school, and sports groups.

Mike Bellotti, head football coach for the University of Oregon, states, "Jonathan is one of the best motivational speakers that I have had the pleasure of listening to in my coaching career." Mike Andrews, director of public relations for Shriners Hospitals, summed up the impact of Jonathan's public speaking: "Seeing and hearing Jonathan is an eye-opening experience. He is a real inspiration." Both authors of this book have had Jonathan as a student and can testify to his dynamic speaking style. A

speech given by Jonathan appears in Appendix A and is available on videotape.

Jonathan emphasizes the importance of "talking about what I know about, something I really care about." He feels that if speakers "feel passionately" about their topic, the other things, such as delivery, will fall into place. Jonathan often is called on to talk to children about living with a disability. He uses a question-and-answer technique to involve the youngsters in the speech. For example, he will ask, "Have any of you ever dropped a glass on the floor? What happened?" The answer is invariably, "It broke." So Jonathan tells his audiences: "Well, my bones kinda break like glass, which is why I tell people, when you carry me, treat me like your best crystal."

Jonathan adds an important thought for beginning speakers. A speech class is an opportunity. Three or four times during the semester you will have the chance to share something important with your classmates. Seize the opportunity to talk about something you really care about. Jonathan puts it this way: "Speaking isn't broccoli; it's fun!"

who blow smoke in my face," not the destruction of the rain forests.

4. *It should be appropriate to the time available.* One limitation of a public speaking class is time. Know what your instructor expects and stick to it. Further, consider the time you have available to prepare. If the speech is due next week, you won't be able to send off for information from your state senator. Pick a topic that you can research in the time available.

5. *It should be manageable.* Don't pick something beyond your abilities or resources. One of your greatest assets in speaking is your own **credibility**, which is the degree to which your audience trusts and believes in you. Nothing will undermine it faster than speaking on a topic with which you are unfamiliar. Know more than your audience. Why else would you speak to them?

6. *It should be worthwhile.* We treat time in our society as a commodity. We bank time, spend time, and buy time. You are angered if someone wastes your time. Don't waste your audience's time. Pick a topic that will inform, persuade, or entertain by presenting them with ideas or information they haven't already heard. Just as we hate to hear an old joke told over again, we don't like to hear for the umpteenth time that we ought to recycle our aluminum cans, unless the speaker tells us something new and insightful about why we should do just that. If you pick a well-worn topic, then you must give it a different "spin" or focus.

Given all of these limitations, how can you come up with an appropriate topic? We discuss topic selection in more detail in Chapter 7, but here are some basic suggestions.

Suggestions for Finding a Topic

- *Make a personal inventory.* What hobbies, interests, jobs, or experiences have you had that would be interesting to others?

- *Talk to friends.* Perhaps they have ideas to share with you, including topics they would like to know more about.

- *Read.* Newspapers, newsmagazines, and books are filled with ideas. You should commit to reading at least one newspaper a day and one newsmagazine a week while enrolled in this course.

- *Check the Internet.* There are so many subject areas discussed on the Internet, along with interest-based chat groups, if you enjoy "surfing the net," you may well find speech ideas there for the taking.

- *Brainstorm.* **Brainstorming** is a creative process used for generating a large number of ideas. A group of people get together and put forth many varied ideas. One person writes them down. No one is allowed to evaluate the ideas until the group has listed every last one it can think of. Then one or more members go back and critically examine the ideas. When brainstorming, work from the broad topic down to narrower topics. "Wearing seat belts" might seem like an overdone topic. But a speech on how even drivers of cars with air bags aren't fully protected if they don't wear seat belts might be a new slant on an old topic. Use the situation, audience, and your own goals as criteria for judging the possible topics. (The activity on page 53 explains brainstorming in more detail.)

INVENTING YOUR SPEECH

It may seem odd, at first, to think of a speech as an invention. However, just as it was not enough for Thomas Edison to simply have the idea for the light bulb, it is not enough for you to just have an idea for a speech. You need to invest time and effort in inventing the substance of what you plan to say. **Invention** is the creative process whereby the substance of a speech is generated. Where do you go for the substance of your speech? Here are some general suggestions, which we will develop in more detail in Chapter 7.

Developing Resources for Inventing Your Speech

1. *Begin with your own experiences.* Each of us has had experiences that make us unique. Many early speech assignments require you to look no further than things that have happened in your own life. For example, you may be asked to introduce yourself or tell a story about an experience you find significant. You may be able to rely on hobbies or past job experiences for an early informative speech. Even if you cannot rely solely on personal experience, it is the logical place to begin searching for information.

2. *Look to general sources of information.* Books, reference books, general-circulation periodicals (*Time, Newsweek, U.S. News & World Report,* etc.), and even public affairs programs, such as *60 Minutes, Dateline,* or *20/20,* are good places to look for information on topics of general interest. Keep in mind that books may have a long lead time before they are published. Thus, on topics that require up-to-date information, you need to rely on more recent sources, such as periodicals, rather than books. A speech on why the United States got involved in the Vietnam War, for example, might well rely on books and encyclopedias, whereas a speech on the current Bosnian situation would require the most recent sources available.

3. *Interview experts.* Sometimes you can interview an expert on the topic of your speech. You may not have to look any further than the other classes you are taking. An interview with an environmental-science instructor, for example, could provide a wealth of information for a unique speech about recycling. Further, experts often provide leads to other sources of information the speaker can read. Be sure to prepare thoroughly for your interview so that you know what questions to ask. Chapter 7 contains specific guidelines for conducting interviews, which you should consult before interviewing sources for any speech.

4. *Conduct computerized searches.* At one time the beginning public speaker relied primarily on paper indexes, such as the *Readers' Guide to Periodical Literature* or *The New York Times Index.* In some libraries, these may still be the best means of access. However, more and more libraries are providing computerized databases, such as InfoTrac. In addition, many students now have access to the Internet either through their universities or through membership in services such as America Online. Your school may also have access to Lexis/Nexis, a service that allows for searches of newspapers, magazines, wire service reports, court transcripts, law digests, and even television program transcripts. If you have access to such resources, they will provide a systematic way to find articles on your topic. Further, they will save you time and improve the quality of your research.

5. *Consider specialized sources of information.* Every discipline has specialized journals and books, as well as indexes to provide access to them. Chapter 7 discusses some of the more commonly used indexes. If you are dealing with a specialized topic early in the class, you probably should skip ahead to that chapter or meet with a reference librarian to help familiarize yourself with the resources available at your school. You might also consider other types of specialized sources, such as trade publications and government publications, if they are appropriate to your topic. For your early speeches, such specialization probably will not be necessary, but you should be aware that there is more to researching a speech than simply consulting the general books and periodicals found in most libraries.

As you gather information, whether from written sources or interviews, be sure to carefully record the facts and quotations you discover. Note not only what was said but also who said it, when, and where. As we discuss in Chapter 7, documenting your evidence for an audience will build your credibility, which will enhance the likelihood you will be effective in delivering your speech.

ORGANIZING YOUR SPEECH

Someone once said that every speech has three tell 'ems. First you tell 'em what you are going to tell 'em; then you tell 'em; and, finally, you tell 'em what you told 'em. That's a bit simplistic, but nevertheless, it captures the basic idea of the three parts of every speech: the introduction, the body, and the conclusion.

Though there are many ways to organize your speech, one of the most helpful patterns we have found for our own students was developed by Dr. Loretta Malandro for the business executives she coaches. According to Dr. Malandro, the traditional introduction, body, and conclusion of a speech should include six important steps. None of these steps should be skipped, and they should nearly always be presented in the order given here.

Six Steps for Organizing Your Speech

1. *Open with impact.* In this step you capture your audience's attention.

2. *Focus on your thesis statement.* In this step you draw the audience's attention to the central point of your speech.

3. *Connect with your audience.* In this step you let the audience know "what's in it for them."

4. *Present your main points.* In this step you present the body of your speech.

5. *Summarize your main points.* In this step you reiterate the main points of the speech.

6. *Close with impact.* In this step you leave your audience with a lasting impression.[1]

Let's briefly examine each of these steps and how they relate to the traditional introduction–body–conclusion format of a speech. This relationship is illustrated in Figure 2.1 on page 34.

Introduction

To present an effective introduction, you should follow three steps.

Open with Impact   Introduce your presentation dramatically or humorously. There's no surer turnoff than beginning a speech, "Uh, um, well, I guess I'll talk about dorm food today." Begin the speech with something that captures your audience's attention, such as an appropriate joke, a startling statistic, an anecdote, or a reference to current affairs.

FIGURE 2.1

Comparison of the six-step organizational pattern with the traditional introduction–body–conclusion organizational pattern

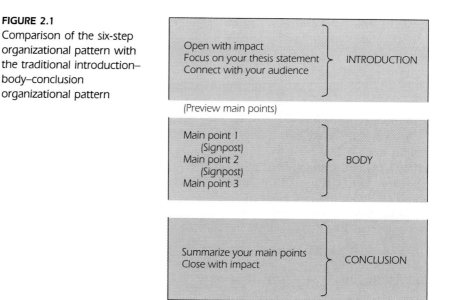

Open with impact
Focus on your thesis statement } INTRODUCTION
Connect with your audience

(Preview main points)

Main point 1
  (Signpost)
Main point 2 } BODY
  (Signpost)
Main point 3

Summarize your main points } CONCLUSION
Close with impact

Focus on Your Thesis Statement   The **thesis statement** focuses your audience's attention on the central point of your speech. For example, if you are opposed to a planned tuition hike on your campus, you should state clearly, "The students of this university should not be forced to pay more for less." On the other hand, you might want to inform your audience about the variety of financial assistance available to them: "With effort and persistence, you can obtain a student loan or scholarship to help meet your college expenses."

Connect with Your Audience   Answer the questions "What's in this for my audience? Why is it in their personal and/or professional interest to listen to me?" For example, will the proposed tuition hike keep some in your audience from completing their degrees? Make the connection to your specific audience clear in the introduction to the speech. This is also a good place to build your credibility as a speaker. Let the audience know you understand their concerns and have their best interests at heart. If you have expertise on the topic, let your audience know this now so that they can appreciate what is to come.

Body

The majority of your speech should develop the thesis you are trying to convey. Usually, the body of the speech is divided into three main points that in aggregate develop the thesis of your speech.

Preview   You should mention all three points briefly before treating each one in detail. This **preview** forecasts the main points of a speech. This is the "tell 'em what you're going to tell 'em" part of the speech. It may be as simple as saying, "I'm going to present three ways to save money on your groceries: clipping coupons, watching for store ads, and buying generic brands." On the other hand, a preview may specifically enumerate the three main points of the speech: "You can save money on your groceries, first, by clipping coupons, second, by watching store ads, and third, by buying generic brands."

Organize Your Main Points   A speech that wanders off the topic or whose main points don't follow a logical pattern of development is likely to lose the audience. The same is true of an overly complex speech. Here are some basic patterns for organizing your main points:

- *Time pattern*   Most stories are arranged chronologically. One event follows another until the climax unfolds. Often speeches deal with topics in terms of past, present, and future.

- *Spatial pattern*   Some topics are best dealt with spatially. A speech on the solar system might begin with the sun and work out to the most distant planets.

- *Categorical pattern*   A lot of topics fall into obvious categories. If I am explaining the federal government to a civics class, for example, I am likely to talk about the legislative, judicial, and executive branches. This is sometimes called a topical pattern of organization. If a topic lends itself to a natural division, this is an excellent way to arrange your speech.

- *Problem–solution pattern*   This is a natural way to organize persuasive speeches and is sometimes called the stock issues approach. What's wrong and why are followed by how to solve it and how the solution will benefit the audience. Many sales pitches are built around a problem–solution pattern. For example, a salesperson selling water softeners would begin with the problems caused by "hard water," such as leaving water spots on dishes and costing more money in detergent. Then she would propose a solution: buying her company's product.

These four ways to organize a speech are summarized in Figure 2.2 on page 36. Other ways to organize a speech are discussed at length in Chapter 8. For now, this will give you a start. The key thing to remember in this regard is to pick a simple pattern and stick with it for the entire speech.

Provide Signposts   We also want to emphasize the importance of using **signposts,** which are transitional statements that bridge your main points. For example, you might say something as simple as, "My second point

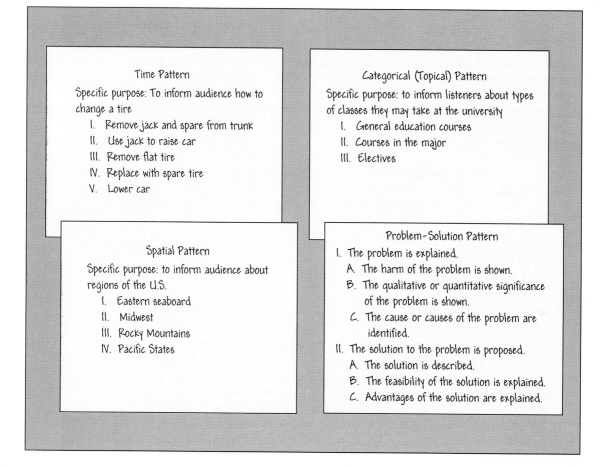

Time Pattern

Specific purpose: To inform audience how to change a tire

I.   Remove jack and spare from trunk
II. Use jack to raise car
III. Remove flat tire
IV. Replace with spare tire
V.   Lower car

Categorical (Topical) Pattern

Specific purpose: to inform listeners about types of classes they may take at the university

I.   General education courses
II. Courses in the major
III. Electives

Spatial Pattern

Specific purpose: to inform audience about regions of the U.S.

I.   Eastern seaboard
II. Midwest
III. Rocky Mountains
IV. Pacific States

Problem-Solution Pattern

I. The problem is explained.
   A. The harm of the problem is shown.
   B. The qualitative or quantitative significance of the problem is shown.
   C. The cause or causes of the problem are identified.
II. The solution to the problem is proposed.
   A. The solution is described.
   B. The feasibility of the solution is explained.
   C. Advantages of the solution are explained.

FIGURE 2.2
Common organizational patterns for a speech.

is . . ." or "Now that you understand the problem, let's examine some possible solutions." The goal in using signposts is to provide your audience with guides along the path of your speech so that they will know where you have been, where you are, and where you are going next.

Conclusion

All too often, speakers invest so much energy in developing the introduction and body of their speeches that they run out of gas at the end. The impact with which you conclude a speech is just as important as the impact with which you began.

Summarize Your Main Points   Tell 'em what you've told 'em. That is the first and most important function of a conclusion. Remind the listeners of what they've heard.

Close with Impact   Just as a salesperson doesn't like the customer to walk out the door without buying something, you don't want your audience to leave without at least thinking about doing what you've asked them to do. So, find a way to reinforce your specific purpose. It's also your last chance to leave a favorable impression. Just as listeners are turned off by an introduction that begins "Today I want to tell you about . . . ," you can undermine the effectiveness of an excellent speech with a poor conclusion, such as "Well, I guess that's about it." Finish with a flourish that is as powerful as your opening.

Ways to Close Your Speech Effectively

- Present a short, memorable *quotation.* This is often an effective way to reinforce your specific purpose and wrap up your presentation.
- Use an *anecdote* or a *story* that illustrates your point. However, it must leave a lasting impression on your audience. A long, drawn out, pointless story will cause your audience to lose interest.
- Make a *direct appeal* or "call to action." Just as a successful evangelist asks the faithful to come forward at the end of a crusade, effective persuasive speakers seek a public commitment from their audience to act on their messages. If you are opposed to a tuition hike, appeal to the audience to contact the board of trustees or sign a petition supporting your position. Perhaps the most famous direct appeal to action was in President John F. Kennedy's inaugural, where he challenged his fellow Americans to "ask not what your country can do for you, but what you can do for your country."[2]
- *Return to your opening.* This is one of the best ways to end a speech because it brings the listeners full circle. Suppose you began your plea for people to sign organ donor cards with the story of a little girl who needed a liver transplant. At the end of the speech you can describe how her life was saved because a donor was found. This gives the speech a sense of wholeness and completeness.

So, conclude your speech by *summarizing* your main points and *closing with impact.*

The box "Sample Speech Outline: Dieting and Physical Activity, by Sally Garber" follows the six steps we have just discussed. Notice how Sally

VIDEO FILE

If you have access to the videotape that accompanies this book, view segment 3, which shows the speech by Sally Garber. This speech is outlined in the box "Sample Speech Outline: Dieting and Physical Activity."

introduces her speech with a thought-provoking question and presents some important statistics that show the topic she is addressing is of widespread concern. Her speech has three clear main points, which she previews for her audience. She cites a number of credible sources, which are also listed in her reference list. Finally, she summarizes and closes her speech with impact. We have noted a number of the features of the outline in the margin. A complete text of Sally's speech appears in Appendix A.

PRESENTING YOUR SPEECH

There's a story told about the great speaker of ancient Greece, Demosthenes, who said that the first, second, and third most important things in rhetoric were—delivery, delivery, and delivery.[3] Although the story is probably apocryphal, it does illustrate the importance of effective delivery. No matter how well thought-out your speech, or how many hours you put in at the library, or how elegant your outline, unless the speech is effectively presented, your message will not have the desired impact. In Chapter 10 we deal at length with the nonverbal nature of delivery, including the important functions it serves for a speaker. In the meantime, however, the following guidelines will help you present your beginning speeches.

Keep in mind that you have three tools as a public speaker: your *voice,* your *face and eyes,* and your *body.* If you manage these effectively, you will be able to get your message across to your audience.

Using Your Voice Effectively

How you use your voice is critical to effective communication. Some basic guidelines will enable you to speak most effectively.

Breathing Properly   Breathe deeply, from your diaphragm. Give your voice enough support to be heard, but avoid straining your voice or shouting.

Speaking Conversationally   Think of public speaking as heightened conversation. Don't attempt to emulate political orators, as most audiences are put off by their techniques. Speak as you do in conversation, but enlarge your voice sufficiently to be heard by all in the room. It is certainly appropriate and even advisable to ask those in the back of the room if they can hear you, should there be any doubt.

Varying Your Voice   Nothing is more deadly to a speech than a monotone voice. Vary the rate at which you speak, the pitch (high or low) at which you speak, and the volume (loudness). The goal is to present your speech enthusiastically, sincerely, and energetically. Let the audience know you care about your topic.

Sample Speech Outline

Dieting and Physical Activity
by Sally Garber

Title of speech.

Specific purpose: To persuade the audience that restrictive dieting is destructive and to empower them to make better lifestyle choices.

Specific purpose is to change both attitudes and behavior.

Introduction

I. **Open with impact:** How many of you took a good look at yourself in the mirror this morning--Did you like what you saw?

  A. Statistics show that a large number of Americans would answer, No.

  B. According to <u>University of California Berkeley Wellness Letter,</u> more than one third of American women and nearly one quarter of men are trying to lose weight at any given time ("A New Spin," 1995, p. 1).

  C. As a society we are not happy with our looks and are spending billions of dollars a year struggling to achieve ideal bodies.

  D. Yet the percentage of overweight Americans continues to increase.

Speech begins with a thought-provoking question.

II. **Focus on thesis statement:** In this struggle is where the problem lies.

III. **Connect with audience:** Our methods behind our motives are destructive; dieting is destructive.

"Focus on thesis statement" and "Connect with audience" are labeled.

Body

(**Preview:** Today we will take a look at the issue of restrictive dieting. We will explore some recent trends in dieting. We will explore why people turn to dieting, why dieting does not work, and why it is claimed unhealthy and destructive. After discussing the issue, I will then give you some ideas on what you can do to achieve a healthy body.)

Speech is previewed for audience.

I. **Main point:** Every day, Americans struggle with their weight, resulting in desperate attempts to be beautiful.

Main points begin with roman numeral I.

(continued) ➤

Sample Speech Outline (continued)

Direct quotations are indicated by quotation marks, and source is cited in parentheses. Your instructor may prefer a different method of citing sources.

A. "The obese now comprise one third of the American population--58 million Americans, up from just one quarter 15 years ago--with the trend cutting across race, age and gender. Overall, 58 million Americans are overweight, with adults weighing 8 pounds more on average than they did a decade ago," according to Tufts University, October 1994 ("To Diet," 1994, p. 3).

B. So what can be done, one might ask? It all depends on who you ask.
   1. Pro-dieters would simply reply, "Go on a diet."
      a. Anyone who has ever struggled with weight loss could tell you that it isn't that easy.
      b. It sure sounds great, though, according to the recent television advertisements--You can have a shake for breakfast, a shake for lunch, and a sensible dinner, and you'll be on your way to a new you!
   2. Anti-dieters would refute this in saying that this way of thinking is where problems arise.

When a word is added by the speaker to the quotation it is indicated by [brackets]. Omissions are indicated by ellipses . . . .

      a. According to <u>Nutrition Today,</u> April 1993, "treatments [for obesity] based on caloric restriction, or dieting, had only temporary effects . . . . [M]ost persons treated with restrictive diets will regain lost weight" (Foreyt & Goodrick, 1993, p. 4).
      b. Restrictive diets are ineffective.

C. How do we convince people that dieting is counter-productive to their goal of weight loss?
   1. There is a non-dieting approach and it works, but we must first explore why diets fail.
   2. The best way to convince people that it works and that it is ultimately the healthiest way to achieve their goal is to simply give them the facts.

Signposts are transitional statements between main points.

(**Signpost:** So let's explore these facts, why are people turning to diets and why are their weight-loss attempts failing?)

II. Main point: Starting about the beginning of this century, Western civilization began to place an extreme emphasis on becoming thin.

A. This resulted in discrimination against the obese, who came to be judged on their appearance rather than their character.

    1. This has led to a situation today in which unloved and unhappy people feel that the only way to be happy is to lose weight.

    2. The tragedy for the overweight occurs when the desperation to be thin is combined with the thought that diets are effective.

B. The continuing popularity of dieting can be explained by the emotional cycle in which the obese seem to struggle. [Turn on overhead.]

    1. They begin by feeling fat and unloved.

    2. Wanting to be loved and happy they feel that they must lose weight in order to gain their desired emotions.

    3. Through many efforts they realize that their goals are unrealistic, leading them to eventually lose self-control, regaining any weight they may have lost.

    4. This leaves them feeling like failures.

    5. Thus, they are further damaged and the cycle continues until something is done. [Turn off overhead.]

    6. These beliefs that they are failures are rooted in the thought that they fail because they lack willpower, which is not only a falsehood, but it also promotes destructive behavior.

C. At the beginning of a caloric restrictive diet moods are elevated.

    1. Dieters are feeling good about themselves because they are motivated, their energy increases, and weight is lost.

Speaker includes note to herself to turn on the overhead projector.

She also includes note to turn off projector.

(continued) ➤

Sample Speech Outline (continued)

    2. This is where the misconception that diets work
       comes into play.
  D. Soon after weight is lost the restriction of calo-
     ries leads to uncontrollable cravings for high-fat
     foods.
    1. These cravings lead to bingeing and purging,
       starvation, and other extreme serious eating dis-
       orders.
    2. The resulting effect is exactly the opposite of
       what the dieter intended to achieve.
  E. All these facts have led many to believe that re-
     strictive dieting has more negative than positive
     effects.

Would a signpost signaling shift to third main point have helped?

III. **Main point:** Let's explore the alternatives we have to
     achieve a healthier lifestyle and make better choices.
     [Overhead]
  A. First, we must begin by knowing that successful
     weight control is a lifelong commitment, not a se-
     ries of crash diets.
    1. To increase chances of long-term success it is
       important to set realistic goals that lead to
       slow, steady success.
    2. "Gradual changes in diet and physical activity
       which build on success are expected to lead to
       more lasting lifestyle changes," states Nutrition
       Today, June 1995 (Blair, 1995, p. 110).
  B. Second, it is necessary to remember that eating
     should be a pleasurable experience.
    1. Food should be enjoyed.
    2. "[E]veryone should use eating as a positive op-
       portunity to relax as they nourish themselves,"
       according to Tufts University, October 1994 ("To
       Diet," 1994, p. 6).
  C. Along with enjoying your meals, wise food choices
     are equally important.
    1. We have seen that deprivation is not the answer,
       good healthy choices are.

2. It is necessary to reduce daily fat intake in order to achieve a healthier body.

3. Eating less fat will reduce your risk for heart disease, chronic fatigue and diabetes, as well as other major health problems.

4. Eating less fat will increase your energy levels, motivating you to get moving, and to exercise, which brings me to our last requirement, exercise.

D. In order to achieve a healthy body, you must combine physical activity with a healthy eating plan.

1. Weight loss will not happen overnight; and it will not happen depriving yourself of your favorite foods; but it cannot happen until you exercise.

2. Healthy weight loss can occur only when your muscles receive oxygen, you must breathe, you must move.

E. The smallest amount of activity proves beneficial.

1. Begin by doing work in the yard or by taking a walk with a friend or pet, or taking the stairs instead of the elevator.

2. "Periods as short as 8 to 10 minutes that total 30 minutes by the end of the day are adequate," according to Nutrition Today, June 1995 (Blair, 1995, p. 111).

3. The idea of "no pain, no gain," is dead.

   a. Low impact exercise, something as simple as walking or riding your bike instead of driving to school is the answer.

   b. But it must coincide with a healthy eating plan that includes choosing lots of fruits, vegetables, and grains, and definitely not deprivation.

4. There are no more excuses; given these guidelines, it is not impossible to reach your goals.

(continued) ➤

Sample Speech Outline (continued)

Conclusion begins with a summary. However, ask yourself if the main points are really summarized here.

Conclusion

  I. **Summarize:** It is no secret that those who exercise and eat well regularly have a better chance for survival, they need less medical care, have more energy, and enjoy life to the fullest.

 II. **Close with impact:** Believe it or not, living life to the fullest and achieving a healthy lifestyle can be an enjoyable process.

    A. It's not just about losing weight, it's a matter of choices.

      1. It's about feeling good about yourself.

      2. It's about leading a healthy balanced life.

      3. It's about setting and reaching goals in all areas of your life.

    B. So I leave you with this: Enjoy your food; enjoy your exercise, but most importantly, enjoy your life.

References

Speaker lists references at end of speech with full bibliographic citation. We discuss the American Psychological Association method of source citation in Chapter 7. Your instructor may prefer a different method of citing sources. Whatever method is used, accurate source citation is important.

A new spin on yo-yo diets. (1995, January). <u>University of California at Berkeley Wellness Letter,</u> 1, 1-2.

Blair, S. N. (1995). Diet and activity: The synergistic merger. <u>Nutrition Today,</u> 30, 108-112.

Foreyt, J. P., & Goodrick, G. K. (1993). Weight management without dieting. <u>Nutrition Today,</u> 28, 4-9.

To diet or not? The experts battle it out. (1994, October). <u>Tufts University Diet and Nutrition Letter,</u> 12, 3-6.

Using Your Face and Eyes Effectively

The face is one of the most complex and expressive parts of our anatomy, capable of communicating thousands of messages. Use your *facial expression* to reinforce your verbal message. The eyes, in particular, convey a great deal. Consider a person who gazes at you without pause. This will tend to make you uncomfortable. On the other hand, in our North American cul-

Successful public speakers know how to read audience members' facial expressions and adapt to the feedback they provide.

ture, a person who refuses to look at us communicates a negative message. In some other cultures, such as certain Asian societies, no such negative message is communicated by avoiding eye contact. As a speaker communicating to an American audience, therefore, maintain eye contact with your audience. This does not mean staring at just one portion of the room or shifting your eyes randomly. Rather, look at one member of your audience for a few seconds, then shift your gaze to another member, and so on. Be alert for audience responses to what you are saying. Are they restless, interested, puzzled? Such feedback can help you adapt to the audience as you speak.

Using Your Body Effectively

Your body is the third tool you use to communicate your message. Specifically, we will consider *posture, movement, gestures,* and *dress.*

Posture   How do you want to stand during your speech? Some speakers are comfortable behind a lectern, whereas others prefer to move away from it or dispense with it entirely. If you choose not to use a lectern, this can be an effective way of lessening the physical and psychological distance between yourself and the audience. If your preference is to use a lectern, do not use it as a crutch or bass drum. Avoid leaning on or clutching the stand, as well as beating on it with your open palm. Instead, find a comfortable, erect posture, and stand slightly behind the lectern. Remember that to breathe effectively, you need to have good body posture.

Movement   Movement should be spontaneous and meaningful. Though good speakers avoid pacing and random movements, it is perfectly appropriate, in fact desirable, to move to emphasize an important idea or a transition between points. There is no reason a speaker has to be nailed to the floor. Use your body to communicate your message whenever possible and practical.

Gestures   It is common in everyday conversation to gesture with your hands. In fact, try this experiment: Give someone directions from your school to your home *without moving your hands*. You will find it virtually impossible. The key to effective use of gestures in a public speech is that they should be appropriate to the point you are making and clearly visible to your audience. The larger the room, the larger the gesture needs to be for your audience to see it. On the other hand, too many gestures, especially if they appear to be the result of nervousness, such as fidgeting, can be distracting to an audience.

Dress   Your dress as a speaker should be *appropriate* to the situation and the audience. A good rule of thumb is to dress as you might for a job interview. People make instant judgments about other people and, as one shampoo ad proclaims, "You never get a second chance to make a first impression." In no case should your dress detract from the message you want to convey.

Methods of Delivery

There are four common ways to deliver a speech:

- Write out a *manuscript* and read it to your audience.
- *Memorize* your speech and recite it from memory.
- Present a spontaneous, unrehearsed *impromptu* presentation.
- Combine preparation and spontaneity in an extemporaneous *presentation.*

We discuss each type of delivery in turn, along with its advantages and limitations.

Manuscript Delivery   When a speaker uses **manuscript delivery,** the speech is written out completely and read to the audience. Few speakers are very good at reading a speech. In fact, except for politicians and other of-

Microsoft founder Bill Gates dresses informally, yet appropriately, for this presentation of Windows 95.

ficials who rely on ghostwriters to prepare their speeches, most of us will not have occasion to give a manuscript speech.

Though it might seem easy to simply write out your speech in advance and read it to the audience, this is easier said than done. One disadvantage of written speeches is that most people don't write as they speak. Speeches delivered from a manuscript have an artificial quality about them. Sentences are often too long and complex. The audience often loses track of the point being made. "Oral essays" are not an effective way to communicate with an audience.

If the manuscript pages get out of order or some are missing, you may be forced to improvise or stop your speech altogether. During his health-care address to a joint session of Congress in 1993, President Clinton looked at his TelePrompTer only to discover that the wrong speech—his state of the union address—was on the screen. While his aides scrambled to get the right speech up, Clinton had to improvise his presentation for about 10 minutes. A less experienced speaker might have been rattled, but Clinton seemed more amused than flustered, commenting that though the state of the union speech was a good one, he didn't want to give it twice.

Another disadvantage of manuscript delivery is that you lose eye contact with your audience. Not only does this inhibit feedback, it reduces your contact with the audience, which, as we will see later, is a major factor in establishing your credibility as a speaker.

When President
Clinton spoke before
a joint session of
Congress, he was
forced to "wing it"
for about 10 minutes
when the wrong
speech was placed
on the TelePrompTer.

   The principal situation in which you will want to deliver a speech from
a manuscript is if it is critical that you be quoted accurately. For example,
public officials usually will speak from a manuscript to ensure that they are
accurately quoted in the media. For your first speeches, however, you should
avoid the manuscript speech.

Memorized Delivery   An alternative to reading a speech is to memorize it. **Memorized delivery** is a mode of presentation in which the speech is written out and committed to memory before being presented to the audience without the use of notes. This method of delivery does eliminate the problems associated with maintaining eye contact. And, presumably, an able speaker can quickly drop a section of a memorized speech should time run short. But, on the whole, memorized speeches today are confined to the theater and speech tournaments. The reason is simple: Memorization requires an enormous investment of time for even a brief speech. Further, if you forget the speech, you are faced with either a very noticeable silence or "winging it." Finally, memorized speeches usually sound memorized. They are simply oral essays without the physical manuscript.

Impromptu Delivery   When a speaker employs **impromptu delivery,** it is a spontaneous, unrehearsed mode of presenting a speech. Frequently we are called on to give such speeches, though usually we don't think of them as speeches. For example, when your instructor calls on you to explain the day's reading assignment—or when you explain to your bank why you really aren't overdrawn—you are making an impromptu speech. In fact, most of our everyday conversations are spontaneous.

Nevertheless, for most speaking situations, the impromptu method of speaking is of limited usefulness. Even experienced public speakers usually have "canned" or set pieces on which they rely when they are called to make impromptu presentations. For example, candidates for president prepare for their debates for days beforehand. Every conceivable question is asked in rehearsal, and possible answers are practiced. The failure to be ready can court disaster, as President George Bush discovered in the second presidential debate of 1992. When asked by one of the "ordinary voters" gathered for the debate how the deficit had affected him, he seemed surprised by the question. His inability to connect to the concerns of this ordinary citizen helped reinforce an image held by many that he "just didn't get it" when it came to the effect of the economy on average people.

For beginning speakers, impromptu speeches should be approached as a learning tool to enhance the principles that apply to other speeches. To rely on impromptu speeches for all of your assignments is not wise.

Impromptu speaking is discussed in more detail in Chapter 15, but here are a few pointers to keep in mind if you are called on to give an impromptu presentation early in the semester.

Tips for Making an Impromptu Presentation

- **Think about what basic point you want to make about the topic. If you are asked about lowering the drinking age to 18, are you for or against it? If you don't know what your stand is, you might** list the pros and cons of the issue and suggest that the audience needs to reach its own conclusion. If you are not informed on the topic, try linking it to something on which you do have information. Note that most instructors give students a choice from among two or three topics for impromptu speaking exercises. It is not their purpose to embarrass or "stump" the speaker.

- Think of one or more points that support your position. If you want to lower the drinking age to 18, is it because that's the age at which people can vote, sign contracts, and enlist in the armed forces?

- If you have time, think of an attention-getter as an introduction. Recently the United States sent armed forces to Haiti, Somalia, and Bosnia. You might begin your speech: "Many of the men and women who risked their lives in Haiti, Somalia, and Bosnia were 18, 19, or 20 years old. If they could fight for their country, why can't they buy a beer when they return home?"

- State your topic in the introduction—it buys you time and then you are sure the audience knows what you are saying. "I'm in favor of lowering the drinking age to 18, and I have three basic reasons."

- As a conclusion, summarize what you've said. "So, because 18 is the age at which people can vote, sign contracts, and enlist in the armed forces, I believe it's only fair to extend all adult rights to 18-year-olds."

If you do not have time to organize your thoughts, at least take a moment to think of your focus and two or three main points. Believe it or not, in a few seconds you can organize a fairly decent impromptu speech. We engage in spontaneous conversations all the time. Thinking and speaking are not mutually exclusive.

Extemporaneous Delivery   The best mode of presentation for most beginning speakers is **extemporaneous delivery,** which combines careful preparation with spontaneous speaking. The speaker generally uses brief notes rather than a manuscript or an outline. Some instructors require students to first outline their speech in a formal way, in which case the outline should serve as a preparatory tool, not an abbreviated speech manuscript. Other instructors require only that students prepare note cards to help them recall their main and supporting points. For an example of speaker's note cards, see Figure 2.3. Practicing the speech in advance allows you to fix the ideas in your head without memorizing the exact wording.

The extemporaneous method allows you to be prepared yet flexible. If you see from the audience feedback that people are disagreeing with you,

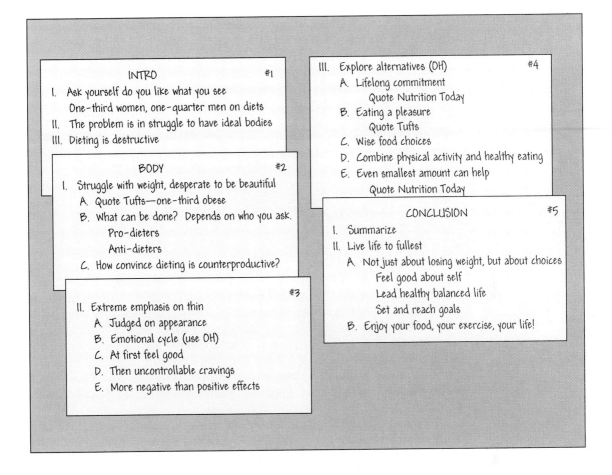

INTRO #1
I. Ask yourself do you like what you see
One-third women, one-quarter men on diets
II. The problem is in struggle to have ideal bodies
III. Dieting is destructive

BODY #2
I. Struggle with weight, desperate to be beautiful
A. Quote Tufts—one-third obese
B. What can be done? Depends on who you ask.
Pro-dieters
Anti-dieters
C. How convince dieting is counterproductive?

#3
II. Extreme emphasis on thin
A. Judged on appearance
B. Emotional cycle (use OH)
C. At first feel good
D. Then uncontrollable cravings
E. More negative than positive effects

III. Explore alternatives (OH) #4
A. Lifelong commitment
Quote Nutrition Today
B. Eating a pleasure
Quote Tufts
C. Wise food choices
D. Combine physical activity and healthy eating
E. Even smallest amount can help
Quote Nutrition Today

CONCLUSION #5
I. Summarize
II. Live life to fullest
A. Not just about losing weight, but about choices
Feel good about self
Lead healthy balanced life
Set and reach goals
B. Enjoy your food, your exercise, your life!

you can reexplain a point or add another example. If the audience seems bored, you might skip ahead to the most interesting example. Most teachers employ an extemporaneous method when lecturing to their classes. Students are invited to interact with their instructor, ask questions, and perhaps challenge a point. An extemporaneous speech should be a true transaction between speaker and listener.

FIGURE 2.3
Speaker's note cards.

SUMMARY

The essential steps in developing an effective speech are: (1) analyze the situation with which you are faced; (2) decide on a purpose; (3) choose a topic that is suitable to both the situation and the purpose chosen; (4) invent the substance of your speech; (5) organize your speech; and (6) present your speech effectively.

In analyzing your situation, consider both the nature of your assignment and the audience you will face. Look for clues that will help you understand your audience, such as common experiences, age, sex, and social status. The general purpose is the primary function of a speech. The three commonly agreed upon general purposes are to inform, to persuade, and to entertain. Six criteria for an appropriate speech topic are that the topic should be (1) interesting to you, (2) interesting to your audience, (3) appropriate to the situation, (4) appropriate to the time available, (5) manageable, and (6) worthwhile. A specific purpose describes your goal or objective in speaking to a particular audience.

There are many ways to come up with an appropriate topic, including making a personal inventory, talking to friends, reading widely, checking the Internet, and brainstorming. The process of inventing your speech includes looking for sources of information for the substance of your speech. Such sources include: (1) your own experiences, (2) general sources of information, (3) interviews with experts, (4) computerized searches, and (5) specialized sources of information. Then you need to develop a clearly organized speech that (1) opens with impact, (2) focuses on your thesis statement, (3) connects with your audience, (4) organizes your ideas with up to three main points, (5) summarizes your main points, and (6) closes with impact. It is useful to provide your audience with a preview of your main points before discussing them in detail. Common organizational patterns include time, spatial, categorical, and problem–solution. Transitional statements, called signposts, help the audience follow your organizational pattern.

In presenting your speech, you have three tools: your voice, face, and body. If you manage these effectively, you will be most likely to achieve your purpose in speaking. Although speeches may be delivered by manuscript, memorization, or in an impromptu fashion, for most speeches we recommend that you use an extemporaneous delivery. This involves fully preparing your speech, reducing it to note cards, and presenting your speech in a spontaneous fashion.

Check Your Understanding: Exercises and Activities

1. Write a one- or two-page analysis of the audience for your first speech. What characteristics do your classmates seem to have in common? Are they similar to or dissimilar from you in age, social status, and background? What assumptions can you make about them based on their attendance at your university or college? How will what you know about your classmates affect your choice of speech topic and specific purpose?

2. Come up with three possible topics for your first speech. For each topic, consider whether it is (a) interesting to you, (b) interesting to

your audience, (c) appropriate to the situation, (d) appropriate to the time available, (e) manageable, and (f) worthwhile. Based on this analysis, which topic do you believe is best for your first speech?

3. Once you have selected the best topic, determine what general purpose it would fulfill and phrase a specific purpose that you would hope to achieve in presenting the speech.

4. Make a list of appropriate sources for information for the topic you have chosen for your first speech.

5. Using the format illustrated in Figure 2.3, prepare an outline that organizes your speech so that it (1) opens with impact, (2) focuses on your thesis statement, (3) connects with your audience, (4) organizes your ideas with up to three main points, (5) summarizes your main points, and (6) closes with impact.

6. View a speech on videotape and then read a manuscript of the speech. Appendix A contains the manuscript of several speeches that are available on the tape accompanying the book. After both reading and viewing the speech, write a short paper, answering the following questions: (a) What seemed to be the greatest strength of this speech? (b) What seemed to be the greatest weakness of this speech? (c) What differences did you note between reading an outline or manuscript of the speech and actually seeing the speech delivered?

   Alternatively, review the manuscript of a famous speech, such as Martin Luther King, Jr.'s, "I Have a Dream" or Mary Fisher's speech on AIDS. Then answer questions (a) and (b) above.

7. In a group of about five students, brainstorm different possible speech topics for about 15 to 20 minutes. During brainstorming the following rules apply:

   • The goal is quantity of ideas—even silly ideas should be listed.

   • No criticism or evaluation is allowed during the brainstorming process.

   • One person is designated to write down every idea. Ideally, use a chalkboard or an easel to write down ideas so that everyone can see them.

   • "Hitchhiking" ideas is encouraged. If you can add to or improve on someone else's idea, do it.

   • When you think everyone is out of ideas, try to get at least one more from each group member.

   • After all the ideas are listed, go through the list and select the best ideas. Look for ideas that fit the assignment, are feasible given the time limits, and would be appropriate for this class. Cross off ideas that don't seem to apply.

- Now rank the remaining ideas in order of value. You may want to modify or combine ideas in this process.
- When your instructor calls for your group to report, give the class your five best ideas. If there are five groups, that would mean 25 ideas listed for the class as a whole.

As time permits, discuss the ideas in class. Which ones are most promising? How well do these possible topics fit the assignment? Will they be interesting and worthwhile for the members of the class? If you have an upcoming speech assignment, you might find one of these topics to be appropriate. You can also repeat the whole brainstorming process outside of class with some friends to see if you can come up with other topics as well.

Notes

1. The eight-part formula (assuming three main points) was developed by Dr. Loretta Malandro and is taught in her program "Speak With Impact," offered by Malandro Communication Inc., Scottsdale, Arizona.

2. John F. Kennedy, "Inaugural Address," in *American Rhetoric from Roosevelt to Reagan,* ed. Halford Ross Ryan, 2nd ed. (Prospect Heights, Ill.: Waveland Press, 1987), 158.

3. George Kennedy, *The Art of Persuasion in Greece* (Princeton, N.J.: Princeton University Press, 1963), 283.

This speaker
has learned to
constructively control
his anxiety before,
during, and after
his speeches.

3

Coping with Speech Anxiety

OBJECTIVES

After reading this chapter, you should be able to:

- Explain the relationship between arousal and anxiety.
- Define anxiety and distinguish it from speech anxiety.
- Identify common sources of speech anxiety.
- Understand and use skills that have proved effective in controlling arousal and speech anxiety.

KEY CONCEPTS

anxiety

constructive self-talk

coping skills

negative self-talk

physiological arousal

self-talk

speech anxiety

It often begins with butterflies in the pit of your stomach. Then your heart begins to noticeably palpitate. Your head starts to swim, making it difficult for you to concentrate, and a thin veil of perspiration begins to form on the palms of your hands. It may result from being asked to pinch-hit during a game of summer softball, from anticipating an important test you need to pass for your major, or from thinking about an interview for a needed internship.

What is this mysterious "it" about which we speak? **Anxiety** is the word we give to feelings of fear and uncertainty usually accompanied by physical symptoms such as butterflies in the stomach, perspiring, and unsteadiness. Not only is it a fact of life for college students, it frequently is a consequence of the subject of this book. In fact, as pointed out during a segment of ABC's program *20/20,* speech anxiety is regularly experienced by upward of 40 percent of all American adults. **Speech anxiety** refers to the feelings of discomfort that people experience before or during speaking in public.

Our concern in this chapter is the constructive control of speech anxiety before, during, and following your speeches. The information presented will help you to become a better, more confident public speaker. Further, we will present specific **coping skills,** which are mental and physical techniques used to control anxiety before, during, and following a speech. These techniques will help you to become a better speaker even if speech anxiety generally is not a problem for you. Of course, for those with minimal speech anxiety, not all of these methods will need to be employed. We begin by discussing the relationship between physiological arousal and speech anxiety. We then describe the sources of speech anxiety. Finally, we present a number of well-researched techniques and coping skills you can use to become a less anxious and more confident public speaker.

PHYSIOLOGICAL AROUSAL AND SPEECH ANXIETY

The relationship between physiological arousal and speech anxiety is paradoxical. When we speak of **physiological arousal,** we mean the physical changes that occur when a person is aroused, such as increased pulse, greater alertness, and more energy. On the one hand, moderate arousal is necessary to effective speaking. Too little arousal, for example, decreases alertness, motivation, and overall performance.[1] On the other hand, too much arousal can cause constricted muscles and vocal cords, excessive sweating, and nausea. Too much arousal, in other words, can have a disastrous effect on public speaking transactions.[2] Everyone experiences some degree of physiological arousal when he or she speaks or, in some cases, anticipates speaking. This arousal is positive until it is interpreted by the person as uncomfortable.

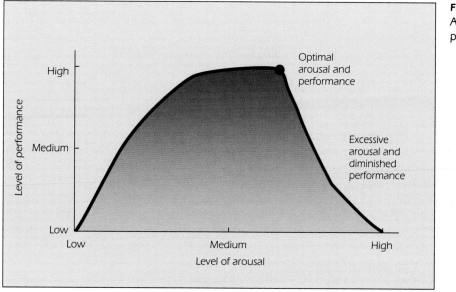

FIGURE 3.1
Arousal and
performance.

The relationship between arousal and speaking is illustrated in Figure 3.1. As you can see, as your level of arousal nears the top of the curve, motivation, alertness, and the potential for effective speaking are positively influenced. However, when your level of arousal begins to exceed this point, motivation, alertness, and the potential to speak effectively steadily decline. The optimal level of arousal is not the same for every person. However, the same factors influence the level of arousal each of us experiences.

The level of arousal you experience before, during, and following a speech will depend on the emotions you are experiencing. Of the many emotions that can influence your level of arousal in this respect, anxiety is the most common. Potentially, it also is the most troublesome.

As noted at the beginning of the chapter, anxiety is a type of fear and uncertainty usually accompanied by physical symptoms. Medical authorities note that such anxiety involves a sense of dread and distress over perceived threats, whether real or not, to either mental or physical well-being.[3] It is well documented that the more anxious we are about something, the greater are the chances that we will experience a performance-detracting level of arousal.[4]

The fear of speaking publicly is a specific type of anxiety. Generally, it is felt before, during, and following a public speech. Public speaking anxiety also shows itself in two major ways. The first is mental. Before a speech it is characterized by such things as excessive worrying, the inability to concentrate, and procrastinating about preparing the speech. During a speech it can take the form of feeling helpless, thinking highly negative thoughts, and erroneously believing that the audience wants the speaker to fail. Following a speech, it commonly expresses itself in terms of self-criticism, unjustified feelings of embarrassment, and the inability to listen to feedback about the speech.

The second and most easily recognized way speech anxiety shows itself is physical.[5] Prior to speaking, for example, an anxious person stereotypically has butterflies in the stomach. While he or she is giving a speech, anxiety can involve excessive perspiration, blushing, forgetfulness, trembling hands, and poor eye contact, among other symptoms. After sitting down, moreover, the anxious speaker may feel physically exhausted, mentally drained, and unable to focus on constructive feedback.

In the context of public speaking, mental and physical anxiety interact with one another. If you are so anxious prior to giving a speech that you procrastinate and do not adequately prepare, you likely will experience symptoms of physical anxiety as you begin to deliver your speech. In turn, as you begin to sense the telltale symptoms of physical anxiety, the more likely you will begin to mentally interpret your presentation in a negative light.

Therefore, optimizing your success as a public speaker depends on your ability to achieve and maintain an optimal level of arousal during all phases of the preparation and delivery of your speech. Before examining the sources and remedies for public speaking anxiety, you may want to evaluate your speech anxiety by filling out the self-assessment exercise in the box "How Anxious Are You About Public Speaking?" on pages 62–63.

RECOGNIZING THE SOURCE OF YOUR ANXIETIES

Not all people have the same reason for being anxious about speaking in public. The underlying sources of mental and physical anxiety are varied. Still, research over the past three decades has given us a good picture of the most common sources of our anxieties about speaking in public.[6] This picture includes a pessimistic attitude toward speaking, inadequate preparation and practice, negative or insufficient experience, unrealistic goals, inaccurate perception of the audience, negative self-talk, and misdirected concerns. Let's discuss each of these sources of anxiety in turn.

Pessimistic Attitude Toward Speaking

The first and most immediate source of anxiety is your perception and reaction to the situation you face. Though actual physiological arousal is neither positive nor negative in itself, your perception of it can be either positive or negative. If you perceive and react to a situation positively, the arousal you feel will be perceived as a pleasant rather than aversive sensation. What's more, it is not likely to exceed its optimal level. Conversely, if you perceive a situation negatively you will perceive the arousal you feel as an unpleasant, even worrisome sensation. This increases the probability of arousal exceeding the optimal level, as you become more and more anxious, further pushing your physiological arousal level.

Research shows that the difference between being positively excited or negatively threatened by a situation such as public speaking is not a matter of arousal per se. It is a matter of how the arousal is initially interpreted. Consider riding a roller coaster. Some people love it, others hate it. If you were to measure arousal while people actually rode a roller coaster, however, you would find, in the beginning, very little difference in their level of physiological arousal. But as the ride progressed and their positive or negative interpretation of the experience began to kick in, differences in arousal would begin to appear.

So it is with public speaking. If you perceive it as an opportunity to become a more skilled communicator, chances are you will be able to maintain an optimal level of arousal before, during, and following your speeches. Of course the reverse also is true. If you perceive public speaking as an anxiety-producing task you prefer to avoid, you probably will become so aroused that you experience the mental and physical signs of anxiety we discussed earlier. The question we now need to address, then, is why some people perceive and react to public speaking so negatively.

Inadequate Preparation and Practice

An obvious reason for viewing the speech transaction as aversive is inadequate preparation and practice. Whereas most students would never dream of entering an athletic competition or taking a test crucial to their success in their major without preparation and practice, many seem to think that public speaking is different in this regard. So they put off preparing and practicing their speech until the last moment. Then they wonder why the act of speaking itself was so traumatic.

Minimizing the importance of preparation and practice to the speaking experience only increases the amount of uncertainty surrounding the speaking assignment. Further, this uncertainty is one of the chief causes of the excessive arousal and anxiety that students feel in the course of speaking in public. Frequently, then, the real source of their discomfort is a result of their own shortsightedness.

Sometimes students recognize the importance of preparation and practice but simply cannot confront the public speaking assignment. Much like "writer's block," such aversion to preparing and practicing a speech occurs because students are afraid to get started. Perhaps they fear failure or they just don't know where to begin. Whatever the reason, procrastination is a sure source of speech anxiety.

How Anxious Are You about Public Speaking?

The following is a self-report measure of public speaking anxiety. Respond to each statement honestly and work quickly. Indicate the extent to which you agree or disagree and score yourself as follows: Strongly Agree = 1, Agree = 2, Undecided = 3, Disagree = 4, Strongly Disagree = 5.

_____ 1. While preparing for giving a speech I feel tense and nervous.

_____ 2. I feel tense when I see the words *speech* and *public speech* on a course outline when studying.

_____ 3. My thoughts become confused and jumbled when I am giving a speech.

_____ 4. Right after giving a speech I feel that I have had a pleasant experience.

_____ 5. I get anxious when I think about a speech coming up.

_____ 6. I have no fear of giving a speech.

_____ 7. Although I am nervous just before giving a speech, I soon settle down after starting and feel calm and comfortable.

_____ 8. I look forward to giving a speech.

_____ 9. When the instructor announces a speaking assignment in class I can feel myself getting tense.

_____ 10. My hands tremble when I am giving a speech.

_____ 11. I feel relaxed while giving a speech.

_____ 12. I enjoy preparing for a speech.

_____ 13. I am in constant fear of forgetting what I prepared to say.

_____ 14. I get anxious if someone asks me something about my topic that I do not know.

_____ 15. I face the prospect of giving a speech with confidence.

_____ 16. I feel that I am in complete possession of myself while giving a speech.

_____ 17. My mind is clear when giving a speech.

_____ 18. I do not dread giving a speech.

_____ 19. I perspire just before giving a speech.

_____ 20. My heart beats very fast just as I start a speech.

_____ 21. I experience considerable anxiety while sitting in the room just before my speech starts.

_____ 22. Certain parts of my body feel very tense and rigid while giving a speech.

_____ 23. Realizing that only a little time remains in a speech makes me very tense and anxious.

_____ 24. While giving a speech I know I can control my feelings of tension and stress.

_____ 25. I breathe faster just before starting a speech.

_____ 26. I feel comfortable and relaxed in the hour or so just before giving a speech.

_____ 27. I do poorer on speeches because I am anxious.

_____ 28. I feel anxious when the teacher announces the date of a speaking assignment.

_____ 29. When I make a mistake while giving a speech, I find it hard to concentrate on the parts that follow.

_____ 30. During an important speech I experience a feeling of helplessness building up inside me.

_____ 31. I have trouble falling asleep the night before a speech.

_____ 32. My heart beats very fast while I present a speech.

_____ 33. I feel anxious while waiting to give my speech.

_____ 34. While giving a speech I get so nervous I forget facts I really know.

To determine your score, first total the numbers you gave yourself for statements 1, 2, 3, 5, 9, 10, 13, 14, 19, 20, 21, 22, 23, 25, 27, 28, 29, 30, 31, 32, 33, and 34. Now subtract this total from 132 and add the difference to your total score on statements 4, 6, 7, 8, 11, 12, 15, 16, 17, 18, 24, and 26. Your score should be no higher than 170 and no lower than 34. If your score is higher than 100, you are moderately to highly fearful of public speaking. A score between 80 and 100 means moderate fear, and anything less than 80 means minimal fear. Your score is only an approximation of your speech anxiety and should be regarded as such. Also, know that the vast majority of students who have responded to this measure on many campuses in the United States fall in the moderately anxious range. Super low and super high scores are rare. Whatever score you achieve, you can benefit from the techniques discussed in this chapter.

Copyright by the Speech Communication Association, 1970, from James C. McCroskey, "Special Reports: Measures of Communication-Bound Anxiety," _Speech Monographs_ 37 (1970): 269–77, by permission.

Despite previous bouts with anxiety Barbra Streisand is back speaking and performing in public.

Negative or Insufficient Experience

Your prior experiences with any task influence how you approach and complete your present task. If your past experiences with public speaking proved both successful and personally rewarding, chances are you look forward to your speaking assignments in this class. But if your prior experiences with public speaking were unpleasant, chances are you harbor some doubt about your abilities to succeed in this class. Finally, if you have had little or no opportunity to speak in public, you too may be mildly or even considerably anxious about speaking before your teacher and peers.

If you are in one of these latter two groups, your anxieties are understandable. It is natural to initially perceive a task such as speaking as a threat if your past experience with the task seemed more punishing than rewarding. It also is natural to feel anxious about a task with which you have little or no familiarity. But the fact that your past efforts as a speaker were unrewarding, or even traumatizing, need not mean that your efforts in this class will prove likewise. As we discuss in the next section, dwelling on unpleasant experiences in your past can be a major obstacle to self-improvement.

By the same token, the fact that you think you have had little experience with the skills necessary to effective public speaking shouldn't make you overly anxious. As pointed out earlier, public speaking is an extension and refinement of the communication skills you put to use daily. Through your class and this book you can learn to successfully extend your everyday communication skills to the task of speaking in public.

Unrealistic Goals

A common source of anxiety for student speakers, especially inexperienced ones, involves the goals they set for themselves. Though it is important to set high goals for yourself, they also should be realistic. Unrealistic goals can lead to irrational fears about the speaking situation. Research shows that people who set realistic goals for themselves are less anxious and more successful than their counterparts with unrealistic goals.[7] This finding also has been reported in studies of elite athletes, business people, and students enrolled in public speaking courses.

Speech-anxious students often hurt themselves by establishing goals that are not only unrealistic but also well beyond their reach. They tell themselves that despite their inexperience and unwillingness to make their speech class a priority, they must be the best in their class or they have to get an A. Such illogical and unrealistic goals, the research shows, harm much more than help students in coping with their speech anxiety.

Inaccurate Perception of the Audience

Another source of speech anxiety involves your perception of the audience. Many beginning speakers view the public speaking situation in general, and their audience specifically, as a threat to their mental well-being. They convince themselves that the members of their audience are just waiting for them to commit some faux pas (social blunder), lose their train of thought, blow a quotation, or mumble through a sentence. Along the same lines, it is not uncommon for beginning speakers to read into the nonverbal feedback they receive from their audience such false conclusions as "they're bored to tears" or "they think I'm terrible." This is anything but the case, of course. Audiences, with rare exception, want speakers to succeed and are silently rooting for them to do so.

In recognition of this fact, consider the case of the late Mary Martin, a well-known and highly praised stage actress. She used to do something before a performance that you may wish to try. Just before going on stage, she would close her eyes, take a deep breath, and say 100 times to herself, "I love my audience." Next she would repeat the process, but this time tell herself, "My audience loves me."

In addition to misperceiving their audience as a threat, beginning speakers may convince themselves that their audience expects more from them than they can deliver. Such expectations about an audience can easily become a self-fulfilling prophecy. These unwarranted expectations also can make you anxious and overly aroused. The students you face share the same boat with you and want you to succeed as much as you do.

Negative Self-Talk

Closely aligned with the problem of unrealistic personal goals is the more widespread problem of self-defeating patterns of self-talk. **Self-talk** refers to communicating silently to oneself, sometimes referred to as intrapersonal communication. **Negative self-talk,** a self-defeating pattern of intrapersonal communication, including self-criticizing, self-pressuring and catastrophizing statements, can result from several causes, including the following:

- undue worrying about your speech, including unnecessary comparisons of your speeches to those of other students before the fact
- dwelling excessively on negative past experiences with public speaking
- spending too much time thinking about the alternative approaches you might take in preparing your speech
- preoccupation with feelings of mental and physical anxiety such as trembling hands and a racing heart
- thinking about the worst and usually most unlikely consequences of your speech—people laughing at you or ridiculing your performance
- thoughts about or feelings of inadequacy as a public speaker

Such negative thinking usually leads to three types of negative self-talk: self-criticizing, self-pressuring, and catastrophizing. Let's look at each.

Self-Criticizing Though realistic self-evaluation is important to self-improvement, it is well documented that many of us berate and derogate ourselves without sufficient cause. Without much evidence at all, we say all sorts of negative things about ourselves.

Not just students but people in all walks of life tell themselves they are poor speakers. Many of them do so, moreover, despite the fact that they have never received any training in public speaking and have had few if any opportunities to speak in public. Thus their lack of skill doesn't justify their self-criticism.

Self-Pressuring   We also bring undue and added pressure on ourselves through our self-talk, never once thinking about whether such pressure will help us to perform better. We tell ourselves, for example, that "we must be the best speaker in the class" without first considering why. As it is, you invariably will experience some degree of pressure and arousal when speaking publicly. A small amount of pressure can help you reach the optimal level of arousal that will help you deliver your speeches effectively. If you feel no pressure at all, you will lack the motivation to properly prepare and practice. But if you tell yourself that anything but being the best isn't good enough, it frequently will hurt rather than help your speaking.

Catastrophizing   Finally, we may blow things out of proportion when talking to ourselves. For example, a speech becomes the worst thing that has ever happened to you, something that you will never be able to live down for the rest of your life, or important enough to hate yourself should you receive a low grade.

As was the case with unrealistic goals, this kind of self-talk increases arousal and speech anxiety. The more negative your self-talk is, the more probable it is that you will exceed your optimal level of arousal. Fortunately, substituting constructive self-talk for negative self-talk is one of the easiest and best ways you can control your level of arousal while preparing and delivering your speeches. We discuss the specifics of this process later in the chapter.

Misdirected Concerns

Finally, recent research suggests that students who are highly anxious about speaking express very different concerns about an upcoming speech than do those who are only moderately anxious.[8] For example, researchers found that highly anxious students were most concerned with how they would be evaluated, how long they should speak, what specific topic they should choose, whether they could use notes, and how long they had to prepare. In short, these students were concerned primarily with immediate factors that affect how they would be evaluated in the classroom situation. These concerns are classic signs of mental anxiety. Moreover, they suggest that truly anxious students may be so preoccupied with themselves, they will neglect the public speaking situation itself.

These researchers also found that students who reported little anxiety about speaking were most concerned with factors that would enable them to successfully attain their goals as speakers. In fact, these are the kinds of issues that even professional and highly paid speakers want to know about—

for instance, the arrangement of the room, the availability of a microphone, and whether the audience would ask questions. To get a clearer idea of what lies behind your anxiety, see the box "What Are the Sources of Your Speech Anxiety?"

CONTROLLING THE SOURCES OF YOUR SPEECH ANXIETY

In the past 20 years, researchers have learned much about the control of arousal and anxiety. In the process, they have also learned that anyone can benefit from following certain arousal- and anxiety-controlling steps regardless of their individual level of anxiety about speaking in public. Let's now look at each of these steps.

Develop an Optimistic Attitude Toward Speaking

To begin with, the slightest shift in our point of view can drastically change the way we see things. For example, shifting your point of view about public speaking from one of performance to one of communicating can make a tremendous difference in the way you look at and respond to the speech transaction.

The first step in controlling speech anxiety for many people, then, requires that they start thinking about public speaking differently. Instead of thinking of it as a public performance during which they will be "on stage," for instance, they might be better off viewing it as a slightly different and more formal way of carrying on a conversation with a group of interested friends or perhaps telling them a story. Certainly the latter is a more inviting view of the speech transaction.

Research shows that this kind of thinking works because it forces people "outside the box" they customarily stay within. Once outside the box, moreover, people begin to understand not only that there are multiple ways to view a task but that these alternative ways of viewing a task actually influence the way they complete it.

Don't Procrastinate Preparing Your Speech

The second step in controlling arousal and anxiety is to commit to preparation well in advance of the actual speech. Although only you know how much time you need to prepare, our experience as instructors is that students usually need more time than they think they do. As we have said, most students do not have a great deal of experience in public speaking, nor are most students exceptionally skilled in public speaking at the outset.

Preparation begins with making sure that you clearly understand the nature of the speech you are asked to share, the conditions under which it

What Are the Sources of Your Speech Anxiety?

Listed below are common sources of speech anxiety. As you read each item, consider how much it contributes to the anxiety you experience about public speaking. Rate each item on a scale of 1 to 10, from least important to most important.

Sources of Speech Anxiety	*Least Important / Most Important*									
	1	2	3	4	5	6	7	8	9	10
Your attitude toward speaking	—	—	—	—	—	—	—	—	—	—
Lack of preparation and practice	—	—	—	—	—	—	—	—	—	—
Previous experiences with speaking —lack of or bad experiences	—	—	—	—	—	—	—	—	—	—
Unrealistic goals	—	—	—	—	—	—	—	—	—	—
Perception of your audience as hostile or unsympathetic	—	—	—	—	—	—	—	—	—	—
Negative self-talk	—	—	—	—	—	—	—	—	—	—
Misdirected concerns with how you will be evaluated	—	—	—	—	—	—	—	—	—	—

Rearrange the items in order of importance. Use this hierarchy to better understand the sources of your speech anxiety. What steps can you take to address and change your patterns of thought and behavior?

1. _____
2. _____
3. _____
4. _____
5. _____
6. _____
7. _____

will be shared, and the expectancies that will guide your instructor's evaluation. If you have a *clear* understanding of what is being asked of you, you will be less likely to procrastinate, so make sure you have all the information you need to get off to a good start.

Preparation also involves making sure that you neither waste your or your audience's valuable time. This means such things as topic selection, deciding on a general purpose, organizing your message, and gathering evidence should be undertaken with considerable care. Nowhere is such care more apparent than in the time you spend in selecting a topic and researching it. Hastily selected and poorly investigated topics not only are easily discerned, they also tell your audience that they didn't merit the time necessary to genuinely prepare. The response you receive from the audience, moreover, likely will make you more aroused and anxious.

Look for Opportunities to Gain Speaking Experience

Of course you have made the first step to gaining public speaking experience by enrolling in this class. Realistically, however, you probably will be able to give only four to six speeches during the course of an academic term. To build up your repertoire of public speaking experience, you should seek out other opportunities to speak. Many colleges and universities offer a competitive speech team. Though this might seem intimidating at first, competition is geared to levels of experience, with beginning speakers normally placed at the "novice" level. There may also be other opportunities to speak on your campus or in your community. Some communities have a Toastmasters International club, which provides an opportunity to gain a great amount of experience in a group devoted to building public speaking confidence.

Once you complete this class, your education in public speaking is not over. You may wish to take more advanced courses or pursue other ways of building your speaking experience, such as competitive speaking or Toastmasters. Just as you would not consider yourself a fully developed golfer after a few months of lessons, you will become a better speaker only if you continue to practice and hone your skills. And as you gain experience, you will overcome one of the principal sources of speech anxiety.

Set Realistic Goals

Usually this begins with an assessment of the unrealistic goals which lead to irrational fears that misguide anxious speakers in the preparation, presentation, and evaluation of their speeches. For example, research shows that anxious speakers often report that they are afraid because they believe that they must be perfect and they must be the best. No one is perfect. To think that *you* always must be perfect simply isn't realistic. By the same token, it is impossible for anyone to be the best at everything. Moreover, unnecessary and anxiety-arousing comparisons arise between people when they tell themselves they always must be the best.

In a public speaking class, you have the opportunity to work on improving your public speaking incrementally. You do not need to be a perfect or ideal speaker with each speech. Rather, as you approach each assignment, focus on one or two areas that you feel are most in need of improvement. Perhaps in a particular speech you'll want to focus on organization, in another on delivery skills, and in another on your use of visual aids.

Realize the Audience Wants You to Succeed

Just as anxious speakers set unrealistic goals for themselves, research shows that they often report that they are afraid because they believe that their audience will ridicule them and they will look ridiculous. These fears are as irrational as expecting perfection in yourself as a speaker. For example, as an audience member, do you routinely ridicule the speaker or performer? Of course not. And audiences don't want to be made uncomfortable. As a result, when a single audience member tries to ridicule a speaker or performer with heckling, it usually is the heckler who becomes the object of audience scorn.

Probably no situation will provide you with as supportive an audience as your public speaking class. Remember, every member of the class faces exactly the same challenges you do. If you do make a mistake when giving a speech, their reaction is far more likely to be empathy and support than ridicule. In fact, in many public speaking classes, it is customary for every speaker to receive a round of applause on the completion of each speech.

Practice Constructive Self-Talk

Another step to take in your efforts to control arousal and anxiety involves constructive self-talk. **Constructive self-talk** is the use of positive coping statements instead of negative self-talk. Just as researchers have found that anxious speakers set unrealistic goals and inaccurately perceive their audiences, they have also found that speakers fear they will make extreme and obvious mistakes. This, too, is an irrational fear. Why should you appear any more ridiculous or make more mistakes than your classmates? If you've followed our advice for preparing and practicing your speech, you should neither appear ridiculous nor make more mistakes than other speakers. All speakers, including the most polished and practiced, make mistakes. The difference is that this latter group doesn't dwell on them, preferring to treat mistakes as an inevitable part of the process of public speaking. Polished and practiced speakers, in other words, know that no one is perfect—including themselves.

Once unrealistic goals and irrational fears about speaking have been confronted and exposed as such, constructive self-talk becomes a genuine possibility. Table 3.1 on page 72 shows examples of positive coping statements. Note that positive coping statements (1) accentuate your assets—not your liabilities; (2) encourage you to relax; and (3) emphasize a realistic

TABLE 3.1 Positive Coping Statements for Speeches

Before speech	During speech	After speech
Task statements	*Task statements*	*Context statements*
What do I have to do?	Keep using coping statements.	It wasn't as bad as I feared.
Remember to use coping statements.	Speak slowly, it helps.	It was not a big deal.
Speak slowly and I'll be fine.		Each time will get easier.
Context Statements	*Self-Evaluation*	*Self-Evaluation*
It's only my class.	How am I doing?	What did I do well?
It's only one speech.	So far so good.	I used coping statements.
We're all in the same boat.	I've started and it was okay.	I spoke.
I know as much as anyone.	I was anxious, but now I've calmed down.	I spoke slowly.
I can't be any worse than previously, only better.	This is a little easier than I thought.	What do I want to improve next time?
		Remember to speak slowly and rehearse my statements.

rather than catastrophic assessment of your situation before, during, and after your speech.

Instead of telling yourself you'll look ridiculous or sound funny, positive coping statements suggest you're attractive and sound sensible. Instead of telling yourself you must present the best speech in your class, positive coping statements suggest you should give the best speech of which you are capable. And instead of telling yourself you were terrible, positive coping statements suggest you'll get better with preparation, practice, and coaching.

Overcoming negative self-talk requires commitment and routine practice. Learning to substitute positive coping statements for negative self-talk also requires dedication and stick-to-itiveness. Thus, what you get out of this particular technique will very much depend on what you put into it.

Direct Your Concerns at Important Issues

As noted earlier, overanxious speakers tend to focus on concerns related to the evaluation of their presentation rather than the overall speech situation. Though it is certainly important that students know how they will be evaluated and what the instructor expects of them, an exclusive focus on such concerns is a case of the proverbial "missing the forest for the trees." Focus on your goal as a speaker and what you want to accomplish in a given

situation. Ask yourself what your audience is like, what they expect, and how you can best meet their needs. Find out about the arrangement of the room, whether the audience will have an opportunity to ask questions, and the like. These factors are directly related to accomplishing your specific purpose, rather than getting a good grade. Our experience as instructors suggests that it is not the student who is overly concerned with the mechanics of evaluation who does best in our classes. Rather, students who do their best to manage the larger speech situation are most likely to give a successful speech.

In sum, then, there are numerous approaches to controlling the most common sources of speech anxiety. Experiment with them to see which ones help you the most. As a reminder, we list them below.

Tips for Controlling the Sources of Speech Anxiety

- **Develop an optimistic attitude toward speaking.**
- **Don't procrastinate preparing your speech.**
- **Look for opportunities to gain speaking experience.**
- **Set realistic goals.**
- **Realize the audience wants you to succeed.**
- **Practice constructive self-talk.**
- **Direct your concerns at important issues.**

TECHNIQUES FOR CONTROLLING ANXIETY AND AROUSAL

The preceding section focused on directly attacking each source of public speaking anxiety. Nevertheless, regardless of how irrational some of the fear may be, or how often you are reassured that your audience will be supportive, you may still experience symptoms of speech anxiety and heightened arousal. The techniques we now discuss do not depend on identifying particular sources of anxiety. Rather, you should think of these as general techniques for coping with speech anxiety. In addition, because they treat the symptoms directly, these techniques are applicable to other anxiety-producing situations, such as athletic competition and public performances.

Using Visual Imagery and Practice to Enhance Performance

Using visual imagery is the opposite of rehearsing your speech. Instead of practicing your speech out loud, it involves visually imagining yourself confidently and successfully giving the speech. At the 1984 Winter Olympiad, TV viewers were treated to a picture of skiing greats Phil and Steve Mahre using this skill prior to their medal-winning performances in the two slalom events. Viewers saw the Mahre brothers, seated and with eyes closed, leaning left and right with clasped palms extended in front of them. They were visually imagining themselves confidently and successfully mastering the slalom courses they were about to ski. Other athletes use these techniques too; see the box "Body Talk: Kristi Yamaguchi."

More to the point of this book is the case of Dr. Loretta Malandro. The founder of a successful communication consulting firm, Dr. Malandro travels worldwide as a professional speaker. One of the things she tries to do before each speaking engagement is to visually imagine herself giving the speech. Even if it means getting up before the first light, for example, she tries to run five miles and visualize her upcoming presentation as she runs. Because Dr. Malandro does this routinely, she sees not only herself as she shares her message, but also the positive feedback she is receiving from her audience.

Visual imagery is used extensively in competitive sports such as skiing, gymnastics, and figure skating. It is a highly effective complement to actual practice. Study after study has demonstrated that when used in combination with practice, visual imagery significantly enhances performance. That's why it is part of the routine practice of Olympic athletes in events ranging from archery to weight lifting.

Because it is yet another way that you can reduce your uncertainty about an upcoming speech, visual imagery also can assist you in controlling your level of anxiety and arousal. This technique works best when you are in a relaxed state and familiar with the content of your speech. It involves controlled visualization of your actual speaking situation, which will require practice on your part. The idea is to see yourself during all phases of your speech. For example, you might first visualize yourself seated at your desk, relaxed but appropriately aroused as you wait your turn to speak. Next, you might visualize yourself leaving your desk, moving to the front of the room, confidently facing your audience and introducing your speech.

Body Talk: Kristi Yamaguchi

I usually get by myself before I go out for a routine. I walk through the program, visualizing myself completing all the moves. Right before a performance, I start talking to myself: "Okay, get out there, skate like it's an everyday practice."

When I start, I try to block out everything around me: the TV cameras, the audience—everything. I focus on the music and the program. By the halfway point I can tell whether it's going to be a good performance or a not-so-good one. Last year at the U.S. Nationals I could tell I was skating slowly but I couldn't do anything about it. Maybe I was a little more nervous than usual. It felt like I was skating through peanut butter.

Skating is unique. You need strength to make the jumps and stamina to keep the program moving, and you have to perform and project toward the crowd. I put in three hours on the ice every day. When I'm getting near to a competition I do back-to-back run-throughs of the program to build stamina. For strength I started a weight-training program last year. During the summer there are also classes off the ice in ballet. And I do a half-hour to an hour a day of aerobics, either riding a bike or Rollerblading.[1]

The techniques Kristi Yamaguchi uses illustrate the importance of practice and mental imaging in dealing with anxiety. Notice that she mentally rehearses her moves right before a performance. She also engages in constructive self-talk when she tells herself that a competition is like an everyday practice. Although a speaker cannot block out the audience, as can a skater, a speaker must block out distracting stimuli and focus on the situation at hand. And even though Kristi's experience at the U.S Nationals was less than ideal, she didn't let it discourage her—as evidenced by the Gold Medal she won at the following Olympics.

_____

[1] American Health © 1992 by Steve McKee.

From here on, you would visualize yourself speaking—moving, gesturing, and making eye contact with individual members of your audience right up to your conclusion. Finally, you would see your audience and teacher enthusiastically responding to your presentation. Once you become adept at visualizing, you can even add sound to the picture in your mind's eye. Hearing yourself take command of an audience as you turn a phrase or smoothly make a transition from one point to another will enhance the impact of visual imagining.

To be most effective, this skill works best as a complement to actual practice. To maximize the enhancement of public speaking skills, therefore, you will also need to rehearse your speech. You can practice in front of

Practicing your
speech is essential to
building confidence.

friends, record your speech on videotape so that you can see the dynamics
you may wish to modify, or practice in other ways. Regardless of how you
practice, here are eight steps that will help you make the most of your practice time.

Steps for Practicing Your Speech

1. Find a place where you will not be disturbed.
2. Set up the area as similar to the actual speech situation as possible. If you will be using a lectern, for example, use some object
   (like a chair or stool) to represent the lectern.
3. Practice alone first, only later in front of friends. Or tape-record
   your practice for later review.
4. Run through the whole speech at least once to see what areas
   need work.
5. Practice particular sections of the speech that are giving you trouble. Get these down "pat."
6. Go back and run through the entire speech again.
7. To work on nonverbal aspects of delivery, use a mirror or video-

tape yourself, if possible. At a minimum, try to tape-record your speech.

8. **Finally, be sure to try a run-through with an "audience" of friends, roommates, or classmates.**

Allow yourself plenty of time for practicing your speech. Make sure you have the speech ready a couple of days before it is due so that you can practice and, if necessary, revise it. Be sure to time the speech to make sure it fits the time limits of your assignment. And remember, practice doesn't make perfect, it makes permanent. So it is not just how much you practice, but how well you practice, that will make a difference in your success.

Making Effective Use of Relaxation Techniques

Butterflies, a racing heart, trembling hands, and weak knees are the result of the excessive adrenaline that is pumped into your system when you are overly aroused. The best way to prevent these symptoms is to condition your body to relax in situations that are, characteristically, overly arousing. You can accomplish this in one of several ways.

Exercise   The first way to help your body relax is to engage in some form of intense exercise one to two hours before you speak. The effects of physical exercise on physical and mental well-being are well known. Intense exercise assists us in decreasing signs of stress and has been linked to improved thinking and performance, regardless of the task.

Relaxation Imagery   If exercise is either inconvenient or impractical, another way to induce relaxation before you speak is to use relaxation imagery. Imagery is not the same as merely thinking. Imagery involves pictures, whereas thinking is a verbal process. Relaxation imagery involves visualizing pleasant and calming situations. Lying in a hammock or on the beach during a warm summer day are but two examples of such pleasant and calming situations. If you were to visually linger on such situations, you would find your body becoming increasingly relaxed. As a result, you would significantly lower the level of arousal customarily felt as a result of the day's activities.

This latter point is important. As a busy college student, you may find your upcoming speech to be the most significant but not the sole source of arousal you experience during the day. By practicing relaxation imagery before you speak, therefore, you can reduce the arousal that began to climb with the start of your day.

Muscular Relaxation   This technique involves systematically tensing and relaxing the various muscle groups. It usually begins with the muscles in your

VIDEO FILE

If you have access to the videotape accompanying this book, view segment 4. Compare the relaxation techniques discussed in this chapter with those illustrated on the tape. After reading this chapter and before your next speech, review this segment and apply at least one relaxation technique to your own presentation.

Physical exercise
before speaking can
reduce feelings of
anxiety.

face and neck, then gradually moves to your middle and lower torso. The idea behind this technique is to teach your body the difference between tension and relaxation. By first tensing and then relaxing your muscles systematically, you can also condition your muscles to relax even under the most stressful circumstances.

There's a good reason for practicing muscular relaxation. When we tense up, the range of movement in our muscles is restricted. They don't work as they are intended. In a game of basketball, we sometimes see this when a free-throw shooter hits the front of the rim, loses "touch," or puts up an air ball. With a speaker, we sometimes see this either in the absence of movement or gesturing or in movement and gesturing that are awkward and unnatural.

Combining Techniques

Visual imagery and relaxation techniques work best when used in combination. By combining relaxation imagery with visual imagining of your speech, you can enhance the effectiveness of both techniques. You will come to associate the speaking situation with relaxing images rather than anxiety-producing ones.

These techniques also work best when they become a habitual routine that you practice as you prepare to speak. Elite athletes don't use them only before they are about to compete. Speakers shouldn't put off using them, moreover, until the night before they speak. The research is clear. These techniques will serve you well only if you commit to their systematic use. We suggest that you develop a routine like the one that follows.

Five Steps to Reducing Speech Anxiety

1. **Immediately begin to analyze your goals. Ask yourself if they are realistic given your experience and commitment to this class.**

2. **Begin today to assess the degree to which you routinely engage in negative self-talk. Write down the self-criticizing, self-pressuring, and catastrophizing statements you routinely make to yourself. Describe in writing how these statements affect your level of arousal and anxiety before, during, and following your speeches.**

3. **Make a list of the positive coping statements you could substitute for the negative ones you now make. Begin to use these statements as you prepare and practice your speech.**

4. **Once you're confident that you have thoroughly prepared your speech, find a quiet time in which you can both practice relaxation imagery and visually rehearse your speech. Do this for 15 minutes every other day, actually practicing your speech in between.**

5. **Use your positive coping statements as you are about to speak, while speaking, and after speaking.**

Postpresentation Techniques

As important as it is to use these techniques prior to and during your presentation, it is equally important to use anxiety-reducing techniques after your presentation. We offer several techniques to reduce your anxiety after your presentation.

Techniques for Reducing Postpresentation Anxiety

- **Describe to yourself what you did well.**
- **List areas in which you still hope to improve. Write down at least three realistic goals for your next presentation.**
- **Engage in positive self-talk, such as "It wasn't as bad as I thought," "I did okay," "People smiled at me and gave me positive feedback."**
- **Breathe deeply, practice muscular relaxation.**

SUMMARY

Speech anxiety is a result of our subjective interpretation of the arousal we experience when called on to speak publicly. Although some degree of arousal is necessary to prepare and deliver an effective speech, too much of it can lead to psychological side effects, such as excessive worry, and physical side effects, such as trembling hands. Too much arousal can lead to a debilitating level of speech anxiety.

To control speech anxiety, you must learn to control the arousal you feel before, during, and after a speech. This learning process begins with a search for the source of your speech anxiety. The most common sources are a pessimistic attitude toward speaking, inadequate preparation and practice, negative or insufficient experience, unrealistic goals, inaccurate perception of the audience, negative self-talk, and misdirected concerns.

Once the source or sources of speech anxiety have been discovered, there are several ways in which its negative side effects can be overcome. Research demonstrates that the most effective ways to manage such anxiety include attacking the source of the anxiety directly. This involves developing an optimistic attitude toward speaking, not procrastinating the preparation of your speech, looking for opportunities to gain speaking experience, setting realistic goals, realizing the audience wants you to succeed, practicing constructive self-talk, and directing your concerns at important issues. More general ways to control speech anxiety and the accompanying arousal include using visual imagery and practice and teaching your body to relax under stressful conditions. Finally, research suggests that these techniques work best in combination.

Remember, some level of arousal when you speak is natural. Moderate levels of arousal, moreover, are necessary for effective speaking. Too much arousal, though, is the difference between being "psyched up" and "psyched out" by the speeches you have yet to share.

Check Your Understanding: Exercises and Activities

1. In a short paper, describe the relationship between physiological arousal and speech anxiety and give examples of both physical and mental symptoms of anxiety. Be sure to define anxiety and distinguish it from speech anxiety.

2. The chapter lists seven common sources of speech anxiety and steps for controlling them. For your next speaking assignment, identify at least one such source of anxiety that concerns you and make an effort to remedy it. For example, if you have a tendency to procrastinate, make sure you start your speech sooner than usual. After the speech, assess how the remedy worked in alleviating at least one source of public speaking anxiety.

3. Before your next speech, make a list of the negative self-talk you have engaged in regarding speech assignments. Then come up with a series of constructive self-talk statements you will use in preparing for and while giving your next speech. Your instructor may ask you to turn in your list prior to speaking.

4. Two of the most convenient relaxation techniques you can use are relaxation imagery and muscular relaxation. Both initially require a quiet place and time where you will not be interrupted. This exercise allows you to practice relaxation on your own or with a friend. It is sometimes useful to have someone read the steps to you so that you can completely relax.

   (1) Find a reclining chair or couch where you can make yourself comfortable.

   (2) Lower or turn off bright lights.

   (3) With your eyes closed, tense and then relax your muscles in this order: face, neck and shoulders, biceps and triceps, forearms, wrists and hands, chest, solar plexus, buttocks/hamstrings, quadriceps, calves, ankles and feet.

   (4) Once completely relaxed, imagine a peaceful setting in which you feel calm. Learn to hold this image for as long as you can. After a minute or two move on to step 5.

   (5) Imagine your speech class. If you feel any sign of anxiety, return to the preceding image.

   (6) Continue to imagine your speech class and add yourself to the picture. See yourself calmly seated, enjoying others as they speak.

   (7) See yourself writing down the requirements of an assigned speech. See yourself involved with the various stages of preparation, including seeing yourself practice.

   (8) See yourself waiting to be called on, aroused but not anxious.

   (9) See yourself walking to the front of the room, turning to face your audience, smiling and opening your presentation with impact.

   (10) See yourself speaking energetically, gesturing, and using your eyes, face, and voice.

   (11) See students and your instructor listening attentively.

   (12) See yourself concluding and your audience responding with genuine applause.

   Practice this series of steps at least twice a week for between 15 and 25 minutes each time. Remember that any time you begin to feel anxious during this exercise, replace whatever image you're holding with a pleasant and relaxing one.

Notes

1. R. M. Yerkes and J. D. Dodson, "The Relation of Strength Stimulus to Rapidity of Habit Formation," *Journal of Comparative Neurology and Psychology* 18 (1908): 459–82.

2. William J. Fremouw and Michael D. Scott, "Cognitive Restructuring: An Alternative Method for the Treatment of Communication Apprehension," *Communication Education* 28 (1979): 129–33.

3. C. L. Thomas, *Taber's Cyclopedic Medical Dictionary,* 12th ed. (Philadelphia: F. A. Davis, 1973), A-101.

4. Michael D. Scott and Louis Pelliccioni, Jr., *Don't Choke: How Athletes Can Become Winners* (Englewood Cliffs, N.J.: Spectrum Books, 1982).

5. William J. Fremouw and M. G. Harmatz, "A Helper Model for Behavioral Treatment of Speech Anxiety," *Journal of Consulting and Clinical Psychology* 43 (1975): 652–60.

6. J. A. Daly and J. C. McCroskey, eds., *Avoiding Communication: Shyness, Reticence and Communication Apprehension* (Beverly Hills, Calif.: Sage, 1984).

7. Albert Ellis and Robert A. Harper, *A New Guide to Rational Living* (Hollywood, Calif.: Wilshire Book Company, 1975).

8. Joe Ayres, "Perceptions of Speaking Ability: An Explanation for Stage Fright," *Communication Education* 35 (1986): 275–87; Michael Beatty, "Situational and Predispositional Correlates of Public Speaking Anxiety," *Communication Education* 37 (1988): 28–39; Bruskin Associates, "What Are Americans Afraid Of?" *The Bruskin Report* 53 (July 1973); J. A. Daly, A. L. Vangelisti, H. L. Neel, and P. D. Cavanaugh, "Pre-Performance Concerns Associated with Public Speaking Anxiety," *Communication Quarterly* 37 (1989): 39–53.

Listening is an important part of the speech transaction.

4

Listening

OBJECTIVES

After reading this chapter, you should be able to:

- Explain what listening involves.
- Describe the significant role that listening plays for both speakers and audience members.
- Recognize and demonstrate the difference between hearing and listening.
- Identify common misconceptions about listening.
- Exhibit behaviors consistent with those of an active listener.
- Demonstrate discriminative, comprehensive, appreciative, therapeutic, and critical listening skills.
- Identify and overcome obstacles to listening.

KEY CONCEPTS

active listening
appreciative listening
comprehensive listening
critical listening
culture
discriminative listening

listening
meta-communication
selective attention
selective perception
sensorial involvement
therapeutic listening

Nationally syndicated humorist Dave Barry wrote about traveling in Japan. In describing how "the Japanese tend to communicate via nuance and euphemism," he described an encounter between his wife, Beth, and a Japanese travel agent just prior to their trip.

BETH:	. . . and then we want to take a plane from Point A to Point B.
TRAVEL AGENT:	I see. You want to take a plane.
BETH:	Yes.
TRAVEL AGENT:	From Point A?
BETH:	Yes.
TRAVEL AGENT:	To Point B?
BETH:	Yes.
TRAVEL AGENT:	Ah.
BETH:	Can we do that?
TRAVEL AGENT:	Perhaps you would prefer to take a train.
BETH:	No, we would prefer to take a plane.
TRAVEL AGENT:	Ah-hah. You would prefer to take a plane?
BETH:	Yes. A plane.
TRAVEL AGENT:	I see. From Point A.

This exchange continued along these lines with Beth seeking an answer to what she perceived to be a straightforward and easily answered question. Hearing none, she broke off the exchange perplexed by what she perceived to be the agent's evasive and unresponsive behavior.[1]

This scenario can be common between communicators from different societies that have different norms for appropriate communication behavior. In this case, it wasn't that the Japanese agent was purposely trying to evade Beth Barry's question. To the contrary, coming from a society where it is impolite to tell others "no" explicitly, the agent was trying to assist her in coming to the realization that her request was impossible because there was no plane between points A and B. To come to such a realization, though, Beth Barry also would have had to realize that to understand the Japanese it is not enough to *hear* the content of the message. You must *listen* for the nuance of the message as well.

Of course, we don't need a cross-cultural example to know that simply hearing what people say isn't the same as listening to them. Most of us have had plenty of experiences where our understanding of what we heard didn't correspond to the message the speaker intended. This is because while we may have heard what was said, we weren't listening for the underlying message that was being sent. *Hearing* is a physical process that in no way guarantees understanding. To gain understanding, we must do more than hear the words—we must *listen*.

Listening is both physical and psychological. Listening also is one of those things to which we all pay lip service. Yet how many of us truly understand what it means to listen, what listening involves, and what significant role it can play in making us more competent communicators, both as speakers and interested audience members? Research suggests that fewer of us understand than we might think.

Listening to other people is essential not only to our daily lives but also to our development as speakers. Further, the information we receive in our daily lives is often rich in cues about the nature of our potential audiences. Thus we are more likely to achieve our speaking goals if we have listened carefully to the people around us.

The ability to listen effectively is important to succeeding (1) in school, (2) at work, (3) in relationships with friends and family, and (4) in situations where we need to share information with others. First, to see how effective listening is essential to learning, consider the fact that as a college student you are exposed to hundreds of hours of lectures, group discussions, and mediated communication. The ability to process and absorb information is the essence of learning. Not every professor is a brilliant speaker, holding your attention with ease. You need to listen especially well if you are to obtain the maximum benefit from your college career.

Second, effective listening is essential to success in the work force. One of the key complaints of many employers is that employees do not listen effectively, costing millions of dollars each year in mistakes and inefficiencies. Among the skills employers value in listeners are "listening for content; listening to conversations; listening for long-term contexts; listening for emotional meaning; and listening to follow directions."[2]

Third, listening is essential to interpersonal communication, especially in families. How many times have you heard children or parents complain that no one listens to what they say? In interpersonal contexts, listening must go well beyond content, focusing on the emotional and relational components of the communication transaction.

Finally, listening is essential to effectively communicate information to others. You need to adapt your own messages to the feedback you receive from others. Understanding what others need is essential to successfully influencing their beliefs, attitudes, and actions through the speeches you share.

As you can see in Figure 4.1 on page 88, which shows the types of communication activities in which people engage daily, listening is by far the most dominant. But it also may be the one with which people are least skilled. The average listener remembers only about half of what was said immediately after it was said. And, as if that weren't bad enough, after 48 hours the average listener remembers only about one quarter of what was said.[3]

In this chapter we discuss the nature of listening, listening to the internal dialogue, misconceptions about listening, obstacles to effective listening, types of listening, and a series of interdependent techniques you

FIGURE 4.1
Listening relative
to other types of
communication.

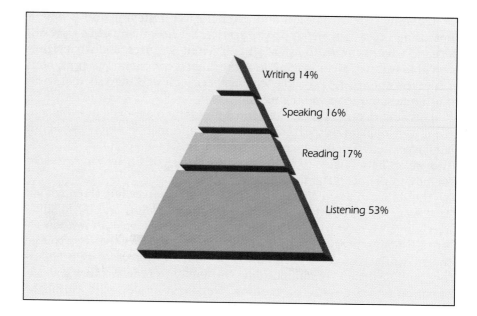

can begin to use immediately in the effort to improve your listening behavior.

THE NATURE OF LISTENING

There is no universally accepted definition of listening. For our purposes, though, **listening** is the process of receiving, attending to, and assigning meaning to aural as well as visual and tactile stimuli.[4] Important to this comprehensive definition is the idea of **active listening,** which involves conscious and responsive participation in the communication transaction.[5] Such active and complete participation encompasses the following:

- selective attention
- sensorial involvement
- comprehension
- retention

Recall from Chapter 1 that the speech transaction is influenced by perception. What's more, people tend to perceive messages selectively. **Selective perception** is the tendency to ascribe meaning to a message that corresponds to our predispositions. A related type of selectivity is **selective attention,** which means that we make a conscious choice to focus on some

Drawing by Ziegler; © 1982 The New Yorker Magazine, Inc.

people and some messages, rather than others. **Sensorial involvement** means that we listen with all of our senses, not simply our sense of hearing. **Comprehension** is the act of understanding what has been communicated. And **retention** is the act of storing what has been communicated in either short- or long-term memory. Whereas the latter two processes are probably familiar to you, the first two, selective attention and sensorial involvement, deserve careful consideration.

Selective Attention

We are most likely to seek out and pay attention to speakers and messages that we perceive to be reinforcing. A person whose speech reflects our viewpoint, therefore, is more likely to get our undivided attention than one whose speech presents a diametrically opposed viewpoint. Similarly, professors whose lectures involve your major are more likely to "have your ear" than those who lecture on topics outside your major.

Understanding selective attention is important to your development as an audience-focused speaker and as an attentive and responsive audience member. You cannot learn to effectively communicate to your audience, for example, unless you first selectively choose to pay attention to the thoughts and concerns of the people in it. You can't be a responsive audience member unless you make the conscious choice to pay attention to what a speaker shares. Listening to others speak, moreover, is one of the best ways to improve on your own speaking ability. For instance, listening for such things as the developmental pattern a speaker follows, changes in pitch and rate, and the sources a speaker cites can assist you tremendously in preparing and delivering your own speeches. In a sense, listening facilitates the "modeling" of effective speakers and their speeches. However, you first must decide to consciously pay attention—selectively attend—to these models of effective public speaking.

Actually, listening begins within our own minds. We all carry on an internal dialogue. Sometimes this is limited to our own thoughts, whereas at other times, it is in response to what someone else has said. For example, imagine you are about to ask a friend for money. You might hear yourself saying silently, "Oh no, he'll never loan me the money. All I will do is tick him off." On the other hand, you might think, "I've helped her out before. She knows I'm good for it. What have I got to lose?"

Sometimes we listen to our thoughts in response to another's words, although we don't verbalize them. For example, suppose you listen to someone speaking about a controversial topic. If you agree with the speaker, you may find yourself thinking, "Yeah ... yes!" On the other hand, if you disagree with the speaker, you may mentally hear yourself saying things like, "You've got to be kidding." Listening to your own thoughts affects how you listen to others and can interfere with your processing of the message you are receiving. For example, if you think you already know what a speaker is going to say, you might say to yourself, "Heard that before," and tune out, missing an important message you did not anticipate. Or thinking about what you are going to say to another person can cause you to miss what he or she is really saying.

Sensorial Involvement

Once you've chosen to pay close attention to the speech transaction, you then need to practice sensorial involvement, that is, involve all of your senses in the transaction. As noted in Chapter 1, every message has two dimensions: a content and a relationship dimension. Reading the text of a speech is not the same as physically participating in the transaction. Reading just text limits us to the *content* of the message and its compositional elements. While *what* a speaker says is important, *how* a speaker says it is equally important. Gestures, movements, facial expressions, and eye contact serve to visually punctuate the content of a speech and suggest nuances of meaning. The reaction of people to a speaker's message and the physical setting in which it's shared also affect the meaning of the message.

To truly appreciate the speech transaction, therefore, you need to involve as many of your senses as you can. Not only must you try to hear what is being said, but you also must try to see and feel what is being said. Only then will you be in a position to measure the totality of the message that has been communicated.

SPEAKING OF . . .

Misheard Lyrics

This list of "misheard" lyrics is reprinted with permission of Simon & Schuster from *'Scuse Me While I Kiss This Guy and Other Misheard Lyrics* by Gavin Edwards, copyright ©1995 by Gavin Edwards, in which he reveals what people thought they heard in popular song lyrics. The title, by the way, comes from a mishearing of a Jimi Hendrix lyric, "'Scuse me while I kiss the sky."

Misheard lyric:
  "The girl with colitis goes by."
Correct lyric:
  "The girl with kaleidoscope eyes."
        —The Beatles

Misheard lyric:
  "And doughnuts make my brown eyes blue."
Correct lyric:
  "And don't it make my brown eyes blue."
        —Crystal Gayle

Misheard lyric:
  "They sent you a tie clasp."
Correct lyric:
  "They said you was high class."
        —Elvis Presley

Misheard lyric:
  "I'll never leave your pizza burnin'."
Correct lyric:
  "I'll never be your beast of burden."
        —The Rolling Stones

Misheard lyric: "Mice aroma."
Correct lyric: "My Sharona."
        —The Knack

Misheard lyric:
  "Baking carrot biscuits."
Correct lyric:
  "Takin' care of business."
        —Bachman-Turner Overdrive

MISCONCEPTIONS ABOUT LISTENING

There are a number of common misconceptions about effective listening. In this section we detail several of these, including the idea that listening is easy, automatically results from intelligence, does not need to be planned, and can be improved through improving reading.[6] Some humorous examples of mishearing are listed in the box "Misheard Lyrics." Unfortunately, failure to listen can also have disastrous consequences.

"It's Easy to Listen"

Some people think that listening is like breathing—that they are born competent listeners. Of course, that is just as fallacious as assuming that because they breathe, they breathe well enough to become professional singers. Just because someone can carry a tune and sing in the shower, it doesn't mean the person is ready for the New York Metropolitan Opera. Similarly, just because we've heard others talk to us all of our lives, it does not mean we are effective listeners. Quite the contrary, our complacency about listening is one of the very things that makes us susceptible to poor listening habits.

"I'm Smart, So I'm a Good Listener"

As the following example will show, even highly intelligent people can fail to listen. Submarine crew members are among the most intelligent, tested, and trained members of the navy. But failure to listen caused the submarine U.S.S. *Stickleback* to collide with a destroyer escort and sink off Hawaii in May 1958. Although no personnel were lost, tragedy was narrowly avoided. And it all happened because an electrician's mate thought he heard the order "Come on" when the actual order was "Come off." Instead of turning his rheostat *down,* as he was ordered, therefore, he turned it *up,* tripping the circuit breakers, cutting off power, and causing the sub to lose control, plunging directly into the path of the destroyer escort.[7]

Despite what we may think, intelligence far from guarantees effective listening. While some highly intelligent people have been trained to use effective listening skills, equal numbers have not. As the U.S.S. *Stickleback* incident illustrated so well, moreover, some people may fail to listen carefully in spite of their intelligence.

"There's No Need to Plan Ahead"

A third common misconception is that listening just happens—that there's no need to plan for it. Of course, sometimes you will end up listening to an unexpected conversation. But if you know in advance that you will be in a listening situation such as the one you face in your speech class, you should plan ahead. For example, in most introductory speech courses, students provide each other with both oral and written feedback. Who do you think will do a better job: the student who prepares in advance, including a review of criteria for the speech, checklists for speech evaluation, and a clear understanding of the speech assignment, or the one who shows up to class only to be surprised by the fact that he or she will be responsible for providing classmates with feedback about their speeches? Finally, when the tables are turned, whose speeches do you think most likely will benefit from the critical evaluation of the speech by classmates?

"I Can Read, So I Can Listen"

Although one might assume that reading and listening skills are correlated, that is not the case. In fact, the skills required are quite different. The reader controls the pace of communication, whereas a listener is at the mercy of

In a bar, listening is extremely difficult because of physical conditions.

the person speaking. A reader can reread a confusing passage, whereas a listener may have only one chance to get the point. Reading is typically a solitary activity; listening most often takes place in groups where it might be hard to hear the speaker or there might be distractions. Listening skills, as you can begin to see, require development in their own right.

OBSTACLES TO LISTENING

There are several factors that can intervene to prevent effective listening. Six of the most important obstacles to listening are physical conditions, cultural differences, personal problems, bias, connotative meanings, and anxiety.[8] Most of these obstacles are directly influenced by our perceptions. Thus the discussion of perception and communication in Chapter 1 directly relates to problems in listening.

Physical Conditions

The physical environment clearly affects our ability to listen. Among the factors that can inhibit listening are noise, an unpleasant room temperature, poor lighting, physical obstacles, and uncomfortable chairs. A noisy, hot, poorly lit room, with a post blocking your view and hard chairs, is hardly an ideal listening environment. On the other hand, a quiet, well-lit

Cultural differences can affect our ability to listen effectively.

room, with a clear line of sight, comfortable (but not too comfortable) chairs, and a pleasant temperature, allows you to concentrate on the speaker. Although there is usually not much the listener can do about the physical environment, certainly being aware of its impact on listening helps you know how much you need to focus. In addition, you can often choose your location to listen. Students who sit in the back of the classroom, where their view is limited, often are tempted to let their attention drift. Those who move front and center clearly are interested in listening to what is said.

Speakers may be able to mediate the impact of the physical environment on audience listening. They can raise their voice so that it is more audible, move toward audience members in the back of a room, and use attention-getting devices such as questions.

Cultural Differences

Communication patterns vary from culture to culture. **Culture** is a learned system of language, beliefs, customs, and values with which specific people identify. For example, the relative importance of the *context* in which listening takes place differs from one culture to another. As anthropologists Edward T. Hall and Mildred Reed Hall define **context,** it is the information that surrounds an event and contributes to the meaning of that event.[9] For example, suppose you receive a message on your answering machine from a relative you almost never hear from except in an emergency. The message simply says, "Call me right away." Needless to say, you would be alarmed, because you know this person never calls you unless there is a serious problem. On the other hand, if you received the same message from a friend who likes to get together with you, you might assume he or she just wants to set up a meeting. The same message has a very different meaning because of the context in which it occurs.

Some cultures rely more than others on unspoken information contained in the context to determine the meaning of the message. In high-context (HC) cultures, such as Japan, the Arab states, and the Mediterranean countries, the context of statements can be extremely important. Much of the meaning in such cultures is carried not only by words spoken but also by the situation in which they are uttered. On the other hand, in low-context (LC) cultures, such as the United States, Germany, and most northern European countries, people rely less on the overall communication situation and more on the words spoken to convey meaning.

When low- and high-context people communicate with each other, the results can be frustrating. Hall and Hall note that

> HC people are apt to become impatient and irritated when LC people insist on giving them information they don't need. Conversely, low-context people are at a loss when high-context people do not provide *enough* information. . . . Too much information frequently leads people to feel they are being talked down to; too little information can mystify them or make them feel left out.[10]

Although we cannot give you any simple rule of thumb for dealing with cultural differences in listening, our best advice is to be aware of the culture of the person(s) to whom you are listening or speaking and take differences from your own culture into account. If you expect to be listening or speaking to someone from a different culture, which is increasingly likely on a college campus, learn as much as you can in advance about the person's culture.

Personal Problems

Most people have had the experience of being so preoccupied with a personal problem they couldn't pay attention to what someone was saying. Personal problems can easily detract from listening to what is being said. The best advice for overcoming this obstacle is to recognize the situation and to focus on what is being said, as difficult as that may be. For example, if you were plagued by a personal problem prior to an important job interview, chances are you would tell yourself to "get your act together." You need to do exactly the same thing prior to listening to (or giving) a speech.

Bias

All people are biased, though not to an equal degree. Bias reflects an opinion formed without evidence, usually about a person or group of people. Racial, religious, sexual, and other such biases, while forbidden by law, often exist in the reality of people's opinions. Recognizing bias is an important step to overcoming it.

Bias isn't always based exclusively on false generalizations about groups of people. Prior, but incomplete, knowledge can cause us to form hasty judgments. Consider the case of the bombing of the Federal Building in Oklahoma City in 1995. Such terrorist acts previously were associated with Arab or Muslim terrorist groups almost exclusively. Despite only partial information, many people chose to jump to unsupported conclusions about who was responsible for the Oklahoma City bombing, even calling for military retaliation against Islamic countries like Iran, which, it turned out, had no involvement. They quickly quieted down when a young American was arrested for the crime. Regardless of its source, bias is a serious impediment to listening. To overcome bias, listeners need to first recognize its existence, mentally set it aside, and recognize its irrationality.

Connotative Meanings

Words have both denotative and connotative meanings. The **denotative meanings** of words are those meanings generally agreed on and which are found in the dictionary. The **connotative meanings** are the subjective meanings, often with strong emotional, personal, and attitudinal components.

Consider a word like "mother." The denotative meaning is straightforward—a female parent. Yet the connotations of the word can vary tremendously. For example, some people have a close and loving relationship with their mother, so they might think of being nurtured and feel happy when they hear the word. Others have a strained relationship with their mother, so they might remember being rejected and feel angry. Adopted children and step-children might have yet other associations. And, of course, there is the street slang meaning of mother that is anything but loving.

Understanding that people may have very different connotations for the same word is essential to overcoming this obstacle to effective listening. Listeners need to recognize their own "trigger words" which may have great emotional content for them, but not necessarily for everyone else. What's more, speakers need to avoid words that are connotatively confusing, if they are to make their meaning clear.

Anxiety

As discussed in Chapter 3, anxiety significantly detracts from our ability to process the information to which we are exposed. Anxious speakers often

TABLE 4.1 Common Types of Listening

Type	Goal	Example
Discriminative listening	To recognize meaning based on variations in audible or visible signals	Listening for difference between verbal message and facial expression
Comprehensive listening	To understand	Listening to lecture on Einstein's theory of relativity
Appreciative listening	To experience stimulation and enjoyment	Listening to music
Therapeutic listening	To help people express their feelings in a nonevaluative and non-threatening environment	Therapist listening to client
Critical listening	To arrive at an informed judgment	Listening to candidates to assist you in voting

are unable to focus on audience feedback as they speak or actively listen to an instructor's feedback when finished speaking. Likewise, anxious audience members have difficulty listening actively. To evaluate yourself in this area, see the box "What Is Your Level of Receiver Apprehension?" on pages 98–99.

TYPES OF LISTENING

Just as there is no single style of effective speaking, there is no single type of listening that is appropriate in each and every situation. There are five common but different types of listening: discriminative, comprehensive, appreciative, therapeutic, and critical.[11] Let's look at each in detail, as well as suggestions to improve your skills at each type of listening. Table 4.1 gives the goal and an example of each type of listening.

Discriminative Listening

This type of listening is the one on which all others are based. **Discriminative listening** distinguishes auditory and/or visual stimuli.[12] As infants we begin to listen discriminatively, learning first to recognize parental voices, then sounds, words, and eventually the complex structures of language. Visual stimuli, such as facial expression, gesture, and movement, become part of meaning for us, as does touch. The careful listener is

SELF-ASSESSMENT

What Is Your Level of Receiver Apprehension?

The following statements apply to how various people feel about receiving communication. Although this measure was developed specifically for persons without hearing disabilities, people who are hard of hearing may think about analogous situations in which they become anxious while receiving messages through nonaural means, such as sign language, closed caption, reading lips, or via a TDD. Indicate if these statements apply to how you feel by noting whether you (5) strongly agree, (4) agree, (3) are undecided, (2) disagree, or (1) strongly disagree.

_____ 1. I feel comfortable when listening to others on the phone.

_____ 2. It is often difficult for me to concentrate on what others are saying.

_____ 3. When listening to members of the opposite sex I find it easy to concentrate on what is being said.

_____ 4. I have no fear of being a listener as a member of an audience.

_____ 5. I feel relaxed when listening to new ideas.

_____ 6. I would rather not have to listen to other people at all.

_____ 7. I am generally overexcited and rattled when others are speaking to me.

_____ 8. I often feel uncomfortable when listening to others.

_____ 9. My thoughts become confused and jumbled when reading important information.

_____ 10. I often have difficulty concentrating on what others are saying.

_____ 11. Receiving new information makes me feel restless.

_____ 12. Watching television makes me nervous.

_____ 13. When on a date I find myself tense and self-conscious when listening to my date.

sensitive to both verbal and nonverbal nuances of messages. This is especially true for public speaking. Listeners in the audience need to look beyond just the words of a speaker's message. By the same token, speakers need to discriminatively listen to the entire message received from the audience. This means they should listen not only for aural feedback but for feedback from nonverbal sources as well. This includes, for example, the expressions on audience members' faces, their body orientation, and head movement such as nodding in agreement. Listed below are some skills that will help you improve your discriminative listening.[13]

_____ 14. I enjoy being a good listener.

_____ 15. I generally find it easy to concentrate on what is being said.

_____ 16. I seek out the opportunity to listen to new ideas.

_____ 17. I have difficulty concentrating on instructions others give to me.

_____ 18. It is hard to listen or concentrate on what other people are saying unless I know them well.

_____ 19. I feel tense when listening as a member of a social gathering.

_____ 20. Television programs that attempt to change my mind about something make me nervous.

To determine your score, first total the scores you gave yourself for statements 2, 6, 7, 8, 9, 10, 11, 12, 13, 17, 18, 19, 20, and *add* 42 to that total (maximum 107, minimum 55). From this result, *subtract* the total of the scores you gave yourself for statements 1, 3, 4, 5, 14, 15, 16. Your score should be in the range of 20 to 100. The higher your score, the more apprehensive you are about listening. Scores above 80 indicate a relatively high level of receiver apprehension. A mid-range score would be about 60. Scores below 40 would indicate a relatively low level of receiver apprehension.

Based on your score, what sorts of listening behaviors do you think you could improve? For example, do your answers suggest a need to work harder at concentration? Should you seek greater opportunities to practice listening skills and learn new information? Could the same type of relaxation exercises suggested in Chapter 3 be useful in listening situations, as well as when you are a public speaker?

SOURCE: Copyright by the Speech Communication Association, 1975, from Lawrence R. Wheeless, "An Investigation of Receiver Apprehension and Social Context Dimensions of Communication Apprehension," *The Speech Teacher* 24, (1975): 261–68, by permission.

Tips for Improving Discriminative Listening

- *Learn to recognize sound structures of language.* Fortunately, most people have mastered this by the time they reach school age. However, if you must listen to someone speak a language that is your second language, you will be frustrated until you have mastered the structure of sound in that language.
- *Learn to detect and isolate vocal cues.* This involves becoming sensitive to vocal inflection, pitch volume, intensity, and the like, which can affect meaning.

- *Practice understanding different dialects.* As our nation becomes increasingly diverse, you will encounter numerous different dialects within the community of English speakers. Understanding someone from a different region, for example, requires concentration and is enhanced by familiarity with the dialect.

- *Learn to detect and isolate visual cues.* Often we can learn as much about a message from what we see as what we hear. The face, for example, can be particularly revealing about a person's emotional state.

Comprehensive Listening

Once discriminative listening has occured, the next step is **comprehensive listening,** which is listening targeted at understanding.[14] Successful comprehensive listening demands that your understanding of a message closely approximates that of the source of the message. How well you comprehensively listen depends on several factors. Chief among them are vocabulary, concentration, and memory.[15]

Vocabulary   Obviously, you cannot comprehend something for which you don't have meaning. Thus a limited vocabulary has the undesirable effect of limiting your ability to comprehensively listen to messages. In fact, failure to master the necessary vocabulary can lead to disaster. For example, both of the authors of this text were high school debaters. One of us recalls a particularly embarrassing incident which resulted from not knowing the meaning of the word *superfluous.* Unaware that the other team's plan to remove all "superfluous United States tariffs" meant that they would remove only the unnecessary ones, the author's team produced several examples of tariffs that were essential to American industries. During cross-examination, an opposing team member asked the author, "Do you know what *superfluous* means?" Of course, the author did not know. When the opposition pointed out that every tariff the author's team had cited was, by definition, *not* superfluous, and that only superfluous tariffs would be removed, the debate was, for all practical purposes, lost. Needless to say, a dictionary became standard material for all future debates.

Concentration   A second important factor for comprehensive listening is concentration. As we know all too well, our minds are easily distracted from the task at hand. If you doubt that, think back to the last time you immediately forgot the name of someone to whom you had just been introduced.

There are two types of concentration: wide-band and pinpoint (Figure 4.2). Whereas pinpoint concentration is most relevant to critical listening, wide-band concentration is most central to comprehensive listening. **Pinpoint concentration** focuses on specific details. **Wide-band con-**

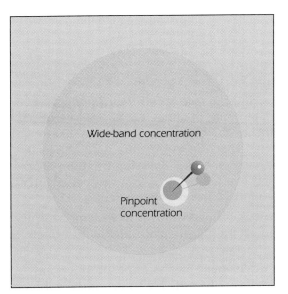

FIGURE 4.2
If you were listening to a symphonic orchestra, you would use wide-band concentration to focus on the total sound of the orchestra. Pinpoint concentration would involve focusing on a single section of the orchestra.

Wide-band concentration

Pinpoint concentration

centration focuses on patterns rather than details. As a result, wide-band concentration assists you in listening for the tone of the speech, or its larger meaning in a particular context.

Both types of concentration, however, demand that you try to block out stimuli that compete with the message on which you are trying to focus. These competing stimuli range from the obvious, such as a heavy-metal band playing in the free-speech area outside your classroom, to the subtle, for example, the gastrointestinal growls your stomach makes when you are hungry.

Memory   Closely related to concentration is the third factor that influences comprehensive listening—memory. Often the failure to remember reflects the fact that you also failed to concentrate. Consider the example of forgetting the name of someone to whom you have just been introduced. Although this very common experience simply may be the result of "mental laziness," most often it is the product of the anxiety accompanying the situation. Both anxiety and preoccupation with feelings of anxiety have a devastating effect on our powers of concentration and memory. As you are being introduced to someone, you may be too busy thinking about how you are being perceived to concentrate on the person's name. It isn't that you forgot the name—it's that you didn't listen for and process the name in the first place.

Much of your day is spent in situations that require comprehensive listening. And nowhere is this more likely to be true than in your speech class.

Here are some skills that will help you improve your comprehensive listening.[16]

Tips for Improving Comprehensive Listening

- *Utilize the time difference between speech and thought effectively.* While most people speak at a rate of about 125 to 150 words per minute, the human brain has the capability to process 400 to 500 words per minute, although that is possible only with a special process known as "compressed speech." By using the time differential to think about what you are hearing, you can better interpret and understand the significance of what is said.

- *Listen for main ideas.* Don't get bogged down in insignificant detail. Rather, focus on understanding the main ideas and principles a speaker is discussing.

- *Listen for significant details.* Though not as important as main ideas, some details are fairly significant. Try to determine which details are illustrative of the main ideas and have significance in understanding what is being said.

- *Learn to draw valid inferences.* What does it all mean? Try to determine what conclusions you can draw from the speech.

Appreciative Listening

Appreciative listening involves obtaining sensory stimulation or enjoyment from others.[17] This could include listening to music, drama, poetry, or a speech to entertain. Though it might appear that such listening "just comes naturally," the fact is that you can enhance your pleasure by expanding your listening experiences, improving your understanding of what you are listening to, and developing your powers of concentration. Music appreciation classes, for example, help students learn what to listen for in different kinds of music.

This is also true of your speech class. Learning about the various types, styles, and structures of speeches should assist you in appreciating what a rarity a good speech is. Learning how important it is to construct and share a good speech, moreover, should only reinforce your appreciation and give you a more finely tuned ear. Here are some skills that will help you improve your appreciative listening.[18]

Tips for Improving Appreciative Listening

- *Use opportunities to gain experience with appreciative listening.* Listening appreciatively, as with all forms of listening, requires experience with different situations.

- *Be willing to listen appreciatively to a variety of writers, speakers, composers, and so on.* Even if you've developed preconceptions about a particular composer or type of music, for example, be willing to listen with an open mind. You may not appreciate Beethoven, and someone else may not appreciate The Black Crowes. Chances are that with a proper frame of mind you can learn what it is that makes them both appealing to large numbers of people.

- *Develop the ability to concentrate while listening appreciatively.* Many forms of appreciative listening depend on not letting your mind wander. Of course, the greater your experience with a variety of situations that involve listening, the more ability you will have to concentrate on the important aspects of the experience.

Therapeutic Listening

Therapeutic listening helps someone talk through a problem.[19] It is the sort of listening that occurs when a therapist listens to a client to help the client overcome his or her difficulties. It also can be a valuable skill when interviewing people as part of the preparation of a speech. This is particularly so, in fact, if the topic you are researching is a sensitive one with which the interviewee has personal experience. Using nonevaluative and nonthreatening ways to help people express their feelings is the hallmark of therapeutic listening. Therapeutic listening requires that listeners focus their attention fully, including showing attentiveness verbally and nonverbally, and demonstrate empathy for the speaker. When you are listening this way, pay particular attention to emotive words that convey such things as anger, tension, and feelings of powerlessness. Also, recognize that you are probably less likely to hear words that convey negative feelings than those that convey positive ones. Finally, therapeutic listening can provide insight into what audience members are like. Here are some skills that will help you improve your therapeutic listening.[20]

Tips for Improving Therapeutic Listening

- *Focus your full attention on the message sender.* If you allow your attention to wander, you do not just hurt yourself, you undermine the very purpose of listening therapeutically

- *Demonstrate attending behaviors, both verbally and nonverbally.* Convey your interest. Nodding, gesturing, providing verbal feedback—all tell the person you are listening and that you care.

- *Develop a supportive communication climate.* Avoid making judgmental statements. Stick to descriptive and nonevaluative remarks. One way to do this is to listen with empathy, which means show that you understand what the other person is going through. Indifference or hostility can be very destructive to the communication transaction in any case, but particularly so in therapeutic listening.

- *Respond appropriately—be a sounding board.* But don't try to play amateur psychiatrist.

Critical Listening

Critical listening, which is an extension and refinement of the other types of listening described in Table 4.1, often requires skills similar to those required by appreciative, discriminative, comprehensive, and therapeutic listening. There is a crucial difference, however: **Critical listening** is listening for the purpose of making reasoned judgment about speakers and the credibility of their messages.

Much of the daily information we receive is targeted at influencing us, as well as making us compliant to the wishes of others. If information directed at influencing us or making us comply was always in our own self-interest, this wouldn't be a problem. Of course, this is anything but the case. Cigarette advertising, for example, is notorious for encouraging people to pursue a habit that can cost them their health or even their life. Beer companies, moreover, glamorize drinking to excess, even though alcohol is the single most abused substance in the United States.

Thus learning to listen critically is a form of self-protection. It guards us against being taken advantage of by unscrupulous salespeople, politicians, and plain old con artists. But learning to listen critically also enhances our ability to communicate while delivering a speech.

At a minimum, critical listening involves focusing on both the speaker and the message in the attempt to verify the validity of what is being said. Is the speaker competent and trustworthy? If you think so, what evidence has been given to you that would make this the case? Is the message directed at getting you to change, stay the same, or buy something? Is it merely informative, or is it argumentative? In either case, how do you know the information is representative of the facts? Is it logical? Is it supported with evidence, and are the sources clearly cited?

Here are some skills that will help you improve your critical listening.[21]

Tips for Improving Critical Listening

- *Consider the credibility of the source.* How much confidence do you have in the good will, trustworthiness, and competence of the person to whom you are listening?

- *Recognize that credibility of sources can influence you.* Although credibility is important and can be influential in and of itself, do

Liquor ads ignore the problems associated with abuse of alcohol.

not let another person's judgment automatically replace your own thinking. Even the most credible sources can be wrong.

- *Evaluate the validity of arguments.* Are the arguments presented reasonable? Don't be afraid to question the logic of a speaker if it seems fallacious.

- *Evaluate the evidence presented in support of arguments.* Is the evidence presented believable, from reliable sources, and documented for you?

- *Recognize fallacies of reasoning.* In Chapter 14 we discuss a number of ways arguments that appear to be valid can be deceptive or fallacious.

- *Identify emotional appeals.* Determine the type of emotions the speaker appeals to. Are these appeals ones with which you are proud to identify? Whereas appealing to legitimate human emotions is a necessary aspect of persuasion (as we see in Chapter 13), misguided appeals can be destructive. Use of appeals to hate, irrational fears, and prejudice should be rejected.

The critical perspective you bring to bear when listening to speakers and their messages is just as relevant to you and the message you ultimately share with others. Thus, learning to listen critically to others will assist you in becoming more objectively critical of yourself. This will assist you in both the preparation and delivery of your own speeches because it will force you to apply a similar set of critical questions to yourself.

TECHNIQUES TO IMPROVE YOUR LISTENING SKILLS

To begin with, no one can make you listen. The decision to actively attend to speakers and their messages is yours and yours alone. The same is true for speakers listening to their audiences. All the techniques in the world, therefore, won't help you become a better listener unless you consciously choose to attend to a specific speaking transaction.

The techniques that follow are best viewed as a collection or system of techniques that are interdependent. Your skill in using one of these techniques, consequently, will have a direct bearing on your skill in using them all. The techniques we discuss are setting goals, blocking out distracting stimuli, suspending judgment, focusing on main points, recognizing highlights and signposts, taking effective notes, being sensitive to meta-communication, paraphrasing, and questioning.

Setting Goals

The first technique is straightforward: Establish a goal you hope to achieve as a consequence of listening. This goes back to the types of listening described earlier. The goal of therapeutic listening is not the same as the goal of critical listening.

Your goal will guide your behavior as you listen. When you are listening critically, for example, much of your attention will be focused on distinguishing what part of a speaker's message is fact from what part of it is opinion. In contrast, when you are listening therapeutically, much of your attention will be focused on what the message suggests an interviewee or a speaker is feeling.

The listening goal established tends to dictate the listening behaviors in which people engage. Thus, when people fail to establish a goal at the outset of the listening process, they run the risk of focusing on what is peripheral rather than central to their needs.

Blocking Out Distracting Stimuli

The second technique is even more straightforward than the first. To listen actively, you must clear your mind of distracting stimuli. Trying to force yourself to rid your mind of distracting thoughts, however, is not the answer. Relaxation may be.

Research suggests that a relaxed mind is a receptive mind. Moreover, we know that there is a mind–body relationship in this regard. When the body feels relaxed, so does the mind. As a result, anything you do to promote self-relaxation prior to listening should help you diminish the potential impact of distracting stimuli. In Chapter 3 we provided a number of ways to help you relax before speaking. The same techniques can also help you relax so that you can become a more receptive listener.

Suspending Judgment

As the Oklahoma City bombing example illustrated, people can be excessively judgmental, even when they have been provided with little concrete evidence on which to base their judgments. People cannot listen when they prematurely judge others and their messages. They may hear what they want to hear, but they cannot listen. Comprehensive listening and critical listening especially demand an open mind.

In the attempt to suspend judgment when you are listening to a speaker, you can do three things. First, recognize and accept the fact that you and everyone else bring subjective experience and bias to the speech transaction. This subjective experience colors and filters your perceptions of the speaker and the message. Second, try not to judge a book by its cover. Stereotypes on the basis of physical appearance are notoriously unreliable. Finally, try to process the message rather than immediately reacting to the speaker and the message.

Focusing on Main Points

You may also find it helpful to prioritize what you listen for in a communication transaction. The content of all messages varies in importance. Some ideas expressed are central, whereas others are more peripheral. As mentioned earlier, listening to the main ideas in a message is most important.

Some students make the mistake of trying to write down verbatim everything a professor says in class. They risk missing the main points of a lecture. For example, one of the authors had a classmate in college who tape-recorded and then transcribed every class lecture. Despite an extraordinary effort on her part, she rarely earned better than a C. Why? Because she focused so much on trying to record and memorize every word her professors said, she never learned to separate the important points from insignificant ones.

Recognizing Highlights and Signposts

Two things you can look for in the attempt to make sure you are listening for main ideas are highlights and signposts. Highlights and signposts also are something you'll want to include in your own speeches to assist the listeners in your audience. The best speakers go out of their way to highlight what is most important in their message. They might say:

> "Of the three ideas I've shared, this one is far and away the most important.
>
> "In my mind, the most precious freedom we enjoy is the freedom of speech."
>
> "How can anyone ignore the magnitude of environmental problems caused by automobiles?"

Signposts are transitional statements that tell people when one main idea is ending and another is beginning. Examples of such signposts might be:

> "Having established the importance of a speaker's credibility, let's now look at . . ."
>
> "This key to understanding the poetry of Edgar Allen Poe leads me to my second point about the interpretation of *The Raven*."
>
> "Equally important to this idea is the notion that an open society demands a free press."

Taking Effective Notes

Much as professors might like to think otherwise, not every word they utter in their lectures deserves to be recorded. Yet they routinely have to ask students to quit writing, sit back in their seats, and listen to an idea before writing it down. Effective note-taking is a science. Like any other science, it demands an appropriate methodology. Ralph G. Nichols and Thomas R. Lewis, two of the earliest researchers on the process of listening, describe four basic note-taking methods for listening to speeches and lectures.[22] They point out that no one method will work with every situation. The four methods are outlining, annotating of a book or manuscript, précis writing, and recording fact versus principle.

Outlining   We will discuss outlining from the point of view of the speaker at greater length in Chapter 8, so we won't go over the details of the process here. Basically the listener tries to capture the main points of the speech as they are presented, as well as the subordinate or supporting ideas under each point. A well-done outline is a good guide to what has been said. But outlining requires considerable effort on the part of the listener and can distract attention from what is being said. It also depends on the speaker using clear signposts and a consistent organizational pattern. Trying to outline a disorganized speech is the height of frustration.

Annotation   This technique works well only when a speaker or lecturer is going over material you have already read. For example, if a literature professor is discussing a short story you have been assigned to read, you would write marginal comments called annotations along the place in the book the professor is discussing. Although the technique does not require great effort on the part of the listener, it can be messy and there is no way to organize your notes for later review.

Précis Writing   With this technique, you listen for a few minutes, get the gist of what the speaker is saying, and then write a brief paragraph to yourself summarizing what has been said. This technique involves alternating between intense listening for three- or four-minute intervals and brief periods of note-taking. While listening to the speaker, you should be focusing on what is being said and how to summarize it for your notes. Though the notes produced are brief, clear, and easy to review, the downside is that you must divert your attention from the speaker to write your précis.

Recording Fact versus Principle   First, you divide your page vertically down the middle. On the left write "facts," on the right "principles." As you listen to the speaker, list each important fact presented on the left, numbering them 1, 2, 3, and so on. On the right, list only broad general principles, using roman numerals (I, II, III, etc.) to distinguish them from facts. Under each principle, list the numbers of facts that correspond to the principles. This method of note-taking is illustrated in Figure 4.3 on page 110. The system avoids excessive writing and requires the listener to think about what the speaker has said. In addition, you can leave space at the bottom for ideas and questions that occur to you as you listen. Although this is a very useful technique, it works better for the social sciences and humanities than for the natural sciences.

Whatever note-taking system you employ, the important thing is to focus attention on the speaker's ideas and try to think about what is being said, not simply try to produce a transcript. Writing down too much can cause you to miss the most important ideas and get bogged down in minute details.

Being Sensitive to Meta-Communication

Another important technique involves listening for meta-communication. **Meta-communication** is the message about the message. It is generally conveyed nonverbally. You can listen for meta-communication in a speaker's eyes, voice, gestures, movements, posture, and use of time. You can also listen for meta-communication in other people's reaction to your message.

Chief among the reasons for listening carefully to meta-communication is cross cue–checking. **Cross cue–checking** involves gauging what a person says verbally against the nonverbal behaviors that make up meta-communication. Cross cue–checking enables people to ferret out the subtleties in a speaker's message—for example, irony, sarcasm, and sometimes

FACTS	PRINCIPLES
1. 1455, Gutenberg invented moveable-type printing	I. Technological developments in communication have accelerated at an ever more rapid pace.
2. 1920s, first radio broadcasts	
3. 1952, 9% of households had TV	(1, 2, 3, 4, 5, 6)
4. 1960, 85% of households had TV	
5. 1980s, 1.1% of households had VCRs	
6. 1995, 67% had VCRs	II. TV & radio are becoming more important to average Americans than print.
7. Average American watches TV 7 hours a day	
8. 96% of population listens to radio	(7, 8, 9)
9. Newspaper subscriptions per household are about half of what they were in 1960	
	IDEAS & QUESTIONS
	Has the increase in VCRs cut into broadcast TV?

FIGURE 4.3
Recording fact vs. principle while listening.

Listening should be both an aural and visual process. What do you "hear" in this speaker's meta-communication?

deception. Meta-communication is a potentially rich source of meaning. Because shared meaning is the bottom-line goal of listening, it would make no sense to ignore this source.

A word of caution is in order. At the outset of this discussion, we stated that the preceding techniques are interdependent. This is especially true of this last technique. Never infer the meaning of a speaker's or audience member's message on the basis of meta-communication alone. It is not a substitute for the spoken word. It also can be tremendously misleading when isolated from its spoken counterpart.

Paraphrasing

One of the techniques you may use when researching your speeches is the interview. Successful interviewing depends on active listening. A key element of active listening is to seek confirmation from people that their message has been understood. The techniques of paraphrasing and questioning (discussed next) are valuable tools for ensuring accurate communication. Moreover, paraphrasing encourages the interviewee to talk because it reinforces the fact that you are actively engaged with what is being said.

To paraphrase a message, you need to briefly repeat in your own words the essence of what has been said. Paraphrasing should be nonevaluative. Your goal is not to convey your opinion of what was said, but merely to confirm that you understand it. Often you will paraphrase not only the denotative content of the message but the emotional aspects as well. For example: "What I'm hearing you say is . . . ," "Let me make sure I understand what you are saying . . . ," "You seem to be feeling. . . ."

Questioning

Similar to paraphrasing, questioning is another way of determining if you correctly understand the message. But rather than simply repeating back what you think you have heard, you ask the other person for information as well as confirmation. Avoid hostile and loaded questions. A *hostile question* signals your strong disagreement with the other person; for example, "How can you possibly say such a stupid thing?" *Loaded questions* assume something that is not necessarily the case. The classic loaded question is "Have you stopped beating your wife (or husband)?" Your goal is not to embarrass or trap people, but to give them an opportunity to clarify and elaborate on what they have said.

When listening to a speech, you should not interrupt to ask a question unless the speaker has clearly indicated a willingness to take questions during a presentation. Even then, the common courtesy of raising a hand to indicate you wish to ask a question is recommended. Some public speakers ask people to hold their questions until the end of a speech. When interviewing people, of course, the flow of questions is much freer. But you should still wait until the opportunity arises to ask your question without interrupting the other person midsentence. Often, paying close attention to nonverbal behaviors will help you know when it is appropriate to interrupt with a question. A pause, a glance, or a facial expression that indicates finality are all ways of signaling that a person is waiting for a response.

SUMMARY

Listening is but one more skill necessary to becoming a competent speaker and audience member. Hearing and listening are not the same thing. Listening is the process of receiving, attending to, and assigning meaning to aural as well as visual and tactile stimuli. Active listening involves conscious and responsive participation in the communication transaction. Selective attention involves making a conscious choice to focus on some people and some messages, rather than others. Sensorial involvement means that you listen with all the senses, not simply the sense of hearing. Comprehension is the act of understanding what was said. Retention is the act of storing what was said in either short- or long-term memory. Listening begins in your mind with an internal dialogue.

There are quite a few misconceptions about listening. Many people think listening is easy, whereas it requires effort. Intelligence is no sure guarantee of effective listening. Those who believe there is no need to plan ahead are misguided. And though it might seem that reading skills correlate with listening skills, such is not the case.

Obstacles to effective listening include physical conditions, cultural differences, personal problems, bias, connotative meanings, and anxiety.

There is more than one type of listening. Discriminative listening distinguishes auditory and/or visual stimuli. Comprehensive listening is targeted at understanding. Appreciative listening involves obtaining sensory stimulation or enjoyment through the words and experiences of others. Therapeutic listening provides someone with the opportunity to talk through a problem. Critical listening has the purpose of making reasoned judgment about speakers and the credibility of their messages.

Once you have made the conscious choice to actively listen, however, there are several techniques you can use to increase your overall listening skill. These include setting goals, blocking out distracting stimuli, suspending judgment, focusing on main points, recognizing highlights and signposts, taking effective notes, being sensitive to meta-communication, paraphrasing, and questioning.

Remembering that we will spend far more of our communication lifetime as a listener than as a speaker, it is important that we work on mastering listening skills. Communication is a two-way street, and the person who ignores the importance of listening is in danger of a head-on collision.

Check Your Understanding: Exercises and Activities

1. In a short paper or speech, describe an incident where your message was misunderstood or where you misunderstood another person's intended message. Were there any tip-offs that the speech transaction was not effective? How could the misunderstanding have been avoided?

2. Planning for upcoming listening situations is important. Consider one of your classes in which the instructor regularly lectures. In what ways can you prepare for listening to the next lecture? Are there any specific listening obstacles you need to overcome? After attending the lecture, see if your understanding was enhanced by your preparation for the class.

3. In a short paper, describe a situation you have experienced in which bias affected the listening process. Choose a situation in which you

feel your meaning was distorted due to bias or a situation in which you feel your own biases handicapped you in the listening process.

4. Make a list of 10 words that have varying connotations to different people or in different situations. Be prepared to share your list with classmates in small groups or before the full class, depending on your instructor's directions.

5. Describe three times in a given day in which you engaged in critical listening. Be prepared to share your list with classmates in small groups or before the full class.

Notes

1. Dave Barry, *Dave Barry Does Japan* (New York: Random House, 1992), 35–36.

2. Anthony P. Carnevale, Leila J. Gainer, and Ann S. Meltzer, *Workplace Basics: The Skills Employers Want* (Washington, D.C.: American Society for Training and Development and U.S. Department of Labor, 1988), 12.

3. Lyman K. Steil, L. Barker, and Kittie W. Watson, *Effective Listening* (New York: Random House, 1963).

4. Andrew D. Wolvin and Carolyn Gwynn Coakley, *Listening,* 3rd ed. (Dubuque, Iowa: William C. Brown, 1988), 93.

5. Wolvin and Coakley, *Listening,* 115.

6. Melvin L. DeFleur, Patricia Kearney, and Timothy G. Plax, *Fundamentals of Human Communication* (Mountain View, Calif.: Mayfield, 1993), 112–13.

7. Robert Haakenson, *The Art of Listening* (Philadelphia: Smith Kline & French Laboratories, n.d.), 3.

8. DeFleur, Kearney, and Plax, *Fundamentals of Human Communication,* 113–17.

9. Edward T. Hall and Mildred Reed Hall, *Hidden Differences: Doing Business with the Japanese* (Garden City, NY: Anchor Press/Doubleday, 1987), 7.

10. Hall and Hall, *Hidden Differences,* 10–11.

11. Wolvin and Coakley, *Listening.*

12. Wolvin and Coakley, *Listening,* 140.

13. Wolvin and Coakley, *Listening,* 146–50.

14. Wolvin and Coakley, *Listening,* 188.

15. Wolvin and Coakley, *Listening,* 189–206.

16. Wolvin and Coakley, *Listening,* 207–25.

17. Wolvin and Coakley, *Listening,* 320.

18. Wolvin and Coakley, *Listening,* 330–33.

19. Wolvin and Coakley, *Listening,* 236.

20. Wolvin and Coakley, *Listening,* 243–74.

21. Wolvin and Coakley, *Listening,* 287–313.

22. Ralph G. Nichols and Thomas R. Lewis, *Listening and Speaking: A Guide to Effective Oral Communication* (Dubuque, Iowa: William C. Brown, 1954), 41–53.

PART TWO

Adapting to the Audience

Effective public speakers focus their analysis on the audience they will be addressing.

5

Audience-Focused Speaking

Mastering the Rhetorical Situation

OBJECTIVES

After reading this chapter, you should be able to:

- Discuss the historical development of the study of the rhetorical situation.
- Define the nature of the rhetorical situation.
- Identify the goals, audience, and constraints you face as a speaker.
- Describe how you can analyze the cultural, demographic, and individual diversity that characterizes today's audiences.
- Explain the relationship between general speech purposes and various rhetorical situational factors.
- Be able to evaluate the effectiveness of your speeches in terms of how they help you achieve your goals.

KEY CONCEPTS

attitude
audience diversity
behavioral intention
belief
canons of rhetoric
constraint

cultural diversity
demographic diversity
demographics
rhetorical situation
values

By all accounts, May 3, 1980, was a wonderful spring day in Fair Oaks, California, a suburban neighborhood just outside the state capitol in Sacramento. It was the kind of day you would expect to see a young girl strolling along the street with a friend, headed in the direction of their school where the annual spring carnival was being held.

And that's exactly what 13-year-old Cari Lightner was doing at one o'clock in the afternoon that day, walking with a friend inside the bike lane that paralleled the street leading to her school and the carnival both of the girls were anxious to attend. But that was not to be.

Behind the two girls, out of earshot and out of view, a man who only two days earlier had been released from jail for his fourth arrest in four years for drunk driving was not only wasted again but also behind the wheel of a car. Whether he was too drunk to see the two girls in front of him or simply too drunk to steer a straight line we will never know.

But of this much we are certain. In four days time he would be arrested again and charged with three felonies as a result of hitting Cari Lightner with such force that it threw her body 120 feet from the point of impact. The charges themselves: felony drunk driving, felony hit and run, and felony vehicular manslaughter.

Although he was convicted, the sentence hardly seemed fitting, given his record of drunk driving and his responsibility in the death of an innocent 13-year-old girl. He spent a total of only eight months in a work camp and eight more in a halfway house. And, as if that weren't chilling enough, upon his release he was notified that with proof of insurance, his driver's license would be reinstated.

As parents will quickly tell you, the death of a child is their worst nightmare. For Cari's mother, Candy Lightner, however, this nightmare was compounded by what she perceived to be an injustice of the highest magnitude. Rather than wallow in her grief and rage, though, Lightner decided to do something about the then too lenient and tolerant attitudes of lawmakers and society toward those who repeatedly drove while intoxicated. As a direct result of that commitment, she not only founded Mothers Against Drunk Driving (MADD) but also spearheaded a campaign first in California and then across the nation that radically changed both state and federal laws regarding drunk driving. In the process, she also gave hundreds of speeches to diverse audiences with varying views about the problem she saw and wanted to solve.

Although Candy Lightner's example may seem far removed from the speaking situations you face, the process she had to go through to become an opinion leader isn't that different from the one you'll need to go through in your efforts to lead opinion. Just as Candy Lightner had to carefully analyze the situation she faced in the effort to change the laws about drunk driving in this country, so too must you carefully analyze the situation you face as a speaker to succeed with your audience now and in your future.

This chapter focuses on situations you will face as a speaker and the analytical skills you will need to master them. Rhetorical scholar Lloyd Bitzer defined a **rhetorical situation** as "a natural context of persons, events, objects, relations, and an exigence [goal] which strongly invites utterance."[2] We begin by briefly telling you about our rhetorical heritage and how it led to the development of the concept of rhetorical situation. We next look at the basic elements of rhetorical situations; the importance of thinking through your speaker goals in the rhetorical situation; the relationship between speaker goals and audience analysis, including assessing and responding to audience diversity; and the set of constraints you'll need to plan for in the rhetorical situation.

OUR RHETORICAL HERITAGE

Although the specific term *rhetorical situation* wasn't coined until the late 1960s, its roots can be traced to ancient Greece and the fifth century B.C. Then as now there was a need for public speaking skills because democracy required people to deliberate about public policy. Further, there were no lawyers, and people had to plead their own case in court. A group of teachers of rhetoric, known as *Sophists,* taught the skills of speaking for a fee. Plato opposed their approach to rhetoric as lacking in regard for the truth and proposed his own philosophy of rhetoric in two dialogues, the *Gorgias* and the *Phaedrus.* Plato believed that one should first discover the truth philosophically and then use rhetoric only in service to truth. In Chapter 6 we discuss the controversy between these schools of rhetoric in more detail.

Plato's famous student Aristotle brought order and systematic focus to the study of the rhetorical situation. Aristotle wrote the *Rhetoric,* probably the most influential book on the subject to this day. Aristotle defined rhetoric as the "faculty of observing in any given case the available means of persuasion."[3] He specified that rhetoric consisted of three modes of proof: *ethos,* the personal credibility of the speaker; *pathos,* the putting of the audience into a certain frame of mind; and *logos,* the proof or apparent proof provided by the actual words of the speech (*logos* being the Greek word for "word"). In many ways this classification foreshadows much of contemporary communication research, with its emphasis on source credibility (*ethos*), audience analysis and reaction (*pathos*), and message construction (*logos*).

The study and practice of rhetoric was further refined by Roman rhetoricians such as Cicero and Quintilian, who developed the **canons of rhetoric,** classic laws of invention, arrangement, style, delivery, and memory. *Invention* concerns the creative enterprise of discovering the materials to be used in the speech. *Arrangement* refers to how the speech is organized. *Style* deals with the way language is used in the speech. *Delivery* concerns the actual presentation of the speech. Finally, *memory* is concerned with ways to learn to recite a speech by heart. With the exception of memory, public speaking instruction to this day is largely concerned with these canons. A glance at the table of contents of this or any other public speaking book will find chapters concerned with gathering the materials for your speech (invention), organizational patterns (arrangement), language use (style), and nonverbal communication (delivery). Memory is largely confined to forensic competition, although making your speech memorable to your audience is also a focus of most public speaking books.

After the Roman period, the study and practice of rhetoric went into a period of decline. As Europe plunged into the Middle Ages, the need for a complete rhetoric was diminished, as human affairs were largely governed by church dogma. Eventually, rhetoric came to be associated almost entirely with matters of style. It is largely from this period that rhetoric came to be associated with empty words, signifying nothing.

With the coming of the Enlightenment, rhetoric was rediscovered. There is not sufficient space here to chronicle all the theorists who revived rhetoric. Particularly noteworthy, however, are the trio of Hugh Blair, George Campbell, and Richard Whately, who wrote in the late 18th and early 19th centuries. Blair concerned himself largely with style. Campbell was a proponent of a type of psychology emphasizing discrete mental faculties, returning rhetoric to a concern with the audience and pathos. Whately revived the concern with invention. His treatise on the *Elements of Rhetoric* gave a new importance to logic and reasoning in rhetoric.

By the early 20th century, departments of speech began to emerge as discrete entities. Theorists again began writing about rhetoric and rhetorical theory. But one of the important features of the study of rhetoric in the 20th century was a return to its fifth century B.C. roots in ancient Greece.

Given this rich history, rhetorical scholar Lloyd Bitzer was following well-established tradition when he sought in 1968 to ground rhetoric in situational factors. Recall that Bitzer saw rhetoric as a response to a situation that strongly invites utterance. The elements of that situation include an exigence (goal), an audience, and a set of constraints that set the parameters for the rhetorical response.

GOALS AND THE MOTIVATION TO SPEAK OUT

Let's begin with what motivates you to speak out. Motives are the things that drive us to confront and hopefully master the rhetorical situation. Motives can be as selfish as convincing people to help you complete a task that will benefit only you. But motives also can be as altruistic as convincing the fortunate to share what they have with those less blessed. So what specifically motivates you? A good grade? Meeting still another requirement

Mary Fisher, who contracted the HIV virus from her husband, riveted the 1992 Republican convention with her speech about AIDS.

for graduation? How about self-improvement? In the effort to truly understand what motivates you, you need to thoroughly analyze the goal or goals you hope to achieve as a result of speaking.

A goal is an end. When we fully understand our speaking goals, they tell us about the destination we hope to reach as a result of speaking publicly. But we need to be careful in this regard. People commonly make mistakes in analyzing and identifying their speaking goals. When Candy Lightner started out, she mistakenly thought her immediate goal was to convince lawmakers to approve legislation changing drunk-driving laws. She also was frustrated early on in her efforts as a result of this mistaken goal. She couldn't even get in to see lawmakers, much less convince them to approve legislation that would change the laws.

On reflection, Lightner realized she had a more immediate goal. She needed to build a base of support that in the long run would become so powerful and attention getting that legislators could not afford to dismiss it. As a result, she placed a personal ad in the newspaper inviting people who had been victimized by drunk driving to call her. The response was enormous, and the organization we now know as MADD began to take shape.

Short-Term and Long-Term Goals

As Lightner learned early on in her campaign, some goals are short-term and others are long-term. Recognizing the difference is central not only to goal analysis but to your mastery of the rhetorical situation as well. **Short-term goals** are those ends you can accomplish in the near future. **Long-term goals** are ends that you can hope to achieve only over an extended period of time. Generally speaking, the realization of your short-term speaking goals should increase the chances of realizing your long-term goals. Simply identifying what you need to accomplish in the short-term, moreover, forces you to stay in the moment. Although it's good to think about an imagined future, it's what you do in the here and now that will first determine whether your goal becomes a reality.

Incremental Goals

Your analysis also requires thinking about goals in order of difficulty of achievement. The shop-worn but accurate saying that "a journey of 1,000 miles begins with a single step" is apropos here. Just as it makes good sense to go after short-term goals before long-term ones, it also makes good sense to first go after those goals you have the greatest chance of achieving. Typically this means organizing your speaking goals incrementally, from least to most important. **Incremental goals** are those steps you must complete to accomplish your long-term goal.

Consider again the case of Candy Lightner. She and the people who joined with her to form MADD had to ask themselves: How do we get from where we are to where we want to be? What are the incremental steps necessary to achieve our short- and long-term goals? The situation faced by MADD was complicated. Just to obtain a hearing on their proposals required legislative help. Lightner initially did not even know who represented her in the state legislature. Ultimately, however, she found supporters, such as Assemblywoman Jean Morehead, who assisted her in drafting and proposing legislation. But before going to the government, Lightner had to form an organization, encourage members to join, obtain financial support, and gain public attention. These are all steps she was able to accomplish through a combination of speeches, press conferences, news releases, and articles in various media. For example, magazines published by insurance companies carried articles on her organization. As you can see, then, mapping out the steps to achieving your goals is essential to mastering the rhetorical situation you face. (For more on Candy Lightner, see the box "Achieving Goals: Candy Lightner, Then and Now.")

Achieving Goals: Candy Lightner, Then and Now

Tragedy can turn a life in directions unexpected. So it was with Candy Lightner. Her daughter Cari's death not only empowered her to found and lead a movement that affected the drunk-driving laws in all 50 states, but changed her life's vocation. In 1980 she left real estate to found MADD. As the *Sacramento Bee* put it, "Lightner, formerly shy and quiet, became a human dynamo and a galvanizing public speaker." Five years later, she left the presidency of MADD as professional leadership took over the organization. In 1991 she became head of a political action committee called Americans Against Crime. Later she briefly served as an advisor and spokesperson for the alcoholic beverage industry, an action which some criticized as hypocritical, although her goal was promoting responsible drinking and designated driving.

Currently, Lightner is the president of the American-Arab Anti-Discrimination Committee (ADC). As an Arab-Lebanese American, Lightner is in a position to take on a new rhetorical challenge—discrimination against Arabs. She recalls her own experiences as a little girl: "I was just starting first grade. Another little girl's mother wouldn't let her play with me." Among her successes as president of ADC was easing anti-Arab stereotypes in the Disney film *Aladdin*. She got the phrase ". . . they cut off your ear / if they don't like your face" deleted from a song planned for the film.

Lightner's example is not an isolated one. Other people who have been thrust into rhetorical situations as a result of tragedy or outrage include gun-control advocate Sarah Brady, the wife of former Reagan press secretary James Brady; victim's rights advocate John Walsh, the TV host of *America's Most Wanted;* and Denise Brown, sister of Nicole Brown, who now speaks nationally about spousal abuse.

Source: Walt Wiley, "Candy Lightner's New Cause," *Sacramento Bee*, 18 October 1994, B1, B4.

ANALYZING YOUR AUDIENCE

VIDEO FILE

If you have access to the videotape that accompanies this book, view segment 5, which covers audience analysis.

So far we have said that rhetorical situations first must be analyzed in terms of the goals you hope to achieve. Any hope you have of achieving your speaking goals, however, depends on whether there is an audience "capable of being influenced by discourse and of being mediators of change."[4]

Audience analysis begins by knowing who your audience is. Then you need to know what power they have to help you achieve your goals. You also need to know whether they favor, oppose, or are indifferent to those goals. Finally, you need to analyze audience diversity—culturally, demographically, and individually.

Audience Selection

In some situations, you will be in a position to choose the audience or audiences for your speeches. For example, if you are seeking donations for your university, you might choose to address a group of current students, recent graduates, or parents of students, to name just a few possible donors. But in many cases you have no choice about which audience you will address. If your fraternity or sorority needs to renew its use permit from the city, you will have to convince the appropriate city agency to issue a renewal. Of course, in your public speaking class, your peers are your audience. Short of changing class sections, you will not be able to select another audience. However, the principles of audience selection we will discuss also apply to topic selection for a fixed audience. It makes sense to pick topics appropriate for your classmates.

Whether you can choose an audience or must deal with one fixed by circumstances, it is important that you analyze prospective audience members in order to understand how to reach them and motivate them to act in ways that will help you achieve your speaking goals.

Although there are many potential audiences you might address in a speech or series of speeches, audience selection is most profitably based on answers to the following questions:

- Who favors your goal? Who is opposed? Who is undecided?
- Who has the power to help you achieve or to prevent you from achieving your goal?

Once again, let's see how these factors might apply to the MADD campaign.

Who Favors/Opposes Your Goals?   Although you might think that everyone would favor saving lives, not everyone agreed with MADD's specific goals. For example, trial lawyers who defended accused drunk drivers stood to lose financially if tougher laws were passed. Some judges opposed having mandatory sentences imposed, which would decrease their discretion over sentencing, as well as potentially overload the court system. There were also millions of Americans who were not aware or appreciative of the magnitude of the drunk-driving problem.

The people who formed the core of MADD were the families and friends of victims of drunk drivers. They were also more numerous than you might imagine, given the fact that a quarter of a million people had died from alcohol-related accidents in the decade preceding MADD's formation.

Although they were not affected in the same way the families of victims were, insurance companies spent millions of dollars every year paying claims to the victims of drunk drivers and their survivors. As a result, one insurance company even went so far in its support as to provide Candy Lightner with office space. And several other companies publicized her cause in their company publications. By tapping into the people in the insurance business who were likely to help her achieve her goals, Lightner found what proved to be a key to building an effective grass-roots organization.

In analyzing your selected audience, you need to be realistic in terms of how you deal with people who support you, those who oppose you, and those who are undecided. Not every audience is susceptible to changing its viewpoint, even when to do so seems to make perfect sense. Thus it is more profitable to plan on speaking to either supporters or those who are at least willing to be persuaded. This means that selecting your audience and adapting to it is often one of the most important decisions you'll face as a speaker.

Who Has Power?   One of the things you must learn to accept is that not everyone who agrees with you will be in a position to help you achieve your goals. Conversely, not everyone who is against you will have the power to impede you from achieving your goals. Some drunk drivers might have opposed MADD's goals, but they were hardly in a position to speak out in favor of the right to kill people while intoxicated.

In your case, there also will be people who are not directly concerned with your topic, but who can be essential to achieving your goals. For example, newspaper and television reporters normally try to maintain some semblance of objectivity in their reports. Yet the publicity they can give your cause can be essential to reaching your desired goal. MADD learned, for example, that family members who had been victimized by drunk drivers were more likely to be covered by the press than people who had not been personally affected. Knowing who is in a position to help or hinder you is essential to effective audience selection.

As Figure 5.1 on page 126 illustrates, there are four possible types of audiences in terms of power and willingness to be influenced. Only audiences in the highlighted box—that is, those with both power and the willingness to be influenced—can help you achieve your goals. Depending on your goals, these boxes may be very different in relative size. On some topics only a very limited number of people may fit in this group, such as the nine members of the U.S. Supreme Court. On other topics almost everyone may be a potential audience member as is the case with a presidential election. The key, therefore, is to find those audience members with both power and an open mind, and target your message to them.

Although your audience in a basic speech class is a given—your classmates—you probably do have the power to select your topics. You should pick topics on which your classmates can be influenced and have some power to act. For example, though your classmates cannot directly vote on legislation in your state legislatures, they can write letters in the attempt to influence the legislators who will vote on the matter. For you to attempt to influence your classmates on a topic concerning legislation you support, therefore, would make good sense.

FIGURE 5.1
Types of audiences.

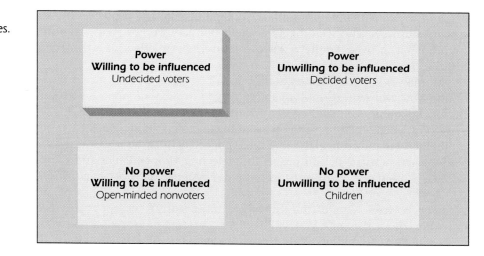

Audience Diversity

Audience diversity refers to the cultural, demographic, and individual characteristics that differ among audience members. Once you know what audience you will be addressing, your task becomes more complex. Today's audience, whether selected or assigned, is a diverse one. This will increasingly become the case as you complete your education and pursue your career. There are many ways to break down audience diversity for the purpose of analysis.

In Figure 5.2, we have divided audience diversity into three types—cultural, demographic, and individual. Recognize that these types overlap with each other and are interdependent rather than independent. For example, the demographic characteristics "religion" and "language" are also cultural characteristics, just as the demographic characteristics "gender" and "age" are also individual characteristics. Still, this division is a useful way to start. Don't let yourself get trapped, however, into thinking that knowing one or two things about the make-up of your audience is sufficient to succeed.

Cultural Diversity   Culture, as you may recall from Chapter 4, is a learned system of language, beliefs, and customs with which specific people identify. **Cultural diversity,** therefore, refers to differences among people in terms of language, beliefs, and customs. At the most basic level, you need to familiarize yourself with the cultural diversity inherent in your audience.

Because culture is learned, what is appropriate in one culture may not be appropriate in another. The list of specific things that make one culture unique from another is inexhaustible. What's more, recognizing and responding to cultural diversity does not demand that you try to learn everything that is most peculiar about a specific culture. To the contrary,

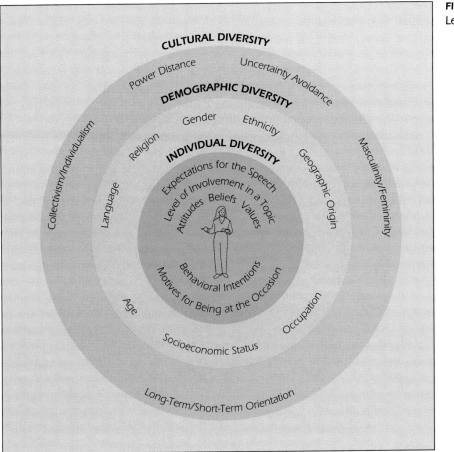

FIGURE 5.2
Levels of diversity.

discovering what is *common but variable* among cultures is the key to culturally responsive speaking.

Dutch communication scholar Geert Hofstede says that all national cultures vary in terms of four dimensions: "*power distance* (from small to large), *collectivism* versus *individualism, femininity* versus *masculinity,* and *uncertainty avoidance* (from weak to strong)."[5] In addition, Hofstede notes that a fifth dimension has been recently discovered, *long-term orientation* versus *short-term orientation* to life.[6] Cultures vary in their positions on these dimensions—for example, the degree to which they accept a large degree of power inequality or the degree to which they favor rugged individualism over collectivism. Your competence in identifying and adapting to cultures that differ on these dimensions will have an important effect on how well you adapt to the cultural diversity of your audience.

Power Distance   Power distance is defined by Hofstede as "the extent to which the less powerful members of institutions and organizations within a country expect and accept that power is distributed unequally."[7] All societies are unequal, some more than others. However, different societies handle inequality in different ways. For example, there are large power distances in countries in Latin America, Asia, and Africa and in some European countries such as Spain. On the other hand, countries such as the United States and Great Britain and some parts of Europe have smaller power distances. Sweden, for example, is an egalitarian country with a small power distance, whereas France has a large power distance.

These differences have important implications for you as a public speaker. For example, suppose you are a manager in an international organization announcing company downsizing. You could not assume that an audience from a small-power-distance culture, such as Sweden, would react in the same way to your speech as those from a large-power-distance culture, such as France. Similarly, teachers are treated with deference in large-power-distance cultures, whereas they are treated as equals in small-power-distance cultures. For example, a professor from a French university teaching in the United States might be surprised to be called by his or her first name, though such a practice is not uncommon at American universities.

Further, power distance can vary within a larger culture, for example, by social class, educational level, and occupation. Of course, in most societies these factors are closely linked. People with higher levels of education tend to belong to the middle or upper social class and hold the most powerful positions. Generally, those occupations with the lowest status tend to have the largest power distance, and those with the highest status tend to have the smallest power distance. Thus, whereas a factory manager might expect workers with little education who occupy the lowest ranks to accept her authority with little questioning, the president of a university might expect her highly educated faculty members to demand a share in the governance of the institution.

Collectivism versus Individualism   The second dimension common to all cultures is collectivism versus individualism. Hofstede explains: "Collectivism stands for a society in which people from birth onwards are integrated into strong, cohesive ingroups, which throughout people's lifetime continue to protect them in exchange for unquestioning loyalty."[8] In an individualistic society, on the other hand, "Everyone is expected to look after himself or herself and his or her immediate family only."[9] Some cultures, notably Asian and Native American, believe the good of the many far outweighs the good of the few. In these collectivist cultures, people shun the individual spotlight. Singling out a member of a collectivist culture while you're giving a speech is likely to embarrass the person.

In cultures where so-called rugged individualism is admired and encouraged, the opposite is true. In the United States, for example, the dominant culture is very individualistic. We champion lone-wolf entrepreneurs who strike it rich, quarterbacks who stand alone in the pocket, and politicians who march to the beat of a different drummer. There is evidence to believe, in fact, that the United States is the most individualistic nation on earth.[10]

This may be changing given immigration patterns and birth rates. Census data show that more people from collectivist cultures reside in the United States today than at any other time in history. American college students today find that people from collectivist cultures are an increasing part of their audience, a fact that must be included in the analysis of the rhetorical situation. To find out where you stand as an individual on this dimension, see the box "How Collectivistic or Individualistic Are You?" on page 130.

Femininity versus Masculinity   The third dimension of culture in Hofstede's scheme is femininity versus masculinity. Hofstede explains: "Femininity stands for a society in which social gender roles overlap: both men and women are supposed to be modest, tender, and concerned with the quality of life."[11] Masculinity, on the other hand "stands for a society in which social gender roles are clearly distinct: men are supposed to be assertive, tough, and focused on material success. . . ."[12] The United States ranks relatively high on measures of masculinity. Comparing the scores on an index of masculinity, the United States is ranked 15 out of 53 countries—with Japan the most masculine and Sweden the most feminine. The most feminine cultures are found in Scandinavia and tend not to assign one set of roles to men and another set of roles to women. In these cultures, the professional role a person assumes is a product of ability rather than biological sex. Thus, when imagining a physician or chief executive officer of a company, people don't automatically see a man. In imagining a nurse or secretary, they don't automatically see a woman.

The opposite is true for many other cultures. Some go to extremes in the degree to which one's sex decides one's role. In contrast to Scandinavia, countries such as Japan, Austria, and Venezuela have few women in positions of corporate or public authority. Women are assigned roles out of view and out of power.

This dimension is important to analyzing your audience and constructing your speech. An audience of Japanese men, as a case in point, would be polite but predictably unreceptive to a woman speaking on a topic such as re-engineering the Japanese corporation. By the same token, a Scandinavian audience would derogate the credibility of a male speaker suggesting women belong in the home.

This dimension can be important in a number of settings. For example, in masculine cultures, children in school tend to speak out and compete openly. Failure is viewed as a disaster and can even lead to suicide. Boys and girls tend to study different subjects. On the other hand, in feminine cultures, students tend to behave less competitively, failure is not viewed as a

How Collectivistic or Individualistic Are You?

The purpose of this questionnaire is to help you assess your individualistic and collectivistic tendencies. Respond by indicating the degree to which the values reflected in each phrase are important to you: "Opposed to My Values" (answer 1), "Not Important to Me" (answer 2), "Somewhat Important to Me" (answer 3), "Important to Me" (answer 4), or "Very Important to Me" (answer 5).

_____ 1. Obtaining pleasure or sensuous gratification

_____ 2. Preserving the welfare of others

_____ 3. Being successful by demonstrating my individual competency

_____ 4. Restraining my behavior if it is going to harm others

_____ 5. Being independent in thought and action

_____ 6. Having safety and stability of people with whom I identify

_____ 7. Obtaining status and prestige

_____ 8. Having harmony in my relations with others

_____ 9. Having an exciting and challenging life

_____ 10. Accepting cultural and religious traditions

_____ 11. Being recognized for my individual work

_____ 12. Avoiding the violation of social norms

_____ 13. Leading a comfortable life

_____ 14. Living in a stable society

_____ 15. Being logical in my approach to work

_____ 16. Being polite to others

_____ 17. Being ambitious

_____ 18. Being self-controlled

_____ 19. Being able to choose what I do

_____ 20. Enhancing the welfare of others

To find your individualism score, add your responses to the *odd-numbered* items. To find your collectivism score, add your responses to the *even-numbered* items. Both scores will range from 10 to 50. The higher your scores, the more individualistic and/or collectivistic you are.

catastrophe, and boys and girls tend to study the same subjects. Obviously, teachers need to know which type of culture they are dealing with if they are to be effective.

Uncertainty Avoidance The fourth dimension Hofstede discusses is uncertainty avoidance, which is "the extent to which the members of a culture feel threatened by uncertain or unknown situations."[13] As a student you know all about uncertainty and the feelings of discomfort that can accompany it. Instructors who are vague about assignments, tests, due dates, and evaluation not only create uncertainty but also are the ones you try to avoid. Just as people vary in terms of the amount of uncertainty they can tolerate, so it is with whole cultures. People who live in "low uncertainty avoidance cultures" have considerable tolerance for the kind of ambiguity that can drive some people nuts.

The greatest difference among cultures on this dimension exists between Asian (except Japan and Korea) and European ones. Hofstede says this is likely the result of the different directions the ancient Chinese and Roman Empires took in making laws. In the Chinese Empire, laws were loosely defined and seldom codified. Thus, lawbreakers could not reliably predict their punishment. Conversely, the Roman Empire codified its laws and enforced them rigidly. Thus, lawbreakers knew exactly what they could expect for committing a specific offense.

Cultures whose roots can be traced to the Chinese Empire have a predictably higher tolerance for living with uncertainty than cultures whose roots can be traced to the Roman Empire. Further, tolerating uncertainty with respect to the law appears to have generalized to tolerating uncertainty in general in these cultures. This is important for speakers to know. People from cultures high in tolerance for uncertainty are less likely to be bothered by ambiguities or loose ends following a speech. People from cultures low in tolerance for ambiguity, however, want a speech to close with concrete recommendations, or better yet, a solid solution to the problem presented in the speech.

Long-Term versus Short-Term Orientation The fifth and final dimension Hofstede discusses is long-term versus short-term orientation to life. "Long-term orientation stands for the fostering of virtues oriented toward future rewards, in particular perseverance and thrift."[14] "Short-term orientation stands for the fostering of virtues related to the past and the present, in particular respect for tradition, preservation of 'face,' and fulfilling social obligations."[15]

Asian countries, such as China, Hong Kong, Taiwan, and Japan, tend to rank very high on the long-term dimension. In fact, this dimension is sometimes called "Confucian" because much of the values, on both sides of the dimension, are the same as the teachings of Confucius. The United

States is in the lower third of countries, and Pakistan is at the bottom of the list, meaning they have a more short-term orientation.

Those cultures with a long-term orientation to life tend to adapt traditions to modern situations, are willing to save and persevere to achieve long-term goals, are willing to subordinate themselves for a purpose, and are thrifty in their use of resources. Short-term–oriented societies respect traditions, are willing to overspend to maintain their lifestyle, expect quick results, and are concerned with "face."

For speakers, therefore, it is very important to know whether their audience members share a short- or long-term culture. Appeals to thrift and patience are likely to be effective in those societies with a long-term orientation, whereas appeals to instant gratification are more effective in societies that have a short-term view of the world. The current debate in the United States over the need to balance the federal budget to protect future generations reflects the results of years of a short-term orientation on the part of American society. That these issues are now being seriously debated suggests that both short- and long-term orientations are competing within the American culture.

These dimensions are *all* important to analyzing cultural diversity. You shouldn't give one greater credence than another. Further, the days of the homogeneous audience are numbered. No longer can one assume a uniform cultural background on the part of audience members. Both now and in your future you can count on audience membership that is not only culturally diverse but also variable with regard to such dimensions as femininity versus masculinity. Thus, developing and delivering a speech that appeals to a majority of the cultures represented in your audience is tougher than ever.

Important as it is to recognize how cultural dimensions like uncertainty avoidance are significant to your audience analysis, you need more specific advice about audience diversity as well. Just because the culture at large is high in uncertainty avoidance, we shouldn't be trapped into thinking that everyone we identify as a member of the culture is so inclined. The formerly collectivist cultures of Eastern Europe, for example, are full of people who are working to make them more individualistic.

It is also important to recognize that the next audience variable we will discuss, demographic diversity, is closely related to cultural diversity. As Hofstede notes, culture operates in a number of layers: national, regional, ethnic, religious, linguistic, gender, generational, social class, and occupational. He points out, "Regional, ethnic, and religious cultures account for differences within countries; ethnic and religious groups often transcend political country borders."[16] Thus, in analyzing the demographic diversity of your audience, you will also be refining your understanding of their cultural diversity on a number of levels.

Students in today's college classrooms represent a wide diversity of ages.

Demographic Diversity   Demographic diversity is the second factor you'll want to examine to better understand your audience and the overall rhetorical situation. **Demographic diversity** refers to the differences among people in terms of demographics. **Demographics** are the basic and vital data regarding any population. Demographic factors include age, socioeconomic status, occupational role, geographic origin, ethnicity, gender, religion, and language.

Age   The age demography of the United States is changing at an accelerated rate. So is the demography of the classroom. It used to be, for example, that traditional college classrooms consisted of a relatively homogeneous group of 18- to 22-year-olds. Today's classroom comprises a much more diverse mix of students. For example, college classes in a state university in the 1990s are likely to be of mixed gender and age. It's common for students to be as young as 17 or as old as 75. As a speaker, you need to take into account this demographic diversity in both the preparation and delivery of your speech. You have to consider not only how 18- to 22-year-olds are likely to respond to your presentation but also how continuing and reentry students are likely to respond. Likewise, you also will have to think through the response of students who may or may not be similar to you or other members of your audience.

This latter fact makes it especially important that you compare your audience with yourself. Some of the most effective speakers are opinion leaders who are similar but not too similar to their audience. Reentry students in their 40s can be somewhat intimidated by speaking to classes of 18- to 22-year-old classmates. Similarly, a 20-year-old asked to speak to a group of middle-aged businesspersons may feel uneasy. In situations where there is a big difference in age between speaker and audience, points of similarity can be stressed. For example, older students speaking to a younger audience can discuss their children, who might be the same age as the rest of the class. On the other hand, younger persons facing an older audience can make reference to parents or grandparents in an effort to find a common thread linking them with the audience.

Socioeconomic Status   Social grouping or socioeconomic status, which is another type of demographic diversity, is not always directly observable. Most universities are working to increase the diversity of their student populations. Thus in your class there may be students who come from impoverished backgrounds as well as students from affluent families. Although you can sometimes make inferences regarding the social status of your audience, these are not always reliable.

Occupation   Demographic diversity also is reflected in one's occupational role. On a residential campus, occupational roles generally are expressed in terms of major. At many schools, however, students already are involved in an occupation and pursuing a degree for purposes of advancement or career change. This is especially true of urban and metropolitan schools in or near major cities.

   Our occupation and the people we routinely come into contact with at work influence how we look at things. People who are self-employed, for example, probably see things differently than do people working in the public sector, at a large corporation, or in the home. Just as it is important for speakers to analyze age and social diversity, so it is with occupational diversity.

Geographic Origin   The heterogeneous make-up of today's audience also is reflected in the geographic origins of the audience members. To understand how important this is to your analysis of the rhetorical situation, look around your campus. The chances are good that your campus reflects national and regional demographic diversity. International student attendance at U.S. colleges and universities is at an all-time high. Faculties are becoming more international as well. Many campuses, especially large urban ones, look like mini-assemblies of the United Nations. To deny or ignore how this national diversity influences people's perceptions of each other, including how you are perceived as a public speaker, is foolish. The same can be said for the regional diversity reflected in your student body. Some campuses are near mirror images of the region in which they exist. Still others look more like international cities than like their regional environment.

SPEAKING OF . . .

Rhetorical Sensitivity

Anyone who listened to sports talk radio during the 1995 World Series knows about the controversy surrounding the Atlanta Braves' "Tomahawk Chop" and the Cleveland Indians' "Chief Wahoo." Both teams were accused of disparaging Native American traditions and tribes. Native Americans and their supporters pointed out that the public would be incensed at a team named after Jews or Blacks or Asians. Others thought Native Americans were being overly sensitive. They pointed out that no one complains about Notre Dame's "Fighting Irish."

Rhetorical scholar Roderick Hart suggests that this kind of scenario begs for what he calls *rhetorical sensitivity*. People who are rhetorically sensitive routinely take other people's point of view into consideration before speaking or acting. Do you think the baseball teams and their fans were rhetorically insensitive? Were you offended by their behavior? If so, what would you suggest they change?

SOURCE: Roderick P. Hart and Don M. Burks, "Rhetorical Sensitivity and Social Interaction," *Speech Monographs* 39 (1972): 75–91.

Ethnicity   Just as national and regional diversity are features of your campus, so too is ethnic diversity. With the exception of Native Americans, the ancestry of the people on your campus usually can be traced to other continents and countries. Although your ethnic origins may be unimportant to you personally, the ethnic origins of many of your classmates may be significant to their self-concept. These same classmates may be actively involved in maintaining and passing on the traditions that define their ethnicity. Thus, if you are ignorant of the ethnic diversity present on your campus, you may inadvertently violate or be insensitive to one or more of these traditions (see the box "Rhetorical Sensitivity").

Gender   Gender's influence on how people perceive themselves and others is a subject receiving considerable scholarly attention. As scholars such as Julia Wood point out, gender is much more than your biological sex.[17] Gender is the blend of social and cultural characteristics that are associated with maleness or femaleness in a particular culture. Individuals learn gender roles—the expectations their cultures have of them as males or females—in the course of growing up.

As you look out at an audience, you can usually tell who is male and who is female by such outward signs as dress and hair style. But this distinction gives you little information about gender-based diversity. You can't tell what part of the United States or what country audience members come from, what their community and family values are, or what their personal preferences and opinions are. Even in an all-female or all-male group, such as a sports team or a men's or women's chorus, there may be great diversity among members. Thus, basing an audience analysis on how many women and men are in it is ineffective. In no way would it approximate the gender-based diversity of today's audience.

Religion Religious diversity is still another form of demographic diversity for you to consider. Even at well-known sectarian universities like Notre Dame, you will find diversity in the religious beliefs of groups of students. Of course at public colleges and universities this is even more so. In some cases, a person's religion can be identified on the basis of apparel and appearance. Such cases include the Amish, Hasidic Jews, some Muslims, and Hindu Sikhs. Usually, however, the religious diversity on your campus or at work will not be outwardly visible. You cannot tell a devout Catholic from an atheist by outward appearances. We cannot emphasize enough, therefore, how important it is for you to consider religious diversity as an inherent feature of your rhetorical situation.

Language Finally, there is language diversity. As illustrated in Chapter 1, people often use their language group to distinguish themselves from other groups. Such is the case with the residents of Boonville, California. If you asked for directions in this small Mendocino County town, a native in his mid-70s might reply: "Take your wee moshe, pike toward the Deep End, and you'll deek on the Big Crik chiggrul and sluggin' region. And jape easy!"[18] You would have encountered one of the few living speakers of a home-grown American language known as Boontling, which evolved in the isolated community of Boonville in the late 19th century. By speaking the lingo, residents could "shark" (play games) with "bright-lighters" (city slickers) passing through town.[19] The culture of the town was bound up with its own unique language. Today, however, only a few older native speakers still know how to speak Boontling. With the coming of modern transportation and communication, the language is dying out.

Language groups are not necessarily based on geographic location or boundaries. Some languages and vocabularies develop around an activity or interest. Surfers and sail boarders, snow boarders and skiers all have a vocabulary peculiar to their sport. The same can be said about computer hackers, photographers, and serious backpackers. What's more, these groups use their vocabulary not only to identify their own kind but also to differentiate themselves from others.

Individual Diversity Up to this point, we have talked about diversity in collective terms such as cultures and demographic groups. But as you well know, what makes humans truly unique is the fact that despite their cultural and demographic characteristics, they still can be individuals. It is at this level that diversity is both most meaningful and most difficult to assess. Individual diversity is deeply embedded in our beliefs, attitudes, values, behavioral intentions, level of involvement in a topic, motives for being at the occasion, and expectations for the speech.

Beliefs We all hold certain beliefs, attitudes, and values about a variety of topics. A **belief** is "an assertion about the properties or characteristics of an object."[20] Some beliefs are relatively obvious and incontrovertible. For example, we all (presumably) share a belief that the Earth is round. On the other hand, some beliefs are very controversial—for instance, those concerning life after death, abortion, and evolution. When you are dealing with matters on which people hold different beliefs from your own, you face a serious obstacle. You must either change their relevant beliefs or convince them that such beliefs are not relevant and not necessarily in opposition to your own point of view.

Social psychologist Milton Rokeach pointed out that some beliefs are more resistant to change than others.[21] *Primitive beliefs,* also known as type A beliefs, are learned by direct contact with the object of belief and reinforced by unanimous social consensus. An example would be the belief that "death is inevitable." Primitive beliefs based on direct experience, but not subject to social support, are called *zero consensus,* or type B, *beliefs.* These beliefs are also very resistant to change. For example, "I like myself" is a type B belief; it is not reinforceable by social consensus. Together, type A and B beliefs are *core beliefs,* which are very resistant to change. The next two types of beliefs are known as *central beliefs* and are still very resistant to change. Type Cs are *authority beliefs.* For example, one's belief in the truth of the Bible or the Koran would be a type C belief. Type Ds are *derived beliefs,* based on authorities' beliefs. For example, the belief in the infallibility of the pope is a derived belief.

Together, type C and D beliefs are more central to a belief system than the final type of beliefs, type E, or *peripheral beliefs.* For example, someone might like rap music whereas another detests it. These are the most inconsequential of beliefs. Figure 5.3 on page 138 illustrates the relationship among these levels of belief. Clearly your chances of changing an audience member's core beliefs are far less than changing central or peripheral beliefs. Changing a type D belief requires an understanding of the type C belief from which it is derived. Thus, one might point to scripture to try to change a believer's views on a religious matter, but such an argument would have no impact on an atheist.

Attitudes An **attitude** is "a learned predisposition to respond in a consistently favorable or unfavorable manner with respect to a given object."[22] Attitudes are not simply beliefs but rather ways of potentially responding to various objects, based in part on one's beliefs about those objects. Over the course of our lives, we develop innumerable attitudes on everything from our favorite brand of soft drink to the burning political issues of the

FIGURE 5.3
A belief system.

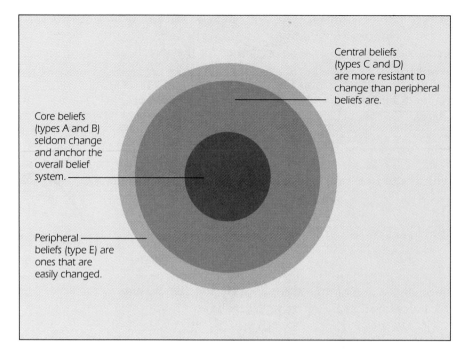

Central beliefs
(types C and D)
are more resistant to
change than peripheral
beliefs are.

Core beliefs
(types A and B)
seldom change
and anchor the
overall belief
system.

Peripheral
beliefs (type E) are
ones that are
easily changed.

day. These attitudes mediate how we respond to the messages we hear. Thus, knowing your audience's attitudes toward your topic is crucial to your success as a speaker.

Of course, it is entirely possible in a diverse audience to have different and even conflicting attitudes among members of the same group. The more you know about the predominant or prevailing attitudes of the group, the better are your chances of convincing at least a majority of the audience of your position. When an audience is fairly evenly divided, you need to attempt to find some middle ground. Finding areas of common agreement while recognizing and respecting differences of opinion is essential to dealing with an audience of mixed attitudes.

Values **Values** are "more general than attitudes." They are "enduring beliefs that hold that some ways of behaving and some goals are preferable to others."[23] Underlying opposition to capital punishment, for example, is not only a belief regarding the improbability that it functions as a deterrent but also a value system about the preservation of human life.

According to Rokeach, some values are terminal whereas others are instrumental.[24] *Terminal values* are those that concern "end states of existence." Examples of terminal values include a comfortable life, an exciting life, a sense of accomplishment, a world at peace, a world of beauty, equality, family security, freedom, and happiness. *Instrumental values* concern "modes of conduct." These are guides to behavior, the means to achieve the ends specified in the terminal values. Examples of instrumental values include ambitiousness, broad-mindedness, capableness, cheerfulness, cleanliness, courage, forgiveness, helpfulness, and honesty.

Although one might not always agree with Rokeach's classification—for example, honesty can certainly be viewed as an end in itself—the basic notion is useful. Some values are desirable in and of themselves, whereas others are instruments for achieving higher, terminal values. For example, forgiveness and courage may be seen as a means to achieving a world at peace.

Values, particularly terminal values, are very difficult to change because they are learned at an early age and widely shared among people. Such values as fairness, justice, life, our nation, and so on not only are fundamental but also were taught to us in our most formative years. In fact, our basic value system probably is pretty well determined by the time we finish kindergarten, as Robert Fulghum pointed out in his best-selling book, *All I Really Need to Know I Learned in Kindergarten.*[25]

Speakers are best advised to appeal to known values shared by the audience rather than trying to convince their audience to adopt new values. There are occasions, however, when speakers are called on to strengthen and reinforce values. A Fourth of July speech, a eulogy, or an inspirational speech can be thought of as fulfilling a value-strengthening function. For the most part, however, speakers need to treat values as a given and build on them. For example, Martin Luther King, Jr.'s, "I Have a Dream" speech was not so much a call for new values as for Americans to live up to the values stated in the Declaration of Independence and the Bill of Rights. The same was true of Louis Farrakhan's speech at the 1995 Million Man March, which called for a return to core values among African Americans.

Behavioral Intentions   A **behavioral intention** is a person's subjective belief that he or she will engage in a specific behavior.[26] Behavioral intentions usually can be inferred from a person's beliefs, values, and attitudes. Intentions are just that: Intentions! Not everyone behaves in accordance with their attitudes, beliefs, and values. For example, most Americans oppose discrimination in the workplace and endorse equal opportunity for persons of all races and genders. Yet reality does not reflect these attitudes. Women in America still make only "72 cents for every dollar a man takes home," and only 3 percent of top executive jobs are held by women.[27]

The important point for you as a speaker is that it is not enough to simply obtain a statement of behavioral intentions from an audience. Ideally, you want to empower your audience to behave in accordance with those intentions. Although this is not always easy, one technique involves actually having audience members make public commitments. At the end of his sermons, for example, Reverend Billy Graham doesn't conclude with,

"Having said that, I hope all of you will consider accepting Jesus Christ as your personal savior." Instead, he calls on people to rise from their seats and join him at the platform to convert. Graham recognizes what the research repeatedly demonstrates: Commitments made in the presence of others are even more difficult to break than private ones. Thus, the more speakers encourage audience members to publicly commit to a certain behavior, the more likely their goals will be achieved.

Level of Involvement in the Topic   Two persons may hold roughly the same beliefs, attitudes, and values regarding a topic and yet be quite different in how easily they are influenced. When Candy Lightner spoke to families of those killed or injured by drunk drivers, these people had direct personal involvement with the topic. You would expect them to respond more favorably to her message than someone who only empathized on an intellectual level with her views on the topic. And they did respond more favorably. It is not just a matter of what attitude people express on a topic, then. You also need to assess how involved they are with the topic. The more involved people are, the more they interpret messages that disagree with their own position as discrepant from their own. This is known as a *contrast effect.* On the other hand, people also *assimilate,* which happens when they perceive messages that are reasonably close to their own as more similar than they actually are. Thus, highly involved persons tend to polarize views—you are either with them or against them. As a speaker, you should try to keep your messages within the latitude of acceptance of highly involved people. Your disagreement should be sufficiently mild that it will not be rejected out of hand.[28]

Highly ego-involved persons normally have a very narrow latitude of acceptance of positions different from their own, and they have wide latitudes of rejection. In fact, they may well perceive positions different from their own as more extreme than they really are. On the other hand, persons with low levels of ego involvement likely have wide latitudes of noncommitment and narrow latitudes of rejection. Simply put, they are much more likely to listen to opposing views than to reject them out of hand. In Figure 5.4, person A tends to have very little room for noncommitment and probably is highly ego involved in the topic. Person B, on the other hand, while holding the same most preferred position as A, has a much wider latitude of noncommitment and is thus more open to different ideas on this topic.

Often a speaker needs to make an uninvolved audience feel more involved in her topic. In the case of MADD, it was not that most people favored drunk driving—just about everyone would have said they were against drinking and driving. However, many jurors in drunk-driving cases who had themselves driven after having a few drinks actually felt more sympathy for the accused drunk driver than for the victim. "There but for the

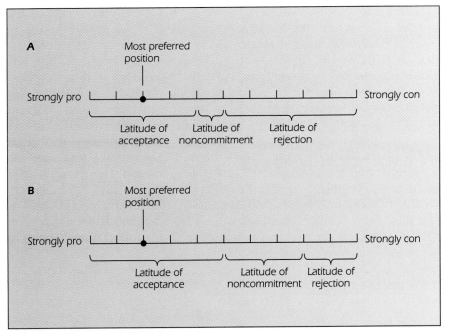

FIGURE 5.4
Latitudes of acceptance, rejection, and noncommitment.

grace of God go I" was the common reaction of many jurors to the plight of the accused. MADD needed to make people feel "But for the grace of God that victim could have been my child or loved one." Most people had never been involved directly as a victim of drunk driving. By telling her story and making the audience realize the pain she had suffered at the loss of her daughter, Candy Lightner created a vicarious involvement with the plight of the victim.

Motives for Being at the Occasion Why are audience members attending your speech? In most classroom situations, the answer is simple: because they have to be. In that situation, you have to work harder at holding their interest and connecting to their needs than if the audience had come especially to hear you speak. In Chapter 8 we offer some suggestions that will help you connect with an audience and gain their attention. Even an audience who has come to hear you needs to be held. It is easy to lose an audience and very difficult to recapture their attention, as any experienced speaker can testify.

Expectations for Your Speech If audience members expect to be entertained, and you deliver a serious speech on the dangers of ozone depletion, you are unlikely to receive a favorable reception. Similarly, if most audience members expect a serious lesson on a topic not to be taken lightly, you owe it to them to meet this expectancy. Always strive to match your speech as much to the audience members' expectations as is possible while still achieving your goals. (For another way to achieve speech goals, see the box "Violating Audience Expectations.")

Generally, speeches contrary to a majority of audience members' expectations may backfire or, at the very least, be apathetically received. For example, the authors attended a graduation ceremony where the speaker used the opportunity to preach his view on "political correctness." While family and friends were there to honor and celebrate the graduates' accomplishments, they were instead treated to a political statement. Whereas such an address might have been appropriate at a meeting of the faculty senate, it missed the mark for the assembled graduates and their guests. The fact that the audience prematurely applauded and shouted loudly at what they thought was the conclusion of his speech reinforced how inappropriate the address was.

CONFRONTING CONSTRAINTS

Obviously, there is more to the rhetorical situation than the cultural, demographic, and individual characteristics of your audience. There are certain constraints on action that we all face. A **constraint** is a limitation on one's choices. Among the common constraints you may face in a rhetorical situation are the facts pertaining to the situation, legal constraints, ethical constraints, nature of the occasion and circumstances, traditions, time factors, and resource factors. Let's examine each of these.

Facts Pertaining to the Situation

Former President Reagan once observed that "facts are stubborn things." Although some people seem oblivious to the facts governing their situation, sooner or later they must face reality. Candy Lightner used the facts—a quarter of a million deaths at the hands of drunk drivers in a decade—to her advantage. Those who tried to ignore these facts eventually were forced to yield. As a speaker, you should always try to fully understand the facts of your situation before speaking.

Legal Constraints

We all must abide by certain legal constraints in our speaking. Libel and slander laws, for example, proscribe certain types of speech. There are also laws that cover when and where one may peaceably assemble. Some anti-abortion activists have been successfully prosecuted, for example, for

Violating Audience Expectations

There are some cases where violating audience expectations may be appropriate. For example, communication professor Michael Burgoon, of the University of Arizona, has repeatedly found that some communicators can not only get away with violating an audience's expectancies but also win their favor in the process. The catch, though, is that these communicators typically are given idiosyncratic credits as a result of some recognizable accomplishment, for example, winning an award or setting a record. Also, sometimes it is useful to speak to a hostile audience and violate their expectancies if a larger, more general audience will also be made aware of your speech.

Thus, for example, presidential candidate Governor Bill Clinton defended his avoidance of service in Vietnam before the American Legion and John F. Kennedy defended his Catholic faith before an audience of Protestant ministers in Houston. In both cases, the "courage" shown by facing a potentially hostile audience and telling its members something they did not want to hear led to favorable coverage by the press at large.

Can you think of a rhetorical situation where, as an audience member, a speaker violated your expectancies? What effect did the violation create? Did you learn any specific lessons from this experience? What were they?

SOURCE: Michael Burgoon and Gerald R. Miller, "An Expectancy Interpretation of Language and Persuasion," in *Recent Advances in Language, Communication, and Social Psychology*, eds. H. Gills and R. St. Clair, (London: Erlbaum, 1985), 199–229.

blocking the entrances to abortion clinics. Although the First Amendment guarantees freedom of speech and assembly, these rights are not an absolute license to do what you please.

Some speakers, however, have effectively challenged and even broken the law for a purpose. Following the principles of Mahatma Gandhi, Martin Luther King, Jr., practiced peaceful civil disobedience in the civil rights movement of the 1960s. So strong was his conviction, King was willing to risk great bodily harm as well as jail for his actions. Ultimately, moreover, this self-sacrifice served to sway public opinion to his side.

In your case, it is highly unlikely that you will choose to purposefully break the law to further the cause advanced in one of your speeches. Yet, unless you check on the legal constraints relevant to your situation, you may accidentally break a law of which you are unaware. In our own experience, we've had students show up to class with everything from exotic beers to poisonous pets, both of which are illegal on our campus. We've learned, consequently, that it is necessary for us to check on the topics and plans of our students well before their time to actually speak. So, check with your instructor before you unintentionally pit yourself against the law.

Ethical Constraints

We discuss ethical considerations for public speaking in detail in Chapter 6. At this point, we simply want to alert you to the fact that as a speaker and as a listener, you will face ethical constraints. Although something may be technically legal, that doesn't make it ethical.

One common example of the ethical constraints faced by speakers is the distinction between worthy goals and unethical means for achieving those goals. It is not unusual for people to attempt to justify ethically suspect rhetoric because it serves a noble end. For example, consider Louis Farrakhan and the Million Man March in 1995. To achieve a worthy end, somewhere between 400,000 and 2 million men marched on Washington, D.C., to hear what Farrakhan had to say. But Farrakhan himself has been widely denounced for views that promote black separatism and smack of anti-Semitism. *Newsweek,* for example, reports that he has a "long history of verbal assaults on Jews, Koreans, Palestinian Arabs, homosexuals—and whites in general."[29] If his rhetoric ends up promoting greater self-reliance and responsibility among African American men, is it ethical by virtue of his goal? Or is no end, no matter how noble, sufficient to justify such rhetoric?

Nature of the Occasion and Circumstances

What is the nature of the occasion prompting you to speak? You may recall January 28, 1986, the day on which the shuttle *Challenger* was to launch seven astronauts, including Christa McAuliffe, the first teacher to go into space. Shuttle launches had become so routine, none of the major networks even covered the launch. However, the image of *Challenger* rocketing into the sky, the astronauts' last words "Go with throttle up?" and the terrifying explosion that followed are etched into our collective public memory.

Ronald Reagan gave one of his most moving speeches after the death of the crew aboard *Challenger.* He matched his rhetoric to the solemn occasion he and the nation confronted. Many consider it his finest hour, as he paid homage to the astronauts who gave their lives in the service of science, while rallying the nation to a renewed commitment to space exploration. This speech is reprinted in Chapter 15.

Your speeches most likely will be given to classes during normal class times. Your audience is a captive one. Given that unavoidable fact, you must always decide whether your topic and presentation are appropriate to this context and occasion.

Traditions

Many speeches are governed by tradition. Whereas this is not a major factor in most classroom speeches, it could be when you are called on to speak in situations outside the classroom. For example, many service clubs, such as Rotary or Lions, have a whole set of traditions that may seem puzzling to the outsider. For example, there is a good deal of good-natured poking fun at certain members, "fines" are levied for infractions such as getting your name in the paper, and so forth. Major corporations, such as IBM and Apple, also have their own set of traditions. IBM is formal whereas Apple is much less so. In speaking to either group, therefore, you would want to reflect the appropriate degree of formality expected in terms of dress, demeanor, and style of presentation.

Time Factors

How much time do you have to give your speech? If you have been asked to speak for 5 minutes and you ramble on for an hour, the response will be predictably negative. On the other hand, imagine paying to hear an hour lecture by a major public figure and having the speech end in 10 minutes. You need to know and respect time limits, as well as match how much information you cover in your speech to your allotted time. For instance, it is generally better to cover a narrow topic thoroughly than to try to cover a wide range of points superficially.

Time also is a factor you need to consider in your preparation. If you have a week to prepare a speech, you probably don't have time to write for information from outside sources. If you have a month, you probably do. You also will need time for practice. Because speaking is in part a behavioral skill, it deserves the same degree of practice as shooting free throws, swinging a golf club, or learning a new exercise in gymnastics. Simply put, it cannot possibly be mastered without some degree of repetition. And this means committing time to practice as far in advance of the speech as possible. Relaxation techniques and other approaches to managing anxiety also require time to master.

Resource Factors

Two questions are involved here. First, what resources do you have available to you? Resources include money, information sources, other people who might assist you, and the like. Second, what resources do you need to accomplish your speaking goal? If your resources match or exceed what you need, you are fine. However, if you lack the necessary resources, you must either redefine your goal or obtain more resources. Initially, Candy Lightner lacked the resources necessary to achieve her goal. She had little money, no political connections, and no organization. Thus, her first steps had to be focused on gaining the necessary resources—money from insurance companies and other contributors, political contacts, and members for her organization.

The same principles apply to a classroom speech. Suppose you are assigned to give a speech with at least three visual aids. How do you go about getting these? If you have enough money, you may be able to pay to have pictures enlarged to poster size or overhead transparencies prepared. If not, what alternative resources do you have? If you have a friend who is an art major, perhaps he or she can help you make posters. Whatever your rhetorical situation, you need to give careful consideration to the resources you have or will need to obtain to achieve your goal.

SPEECH PURPOSES

Given the preceding constraints with which you must deal, we can now look at your purpose. All speeches are motivational. Although the three common general speech purposes are to inform, to persuade, and to entertain, each of these purposes still involves motivating your audience. Information without direction is useless to an audience. You may be asking yourself how the rhetorical situation fits into these purposes. Although general speech purposes can be identified for frequently recurring rhetorical situations, each rhetorical situation involves a unique complex of persons, events, objects, relations, and goals. Whether a speech is predominantly informative or persuasive, for example, is not simply a matter of a speaker choosing what he or she wants to accomplish. Rather, it depends on all three elements of the rhetorical situation—goals, audience, and constraints. Table 5.1 lists some of the complexities involved in understanding the dynamics of the rhetorical situation.

To illustrate this point, suppose you are giving a speech about crack cocaine. Speaking to an audience of parents, you might inform them about symptoms of crack use among their own children. To an audience of teenagers, you might seek to persuade them to avoid the drug. For an audience of elementary children, you might seek to persuade them to "just say no" to drugs. The fact that it is difficult to imagine an entertaining speech today on drugs is a sign of how much attitudes have changed regarding drugs as a serious problem. During the '60s and '70s, drugs were frequently the topic of jokes. Two comics of the time, Cheech and Chong, made their reputations with drug-related humor in both their stand-up routines and a series of cheap, still popular, and extremely profitable movies.

The point of this example is that, depending on goals, the audience, and certain constraints, one may take essentially the same topic and shape it to any of the possible general purposes described. Further, it should be

TABLE 5.1 Factors in Determining Speech Purpose

	Purpose		
	To inform	To persuade	To entertain
Goal	Knowledge	Influence on attitude, value, or behavior	Enjoyment
Audience	Uninformed	May be informed, may be hostile	Seeks pleasure, diversion
Message	Noncontroversial	Controversial or reinforcing	Humorous, dramatic
Contexts	Classroom, training session	Political rally, business meeting	After-dinner speech

clear that these purposes are not mutually exclusive. It is difficult to imagine a successful persuasive speech that did not also inform. Clearly an informative speech may also persuade someone to act differently. If we were to inform you about methods for preventing AIDS, you might change your behavior, even without our urging. Speeches to inform or persuade also sometimes contain entertaining moments. In fact, humor, particularly irony, is sometimes very persuasive. Comics such as Bill Maher and Jay Leno typically have a strong political message embedded in their humor. Finally, the building of new attitudes and values is usually a long process. The persuasive efforts of Candy Lightner and other individuals and groups were part of a larger movement that changed America's value systems about alcohol and drug abuse. Rather than something to be tolerated or even laughed at, these problems have become something to be treated seriously.

When you are assigned a speech, therefore, you must take into account the whole rhetorical situation, whether the speech is labeled informative, persuasive, or entertaining. Be particularly careful to consider your audience in this regard. You could deliver the same speech on evolution to a group of biology teachers and a group who believes the Bible is literally true, including God creating the world in six days. Whereas the biologists might see your speech as informative, the other group undoubtedly would see it as an attempt to persuade them to change their beliefs. Same speech—different audiences—different perceived purposes. You cannot merely assume that your audience shares your perception of the purpose of the speech. Only by fully analyzing the rhetorical situation can you be reasonably confident that your intentions are accurately perceived.

Because an audience is made up of many different individuals, a diverse audience may include those who see your purpose as informative while others see it as persuasive. There is nothing wrong with this; in fact, it is inevitable. However, it is best to know this in advance and adapt to that

In the 1960s and
'70s drug use was
frequently treated as
an object of humor.

segment of the audience most relevant to reaching your goal. Thus, though you may want only to inform your classmates who believe in evolution of the latest advances in the theory of evolution, some of your class may disbelieve the theory. For them, you will need to preface your speech by making it clear that you do not intend to challenge their beliefs. On the other hand, if you are seeking to persuade this latter group, then you will need to specifically deal with some of their objections to the theory of evolution. The more heterogeneous an audience, the more difficult it becomes for the speaker to adapt to the rhetorical situation.

Once you have presented your speech, it is important to evaluate what you have accomplished. Talk to members of the audience. Observe the outcome of your speech. If you are seeking to persuade an audience in the short-term, you may want to survey your audience before and after your speech to see if their attitudes have changed. Measuring the extent of long-term persuasion is more difficult because the results may not show up for years. You can usually tell immediately if an audience is entertained. Laughter and applause are often their own reward.

If time permits, don't be afraid to take audience questions. This sort of interaction gives you another chance to make your point. It also helps you know how well you have succeeded. Taking questions in a nonhostile, positive way is to your advantage.

Today drug use is taken seriously as a significant social problem.

In the classroom environment, there are frequently opportunities for classmates and your instructor to critique your speeches orally or in writing. These are valuable sources of feedback. Your goal in this class, presumably, is to become a better speaker. More often than not, one speech is not enough to achieve this goal. Thus, you should view each speech as a step in a process. After each speech, we recommend that you take stock and assess where you are. As you learn from the inevitable mistakes as well as the things you do correctly, your goal should become more attainable. Learning to be an effective public speaker is a dynamic process, and the more open you are to change, the more successful you are likely to become.

SUMMARY

The rhetorical situation is "a natural context of persons, events, objects, relations, and an exigence [goal] which strongly invites utterance." Our rhetorical heritage extends back to fifth-century B.C. Greece. Sophists believed that truth is relative, and they taught public speaking skills for a fee. Plato believed that rhetoric should be in the service only of truth. Aristotle defined rhetoric as "the faculty of discovering in any given case the available means of persuasion." The Romans codified the principles of rhetoric into canons governing invention, arrangement, style, delivery, and memory.

Among contemporary theorists, Lloyd Bitzer has grounded rhetoric in the situation. The rhetorical situation contains an exigence (goal), an audience, and a set of constraints. Carefully analyzing each of these elements is essential to successful public speaking.

A goal is an end that a speaker seeks. Short-term goals are those ends you seek to accomplish in the near future; long-term goals require an extended period of time; incremental goals are steps along the way to a long-term goal.

The audience may be either selected or assigned. The ideal selected audience is one that is willing to be influenced and has the power to help the speaker achieve his or her goals. If the audience is assigned, the speaker should select a topic that is relevant to that group in terms of their ability to act and their willingness to be influenced.

Audience diversity refers to the cultural, demographic, and individual characteristics that differ among audience members. Cultural diversity refers to the differences among people in language, beliefs, and customs. Cultures vary in terms of five dimensions: power distance, collectivism versus individualism, femininity versus masculinity, uncertainty avoidance, and long-term orientation versus short-term orientation to life. Demographic diversity involves differences related to basic and vital data regarding any population, including age, socioeconomic status, occupational roles, geographic origin, ethnicity, gender, religion, and language. Individual diversity is deeply embedded in our beliefs, attitudes, values, behavioral intentions, level of involvement in a topic, motives for being at the occasion, and expectations for the speech.

Beliefs are assertions about the properties or characteristics of an object. Attitudes are predispositions to respond in a consistently favorable or unfavorable manner with respect to an object. Values are more general and enduring than attitudes and hold that some ways of behaving and some goals are preferable to others. A behavioral intention is a person's subjective belief that he or she will engage in a specific behavior. Some audience members may have a greater or lesser level of involvement in a topic than others have. An individual's motives for being at a speech are important to audience analysis, as are individual expectations of your speech.

The rhetorical situation also includes various constraints on the speech, such as factual, legal, ethical, nature of the occasion, traditions, time, and resources. Each of these factors can limit the speaker's choices as well as the likelihood that the speaker will achieve his or her goal.

Although general purposes, such as to inform, persuade, or entertain, can be identified, each rhetorical situation includes goals, an audience, and constraints that define the actual purposes of the speech. Only through careful audience analysis and adaptation can speakers match their speeches to the rhetorical situations they face. Finally, evaluation by self and others is an important part of becoming a better speaker.

Check Your Understanding: Exercises and Activities

1. Given the topic of alcohol abuse, how might you develop your speech presentation differently if your audience were made up of (a) high school students, (b) students your own age, (c) bar and tavern owners in your community, or (d) recovering alcoholics? In a short paper, explain how your approach and purpose would differ in each case.

2. Create a model of your belief system, including your core beliefs, authority beliefs, and representative derived beliefs on one of the following topics: gun control, the importance of voting, abortion, civil rights. What does your belief system say about how susceptible you are to being influenced on the topic selected?

3. Describe a situation where your behavior didn't follow your stated attitudes. What does this suggest to you about using attitudes as your chief guide in predicting people's behavior?

4. Learn as much as you can about the cultural, demographic, and individual diversity of your classmates. Construct a short questionnaire that will guide you in preparing for upcoming speeches. If you know the topic of your speech, include questions about audience beliefs and attitudes regarding that topic. Tabulate the results of your questionnaire. Briefly summarize your findings in writing.

Notes

1. Otto Friedrich, "Seven Who Succeeded; Candy Lightner; 'You Can Make a Difference,' " *Time,* 7 January 1985, 41.

2. Lloyd Bitzer, "The Rhetorical Situation," *Philosophy and Rhetoric* 1 (1968): 5. Bitzer further defines an exigence as "an imperfection marked by urgency; it is a defect, an obstacle, something waiting to be done, a thing which is other than it should be." In this text we prefer to focus on the speaker's goal, which, strictly speaking, is to *overcome the exigence* present in the rhetorical situation.

3. Aristotle, *Rhetoric,* trans. W. Rhys Roberts (New York: Modern Library, 1954), 24.

4. Bitzer, "Rhetorical Situation," 8.

5. Geert Hofstede, *Cultures and Organizations: Software of the Mind* (London: McGraw-Hill, 1991), 14.

6. Hofstede, *Cultures and Organizations,* 14.

7. Hofstede, *Cultures and Organizations,* 262.

8. Hofstede, *Cultures and Organizations,* 260.

9. Hofstede, *Cultures and Organizations,* 261.

10. Hofstede, *Cultures and Organizations,* 53.

11. Hofstede, *Cultures and Organizations,* 261.

12. Hofstede, *Cultures and Organizations,* 262.

13. Hofstede, *Cultures and Organizations,* 263.

14. Hofstede, *Cultures and Organizations,* 261.

15. Hofstede, *Cultures and Organizations,* 262–63.

16. Hofstede, *Cultures and Organizations,* 15–16.

17. Julia T. Wood, *Gendered Lives* (Belmont, Calif.: Wadsworth, 1994).

18. Jennifer Warren, "Boonville's Sprightly Lingo About to Die Out," *Sacramento Bee,* 21 January 1996, A2.

19. Warren, "Boonville's Sprightly Lingo," A2.

20. Sarah Trenholm, *Persuasion and Social Influence* (Englewood Cliffs, N.J.: Prentice-Hall, 1989), 6.

21. Milton Rokeach, *Beliefs, Attitudes and Values* (San Francisco: Jossey-Bass, 1968), 6–21.

22. M. Fishbein and I. Ajzen, *Belief, Attitude, Intention, and Behavior* (Reading, Mass.: Addison-Wesley, 1975), 6.

23. Trenholm, *Persuasion and Social Influence,* 11, based on Rokeach, *Beliefs, Attitudes and Values.*

24. Milton Rokeach, "Change and Stability in American Value Systems, 1968–1971," in *Understanding Human Values: Individual and Societal,* ed. Milton Rokeach (San Francisco: Jossey-Bass, 1968), 129–53.

25. Robert Fulghum, *All I Really Need to Know I Learned in Kindergarten* (New York: Ivy Books, 1988).

26. Fishbein and Ajzen, *Belief, Attitude, Intention, and Behavior,* 12–13.

27. "Trouble at the Top," *U.S. News and World Report,* 17 June 1991, 41–42.

28. M. Sherif and C. I. Hovland, *Social Judgment: Assimilation and Contrast Effects in Communication and Attitude Change* (New Haven, Conn.: Yale University Press, 1961).

29. Howard Fineman and Vern E. Smith, "An Angry 'Charmer,' " *Newsweek,* 30 October 1995, 33.

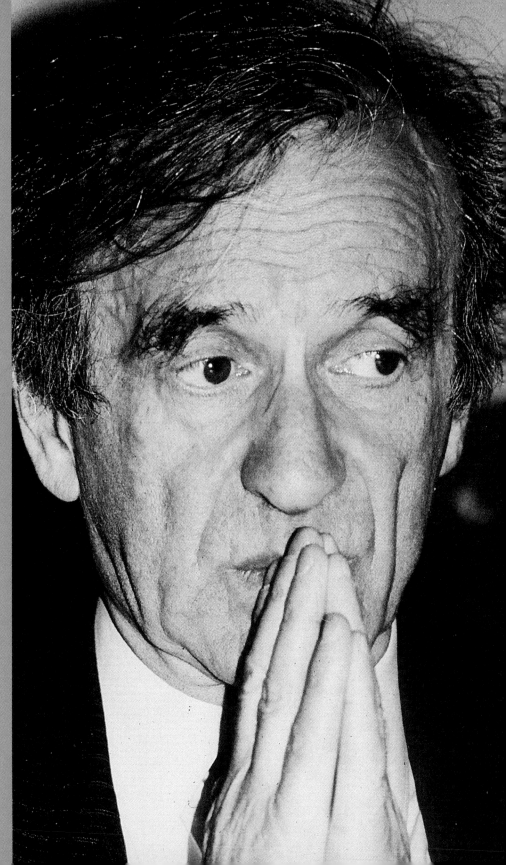

Elie Weisel, Nobel Peace Prize winner, has been a force for ethics as he fights against bigotry and racism.

6

Ethical Speaking

OBJECTIVES

After reading this chapter, you should be able to:

- Demonstrate an understanding of the differences among ethical relativism, universalism, utilitarianism, and situational ethics.
- Apply ethical principles to a variety of different public speaking situations.
- Explain plagiarism and the role of attribution in avoiding plagiarism.
- Explain and apply the basic ethical obligations of both speakers and listeners.

KEY CONCEPTS

categorical imperative	plagiarism
cultural relativism	situational ethics
ethical relativism	trustworthiness
ethics	universalism
good reasons	utilitarianism
goodwill	

Although Mr. Spock believed that the needs of the many outweighed the needs of the one, his shipmates risked their many lives to save him after his "death" in *Star Trek II: The Wrath of Khan*.

You may remember the climactic scene of *Star Trek II: The Wrath of Khan,* when Mr. Spock enters the warp drive chamber of the *Starship Enterprise* to prevent the destruction of the ship, sacrificing his own life to save those of his shipmates. Of course, thanks to the miracles of science fiction, Spock is reborn in the sequel. By *Star Trek IV* he is back to his normal, logical self. Questioned by his human mother, "Does the good of the many outweigh the good of the one?" Spock replies, "I would accept that as an axiom."[2] His mother then informs him that he is alive because the crew of the *Enterprise* violated that axiom. His shipmates risked their *many* lives to save *one* life—his.

In many senses, this question—Does the good of the many outweigh the good of the one?—is at the heart of ethics. **Ethics** is a system of principles of right and wrong that govern human conduct. Mr. Spock is governed by an ethical principle that is not too far from the philosophy of John Stuart Mill, who believed that one should always choose the action that maximizes happiness and minimizes unhappiness for the greatest number of people.[3] Ethical standards and practices should not be viewed as all-or-nothing propositions. In fact, there are degrees of ethical behavior, from highly ethical to totally unethical.[4]

In this chapter we treat ethics as an important concern of all participants in the public speaking transaction, speakers and audience members alike. The same standards that govern our everyday conduct are applicable to the public speaking transaction. In addition, because speakers can potentially influence a great many people, they have to face some special concerns. Thus, we begin this chapter with a review of some basic ethical questions. Next, we suggest a set of norms, or guidelines, for public speak-

ing. We then focus on ethical issues faced by public speakers, including plagiarism. Finally, we discuss specific ethical obligations of both speakers and
listeners.

BASIC ETHICAL QUESTIONS

As a speaker you will often be grappling with topics that involve ethical
considerations: Why should you care about ethics? How will you adapt to
differences in groups and cultures that have different standards of ethical
conduct? Are there some universal principles that simply cannot be com-
promised? What constitutes the greatest good for the greatest number, and
to what extent should some people be asked to sacrifice for the greater happiness? What are the situational constraints that impinge on your ethical
decision making? What means are ethically acceptable in seeking to achieve
ethical ends? These are some of the questions we address in this section.

Why Care about Ethics?

Perhaps the most basic ethical question of all is "Why care about ethics?"
After all, why shouldn't everyone just look out for number one? There is,
of course, no way that reading a book or enrolling in a class will make a
person who doesn't care about ethics into Mother Teresa. However, we believe that most people are fundamentally ethical and seek to do the right
thing. Ask yourself about your own motives. Have you ever sacrificed something you really wanted to help out someone less fortunate than yourself?
Have you ever helped a friend through a difficult situation or talked someone out of harming him- or herself or others? If you have done any of these
or countless other ethical things, you know the feeling that comes from doing what is right. The question is, "How do ethical principles apply to the
public speaking situation?" Our goal in this chapter is to help you answer
that question. It doesn't mean we can give you pat answers for every situation. But we do hope to provide you with guidelines for "doing the right
thing."

Is Everything Relative?

Ethical relativism is a philosophy based on the belief that there are no
universal ethical principles. This theory goes back at least as far as the
Sophists, who believed that truth was relative and depended on circumstances.[5]

The most radical version of relativism asserts that any one person's ethical standards are as good as the next person's. Although this philosophy
has the advantage of simplicity, it makes a civilized society impossible. Life

American women played an important role in Operation Desert Storm, which conflicted with the norms for women in Saudi culture.

would be, essentially, a free-for-all. Even when a group of people hold such a radical view, the consequences for society are potentially disastrous. After all, the Nazis believed they were entitled to enslave and kill Jews and other "undesirables." No doubt the street gangs in many cities believe it is moral to shoot members of rival gangs. Whatever the rationale, an individual- or group-based ethics is untenable.

On the other hand, many people endorse **cultural relativism,** the notion that the criteria for ethical behavior in one culture should not necessarily be applied to other cultures. This was the position of the Sophist Protagoras, who argued that moral laws are based on the conventions of a given society. Examples of such differences among cultures are easy to find. In western cultures, for example, women are held to be, at least in principle, equal to men. In some other cultures, women are subservient to men; this is a fundamental ethical principle. Differences between two cultures were starkly apparent during the U.S. involvement in the Persian Gulf War in 1991. Female American officers often commanded male soldiers, something unthinkable in Saudi Arabia. Saudi women are not even allowed to drive cars, much less serve in the army or issue commands to men. By what right could either culture claim superiority over the other?

Similarly, there are cultural differences in ethical standards governing communication. One such difference involves the extent to which people should be explicit or "brutally honest" in certain situations. In collectivist cultures, "saving face" is important to the good of all society, so people are often indirect and may stretch the bounds of truthfulness in certain situations. To do either in an individualistic culture such as that of the United States could be regarded as unethical communication. Can either culture claim superiority over the routine communication practices of the other? Not really.

At the same time, there are limits to what most people will accept as culturally relative ethics. Even within a society, customs change over time as people reexamine their ethical values. Human sacrifice was once a routine part of some religions, yet no one today would consider such behavior ethical. Less than a century and a half ago, a significant number of Americans believed that slavery was ethical and gave their lives to defend the institution. A mere 50 years ago, during World War II, American citizens of Japanese ancestry were interned in "relocation" camps. And today, female infants are routinely killed or allowed to die in a number of countries around the world. What makes one culture or one time period ethically superior or inferior to other cultures or other times? Or is it all relative?

We need to be careful not to exaggerate cultural differences, however. Philosophy Professor James Rachels, for example, points out that different cultures often agree on underlying principles but disagree on how they are to be applied. For example, he points out that even apparently inhumane practices, such as the Eskimos leaving the elderly to die in the snow, are grounded in the need of the family to survive in a harsh environment. Rachels argues that "the Eskimos' values are not all that different from our values. It is only that life forces upon them choices that we do not have to make."[6]

Are There Rules for Every Situation?

An alternative to ethical relativism is **universalism,** the philosophy that there are ethical standards that apply to all situations regardless of the individual, group, or culture. Immanuel Kant, an 18th-century philosopher, developed such a philosophy. He proposed the **categorical imperative:** *"Act only on that maxim through which you can at the same time will that it should become a universal law."*[7] To will the maxim be universally applicable means that you would want everyone to obey the same rule as you are proposing.

Suppose, for example, that you think it's acceptable for anybody to lie at any time, so you propose, as a universal rule, that lying is permissible for any reason. What would the result be? Lies would deceive no one, because lying had become the rule. Thus, a universal law that lying is permissible would in fact make lies ineffective. Consider voting as another example. You might think you don't need to vote, because your own vote doesn't make a difference. But imagine that as a universal rule: "Since individual votes don't matter, voting is unnecessary." If not voting were a universal rule, democracy would collapse. So Kant gives us a test for specific ethical rules. To be an ethical principle, a rule or maxim must be capable of being applied universally.

One of the most important ethical rules that Kant proposed relates directly to the public speaker. Kant proposed the maxim *"Act in such a way that you always treat humanity whether in your own person or in the person of any other, never simply as a means, but always at the same time as an end."*[8] One practical implication of this maxim is that speakers should treat audience members with respect, not simply as a means of achieving their goals. Conversely, audience members should respect and treat speakers as fellow human beings, not as objects of derision. Obviously, then, tactics that deceive or demean either an audience or a speaker would be unacceptable.

Kant's categorical imperative is not without drawbacks. Consider truth telling. If lying is unacceptable in any circumstance, innocent people may suffer as a consequence. Miep Gies, for example, lied to authorities throughout World War II to protect the Jews she was hiding from the Nazis, including a young girl named Anne Frank. And this isn't an isolated example. History is replete with cases demonstrating that it's sometimes better to bend the truth to fit the situation.

Of course, one can reformulate Kant's rule and say people shouldn't lie except under certain circumstances, such as when necessary to save lives. But that creates another problem: How do we know which actions fall under these conditions? Rachels points out a key problem with Kant's universalism: "For any action a person might contemplate, it is possible to specify more than one rule that he or she would be following; some of these rules will be 'universalizable' and some will not. . . . For we can always get around any such rule by describing our action in such a way that it does not fall under that rule but instead comes under a different one."[9] To examine your own principles, see the box "When Is It Acceptable to Lie?"

Does the Good of the Many Outweigh the Good of the Few?

Another ethical standard, utilitarianism, was proposed by English philosophers Jeremy Bentham, John Stuart Mill, and Henry Sidgwick. **Utilitarianism** is based on the principle that the aim of any action should be to provide the greatest amount of happiness for the greatest number of people. Much like Mr. Spock, these philosophers sought the greatest good for the greatest number. And they specifically defined the good as that which creates happiness—"not the agent's own greatest happiness, but the greatest amount of happiness altogether."[10]

This certainly is a useful standard for the public speaker. Most topics on which you will speak are about choices and trade-offs. If we cut social

SELF-ASSESSMENT

When Is It Acceptable to Lie?

Read the following scenarios carefully. Put a check mark next to the scenarios in which you think it would be acceptable to lie. Be prepared to present your responses in class and to discuss any differences between your responses and those of your classmates.

_____ 1. You know your best friend is cheating on a lover. The lover is suspicious and asks you, "Is Jane/Joe cheating on me?"

_____ 2. The person seated next to you during an exam appears to be copying your answers. As you turn your exam in, the instructor asks, "Was X copying from your exam?"

_____ 3. A casual friend misses several lectures in a class you both attend. He asks to borrow your notes to copy them. You don't want to hand over your hard work, but you also don't want to appear unsympathetic.

_____ 4. A person repeatedly asks you out on a date. You've run out of excuses, but to be honest about it, you find the person completely unattractive.

_____ 5. Your parents have always trusted you. Over a break from school they ask you whether you've experimented with marijuana. Even though you have used marijuana, you are of the opinion that what your parents don't know won't hurt them.

spending to fund a tax cut, some people will suffer while others will benefit. If we crack down on crime and build more prisons, there will be less money for schools and colleges. What constitutes the greatest good for the greatest number? As a speaker, you have an obligation to your audience to thoroughly research your subject to determine what position will ensure the greatest good and to put that greatest good ahead of mere personal gain. If you fail to fully inform your audience of the facts, if you lie to or deceive them, how can _they_ rationally decide what will promote the general good?

Utilitarianism, of course, has its critics. Many would say it promotes ethical relativism. After all, if the greatest good for the greatest number means that some minority of people are oppressed, would not utilitarianism justify that oppression? Could not a Hitler rationalize his extermination of the Jews in the name of the greater good for all of Germany? Certainly that is not what the utilitarians contemplated. But critics of utilitarianism have a point. Seeking the greatest happiness for all does not guarantee that particular individuals will not suffer unjustly.

If you think these issues are mere philosophical musings, think again. Consider the case of a newborn baby who suffered from a genetic abnormality that would cause its death in a short time. The parents wanted to donate the baby's organs to help other ill children. However, in the process of dying, the baby's organs would so deteriorate that they would not be usable for transplantation. The parents sought to have the baby's life support disconnected, but they were overruled by a judge. Here a utilitarian would have no difficulty justifying "pulling the plug." The baby was brain-dead and could enjoy no happiness. Several other babies could benefit from the transplantation of the organs. But those with other philosophical views might argue that all human life is sacred. They could claim that this was the first step on the road to disconnecting life support from viable infants to save the lives of others. These sorts of dilemmas have led to the emergence of a new field, known as biomedical ethics. Many hospitals now have review boards that deal with ethical dilemmas in medicine.

How Do Specific Situations Affect Ethical Principles?

Another approach to ethics is known as **situational ethics.** According to this philosophy, there are overriding ethical maxims, but sometimes it is necessary to set them aside in particular situations to fulfill a higher law or principle, such as love. As one writer put it, "What acts are right may depend on circumstances . . . but there is an absolute obligation to will whatever may on each occasion be right."[11]

Situational ethics is particularly useful in explaining how what appears to be the same kind of act can be ethical in one case and unethical in another. For example, most people agree that giving a speech in the classroom written by someone else is unethical. The principle that a student should do his or her own work is embedded in American education. At the same time, no one expects Jay Leno to write all of his own jokes or the president of the United States to write all of his own speeches. In those situations, everybody knows that Leno has comedy writers and the president has ghostwriters.

Critics of situational ethics argue that this is just relativism in another guise and thus provides no criteria for ethical judgment.[12] However, situationists do not mean we should abandon all ethical principles. As ethicist Joseph Fletcher writes: "The situationist enters into every decision-making situation fully armed with the ethical maxims of his community and its heritage, and he treats them with respect as illuminators of his problems. Just the same he is prepared in any situation to compromise them or set them aside *in the situation* if love seems better served by doing so."[13]

One problem with situational ethics, however, is that it would allow the use of unethical means to achieve ethical goals.[14] That brings us to our final question.

Do the Ends Justify the Means?

You may have heard the old saying "The ends don't justify the means." This means that it is not acceptable to do something wrong just because it will produce a good result. Of course, some people will use a good result as the justification for behavior normally considered immoral. But to do so raises serious ethical concerns. As a speaker you need to concern yourself with both ends (goals) and the means you use to achieve them.

In terms of ends, many of your topics are likely to be about issues of right and wrong, morality and immorality, the weighing of the good of the many against the good of the few. Understanding how people make ethical decisions is important to your choice of topic and the goals you seek. Obviously, the first and foremost ethical obligation of any speaker is to seek ethical ends, that is, to make sure you are striving to achieve a goal that is ethical and just. So, as you choose your topics, adapt to your audience, and seek to fulfill your goals as a speaker, you should always focus on accomplishing ethical ends.

Not only should your goals be ethically sound, but how you seek to reach those goals should also be ethical. Consider the example of a speaker who wants to raise money for a worthy cause, such as finding a cure for AIDS. Certainly the end is admirable. But suppose the speaker knows the audience is strongly homophobic and so tells them that the money will be used for cancer research. Does the end—raising money to fight AIDS—justify the means—lying about how the money will be spent? Would it not be a greater good to educate the audience about AIDS, letting them know that it is not just a disease that gay men get, rather than to give in to their phobia? Further, once you accept the premise that it's acceptable to lie to raise money for AIDS research, why not for the homeless, for the poor, or for communication majors at the local college? No matter what the goal, the ethical speaker uses ethical means to achieve his or her ends.

ETHICAL NORMS FOR PUBLIC SPEAKERS

Developing standards for ethical public speaking is not an easy task. Probably the closest thing to a code of conduct for public speakers is the Speech Communication Association's Credo for Free and Responsible Communication in a Democratic Society, reprinted in the box "Codes of Conduct for Public Speaking" on page 164. More than any specific code of conduct, however, ethical public speakers are guided by the traditional standards of rhetoric that date back over 2,000 years. As explained in Chapter 5, Sophists were known for their philosophical relativism. Some Sophists carried this philosophy to its logical extreme, arguing that virtually any rhetorical deception was justified if it furthered their cause.[15]

SPEAKING OF . . .

Codes of Conduct for Public Speaking

Although it is not a full-fledged ethical code, such as those found in law and medicine, the Speech Communication Association's Credo for Free and Responsible Communication in a Democratic Society forms an important touchstone for the ethical public speaker. Other guidelines that may be of help to the public speaker are found in the American Advertising Association's Code of Ethics, the Code of Ethics of the International Association of Business Communicators, and the Public Relations Society of America's Code of Professional Standards for the Practice of Public Relations.[1]

Credo for Free and Responsible Communication in a Democratic Society[2]

Recognizing the essential place of free and responsible communication in a democratic society, and recognizing the distinction between the freedoms our legal system should respect and the responsibilities our education system should cultivate, we the members of the Speech Communication Association endorse the following statement of principles:

We believe that freedom of speech and assembly must hold a central position among American constitutional principles, and we express our determined support for the right of peaceful expression by any communicative means available.

We support the proposition that a free society can absorb with equanimity speech which exceeds the boundaries of generally accepted beliefs and mores; that much good and little harm can ensue if we err on the side of freedom, whereas much harm and little good may follow if we err on the side of suppression.

We criticize as misguided those who believe that the justice of their cause confers license to interfere physically and coercively with the speech of others, and we condemn intimidation, whether by powerful majorities or strident minorities, which attempts to restrict free expression.

We accept the responsibility of cultivating by precept and example, in our classrooms and in our communities, enlightened uses of communication; of developing in our students a respect for precision and accuracy in communication, and for reasoning based upon evidence and a judicious discrimination among values.

We encourage our students to accept the role of well-informed and articulate citizens, to defend the communication rights of those with whom they may disagree, and to expose abuses of the communication process.

We dedicate ourselves fully to these principles, confident in the belief that reason will ultimately prevail in a free marketplace of ideas.

---

[1]Richard L. Johannesen, *Ethics in Human Communication,* 3rd ed. (Prospect Heights, Ill.: Waveland Press, 1990), chap. 10.

[2]Used by permission of the Speech Communication Association.

Such philosophical relativism ran counter to the philosophy of Socrates, who taught that absolute truth was knowable through a question-and-answer technique known as dialectic. Socrates' student Plato wrote two dialogues, the *Gorgias* and the *Phaedrus,* that expounded this Socratic view of rhetoric. To Plato, rhetoric, as practiced by the Sophists, was a sham, with no truth to it, designed to deceive listeners. In the *Phaedrus,* Plato proposes an ideal rhetoric, one based on philosophical truths. The basic function of this rhetoric is to take the truth discovered through dialectic and energize it for the masses.

The best-known response to Plato came from his student Aristotle, whose *Rhetoric* is probably the most influential book on communication to this day. To Aristotle, rhetoric was not the opposite of dialectic but rather its counterpart. Aristotle did not view rhetoric as either moral or immoral. Rather, it was an art that could be put to both good and bad uses. The moral purpose of the speaker was the determining factor. Aristotle believed that "things that are true and things that are just have a natural tendency to prevail over their opposites."[16] Therefore, he stressed the importance of training in rhetoric. Even arguing both sides of a question was not immoral: rather, it was a way of learning how to refute someone who misstates the facts on the other side of an issue. For Aristotle, in sum, rhetoric was an art, not a sham.

In the first century A.D., the Roman orator and rhetorician Quintilian provided an ethical standard that many emulate to this day. To Quintilian, the ideal citizen-orator is a good person, speaking well. As he put it, "Oratory is the science of speaking well."[17] Further, because no one "can speak well who is not good,"[18] the moral quality of the speaker is not irrelevant. Rather, it is central to the ideal orator.

Today, the issue of ethical standards for public speaking has once again become a central concern for speech communication educators. What constitutes ethical communication? Most of us would agree that speakers should not lie or distort the truth. Beyond that, however, what are the moral obligations of speaker to audience and audience to speaker? Based on the work of the philosophers discussed, as well as several speech communication scholars, we suggest the following norms or guidelines for the public speaker: (1) Be truthful. (2) Show respect for the power of words. (3) Invoke participatory democracy. (4) Demonstrate tolerance for cultural diversity. (5) Treat people as ends, not means. (6) Provide good reasons. Let's look at each of these more closely.

Be Truthful

James Jaksa and Michael Pritchard of Western Michigan University have developed a set of ethical norms for speakers. Three of these seem particularly relevant to us. The first is the norm of truthfulness, which is fundamental to all communication.[19] The speaker caught in a lie loses his or her credibility and the goodwill of the audience, which are essential to belief. As former presidential spokesman Larry Speakes learned, the loss of credibility can be disastrous. After acknowledging in his 1988 book, *Speaking Out*, that he made up quotations and attributed them to President Reagan, he lost his prestigious position at Merrill Lynch. In retrospect he admitted, "It was wrong—wrong then and wrong now."[20]

Of course one does not have to tell an outright lie to deceive listeners. As we discuss in more detail in Chapter 14, distortions and omissions can sometimes be as harmful to the truth as outright lies. If you doubt that, we invite you to check out the "facts" in many political ads. Although most are based on a kernel of truth, often what's left out changes the whole meaning of the ad. We recall one political challenger who showed a video clip of the incumbent saying, "I'll do anything to get re-elected." What the ad failed to mention was that the incumbent was playing the part of the challenger! The video clip was edited to reflect the exact opposite of the meaning intended by the incumbent. Of course the ad didn't lie outright—the words were actually said—but because the context was omitted, the result was the same as a lie.

A speaker who is unsure of the facts must learn the truth before speaking. Even a speaker who is simply misinformed, not consciously lying, can cause considerable harm. One of the authors heard a student speech based on the theory that AIDS is not caused by a virus but is a result of the homosexual lifestyle. That thesis flies in the face of every reputable medical study done on the disease. Documented cases of AIDS transmitted from mother to baby at birth or through blood transfusions clearly disprove the theory. Yet students in the class seemed to believe every word of the speech. Although a guest in the class, the author finally intervened and questioned some of the student's claims. Such misinformation, if believed, can have serious, even fatal consequences for audience members who come to believe they are immune to a lethal disease because they are heterosexual.

Show Respect for the Power of Words

Another norm cited by Jaksa and Pritchard is respect for the word.[21] The power of words is undeniable. Consider the reaction of people to certain emotionally laden words. Even words and usages that were once acceptable, such as referring to a woman as a "girl," or an African American man as "boy," have come to be viewed as sexist and racist. Emotionally charged words can cause severe damage. Consider the effect on the O. J. Simpson jury and the public at large of a racial epithet used by detective Mark Fuhrman, captured on tape and played for the jury and the world to hear.

Although freedom of speech is central to our democracy, the courts have recognized that there are limits. As Chief Justice of the Supreme Court

Revelations during the O. J. Simpson case about Mark Fuhrman's use of racist language shocked the jury as well as the public.

Oliver Wendell Holmes, Jr., once said, freedom of speech does not give you the right to shout "fire!" in a crowded theater. Although Justice Holmes was speaking metaphorically, the principle he was expressing is as relevant to the current debate about speech codes as it was nearly a century ago. The fact that you can say almost anything that comes to mind in this country doesn't make the content of what you say either ethical or wise. The old saying "Sticks and stones can break my bones, but words can never hurt me" is incorrect. In fact, words are very powerful and can cause great harm as well as great good. The ethical speaker recognizes that words have consequences.

Invoke Participatory Democracy

Jaksa and Pritchard discuss the importance of participatory democracy, which rests on a foundation of choice and respect for people.[22] Citizens must have accurate and ample information in order to make informed choices. Further, the golden rule of treating others as we would have them treat us applies to public speaking as well as to interpersonal communication. Speakers should put themselves in the shoes of listeners and ask if they are treating them as they would like to be treated. The ethical speaker recognizes the audience as an equal participant in the communication transaction. Similarly, listeners need to show respect and tolerance for speakers, even if their views are different from their own. Shouting down a speaker, for example, infringes on the speaker's freedom of speech and the public's right to hear a full spectrum of viewpoints.

In other words, ethics in communication is a joint responsibility. For example, there have been many complaints in recent years about negative and deceptive political advertising. Yet political consultants say they are only giving the public what it wants. Although that is no ethical defense for their behavior, we must also realize that deceptive advertising succeeds only because voters fail to protest against it and continue to vote for candidates who engage in such practices.

Demonstrate Tolerance for Cultural Diversity

Clearly, what people regard as ethical or unethical depends a great deal on their culture and the set of beliefs that inhere in it. It is difficult for people to avoid using their own culture's ethical standards when judging the behavior of people in another culture. In North America, for example, we generally like people to be "up front" with us, that is, to communicate honestly and directly, even if we don't like the message. We generally don't want people to beat around the bush on matters we personally perceive as significant.

But what we call beating around the bush is the norm in many cultures around the world. Physicians, businesspeople, and even family members may be less than direct or forthright in their transactions with each other. In Japan, physicians and family members commonly hide the truth from a terminally ill patient. They believe that telling the truth in this case will undermine the power of the person's mind to intervene and perhaps divert the disease's course.

Some cultures, groups, and individuals are more tolerant of diversity than others. In general, Americans have historically been intolerant of behavior that runs counter to accepted norms. As our culture grows more diverse, this lack of tolerance becomes more apparent. Immigrants who accede to American norms are quickly assimilated. Those who don't are often singled out for disapproval. Think about this in terms of cultural relativism. Many of the cultural practices recent immigrants have brought with them are outside the bounds of what the majority of Americans regard as ethical. These cultural practices include religious rituals, food choices, and even dress.

Ethical speakers recognize that the customary criteria they use in making ethical judgments may be inappropriate in judging the behavior of people from other cultures. This tolerance guides ethical speakers in both interpreting and responding to the communication behaviors of those who are culturally dissimilar from them. Tolerance is not synonymous with unconditional approval, however. Ethical speakers may tolerate ethical norms with which they disagree, but they may also engage in constructive dialogue with the individuals who follow those norms.

Treat People as Ends, Not Means

To these principles we wish to add one taken from Kant, namely, that people should never be treated as mere means to an end. Their best interests should be the ends sought by the speaker. Using people as objects, manipulating them even to achieve desirable ends, is never justified. Consider the case of the *Jenny Jones Show,* a TV talk show. In 1994, Jones invited people to go on the air and meet their secret admirers. What the producers didn't tell these people, however, was that these secret admirers could be heterosexual, gay, or lesbian. You may recall the tragic results of this attempt to "entertain" the viewing audience. One guest discovered that his secret admirer was gay and later stalked and murdered the admirer.

Of course the guest's tragic overreaction was also unethical and far out of proportion to the deception perpetrated by Jones. Nevertheless, the television show was widely criticized as having gone too far. Embarrassing people on national TV as a means of simply building program ratings is clearly unethical.

Provide Good Reasons

Another principle of ethical speaking has been articulated by Karl Wallace, scholar and former president of the national Speech Communication Association. Wallace believes that the public speaker must offer his or her audience "good reasons" for believing, valuing, and acting.[23] **Good reasons** are statements, based on moral principles, offered in support of propositions concerning what we should believe or how we should act. Wallace believes that ethical and moral values, as well as relevant information, are the basic materials of rhetoric. Speakers who rely on "good reasons" value all people and the ethical principles to which they adhere. Not only does the use of good reasons help ensure that the speaker uses ethical means, it is also far more likely to be successful in accomplishing the ethical ends sought by the speaker.

SPECIAL ISSUES FOR SPEAKERS

As a public speaker, you face some special issues that might not be as relevant in other communication situations. A speech is a uniquely personal event. Unlike a written essay, for example, in which the author may be unknown to the reader, a speaker stands as one with his or her words. In fact, Aristotle said that character "may almost be called the most effective means of persuasion" possessed by a speaker.[24] Four important issues need to be addressed, therefore, because of their special significance for public speakers: (1) plagiarism and source attribution, (2) building goodwill and trustworthiness, (3) revealing or concealing true intentions, and (4) discussing both sides of a controversial issue.

Plagiarism and Source Attribution

Plagiarism—stealing the ideas of others and presenting them as your own—is highly unethical. What makes it a particular sin for speakers is that they are jeopardizing their most important asset—their character. Few students begin their speech assignment intending to plagiarize. But other pressing assignments, poor time management, sloppy note-taking, or just plain laziness often intervene. Students are tempted to use someone else's words or ideas without credit, assuming that no one will be the wiser. The consequences of such behavior can be severe. An example from the authors' own experience illustrates what can happen.

One of our teaching associates (we'll call him Jack) was ill and asked another TA (Jane) to cover his class. It happened that one of the students in Jack's class was the roommate of a student in Jane's. When Jane heard the same speech in Jack's class that she had heard earlier in the week in her own section, bells went off. Of course, it turned out that one roommate had appropriated the other student's speech. While the plagiarizer was caught red-handed, it didn't end there. The original speech writer was guilty of aiding and abetting the roommate. Both students had to face disciplinary action from the university as well as failure in the class.

Although it's true, of course, that this act might have gone undetected had Jack not become ill, this is not the only way plagiarism is detected. At our university, and we suspect this is true at others as well, professors often talk about speeches they have heard in class. In fact, every speech at our university is recorded on videotape. Over the years, we have discovered several instances of plagiarism. Each time the students have been shocked and repentant. They have come to realize that they have put their college careers at risk for a few extra points on a speech. The negative consequences of plagiarism are not confined to students. Plagiarism can also destroy a career, as described in the box "Plagiarism: Truth or Consequences."

How can you avoid plagiarism? First, you need to recognize that there are varying degrees of the offense. Because plagiarism is a form of theft, we call these variations "the total rip-off," "the partial rip-off," and "the accidental rip-off."

The Total Rip-Off   The case of the roommates who used the same speech is an example of a total rip-off. Here a student simply gives someone else's speech. Usually it is not a speech from a published source, because such speeches don't often fulfill the assignment. Further, if the speech is well known, it is likely to be spotted instantly as a phony. More common is the use of a speech from a classmate who took the class in a previous term or

Plagiarism: Truth or Consequences

Senator Joseph Biden was a leading contender for the Democratic nomination for president in 1988 when he spoke in Des Moines, Iowa, on August 29, 1987. Little did he know that his candidacy was about to unravel.

Biden had seen a videotape of Neil Kinnock, leader of Britain's Labour party, in which Kinnock asked: "Why am I the first Kinnock in a thousand generations to be able to get to university?" Pointing to his wife, he continued, "Why is Glenys the first woman in her family in a thousand generations to be able to get to university? Was it because all our predecessors were thick?" He concluded, "Does anybody really think that they didn't get what we had because they didn't have the talent or the strength or the endurance to the commitment? Of course not. It was because there was no platform on which they could stand."

Biden spoke almost the same words at an Iowa State Fair debate, without attribution: "Why is it that Joe Biden is the first in his family to ever go to a university? Why is it that my wife who is sit-

ting over there in the audience is the first in her family ever to go to college? Is it because our fathers and mothers were not bright?" He concluded: "No, it's not because they weren't as smart. It's not because they didn't work hard. It's because they didn't have a platform on which to stand."

Those purloined words came back to haunt Biden. When newspapers reported the similarities and his political opponents began circulating videotapes comparing the two speeches, his fate was sealed. Soon other instances of Biden's borrowing words from politicians like Robert Kennedy and Hubert Humphrey came to light. Ultimately he was forced to end his quest for the presidency. Although Joseph Biden has remained in the Senate, his hopes for national office appear dead. And it all began when he lifted a few words from Neil Kinnock.

SOURCE: Jack W. Germond and Jules Witcover, *Whose Broad Stripes and Bright Stars? The Trivial Pursuit of the Presidency 1988* (New York: Warner Brothers, 1989), 230–31.

who is in another section. This is clearly academic dishonesty equivalent to cheating on an exam or turning in someone else's term paper. Most universities and colleges suspend or even expel students caught in this sort of dishonesty. If the speech was knowingly given to the plagiarist, the original author can face the same penalties.

Avoiding this type of plagiarism is easy: Don't offer or accept the speech of another person to present as your own. Most students who use other students' speeches do so out of desperation. Our advice is not to put off writing your speech until the last minute. Give yourself as much time to research and prepare as you would to write a paper for an English class. Realize also that giving a speech you don't really know is likely to be a disaster. You will stumble over words and be unable to answer questions. Even if you escape detection, you'll do yourself little good. If you simply cannot get a speech ready to deliver on time, talk to your instructor. Policies will vary, but your own speech, given late, even with a penalty, is far superior to a ripped-off speech given on time.

The Partial Rip-Off   More common than the complete rip-off is the partial rip-off. Here a student creates a speech by patching together material from different sources. Rather than quoting the sources, the speaker presents the ideas as if they were original. The irony is that the speaker has done a lot of work. The problem was not that time ran out. Rather, the speaker wanted to be credited with the ideas.

The way to avoid this type of plagiarism is to give credit to your sources orally and to make sure that your speech is only *partially* made up of material from these sources. Rather than simply using the words of another, tell the audience who made the statement or where the idea originated. Interestingly, research has shown that under many circumstances, citing sources in your speech enhances your persuasiveness.[25] Audiences are impressed that you have done your homework. It is important to cite sources as you speak, not just in the bibliography of your written outline. Only by citing sources orally can you inform your audience of where the words, phrases, and ideas came from, which is what you need to do to build your credibility as a speaker.

Citing sources is important for direct quotations as well as for specific facts, statistics, and ideas derived from the work of others. Thus, you might not quote Martin Luther King, Jr., directly, but you would still refer to him as the author of the idea that people should be judged by their character, not their skin color.

The Accidental Rip-Off   Perhaps the most frustrating thing for an instructor who discovers a student's plagiarism is when the student simply doesn't understand what he or she has done wrong. For example, a student may take significant ideas or even quotes from sources listed in a bibliography accompanying the speech, without saying so in the speech. The student sees no problem, responding, "I did cite my sources—they are right there in the bibliography." For the listener, however, there is no way to know which ideas came from outside sources and which are the speaker's own, as mentioned in the previous section. A common variant of this is that the speaker attributes ideas to a source but actually uses a word-for-word quotation without making that clear to the audience. The written version of the speech outline should include quotation marks to distinguish between paraphrased ideas and direct quotations. Further, you should use "oral" quotation marks. Either state that you are quoting someone, or make it clear from your tone of voice that you are in fact quoting someone else's words. Use such phrases as "To quote Martin Luther King, Jr., . . ." or "As Martin Luther King, Jr., said, . . ."

Finally, be careful of letting ideas become disassociated from their source. We've all had the experience of remembering an idea or a quote but forgetting where we heard it. Unfortunately, the tendency in a speech is to just use the words. By taking careful notes as you research your speech, you are less likely to accidentally borrow an idea from another source without attribution.

Whether a full-scale rip-off, an incremental theft, or an accidental violation, plagiarism is a serious ethical offense for the public speaker. Our best advice is to resist the temptation, cite the sources of your ideas for your audience, and take pride in those ideas that are your own. In Chapter 7 we discuss how to record and cite sources in a speech. But the general principle is to let your audience know exactly where your ideas are coming from.

Building Goodwill and Trustworthiness

A speaker's credibility has several components. Two of the most important are goodwill and trustworthiness. **Goodwill** is the perception by the audience that a speaker cares about their needs and concerns. A speaker who truly cares about his or her audience's needs, and who can communicate that to the audience, not only is more likely to be effective but also is much more likely to behave ethically. There is a huge difference, for example, between the speaker who is trying to put one over on the audience and one who really cares about the well-being of the audience. If speakers apply the principle developed by Kant, of treating people as ends and not means to ends, then that is a mark of goodwill.

Trustworthiness is the perception by the audience that they can rely on a speaker's word. A promise made is as good as done. The effect of a broken promise or a revealed lie on a speaker's trustworthiness is devastating. In recent years, there was perhaps no more prominent broken promise than George Bush's election campaign statement, "Read my lips, no new taxes." Many political observers attributed his defeat for a second term not so much to his having raised taxes but to his having raised them after making an unmistakable promise not to. One reason politicians in general are held in such low regard by the public is that so many of them have broken their promises and become untrustworthy in people's eyes.

As a speaker, you need to realize that you rarely can accomplish your purpose in one speech or even a short series of speeches. Often your goals will require a long-term commitment. And your relationship to your audience needs to be one of trustworthiness. If you violate their trust, not only have you behaved unethically, you have jeopardized your chances of achieving your goals as well. The solution to this problem is twofold. First, don't make promises you cannot or do not intend to keep. And second, if circumstances might require you to deviate from prior promises, make it clear what limits there are on your promise. Had President Bush said, "I'll do everything in my power to resist new taxes," it might have been a different story in 1992.

Revealing or Concealing Intentions

One of the thorniest issues you face as a speaker is whether or not to reveal your intentions to your audience. Sometimes, to begin your speech by announcing a position that you know your audience drastically opposes is to deny yourself the opportunity to be heard. On the other hand, to conceal your true intentions can be unethical, particularly if those intentions violate what the audience perceives as its best interests. In some ways, this decision requires the application of "situational ethics." Consider a couple of examples.

You are speaking to a potentially hostile audience about a controversial issue. Let's say you want to convince a group like the Moral Majority that we should not have state-sanctioned prayer in school. Should you begin by announcing your position? What is the likelihood that your argument would be heard? On the other hand, suppose you begin by describing a scenario in which the state requires everybody in school to study the Koran and pray to Allah. "How would you react?" you ask them. "Well, now reverse the situation," you continue. "What if Moslem students are required to study the Bible and say the Lord's Prayer?" The idea would be to work from a common ground—that Christians should not be forced to pray to a Moslem God—to the logical application of that principle to the issue of state-sanctioned school prayer.

Certainly this approach is no guarantee of persuading the audience of your viewpoint. But it is hard to argue that it is ethically wrong to begin with points of agreement before moving to areas of disagreement. The intentions of your speech are revealed to the audience. When and how those intentions are revealed is a strategic rather than an ethical issue.

On the other hand, consider the case of the person who knocks on your door and asks you if you would be willing to participate in a survey. Sure, you reply, always happy to help out. After going through a series of questions, you realize that the "pollster" is actually a salesperson for an encyclopedia company. Your time has been wasted, and now you have to figure out how to get the person to leave. The clear misrepresentation of intent—pollster as opposed to salesperson—is ethically wrong. And you have been harmed, if for no other reason than the salesperson stole your time. And, as many sellers know, once they get their foot in the door, the likelihood of closing the sale increases.

What makes these two cases different? Both people begin by concealing their intentions, and both eventually do reveal their goals. But in the first case, the speaker does not misrepresent his or her intentions; rather, they are deferred until after some common ground is established. In the second case, a direct misrepresentation is made—there is no poll. While the two cases seem on the surface to be similar, we would argue that the situations are far different and that that difference is ethically relevant.

These types of cases are not always easy or clear-cut. A universal rule —always state your purpose up front—cannot be applied. Speakers must sincerely ask themselves in what ways their interests and those of their audience intersect. They must then decide the best approach to take in any given case, at the same time striving to maintain goodwill and trustworthiness.

Discussing Both Sides of a Controversial Issue

One question with both ethical and practical implications is whether or not you should provide an audience with only your side of an issue or mention arguments on the other side of the issue as well. For a number of years, speech experts answered this question pragmatically: It depends on the make-up of your audience. If the general level of education in your audience is high school or less, stick to your side only. If the level of education in your audience is beyond high school, introduce the other side as well. Of course this raises some real ethical concerns. It smacks of using the audience as a means rather than treating them as ends. Basically, it says if you can fool enough of the people, no need to worry about fooling all of them.

The authors have never thought much of the recommendation to present only one's own side of an issue. What's more, we now have research on our side. This research, which combined the findings of over 25 studies done over the past four decades, suggests that speakers should use a two-sided persuasive message regardless of the audience's level of education. Specifically, the most effective persuasive strategy is to present both sides of a controversial issue along with a refutation of the other point of view.[26] If you think about it, this makes good sense. Only someone living in a complete vacuum is not going to eventually hear the other side of the story. What does it do to the audience's perception of your credibility if they believe they've not been told the whole truth? Two-sided presentations are not only more ethical, they are also more effective. We discuss the issue of "message sidedness" in more detail in Chapter 13.

ETHICAL NORMS FOR LISTENERS

People who find themselves in the primary role of listeners also need to think about their ethical obligations. Remember, audience members are very much a party to the public speaking transaction. When you are a listener, you too bear some responsibility for the consequences of the speech. Thus, we suggest these norms for ethical listening: (1) Take responsibility for the choices you make. (2) Stay informed on the issues of the day. (3) Speak out when you are convinced that a speaker is misinforming or misleading people. (4) Be aware of your own biases.

Take Responsibility for Choices

The first guideline for listeners is to recognize that unless coerced, they are responsible for the choices they make during and following a communication transaction. This means listeners cannot blame a speaker for the decision to riot following a speech or for violating human rights because they were persuaded to do so by a charismatic communicator. Just as the judges at the Nuremberg trials concluded that "following orders" was not an excuse for war crimes, audience members cannot excuse their unethical behavior on the grounds that they were complying with a speaker's request.

Stay Informed

A second guideline, which logically follows from the first, is that listeners are responsible for keeping themselves informed on issues of the day. People who are uninformed about important topics and vital issues are easy prey for propagandists. History is replete with examples of people who have tried to attribute unethical behavior to ignorance, real or imagined. They range from the people who said they didn't know the Nazis were sending millions of Jews to their death during World War II to the pharmaceutical company executives who claimed they were unaware of the terrible side effects of the drug thalidomide. Simply put, ignorance is no excuse for unethical behavior.

Speak Out

The third guideline for listeners is related to the first two. It involves the audience members' ethical obligation to speak up when convinced that a speaker is misinforming or misleading people. Most of us have been in situations where we knew someone was bending the truth, leaving out pertinent details, or passing off another's ideas as original. Under some unique set of circumstances, keeping this knowledge to ourselves may be justified. In most circumstances, however, listeners owe it to themselves and others to speak up. Speaking up can take the form of a question for the speaker following a presentation, asking the appropriate agency for equal time to speak, writing a letter to the editor of a newspaper or magazine, or confronting the speaker one on one. Whatever the appropriate medium, constructive objections are generally preferable to silence.

Be Aware of Biases

The final guideline for listeners concerns their subjective view and the manner in which it biases how they receive and process a speaker's message. Perception is colored by one's experiences, both real and vicarious. Rather than denying the fact, it's much healthier and realistic for us to admit this to ourselves. Only then can we determine how much of our reaction to a speech is based on its content and relational dynamic and how much is attributable to our individual biases.

ETHICAL OBLIGATIONS OF SPEAKERS AND LISTENERS: A SUMMARY

Finally, having discussed the ethical principles underlying all human action, as well as norms specific to public speaking, the special issues faced by speakers, and ethical norms for listening, we offer a summary list of guidelines for both speakers and listeners.[27]

Ethical Guidelines for Speakers

- **Provide truthful, relevant, and sufficient information to allow audience members to make informed choices.**
- **Present "good reasons," not just those that may work. Appeal to the best, not the worst, in people.**
- **Reinforce and be consistent with democratic processes. Recognize the importance of free speech in a democratic society and the right of others to disagree.**
- **Demonstrate goodwill and trustworthiness toward the audience.**
- **Put yourself in the position of the listeners and treat them with the same respect you would expect were the roles reversed.**
- **Recognize that both the means and the ends of a speech should be ethical. Be concerned with the possible consequences of accepting the message as well as with its truthfulness and accuracy.**
- **Take responsibility for your own work. Plagiarism is the ultimate in intellectual dishonesty.**

Ethical Guidelines for Listeners

- **Be aware that all communication is potentially influential and that there are consequences to accepting any message. Ask what influence the speaker is seeking to exert.**

Listeners have an ethical responsibility to listen to opposing points of view with an open mind.

- Stay informed on important topics so that you can judge the accuracy of the communication provided by others. Be willing to independently confirm information that appears questionable.
- Be aware of your personal biases to reduce your susceptibility to appeals to prejudices. Be willing to listen to opposing views with an open mind.

- Be aware of deceptive communication ploys and work to expose those guilty of fallacious reasoning, propaganda ploys, and outright deception. Be willing to speak out in response to deceptive speech.
- Put yourself in the position of the speaker and treat him or her with the same respect you would expect were the roles reversed.
- Provide constructive feedback to the speaker if the opportunity is provided.

SUMMARY

Several basic ethical questions are of concern to speakers: (1) Why care about ethics? Most people fundamentally want to do what is right and so turn to ethical guidelines, including those governing the public speaking transaction. (2) Is everything relative? Ethical relativism answers that there are no universal ethical principles. Cultural relativism is the notion that the criteria for ethical behavior in one culture should not be applied to other cultures. (3) Are there rules for every situation? Universalism answers that there are ethical standards that apply to all situations regardless of the individual, group, or culture. (4) Does the good of the many outweigh the good of the few? Utilitarianism answers that the aim of any action should be to provide the greatest amount of happiness for the greatest number of people. (5) How do specific situations affect ethics? Situational ethics answers that, though there are overriding ethical maxims, sometimes it is necessary to set them aside in particular situations to fulfill a higher law or principle. (6) Do the ends justify the means? The authors argue that speakers should seek ethical ends utilizing ethical means.

While no codified system exists for speakers, useful guidelines can be found in the Speech Communication Association's Credo for Free and Responsible Communication in a Democratic Society. A series of ethical norms for public speaking can be derived from both traditional and contemporary sources. Among these norms are (1) be truthful, (2) show respect for the power of words, (3) invoke participatory democracy, (4) demonstrate tolerance for cultural diversity, (5) treat people as ends, not means, and (6) provide good reasons.

Public speakers face special issues: (1) Plagiarism, the stealing of the words or ideas of another, is considered a serious ethical violation. Audiences, at least in Western cultures, expect speakers to distinguish between their own ideas and those of others through proper source attribution. (2) Building goodwill and trustworthiness is essential to successful and ethical public speech. (3) Whether to reveal or conceal one's intentions can present an ethical as well as practical dilemma for speakers. (4) Giving a two-sided presentation, rather than concealing one side of the story, is both ethically sound and pragmatically more effective.

There are also important ethical norms for listeners. Listeners should (1) take responsibility for the choices they make; (2) stay informed on the issues of the day; (3) speak out when they are convinced that a speaker is misinforming or misleading people; and (4) be aware of their own biases.

Since public speaking is a transaction between speakers and an audience, both parties have ethical obligations.

Check Your Understanding: Exercises and Activities

1. In a brief speech or short paper, explain the reason you believe the best ethical standard for the public speaker is (1) relativism, (2) universalism, (3) utilitarianism, or (4) situational ethics. Define the version of ethics you endorse, and explain why you feel it is the best alternative for public speakers.

2. Read the following cases and answer the questions about each one. Depending on your instructor's directions, either write a short paper responding to one or more of the scenarios or discuss one or more of them in a small group.

   Case A: A student in your public speaking class presents a speech that contains glaring factual errors. As an audience member who is familiar with the topic, you realize that the speaker has not done research and has "made up" certain "facts." What should you do? What do you think the instructor should do?

   Case B: You are preparing a speech arguing against a tuition increase at your college. In your research, you discover strong arguments against your position. Nevertheless, you still believe the tuition increase is a bad idea. Should you share the arguments against your position with your audience, or present only your side of the story?

   Case C: You are required by your instructor to attend a speech outside of class time. You discover on arriving at the lecture hall that the speaker holds views precisely the opposite of your own. What should you do?

   Case D: You are assigned by your teacher to speak for a position you fundamentally oppose on a question about which you hold strong moral beliefs, such as abortion. What should you do?

3. In a short paper, discuss the differences and similarities between the ethical obligations of speakers and listeners. As a speaker, how would you deal with listeners who are unwilling to meet their basic ethical obligations? As a listener, how would you respond to a speaker you felt was unethical?

4. In a short paper, discuss whether you agree with Quintilian that "no one can speak well who is not good." Cite some contemporary or historical examples to support your position.

5. In a short paper, consider the question of whether there can be any situation in which it is ethical to "shock people into action" through the use of especially horrifying or unpleasant images. Give examples to support your position.

6. In your view, what modern politician is most successful at eliciting feelings of goodwill and trustworthiness? Why do you think this person is successful in doing so? Be prepared to discuss your example in class.

7. Administrators, faculty, and students on campuses across the United States are trying to come up with speech codes that strike a balance between First Amendment rights and the right of people in the college community to be protected from hateful and demoralizing language. Working either on your own or in an instructor-assigned group, find out if your school has a speech code that prohibits the use of certain types of words and language. If it does, how would you amend it to fit your or your group's thinking? If it doesn't, what would you include in such a code? Write a short paper on your findings or thoughts, or be prepared to discuss them in class.

Notes

1. *Star Trek II: The Wrath of Khan* (Paramount Pictures, 1982).

2. *Star Trek IV: The Voyage Home* (Paramount Pictures, 1987).

3. Nina Rosenstand, *The Moral of the Story: An Introduction to Questions of Ethics and Human Nature* (Mountain View, Calif.: Mayfield, 1994), 100.

4. J. Vernon Jensen, "Ethical Tension Points in Whistleblowing," in *Ethics in Human Communication*, 3rd ed., ed. Richard L. Johannesen (Prospect Heights, Ill.: Waveland Press, 1990), 281.

5. Samuel Enoch Stumpf, *Socrates to Sartre: A History of Philosophy* (New York: McGraw-Hill, 1966), 35.

6. James Rachels, *The Elements of Moral Philosophy* (New York: Random House, 1986), 21.

7. Immanuel Kant, *Groundwork of the Metaphysics of Morals*, trans. H. J. Paton (New York: Harper & Row, 1964), 88.

8. Kant, *Groundwork of the Metaphysics of Morals*, 96.

9. Rachels, *Elements of Moral Philosophy*, 108–9.

10. John Stuart Mill, *Utilitarianism*, in *Essential Works of John Stuart Mill*, ed. Max Lerner (New York: Bantam Books, 1961), 198–99.

11. William Temple, *Nature, Man and God* (New York: Macmillan, 1934), 405, as cited in Joseph Fletcher, *Situation Ethics: The New Morality* (Philadelphia: Westminster Press, 1966), 27.

12. James A. Jaksa and Michael S. Pritchard, *Communication Ethics: Methods of Analysis,* 2nd ed. (Belmont, Calif.: Wadsworth, 1994), 21.

13. Fletcher, *Situation Ethics,* 26.

14. Fletcher, *Situation Ethics,* 121.

15. Stumpf, *Socrates to Sartre,* 36.

16. Aristotle, *Rhetoric,* trans. W. Rhys Roberts (New York: Modern Library, 1954), 22.

17. Quintilian, *Institutio Oratoria,* trans. H. E. Butler (Cambridge, Mass.: Harvard University Press, 1920), 317.

18. Quintilian, *Institutio Oratoria,* 315.

19. Jaksa and Pritchard, *Communication Ethics,* 65.

20. Larry Speakes, *Speaking Out: The Reagan Presidency from Inside the White House* (New York: Avon Books, 1988), 400.

21. Jaksa and Pritchard, *Communication Ethics,* 64.

22. Jaksa and Pritchard, *Communication Ethics,* 74.

23. Karl R. Wallace, "The Substance of Rhetoric: Good Reasons," *Quarterly Journal of Speech* 49 (1963): 239–49.

24. Aristotle, *Rhetoric,* 25.

25. James C. McCroskey, "A Summary of Experimental Research on the Effects of Evidence in Persuasive Communication," *Quarterly Journal of Speech* 55 (1969): 169–76.

26. Mike Allen, "Meta-Analysis Comparing the Persuasiveness of One-Sided and Two-Sided Messages," *Western Journal of Communication* 55 (1991): 390–404.

27. Several of these speaker and listener responsibilities are also derived from Trenholm, *Persuasion and Social Influence* (Englewood Cliffs, N.J.: Prentice-Hall, 1989), 18–20.

PART THREE

Putting Theory into Practice

Creating a speech begins with a process known as invention.

7

Inventing
Your Message

Genius is one percent
inspiration and
ninety-nine percent
perspiration.
—Thomas Edison

OBJECTIVES

After reading this chapter, you should be able to:

- Explain the benefits of focusing on the audience when you invent a speech.
- Choose an appropriate topic for a speech.
- Formulate a specific purpose for a speech.
- Recognize the types of support you can use for a speech.
- Conduct systematic research to find support for a speech.
- Conduct a meaningful interview with an expert on the topic of a speech.
- Prepare a bibliography for your speech.
- Formulate a research strategy for your speech.
- Record information in a usable form for your speech.

KEY CONCEPTS

Boolean operators
CD-ROM
chat lines
e-mail
Internet
narrative fidelity

narrative probability
online catalog
online service
usenet groups
web browser
World Wide Web

Thomas Edison understood the essence of his inventive genius. Although all great inventions begin with some spark of inspiration, they come to reality only through hard work. The same is true of speeches. Inspiration may get you started, but it won't see you through the home stretch. Hard work is necessary to create a speech out of an idea for a topic, a problem you want to solve, or a persuasive goal you want to accomplish.

This chapter is about the hard work that is essential to transforming thought into public speech. It looks at the process set into motion when your instructor first explains the nature of the speaking assignment you must complete. The specific topics we'll examine include focusing on the audience; choosing a topic; formulating a specific purpose; supporting your speech with examples, facts, statistics, expert opinion, explanations, descriptions, and narratives; finding support, including personal experience and knowledge, library resources, interviews, nonprint media, and the Internet; preparing a bibliography; developing a research strategy; and recording information.

FOCUSING ON YOUR AUDIENCE

As we discussed in Chapter 5, the rhetorical situation you face as a speaker includes your goals, the audience, and constraints. To successfully invent a speech that fulfills your goals, you need to understand whether your audience favors, opposes, or is undecided about your goals. You also need to know what power, if any, they have to help you achieve your goals. You need to understand the diversity of your audience, including cultural, demographic, and individual differences. Understanding your audience does not mean simply telling them what they want to hear; it means knowing whether your basic message is likely to fall on receptive ears or to be tuned out.

In addition to an audience's attitude toward your topic, you need to consider their level of knowledge about and interest in the topic. If they already know most of what you are going to say, they are likely to feel your speech is a waste of time. On the other hand, if the audience members know nothing about your topic, they may not be able to understand your speech. So you need to meet your audience's level of knowledge—presenting them something new and worthwhile, yet not going beyond what they can absorb in a short period of time.

As you select your topic, do your research, and construct your speech, always keep your audience in mind. A focus on audience is the hallmark of the successful speaker.

CHOOSING A TOPIC

As we discussed in Chapter 2, a good speech topic should be interesting to you, interesting to your audience, appropriate to the situation, appropriate to the time available, manageable, and worthwhile. Obviously, a thorough analysis of the rhetorical situation should help you meet these standards. Understanding the needs you share with your audience, the situation, the time available, and your resources should help you in determining a topic your audience is likely to find involving.

The question for many students, though, is "Where do I find the ideas for a speech topic?" An obvious place to begin is with your own interests, experiences, and knowledge. Identifying a topic depends a lot on remembering to look for a topic as you go through the day. For example, you may see a television program, such as *20/20* or *60 Minutes*, that deals with a topic that interests you. Or a magazine or a newspaper may suggest a topic. For example, an article in *Consumer Reports* titled "Selling Green" was the source of an excellent speech for one of our students.[1] Moreover, because the article questioned advertisers' claims that their products were environmentally sound, the topic proved to be of interest to other students.

Television, newspapers, and magazines are but a few of the places where you might find a topic. Others include campus publications, instructors, and fellow students. Computer users who surf the Internet may find ideas there. The number of places to find a good topic, in fact, is limited only by how aware you are of what's going on around you.

FORMULATING A SPECIFIC PURPOSE

In an introductory speech class, the *general* purpose of a speech probably will be assigned. You'll be asked, for example, to present a speech whose purpose is to inform, to persuade, or to entertain. What you will not be assigned is a *specific* purpose, that is, your goal or objective in speaking to a particular audience. If, for example, your general purpose is to persuade, your specific purpose might be "to persuade the audience to vote for candidate X."

SUPPORTING YOUR SPEECH

Although you have a topic and a specific purpose, a speech needs more than your own opinion. You need to find ways to support the points you make in your speech. Possible types of support include examples, facts, statistics, expert opinion, explanations, descriptions, and narratives. The important thing to recognize is that not all forms of support are equal. Not all examples, for instance, carry equal impact.

Examples

An **example** is a specific instance that represents some larger class. Thus, you might cite a recycling program in your hometown as an example of how curbside recycling can work. The test of an example is whether it is actually representative of the larger category. To test whether an example is representative, ask the following questions:

- *What is the relevance of the example to the larger category?* If you are talking about products that are made *from* recycled material, then a cardboard box made from new materials, which could *be* recycled by the consumer, is not relevant to your point.

- *Are there enough instances to support the generalization?* A few years ago, a disposable-diaper manufacturer ran an ad campaign claiming that its diapers could be turned into compost. However, according to a *Consumer Reports* article, only about a dozen cities had the capability to compost disposable diapers.[2] Thus, if you were listing products that could be set out for curbside recycling, disposable diapers wouldn't be a good example.

- *Are the examples typical of the larger category?* One needs to be careful of isolated and atypical examples. Just because one or two politicians are convicted of taking bribes does not prove that most politicians are crooks, despite popular myths to the contrary.

- *Are there counterexamples that disprove the generalization?* A counterexample is an example that contradicts the generalization. Whereas several examples can only suggest the truth of a blanket generalization, even one example to the contrary can disprove it. If a speaker claims *all* American cars are unreliable, then pointing to just one car line, for example, the Saturn, as having been shown to be reliable disproves that generalization. If there are counterexamples, either the generalization is false or it needs to be reformulated to be less inclusive. Thus, a speaker might say, "Many American cars are unreliable," a generalization that one counterexample would not disprove.

Facts

A **fact** is something that is verifiable as true. It is a fact that there are 50 states in the United States. As former baseball great Yogi Berra might say, "You can look it up." On the other hand, the statement that Texas is the best state in which to live is not a fact, though it may be widely believed by Texans.

A fact, of course, is only as good as the source of that fact. To evaluate facts, ask the following questions:

- *Do the facts come from a reliable source?* Encyclopedias, almanacs, authoritative books, and articles are usually reliable. On the other hand, if the "facts" come from someone who has a clear bias about the topic, you should be suspicious. For example, do guns help prevent crime? If you were to believe the National Rifle Association, they do. Gun-control advocates, however, would dispute this "fact." Be sure not only that your audience knows where you are getting your facts but also that these sources are likely to be acceptable to its members.

- *Are the facts verifiable?* You should be suspicious of facts that are difficult to verify. For example, there are widely varying estimates of certain types of crime, such as rape. Part of the discrepancy is that many rapes go unreported. Thus, the number of reported rapes is multiplied by some factor assumed to represent the number of unreported rapes for every reported rape. However, these numbers are impossible to verify for the very reason that the unreported rapes are, by definition, unverifiable. Although these estimates may be useful, they are not "facts" in the sense of being verifiable.

- *Are the facts the most recent available?* Until a few years ago, it was a fact that the Soviet Union consisted of 15 republics. However, the Soviet Union has now disappeared as a unified nation. Some parts of the former nation, such as Chechnya, have even engaged in armed rebellion. The correct facts with regard to what was once the U.S.S.R. are subject to constant change.

- *Are the facts consistent with other known facts?* Facts do not stand alone. You should be suspicious of alleged "facts" that seem to be inconsistent with other known facts. For example, many tobacco manufacturers claim that nicotine is not addictive. However, not only the surgeon general but anyone who has tried to give up smoking can tell you that such a "fact" is suspect. Double-check your sources for possible error. Be particularly careful with secondary sources. If the source of your information has relied on another source rather than gathering it firsthand, that is a secondary source. It is always better to look at primary or original sources of facts, as there may be honest mistakes in transferring information from one source to another. Finally, keep in mind what facts your audience already knows. If your facts are inconsistent with what the audience believes to be true, you have to first convince them that yours are more reliable if you are to have any success.

Statistics

Statistics are numerical data, such as percentages, ratios, and averages, that are classified in a meaningful way. Statistics can be a rich source of information. Yet they also can be confusing and misleading. For example, an American automobile manufacturer announced a survey showing that its cars were preferred overwhelmingly to foreign cars. However, it turns out that the company included only 200 people in its survey, none of whom even owned a foreign car.[3]

We are constantly bombarded by statistics that seem authoritative but are of dubious value. Some questions to ask about statistics are the following:

- *Is the source of the statistics reliable and unbiased?* The tip-off to the problems with the survey on foreign versus American cars is that it was sponsored by an American car company. On the other hand, statistics found in official sources, such as the *Statistical Abstract of the United States,* are less likely to be biased.

- *Were unbiased questions asked?* A poll asking whether or not disposable diapers should be banned was preceded by a statement that disposable diapers accounted for only 2 percent of trash in landfills. Not surprisingly, 84 percent of those polled felt disposable diapers should not be banned.[4]

- *Were the statistics accurately collected?* To be meaningful, statistics should be gathered from a random sample of people representing some larger population. Two hundred people who have never owned a foreign car are hardly representative of the population in general, many millions of whom drive imports. Further, one would need a much larger sample to warrant meaningful conclusions about the population as a whole. How big a sample must be depends on a variety of factors, including how large a margin of error can be tolerated and how evenly divided the sample is.

- *How was the sample selected?* A meaningful poll calls you, not the other way around. Based on sophisticated sampling techniques and

Using a visual aid helps your audience understand statistics.

random selection, a national poll can predict a presidential election with about a four-percentage-point margin of error. But when your local television station or newspaper conducts an "unscientific poll" in which people call in to record their views, the results are meaningless. Only people who are interested in the topic will call, and there is nothing to prevent someone from calling a hundred times. In short, such polls are worse than worthless, because they undermine confidence in legitimate polls.

- *Are the differences in the poll greater than the margin of error?* A good poll will tell you the margin of error. The margin of error increases as the sample gets smaller. Whereas the margin of error for a sample of 1,067 people is about 3 percent, for 150 people the margin of error is about 8 percent.[5] Suppose a poll has a margin of error of four percentage points. Thus, if it shows a political candidate ahead of her opponent by 51 to 49 percent, she could be ahead by as much as 55 to 45 percent, or behind by 47 to 53 percent—or any number in between. Subgroups within a sample may have even greater margins of error than the larger group. For example, large-scale national polls on the Clarence Thomas and Anita Hill controversy showed that most people believed Thomas. However, an ABC–*Washington Post* poll showed 38 percent of women believed Thomas whereas 28 percent believed Hill, a 10-point difference. However, the margin of error of this particular subgroup was reported as 12 percent![6]

- *What are percentages based on?* There's been a 10 percent increase in the rate of inflation! Sounds pretty alarming, doesn't it? However, unless you know what the underlying rate of inflation is, this is a meaningless figure. Inflation rates are themselves a percentage. Say that inflation is running at 4 percent. That means what cost $100 last year now costs $104. A 10 percent increase in the rate of inflation means that it would cost $104.40—not too bad. On the other hand, a 10 percent rate of inflation means that what cost $100 a year ago now costs $110. Sound confusing? It is. The point is that you need to be sure of what percentages are based on before relying on them to prove a point.

This list of questions is not meant to discourage you from using statistics. They can be a powerful form of support. The key is to know what your statistics mean and how they were collected, and to avoid biased sources and questionable sampling techniques. Most important, you need to explain enough about the statistics to your audience so that they will have confidence in the claims you are using the statistics to support.

Expert Opinion

One very useful source of support is **expert opinion,** a quotation from someone with special credentials in the subject matter. Quotations from experts, whether gathered from a personal interview or from written sources, can be a powerful way of supporting your points. However, you need to ask three basic questions about expert opinion:

- *What is the source's expertise?* How do you know this person is an expert? Look to biographical sources (such as *Who's Who*) if you do not know who the person is. Look for marks of expertise, such as academic credentials, official positions, or references from other authorities. Finally, make sure your source is an expert in the subject matter of your speech. It is important to explain to your audience why the person you are quoting is an expert they should believe.

- *Does the expert have a reputation for reliability?* How accurately have the expert's previous statements been? If someone has a record of either false or mistaken statements in the past, it is misguided to rely on that person's statements in the future. For example, the scientists who claimed they had created cold fusion in a bottle were unable to replicate their discovery. It would be a mistake to accept any of their future claims at face value. You may be able to determine the reliability of a source by looking to his or her previously published statements or the reports of other experts.

- *Is the source unbiased?* If a source has a vested interest in one side of a topic, his or her opinions are automatically suspect. Your audience needs to be assured that you are not relying on sources who have an ax to grind.

Explanations

An **explanation** is an account, an interpretation, or a meaning given to something. Detailed explanations may prove useful in a speech. But to be effective, explanations must meet two tests:

- *Is the explanation clear?* A complex or unclear explanation may only confuse your audience. One way to clarify an explanation is to use comparisons and contrasts. Thus, someone might explain a nuclear power plant by comparing it to a tea kettle whose source of heat is a nuclear reaction.

- *Is the explanation accurate?* An explanation that is clear is not necessarily complete or correct. You must also make sure that your explanations are as complete and accurate as possible, given the limitations of a speech situation.

Descriptions

A **description** is a word picture of something. For example, you might describe a place you have visited or researched. During the debate over sending U.S. peacekeepers to Bosnia, many critics supported their objections with elaborate descriptions of the terrain and climate, suggesting that the tanks and heavy armor being sent to protect our troops would not function well in Bosnia.

Descriptions should meet the following tests:

- *Is the description accurate?* Descriptions can be tested for accuracy by comparing them to the thing being described. Thus, for the Bosnia example, looking at pictures of the terrain or consulting an atlas might help verify the accuracy of the descriptions given by opponents of sending troops.

- *Is the description vivid?* To hold an audience's attention, you need to paint a word picture. Consider the words President Clinton used to describe the situation in Bosnia when he proposed sending troops there to uphold the peace treaty:

Skeletal prisoners caged behind barbed-wire fences; women and girls raped as a tool of war; defenseless men and boys shot down into mass graves, evoking visions of World War II concentration camps; and endless lines of refugees marching toward a future of despair.[7]

In speaking to the nation about the need to deploy American troops in Bosnia, President Clinton's words recalled the visual images of suffering in that war-torn country.

This description evokes haunting memories of the pictures that had been telecast around the world of the horrors of the Bosnian war. Further, the president's references to World War II concentration camps created an even more vivid description.

Photographs and other visual materials can sometimes take the place of descriptions in a speech. In Chapter 11, we discuss the use of visual means of support, usually called "visual aids."

Narratives

Narratives are extended stories that are fully developed, with characters, scene, action, and plot. Narratives sometimes provide an effective way of driving a point home to an audience. As Figure 7.1 indicates, an effective narrative builds gradually from the beginning, through conflict, to a climax. The conflict is then resolved, and the ending of the story often ties back into the beginning. For example, consider a story we all remember from childhood, "Little Red Riding Hood." In the beginning she is simply off to deliver a basket of goodies to her grandma. Conflict develops when

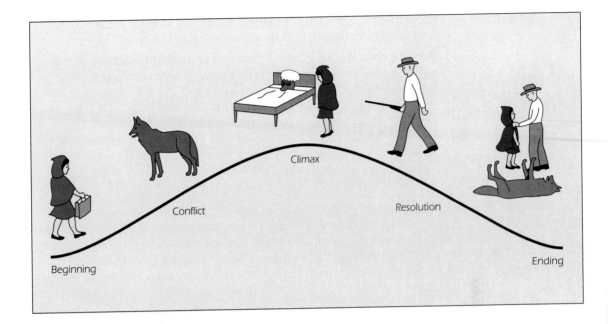

Conflict

Climax

Resolution

Beginning

Ending

Little Red Riding Hood is confronted by the wolf. The climax occurs at Grandma's house when she asks the wolf in Grandma's clothes a series of questions and the wolf answers each by saying, "All the better to (hear, see, eat) you with, my dear." The resolution comes when the hunter arrives to rescue Little Red Riding Hood from the wolf. Finally, the story ends with the demise of the wolf and the freeing of Little Red Riding Hood. Often the ending of a story will tie into the beginning. Little Red Riding Hood has learned a valuable lesson, as have the children who hear the story: Don't trust strangers.

Narratives can be more than a useful supporting tool for a speech; in some cultures, narrative is an organizing principle of speaking. The story-teller in Native American culture, for example, is revered. Award-winning rhetorical scholar Walter Fisher has argued, in fact, that human beings are fundamentally storytellers. Fisher believes that reasoning is fundamentally done in the form of narrative. Even if one doesn't accept his narrative paradigm, it is undoubtedly the case that a well-told story, real or fictional, can captivate an audience. Fisher claims that two basic tests apply to narrative reasoning:[8]

- *Does the narrative have probability?* **Narrative probability** is the internal coherence or believability of a narrative. Does a story make sense in and of itself? We all have had the experience of walking out of a movie totally unbelieving the characters or plot. Perhaps you

FIGURE 7.1
The narrative, or story. Narratives build to a climax which must be resolved by the storyteller.

thought, "No way could it happen like that!" If a story does not seem to make sense internally, it is not going to convince an audience.

- *Does the narrative have fidelity?* **Narrative fidelity** is the degree to which a narrative rings true to real-life experience. Even if a story makes sense internally, it may not make sense in terms of the real world. An audience needs to believe that a story either really happened or at least could happen (if it is a hypothetical story). Although many of Ronald Reagan's stories turned out upon further research not to have really occurred, they had a tendency to ring true, as the box "Storytelling" shows. If events did not happen exactly as Reagan described, they certainly could have happened that way.

When you tell a story to an audience, you should let them know if it is true or hypothetical. But either type of story needs to ring true to their own experience if it is to have impact. Although we may enjoy hypothetical stories for their entertainment value, we don't find these narratives "real." For a speech to have impact, the narratives need to have probability and fidelity.

FINDING SUPPORT

Examples, facts, statistics, opinions, explanations, descriptions, and narratives constitute the supporting materials from which you will construct your speech. The process of gathering these supporting materials is called **research.** There are two basic steps to research. First there is the *search,* whereby you find the sources likely to contain information on your topic. Then there is the *re-search,* by which you examine these sources for materials you can use. Many people mistakenly rely on the first source they find on their topic, jotting down a few notes, and then writing their speech. In other words, they skip to the re-search phase of the process before they have done a thorough search of information available on their topic. To avoid this mistake, which can lead to an incomplete and even deceptive speech, look for as many sources as you can before deciding about the materials on which you'll most rely.

There are innumerable sources to which you can turn to gather materials on your topic, including personal experience and knowledge, library resources, interviews, nonprint media, and the Internet, including the World Wide Web.

Personal Experience and Knowledge

Your own experience and knowledge is frequently the best source to initially consider as you begin to think about constructing your speech. Speaking about matters with which you have firsthand experience person-

Storytelling

Ronald Reagan delighted in telling stories, many of them imaginary. Lou Cannon recounts one of Reagan's most famous made-up stories in his book, *President Reagan: The Role of a Lifetime:*

One of the imaginary stories he liked to tell emphasized the virtues of truth telling. Harking back to his days on the Dixon High School football team, Reagan would say, "I'll never forget one game with Mendota," and then tell a story about acknowledging an infraction of the rules that the referee had not detected. The penalty cost Dixon the game. Reagan would never forget this game because he had invented it.[1]

Was Reagan a liar? Well, not necessarily. As Cannon points out: "Reagan had probably long ago convinced himself of its verity." In any event, it was a moving story with narrative probability, if not fidelity. Ironically, its moral was—to tell the truth!

On another occasion, Reagan told a poignant story commemorating the landing on D-Day at Normandy. He shared the story of one of the men who participated in the assault on Omaha Beach, and he read a letter from the man's daughter. Cannon writes:

PFC Peter Zanatta . . . had survived the assault and promised to return to Normandy after the war to see "the beach, the barricades, and the graves." He never did. When he was dying of cancer three decades later, his daughter Lisa Zanatta Henn had promised to return for him and put flowers on the graves. She had done that this day, and Reagan fought back tears when he read from the letter. "Through the words of his loving daughter, who is here with us today, a D-Day veteran has shown us the meaning of the day far better than any president can. It is enough for us to say about Private Zanatta and all the men of honor and courage who fought beside him four decades ago: We will always remember. We will always be proud. We will always be prepared, so we may always be free."[2]

Much of the power of Reagan's storytelling in this instance lies in the fidelity of this story. It is not made up—it is based on the true account by the daughter of a real-life American hero.

---

[1] Lou Cannon, *President Reagan: The Role of a Lifetime* (New York: Simon & Schuster, 1991), 223.

[2] Cannon, *President Reagan*, 484–85.

ally connects you to your message. What's more, this personal connection may also tell you how to connect your message to the personal and professional needs of your audience. For example, a successful actress, who was enrolled in one of the author's classes at the University of Southern California, gave a speech on how to break into "show biz." Unfortunately, she failed to mention her own experience. Had she done so, her speech would have connected more effectively to the audience, in effect saying, "If I can do this, so can you!"

Even though your personal experience and knowledge is a good source with which to start, don't stop there. No matter how intense your experience or extensive your knowledge, there always is more to learn. In the effort to augment personal experience and knowledge, then, consult other sources as well.

Library Resources

There is no better source for expanding your personal knowledge than your library. The library is the intellectual center of most universities and colleges—the repository of the history of ideas and thought. Although campus libraries vary in their extensiveness and degree of sophistication, the basic principles of a library search are the same.

The first step in using your library is familiarization. Most campus libraries feature guided tours, handouts, and special seminars for groups interested in a particular area of research. Your instructor also may have your class take a library tour or send you on a library scavenger hunt to familiarize you with the library. Whatever you do, though, don't wait until you are facing a deadline before familiarizing yourself with your library. If you didn't do it during your first few weeks on campus, make it a priority now.

We recommend following five steps when you do library research.

Five Steps of Library Research

1. **Select key terms.**
2. **Search the library catalog.**
3. **Search relevant indexes and abstracts.**
4. **Use CD-ROM searches.**
5. **Consult reference books.**

Although you may not need to use each step every time you do library research, it's useful to know about each step and how they are connected. Let's now look at each step in detail.

Select Key Terms A **key term** is a word or phrase used in library catalogs and indexes to identify a subject. Such key terms are like the combination to a safe. If you have the right combination, you can easily open the door; without it, however, your chances of opening the door are slim. Thus, the most effective library researcher begins with a key term or terms on the topic of interest.

The basis of most university library card catalogs and indexes is the *Library of Congress Subject Headings,* which tells you what a term is used for and lists broader topics, related topics, and narrower topics. For example, if you are interested in the topic of "green marketing," you might look under the term *recycling.* The *Library of Congress Subject Headings* indicates that the processing of recyclables is found under the term *recycling,* whereas reclaiming and reuse of larger items is listed under *salvage.* Thus, you would begin your search for sources on "green marketing" with the term *recycling.*

Search the Library Catalog   Although many libraries still use a card catalog to list their book holdings, an increasing number use online catalogs, which ease your task and allow you to construct more complex searches. An **online catalog** is a computerized listing of library holdings. The principles on which the two catalogs are built are the same.

Catalogs are arranged by subject, author, and title. Some online catalogs may also permit searching by call number or combining the search into all categories. Because you are just beginning a search on your topic, it is unlikely that you will know specific authors, titles, or call numbers. Thus, the subject heading is the most likely basis for your search.

You will have used the *Library of Congress Subject Headings* first, so you already know the key term(s) to search for. Let's continue to use the example of recycling. Using that term alone, you might find 80 or more publications. At this point, you could look through the list of books, noting the call numbers of the most likely sources. Titles may suggest whether or not the book would be directly relevant to your topic. Also, you would want to select the most recent books.

If you are using an online catalog, one additional advantage is that you can use what are called **Boolean operators.** These are terms, such as *and, or,* and *not,* used to narrow or broaden a computerized search of two or more related terms. For example, using the Boolean operator *or* to find books listed under either "recycling" or "landfills" might yield an additional 27 books. The Boolean operator *and* allows you to narrow the search to only books that deal with some aspects of recycling. For example, under "recycling and plastics," there might be only two books dealing with both topics. Finally, you can limit your topic to books that do not deal with a certain topic. Using the Boolean operator *not,* you can find all the books that deal with recycling but not aluminum. Finally, you can also further limit your search by specifying items such as the year a book was published.[9]

As you can see, the online catalog provides increased capabilities to expand, limit, and speed up your search. Some online terminals are connected to printers so that you can print out the results of your search and use that to locate the books you need. If you do not have a printed copy of your search, however, you should note the author, title, date, and call number of each source that appears promising. Simply going into the stacks with a series of call numbers can be confusing, as you will soon forget which call number went with which book.

When you visit the stacks, it is a good idea to do a little browsing as well as finding the specific books you have noted. Since books are shelved by subject, it is not unusual to find a book closely related to your topic that you overlooked in your search. This serendipitous search for information often turns up better sources than what you were originally looking for.

One great advantage of going to books for information first is that the authors have done much of your work for you. Most books have a bibliography or footnotes that lead to other sources. Obviously, the more recent the books you read first, the more up to date their bibliographies. In many ways, a researcher is like a detective looking for clues. A good general book on a topic is like a room full of clues. The author will have left fingerprints all over the place. Follow the leads suggested by general books.

Search Relevant Indexes and Abstracts   An **index** is a listing of sources of information, usually in journals and magazines, alphabetically by topic. An **abstract** is a summary of an article or a report. Every topic you can imagine is classified in one or more specialized indexes. A good library has hundreds or even thousands of indexes related to specialized fields. Some indexes both list and abstract articles in journals. On the topic of recycling, for example, a good place to look for information is *Environmental Abstracts*. In addition to abstracting articles from a variety of journals, conferences, and reports, it has a review of the year's key environmental events. In terms of recycling, there are specific listings for recycled products, such as rubber or plastic. Thus, if you were interested in the recycling of plastics, you would find numerous citations in this index.

Of course, not every library has every journal listed in any given index. Thus, you must compare the most promising articles in the index with your library's holding of journals. Some libraries provide listings of the journals they have. The card or online catalog may also list journals. You would look under title, for example, to see if your library had the journal *BioCycle*, which is listed in *Environmental Abstracts*.

For popular journals, the *Readers' Guide to Periodical Literature* is the old standby. It lists articles in publications like *Newsweek*, *Time*, and other popular magazines, common to most libraries.

Major newspapers, such as the *New York Times*, *Wall Street Journal*, and the *Christian Science Monitor*, provide printed indexes that you need to consult before looking through reels of microfilm for newspaper articles on your topic. The computerized database published by InfoTrac includes the *National Newspaper Index*, covering five national newspapers. If this index is available to you, it will make finding relevant newspaper articles much easier than using printed indexes.

Because we cannot list every index here that you would be likely to need, the best strategy is to ask a reference librarian what indexes would be suitable for a given topic and where they are located. Make sure you have narrowed down your topic to something specific before going to the librarian. For instance, "I have a speech to give tomorrow on recycling and I need some help" is less helpful than "I'm doing a speech on recycling, and I want to find out how much of our landfill space is being wasted because people don't recycle."

Use CD-ROM Searches   At one time a computerized search for sources was prohibitively expensive. Fortunately, technology has progressed to the point where money is not the deciding factor in taking advantage of computerized databases. A **CD-ROM** is a compact disc–read only memory, used for storage and retrieval of data. CD-ROM technology has revolutionized computerized searches. Using the same technology as music compact discs, CD-ROMs store information in a compact disc–read only memory format.

The authors searched three databases on the topic of recycling: the *General Science Index (GSI),* the *Public Affairs Information Service Index (P.A.I.S.),* and the *Government Documents Catalog Service (GDCS).* The *GSI* yielded 84 citations under "recycling," 205 under "plastic," and 6 under "recycling and plastic." By narrowing the search to the last term, we avoided sorting through 84 citations on recycling and 205 on plastic to find the ones that dealt directly with the recycling of plastics.

Not all libraries carry the same databases for CD-ROM, so you should consult your reference librarian to learn about what is available at your library.

Consult Reference Books   Frequently you need to find a very specific fact— for example, how much plastic was produced in the United States last year. You could search a dozen articles and never find that number. But a good reference book, such as the *Statistical Abstract of the United States,* puts that kind of information at your fingertips.

Perhaps you need a good quotation to begin or end your speech. Numerous books of quotations are available. In fact, because there are so many, a reference book called *Quotation Location* was written to help you find any of 900 published compilations of quotations.[10]

These are only two of the countless reference books to which you can turn in the effort to track down information. Here are some other reference books to which you also may want to turn:

- **Almanacs and Yearbooks**   *The World Almanac and Book of Facts* provides current information on every topic from abortion to zoology. It also includes a chronology of the preceding year and covers events of the entire world, not just the United States. Another popular annual publication is the *Information Please Almanac.*

- *Facts on File* and *Editorial Research Reports* are useful sources on current events and important public controversies. *Facts on File* provides a weekly digest of world news and has a cumulative index. *Editorial Research Reports* has numerous well-researched reports on topics of public significance. Both of these sources are relatively easy ways to bring yourself up to date on current topics.

- **Biographies,** such as the *Who's Who* series (*Who's Who in America, Who's Who in American Business,* and so on) and the *Dictionary of American Biography,* help you learn about people related to your topic. A *Biography Index* will help you locate articles and books of a biographical nature.

- **Encyclopedias**   Although the information in them is likely to be general and dated, encyclopedias can provide a useful source for your early search. Not only are encyclopedias available in the traditional book form, they are now on CD-ROM. In fact, many computers include an encyclopedia CD-ROM with the original purchase. On the topic of recycling, for example, the *World Book Encyclopedia* has articles on recycling, conservation, and environmental pollution, all of which might prove relevant to this topic.

    You may also want to consult subject-specific encyclopedias. For example, there are encyclopedias dealing with the social sciences, art, education, and science and technology. Do not overlook such specialized encyclopedias in conducting your early search for information. Another useful encyclopedia is the *Encyclopedia of Associations,* which provides the address and phone number of relevant groups, such as the Aluminum Recycling Association. If you have time to write or call for information on your topic, this encyclopedia is a valuable source of associations that might have materials you can use.

- **Atlases** are valuable in learning about the world. By consulting an atlas, you can learn not only where a country is geographically but also important facts about it. For example, the *World Book Atlas* contains not only maps but also a wealth of information about climates, regions of the earth, natural resources, population, and so on. In a rapidly changing world, yesterday's atlases may be out of date, however, so it is important to consult the most up-to-date atlas possible. Because national boundaries can change overnight, newspapers and periodicals are good sources for updated maps about places such as the former Yugoslavia.

Interviews

We put off discussing interviews until now for a reason. Far too often students go into an interview before researching their topic. In a sense, they expect the expert they interview to write their speech for them. Although

Interviews with experts are an excellent source of information for your speech.

interviews with experts can offer useful information and may lead you to other sources of information, they cannot substitute for doing your own research. Thus, an interview should be conducted only after you've been to the library and done the research necessary to ask the interviewee intelligent questions.

Finding potential interviewees on most topics is not as difficult as you may think. On the topic of recycling, you may be able to arrange an interview with the director of a local recycling center. Community leaders, including members of the city council, also may have information on topics such as recycling, traffic congestion, parking, and growth. At a university, most departments have experts on various topics. Often a call to the department asking if there is anyone familiar with your specific topic will elicit a name. In other cases, you may simply want to consult a department's course offerings. Someone who teaches a class on ecology, for example, most likely is an expert in that subject.

Another strategy is to contact organizations that are related to your topic and ask if someone there would be available to interview. For example, if you are researching the effects of secondhand smoke, the American Lung Association is a likely source of potential interviewees.

Sometimes you may already know a person who can help you. We recall the case of one student who was speaking about a "miracle" weight-loss product. After calling the company's home office and getting the runaround, she contacted her local pharmacist. He informed her that the ingredients in the product were in no way capable of helping a person lose weight—in fact, they were potentially harmful. A brief interview with the pharmacist, moreover, gave her information she would have had great difficulty finding on her own.

Once you have decided on a person you would like to interview, the following basic guidelines for before, during, and after the interview should help you proceed.

Before the Interview

- Contact the potential interviewee well in advance. Explain why you want to meet and how much time you think you'll need. If the person agrees to be interviewed, ask for a convenient time and place for a meeting (usually at the interviewee's place of business). If possible, confirm your appointment in writing. Verify where and when you will meet and how much time you have to spend, which will guide you in both formulating questions and ascertaining the number of questions you can reasonably pursue.

- Do some general reading on your topic. Read at least a book or two and some recent articles. This will give you a basis for asking your questions and allow you to concentrate on those things you cannot easily find out for yourself.

- Prepare specific questions in advance. You should attempt to ask open-ended questions, which will allow the interviewee an opportunity to talk at some length. Of course, be prepared to deviate from that list as answers suggest other avenues to follow. But at least you know you won't be wasting time trying to come up with questions on the spot.

During the Interview

- Show up on time, dressed professionally, and ready to begin. Introduce yourself and explain how you will use the interview in your speech. If you are planning to tape-record the interview, be sure to ask for permission. If an interview is by phone, you have a legal obligation to inform the other party if you are planning to tape the conversation.

- Using what you've learned about your topic as a guide, begin with general questions and then work to specific ones. Be sure to let the interviewee talk. Don't monopolize the conversation, as this will defeat the purpose of the interview.

- Ask the interviewee if he or she can suggest other sources of information—books, pamphlets, periodicals, or other experts. Often an expert will lead you to sources you never would have thought of yourself. If you are lucky, your interviewee may even loan you some relevant journals or other publications.

- Use the active listening skills discussed in Chapter 4, especially setting goals, blocking out distracting stimuli, suspending judgment, being sensitive to meta-communication, and using paraphrasing and questioning.
- Either tape-record (with permission) or take complete notes during the interview. If you do not get something down, ask a follow-up question to make sure you get the essential points on paper. If you want to use quotes from the interview in your speech, make sure they are accurate.
- When your time is about up, ask the interviewee if there is anything he or she can add to what has been said. Perhaps there is some area you have completely overlooked.
- Thank the interviewee for his or her time and exit graciously.

After the Interview

- A follow-up thank-you letter is common courtesy and may help you get subsequent interviews.
- Transcribe your tape or your notes while the interview is fresh in your mind. Notes that may have been clear at the moment will quickly fade from memory unless you flesh them out soon after the interview.
- Follow up on leads or other interviews suggested by your interviewee.

Interviews not only can provide a rich source of information but also can add credibility to your speaking. The fact that you have taken the time to speak directly to an expert shows your concern for your audience. Further, your own expertise is enhanced by virtue of the interview. And if you use the interview in presenting your speech, be sure to let your audience know why your interviewee is a credible source on your topic. In the box "The Importance of Interviewing: Professor Rick Rigsby" on page 206, a former television reporter offers some additional advice.

Nonprint Media

We live in a world dominated by multiple channels of information. Many universities have extensive collections of nonprint media, including films, videotapes, recordings, photographs, and other nonprint materials. You may find a film or sound recording that fits your topic. Or photos or slides may be available that you could use as visual aids in a speech.

Of course, nonprint resources should meet the same tests of evidence as other forms of support. For example, photos should accurately represent the whole context in which they were taken. Cropped or altered photos, for example, can create false impressions. If you doubt that, just check the lat-

The Importance of Interviewing: Professor Rick Rigsby

Dr. Enrique D. "Rick" Rigsby is assistant professor of speech communication at Texas A&M University in College Station, Texas. Prior to teaching he was a television news reporter for seven years. Not only did Rick use the interview as a principal technique in television reporting, he continues to conduct interviews as part of his research, as he explains below. We asked Rick to explain the importance of interviewing to students of public speaking.

To appreciate the role interviewing performs, one must understand that we humans tend to be storytelling animals. Everyone has a history filled with commendations, successes, and struggles. These stories are marked by significant dates and may include a supporting cast of characters. The stories develop in basements and ballparks, departments and dormitories. We experience life, record dramas, and share the stories when called upon. Thus, our stories contribute to newscasts, government reports, research projects, even speeches in communication classes!

For the college student preparing a speech, interviewing someone with expertise on the subject might produce insights other sources cannot generate. Make sure to avoid this one pitfall: Refrain from interviewing the person most available. Rather, carefully select the individual who will enhance your work. A simple question to ask yourself is "Will the interview I conduct enlighten the audience about the subject and increase my credibility as a speaker?"

I have used the medium of interviewing in both my collegiate and professional careers. When I was a speech communication major in college, interviewing individuals for speeches allowed me to use real-life adventure to help inform, persuade, or entertain my audience. As a television news reporter, I interviewed thousands of people in a variety of situations. Imagine talking to a person who has just won the lottery or thrown the winning touchdown pass! Getting the right interview can make the difference between a presentation that few hear or a speech that few will ever forget. I continue to use interviewing today. A large part of my job as a college professor is to conduct research. My research focuses on volunteers who participated in the civil rights demonstrations of the sixties. An essential part of my research task is to interview those former protesters and document their stories.

If your future includes the preparation of a presentation, you would be well advised to consider the medium of interviewing as a way of obtaining information. Remember, we're a storytelling culture. But what good is a story if it's never told? You know, interviewing a subject as a part of your speech preparation could make the difference between a mediocre speech and a memorable oration. But don't take my word for it . . . go interview your speech prof!

est supermarket tabloid for pictures of two-headed aliens. Using video- or audiotape also requires that you do not edit the tape in such a way as to change the context.

Sometimes you will see something on television that is directly relevant to your speech. If you can record the program, you can then extract the important information at your own leisure. If you can't tape the program, you may still be able to secure a transcript. Programs such as *Night-line, 20/20, 60 Minutes,* and *Newshour with Jim Lehrer* have transcripts available. The addresses, phone numbers, and transcript prices are given at the end of the program. If you request transcripts, be sure to allow enough time to receive them, however. Sometimes rush orders are accepted. Also, many transcripts are available on the Internet. These transcripts can be downloaded to your computer directly, saving time and money. Again, Internet addresses are frequently provided at the end of the program.

The Internet

One of the most exciting new developments for research is the **Internet,** a collection of computer networks connecting computers around the world. Although it's not exactly a superhighway (at least not yet), the Internet is like a highway in that it allows the user to travel electronically to almost anywhere in the world. The access to information resources it provides is virtually limitless.

Use of the Internet is increasing rapidly. A survey done by Nielsen Media Research for CommerceNet in 1995 reports that 1 in 6 Americans and Canadians over age 16 have access to the Internet.[11] Nearly 11 percent of them had used "the net" in the preceding three months, and 18 million people had used the **World Wide Web,** a collection of thousands of sites called "home pages." Although the survey did not address college students specifically, our experience as professors suggests that college students are increasingly using Internet resources, often available for little or no charge from their campuses. In the 21st century, there is little doubt that the Internet, or its successor, will be one of the principal resources for speakers in inventing their messages.

What's on the Internet? Among the most important resources for speakers are e-mail, chat lines, usenet groups, and the World Wide Web.[12] **E-mail** (electronic mail) is a message sent from one computer, over the network, to one or more other computers. If you know the e-mail address of a source that interests you, contact that source directly. You can e-mail most government, education, and commercial institutions.

Chat lines are real-time discussions with other computer users on topics of common interest. Multiple users can participate simultaneously and respond to each other. Although not necessarily reliable as a source of factual information (unless the participants are experts in the field), chat lines

Doonesbury

BY GARRY TRUDEAU

can certainly help you get ideas for speech topics. Or you can bounce ideas off other people interested in the same topic.

Usenet groups are electronic "newsletters" to which subscribers can contribute. In the field of speech communication, for example, there are usenet groups for those interested in communication theory and research and those interested in academic debate, to name just two areas.

Finally, the most useful aspect of the Internet to speakers is the World Wide Web. Within each home page there are connections to other sites, which can link to even more sites. Sites cover everything from sports to literature. For example, you can find the latest scores of your favorite sports or the entire text of some books on the web. Even items such as atlases, encyclopedias, government publications, and much more may be available through your computer. In a sense, the Internet can be thought of as a "virtual library."

How does the average person connect to the Internet? First, you need a computer. It does not have to be a particular brand; either an IBM-compatible or a Macintosh will do. Second, you need to physically connect your computer to a network or phone line. Many colleges have computers in their labs or even in dorm rooms that are connected to a local network which will provide access to the Internet. Otherwise, you need a modem, a device that connects through ordinary telephone lines. The faster the modem (measured in what is called baud rate), the better.

In order to use the Internet, you need to have an account on the network computer (called a server) that you are connected to, whether directly or by modem. Numerous **online services** are commercially available to connect to the Internet. In addition to access to the Internet, these online services provide news, entertainment, and advertising. Among the most widely used online services are America Online, CompuServe, and Prodigy.[13] Some companies provide a free trial period that allows you to see if you like the service, but after that you pay a membership fee and a rate for the time you use. A cheaper alternative for college students is often to obtain an account with the computer network at their college, which means they are using the college's computer system to connect to the Internet. Even if you don't own a computer, most colleges have computer labs students can use for network access. Check this alternative before shelling out the money to join a commercial service.

Finally, you will need a **web browser,** a program that allows the user to search for and reach World Wide Web sites from his or her own computer. Commercial services usually provide a web browser as part of their package. A widely used program for searching the web, which is usually available at little or no cost to college students, is Netscape Navigator.[14] This program allows you to reach various home page sites with a click of a mouse. What makes this program and others like it so exciting is that, as you read a text, certain words are underlined and in color. By pointing your mouse to the word and clicking, you connect to another site. Like a web, the sites are interconnected in almost infinite ways. For example, if you went to the Shakespeare home page,[15] you would find that you could connect to topics ranging from *Hamlet* to *Romeo and Juliet.* If you are a fan of the comic strip *Dilbert,* you might want to visit the Dilbert Zone,[16] where you can view not only the latest *Dilbert* strip but also read about the strip's creator, Scott Adams, or even purchase Dilbert products. If you are interested in high fashion, perhaps you'd like to visit *Elle* magazine's home page.[17] The list of possible sites is endless.

But how do you learn what web sites exist? One source is friends, including those to whom you connect by e-mail. Usenets frequently provide lists of favorite web sites. Many computer magazines, and even general-circulation magazines, such as *Newsweek,* devote sections to favorite web sites. But more effective are online search engines, such as Yahoo.[18] By entering key search words or clicking your mouse on a highlighted word, you can explore everything from the arts to the sciences.

One caveat is in order regarding the use of Internet resources. Unlike published books and articles, which are usually subject to editing, fact checking, and peer review, the Internet is unregulated. Anyone can say anything and, short of outright pornography, there's no governmental regulation. You must also be cautious with information gathered from the Internet because you have no assurance as to its reliability and verifiability. There have been instances of material being altered on the net. As a speaker you have an ethical responsibility to ensure such information is accurate, even if this requires tracking down the original source of the information. So, all the tests of supporting materials that apply to published materials apply doubly to computer information. Nevertheless, there is also the advantage

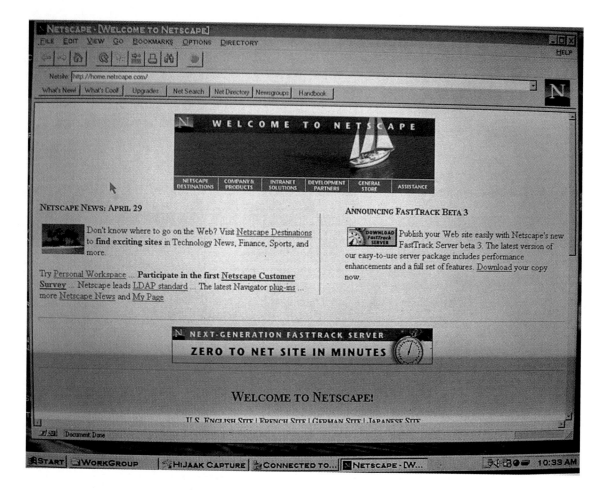

The web browser Netscape Navigator is a popular way to "surf the internet."

that because Internet-based information is unedited and uncensored, you can directly read the ideas of others, even controversial or unpopular ones that would never make it into print. In many ways the Internet is the ultimate marketplace of ideas.

SELECTING SUPPORT FOR YOUR SPEECH

Now that you know where to find material on your topic, you're ready to begin selecting the most promising sources and gathering the information you want to use. This process involves preparing your bibliography, reading the material you've selected, and recording relevant parts so that you can use them when you organize your speech.

Preparing a Bibliography

Before beginning in-depth reading on a topic, you should prepare a pre-liminary bibliography of the sources you have found. You might, for ex-ample, find 20 sources on recycling that look like they will be relevant. Using note cards (4 by 6 inches is a good size), list the following informa-tion about each source:

> for all sources: author(s), preferably by full name, if an author is listed;
>
> for books: the exact title and the following facts of publication: loca-tion, publisher, and date;
>
> for periodicals: the article title, volume number, date, and pages;
>
> for government documents: the agency issuing the document, as well as its full title and date;
>
> for electronic resources: the e-mail address, web site, or path by which the material was located; and
>
> space for additional information as you read the source.

Because you will need all of this information for your formal speech out-line, it is better to list it as you compile it, rather than having to go back to find it later. At the end of this chapter we provide samples of how to cor-rectly cite sources according to the system developed by the American Psychological Association. If you need more space than is provided by one card for recording information that you read, give each source a code num-ber or a short title to use on additional cards from the same source.

Reading Your Sources: A Research Strategy

After accumulating a long list of potential sources, you are faced with the task of deciding where to begin reading. A good rule of thumb is to begin with the most recent and the most general items. Beginning with the most recent can save you a lot of work. An article from this year on recycling may review articles and books written earlier. Not only will this review al-low you to go back and find additional sources of information you may have overlooked, it also will help you avoid dead ends. If you were to be-gin with an article written in 1980, you might try to solve a problem that already has been solved in the years since then.

Among the most recent sources, try to first read those that are general. If you begin with sources that are very narrow, you may invest your energy in something that ultimately proves irrelevant to your speech. General ar-ticles and books on your topic will likely yield relevant material. They will give you the broad view of your topic. If you focus too quickly on a spe-cific part of your topic, you will have no sense of the whole picture.

You can use your preliminary bibliography to prioritize how you go about finding the specific information to use in your speech. Working backward from the present, you can use the bibliography to guide your exploration of the literature on your topic in a productive and efficient manner. In the process, you may discover issues you've overlooked or insights you should consider.

When you are looking at any source, it is not necessary to read it cover to cover. Read introductory and concluding material first to get an idea of what the whole article or book covers. With books, make use of the table of contents and index; this will lead you to the most beneficial parts of the book first.

You should also learn to skim, focusing on main headings, topic sentences, and summary statements, to get a general idea of whether a book or an article is suitable for your purpose. Don't simply rely on titles, which are often misleading because they are so general. Almost any title with the word "communication" in it is a case in point. Because the word is so all-encompassing, you can't always tell if an article is about the kind of communication you have in mind.

Finally, if you are pursuing a topic that is the subject of a scholarly discipline, chances are the articles you begin to find will have been abstracted. Obviously, these indexes—for example, *Communication Abstracts*—can save you considerable time in finding information you can use in your speech.

Recording Information

As you gather materials, carefully record the facts and quotations you discover. It is important to note not only the substance of what was said but also who said it and where. Documenting such information will build your credibility with your audience and enhance your overall effectiveness as a speaker.

One well-established technique is to write important facts, examples, quotations, and statistics on note cards. Cards need to be large enough to accommodate the information, yet small enough so that you won't be tempted to put more than one fact on each card. The advantage of this technique is that you can organize cards in any way that seems logical when you begin writing your speech. A sample note card is shown in Figure 7.2.

Another strategy is to photocopy pages from articles or books that seem particularly useful. Then use a highlighter or marker to identify those things you may wish to use in the speech. At this point, cut out the quotations you plan to use and paste or tape them to cards. Again, be sure to note the source and page number on each card. The advantages of this technique over copying information onto note cards are two-fold. First, it saves time. Second, it ensures that you will accurately quote the source, since handwritten notes may be hard to read or even inaccurate.

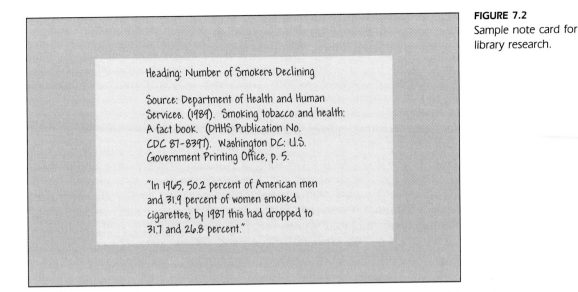

FIGURE 7.2
Sample note card for library research.

Finally, if you are doing a computerized search, such as on the Internet, you may be able to directly download information onto a computer. For example, transcripts of CNN programs can be found by going to their web site and following the instructions of your web browser for downloading files.[19] Although this technique makes for ease in writing your speech, it does not relieve you from reading and absorbing the material, since you will be able to cite or quote only a small portion of it in a given speech.

SUMMARY

The process of inventing your speech is like the process of inventing a new product: You need both a source of inspiration and the willingness to engage in hard work.

You begin by analyzing the rhetorical situation and focusing on your audience. Then you choose a topic and decide on your specific purpose.

Many types of support are effective in speeches. Look for examples, facts, statistics, expert opinion, explanations, descriptions, and narratives to support your specific purpose.

It is important to evaluate supporting material. Ask yourself, are examples relevant, of sufficient quantity, and typical, and are there no counterexamples? Are the facts from a reliable source, can they be verified, are they the most recent, and are they consistent with other known facts? Are statistics from a reliable and unbiased source, were fair questions asked in gathering the data, and were they accurately collected? Also ask how the sample was selected to ensure that it was random and representative. Make sure any differences in the poll are greater than the margin of error and that you know the base of any percentages cited.

Expert opinion depends on the source's expertise, reliability, and lack of bias for its authority. Explanations should be clear and accurate. Descriptions should be accurate and vivid. Finally, narratives must have probability (coherence) and fidelity to the real world.

Before you can gather the materials for your speech, you need to search for them. Possible sources of information for your speech include personal experience and knowledge, library resources, interviews, nonprint media, and the Internet. From these sources you need to prepare a bibliography.

Finally, you need to re-search the topic, which involves examining the sources you've found for materials you can actually use. As you begin reading for information, start with the most general and most recent sources first, as these may lead you to other sources your own search overlooked. Develop a recording system for both sources and data. Either copy information on note cards or use selective photocopying and computer printouts to record information.

Check Your Understanding: Exercises and Activities

1. Check your understanding of the American Psychological Association guidelines for source citations on pages 218–221. Provide a correct source citation for each of the following hypothetical sources, using APA guidelines.

   - A book with one author named Jack Smith, titled College Life, published in New York by University Press in 1995. How would your citation change if Smith were the editor of the book? How would you list a second author, John Q. Doe? How would you list a third author, Mary A. Smith?

   - An article titled Dorm Life in American Universities, by Peter Chu, published in the scholarly journal Universities and Colleges, volume 31, December 1995, pages 24–56.

   - A chapter by Jose Sanchez titled The Nine Lives Myth, appearing on pages 99–109 in the book Cat Stories, edited by Morris T. Katt, published by Feline Press in San Francisco, California, in 1995.

   - An article in Canine Magazine titled Snoopy and Me, by Charlie Brown, pages 56–57, on December 14, 1995, in volume 42. How would you list it if no author were named?

2. A speaker arguing that we should buy American products presents the following example: "I purchased a Japanese car last year. Since I purchased it, I have had nothing but trouble. I think this proves that you should buy American!" Compare this example to the tests of examples discussed in this chapter. Which of the tests does it fail to meet?

3. *Worksheet for speech topic choice:* One way to select an appropriate speech topic is to begin with an inventory of your own interests and those of your listeners as revealed by their self-introductions in class. Under each of the following headings, list at least three things that are important to you and to your audience.

	My interests	Audience interests
Hobbies	_____	_____
	_____	_____
	_____	_____
School	_____	_____
	_____	_____
Work	_____	_____
	_____	_____
Goals	_____	_____
	_____	_____

Situational factors _____ _____

Nature of assignment _____

Time available _____

List of three possible topics _____

_____

_____

4. How would you go about verifying the "fact" that the leading causes of death in the United States are heart diseases, cancer, and infectious diseases? What sources would you consult? Are these in fact the three leading causes of death?

5. Obtain a recent poll (that appears in an article in, for example, *USA Today* or *Newsweek*). Does the poll meet the tests of statistical evidence outlined in this chapter? How large was the sample, and what was the margin of error? Did differences in the poll exceed the margin of error? What, if anything, does the article on the poll not tell you that you need to know to properly test the statistics in the poll?

6. How would you go about determining on what subject Arthur L. Schawlow and Charles H. Townes are experts? (Hint: They won Nobel Prizes for their discovery.)

GUIDE TO SOURCE CITATIONS

(Based on the *Publication Manual of the American Psychological Association*, 4th ed.)

It is important that you fully document the sources of information you use in preparing a speech outline. Cite the source in parentheses in the actual body of the outline by name and date. Put in page numbers for quotations or specific facts, for example, (Jones, 1990, p. 1).

Include a list of references at the end of the outline. Always include the author, date, title, and facts of publication. Personal communications, such as letters, phone calls, e-mail, and interviews, are cited only in the text, not the reference list; for example, J. Q. Jones (personal communication, April 1, 1992). The format varies depending on the type of work referenced. Here are some of the most common types of works you may use in a speech. Notice that APA style does not place quotation marks around the titles of articles or book chapters. Also, titles of books and articles are not capitalized, except for the first word, the first word following a colon, and proper names. Periodical titles are capitalized. Authors are listed by last name first, followed by first and sometimes middle initials.

Books

Single Author

Freeley, A. J. (1990). <u>Argumentation and debate: Critical thinking for reasoned decision making</u> (7th ed.). Belmont, CA: Wadsworth.

Multiple Authors

Germond, J. W., & Witcover, J. (1989). <u>Whose broad stripes and bright stars?</u> New York: Warner Books.

Corporate Author

American Psychological Association. (1994). <u>Publication manual of the American Psychological Association</u> (4th ed.). Washington, DC: Author.

Government Document

Department of Health and Human Services. (1989). <u>Smoking tobacco and health: A fact book.</u> (DHHS Publication No. CDC 87-8397). Washington, DC: U.S. Government Printing Office.

Chapter in a Book

Steeper, F. T. (1978). Public response to Gerald Ford's statements on Eastern Europe in the second debate. In G. F. Bishop, R. G. Meadow, & M. Jackson-Beeck (Eds.), The presidential debates: Media, electoral, and policy perspectives (pp. 81-101). New York: Praeger.

Periodicals

Weekly Magazine

Alter, J. (1988, September 26). The expectations game. Newsweek, 112, 16-18.

If the author is unknown, you would list it as follows:

The expectations game. (1988, September 26). Newsweek, 112, 16-18.

Scholarly Journal Divided by Volume Numbers

Vancil, D. L., & Pendell, S. D. (1984). Winning presidential debates: An analysis of criteria influencing audience response. Western Journal of Speech Communication, 48, 63-74.

[This means the article was published in 1984, in volume 48, on pages 63–74.]

Newspaper

Rosentiel, T. H. (1988, October 14). Minus a Dukakis home run, Bush is called winner. Los Angeles Times, p. A25.

If the author is unknown, you would list it as follows:

Minus a Dukakis home run, Bush is called winner. (1988, October 14). Los Angeles Times, p. A25.

Pamphlet (published by author)

American Diabetes Association. (1987). Diabetes and you. Alexandria, VA: Author.

Internet

As computer sources multiply, the citation format has been evolving. We recommend that you use APA guidelines for the type of publication, adding

the type of medium, the necessary electronic information to permit retrieval, and then the date you accessed the information in brackets. For
example:

Clinton, B. (1995, November 27). Statement by the
president [Online]. Available: http://docs.whitehouse.gov/
white-house-publications/ 1995/11/1995-11-27-presidents-
statement-on-bosnian-peace-keeping-mission.text. [1996,
January 15]

All references are listed in alphabetical order by authors' last names, regardless of type. Works listed by title, where the author is not known, are
placed alphabetically by title. Thus, a reference list might look like the following:

References

Alter, J. (1988, September 26). The expectations game.
Newsweek, 112, 16–18.
American Psychological Association. (1994). Publication
manual of the American Psychological Association (4th ed.).
Washington, DC: Author.
Department of Health and Human Services. (1989). Smoking
tobacco and health: A fact book. (DHHS Publication No. CDC
87-8397). Washington, DC: U.S. Government Printing Office.
Freeley, A. J. (1990). Argumentation and debate: Critical
thinking for reasoned decision making (7th ed.). Belmont,
CA: Wadsworth.
Germond, J. W., & Witcover, J. (1989). Whose broad
stripes and bright stars? New York: Warner Books.
Minus a Dukakis home run, Bush is called winner. (1988,
October 14). Los Angeles Times, p. A25.
Steeper, F. T. (1978). Public response to Gerald Ford's
statements on Eastern Europe in the second debate. In G. F.
Bishop, R. G. Meadow, & M. Jackson-Beeck (Eds.), The
presidential debates: Media, electoral, and policy
perspectives (pp. 81–101). New York: Praeger.
Vancil, D. L., & Pendell, S. D. (1984). Winning
presidential debates: An analysis of criteria influencing
audience response. Western Journal of Speech Communication,
48, 63–74.

Notes

1. "Selling Green," *Consumer Reports,* October 1991, 687–92.

2. "Selling Green," 687–92.

3. Cynthia Crossen, "Lies, Damned Lies—and 'Scientific' Studies," *Sacramento Bee,* Forum, 24 November 1991, 1–2. (Reprinted from the *Wall Street Journal.*)

4. Crossen, "Lies, Damned Lies—and 'Scientific' Studies."

5. Robert S. Erikson and Kent L. Tedin, *American Public Opinion,* 5th ed. (Boston: Allyn & Bacon, 1994), 28.

6. Crossen, "Lies, Damned Lies—and Scientific Studies."

7. Bill Clinton, "Statement by the President" [online] (Washington, D.C.: The White House, Office of the Press Secretary, November 27, 1995) [http://docs.whitehouse.gov/white-house-publications/1995/11/1995-11-27-presidents-statement-on-bosnian-peace-keeping-mission.text].

8. Walter R. Fisher, *Human Communication as Narration* (Columbia: University of South Carolina Press, 1987).

9. Based on Meriam Library, *How to Use the On-Line Catalog* (Chico: California State University, 1991).

10. Patricia McColl Bee and Walter Schneider, *Quotation Location* (Ottawa, Canada: Canadian Library Association, 1990).

11. "Cyberspace Survey Finds That 1 of 6 Uses Internet," *Sacramento Bee,* 31 October 1995, E1.

12. David Wallechinsky, "Be at Home on the Internet," *Parade Magazine,* 19 November 1995, 6, 9.

13. America Online can be reached at 1-800-827-6364; CompuServe at 1-800-848-8199; and Prodigy at 1-800-PRODIGY (according to Wallechinsky, "Be at Home on the Internet," 9).

14. For more information, contact Netscape Communications Corporation, 501 East Middlefield Road, Mountain View, CA 94043, phone: 1-415-254-1900, fax: 1-415-254-2601.

15. http://the-tech.mit.edu/Shakespeare/works.html

16. http://www.unitedmedia.com/comics/dilbert/

17. http://www.ellemag.com/

18. http://www.yahoo.com/

19. http://www.cnn.com/

Organization is one of the most important ingredients in successful public speaking.

8

Organizing
Your Message

OBJECTIVES

After reading this chapter, you should be able to:

- Develop an organizational strategy geared to your audience.
- Refine the specific purpose of your speech.
- Develop a clear thesis statement for your speech.
- Organize the body of a speech, using one of the eight patterns of organization.
- Construct an effective introduction and conclusion for a speech.
- Prepare a formal outline for a speech to your class.
- Prepare and utilize speaker's notes for a speech to your class.

KEY CONCEPTS

categorical pattern
causal pattern
extended narrative
main points
Monroe's motivated sequence
problem–solution pattern

refutational pattern
spatial pattern
subpoint
supporting point
time pattern

It is easier for an audience to follow a speech when they know how it is organized.

In everyday conversation, we often speak in a random and seemingly disorganized fashion. Particularly in interpersonal conversation, one idea will trigger another, which will trigger another, and so on. We all have had the experience of wondering how we ended up talking about the latest music video when the conversation began with a question about weekend plans.

When engaged in casual conversation, we have no reason to worry about structuring our message. In fact, part of the fun of such conversations is that they are spontaneous and unpredictable. If we don't understand what someone has said, we can simply ask the person to explain what was meant. Feedback is immediate, verbal as well as nonverbal.

Unfortunately, as we move from engaging in conversation to speaking in public, such random and unpredictable speaking becomes a hindrance to effective communication. Rather than being fun, listening to the random thoughts of a disorganized speaker is frustrating. As listeners we desire structure. We want to know where speakers are going and when they get there. A "stream of consciousness" public speaker is usually an ineffective one.

In this chapter, we assume that you already have a general notion of what you want to communicate in your speech. But, as Plato implied in the quotation at the beginning of this chapter, simply knowing what you want to communicate is not enough. You need to know how to structure that information for maximal effect. There are some specific things you can do organizationally to help you achieve your goals. They include developing an organizational strategy geared to your audience, refining your specific purpose, focusing on your thesis statement, organizing the body of your speech, introducing your speech, concluding your speech, communicating organization through previews and signposts, and preparing the formal outline and/or speaker's notes.

FOCUSING ON YOUR AUDIENCE

Just as with the process of invention discussed in the preceding chapter, the organization of your speech should be grounded in your analysis of your rhetorical situation, in particular your audience. For example, should you put your best foot forward, so to speak, or save your best for last? A lot depends on the audience. Suppose you have an audience that is either disinterested or hostile. If your most compelling material is saved until the end, you are likely to lose them long before you have a chance to enlighten them or influence their opinion. On the other hand, if your audience already is greatly interested in your topic, you may want to build to a climax so that your best material will be fresh in their minds at the conclusion of the speech. A careful analysis of your audience is also crucial to refining your specific purpose and formulating your thesis statement.

Refining Your Specific Purpose

In Chapter 2, we defined the *specific purpose* as the speaker's goal or objective in speaking to a particular audience. Although you will have a specific purpose in mind before you actually begin to construct your speech, you will need to refine your specific purpose in light of your research and your analysis of the audience. The specific purpose of a speech represents a compromise between the speaker's ideal goal and the constraints of the particular rhetorical situation. Suppose you know the audience is skeptical of your point of view. You may want to refine your specific purpose to a more achievable goal than your ideal. For example, if you want your audience to buy a personal computer, and you know they are largely uninformed and even hostile to the machines, perhaps you should only try to open their minds a little and persuade them to consider trying out a computer. As you develop your specific purpose, keep in mind these factors and the four guidelines listed on the following page.

Guidelines for Refining the Specific Purpose of a Speech

- Describe the results you seek.
- Be as specific as possible.
- Express your goal in measurable terms.
- Set a realistic goal.

The specific purpose of a speech is typically expressed in terms of an infinitive phrase that begins with "to." Specific purposes usually fall into one of the general purposes described in Chapter 2: *to inform, to persuade,* or *to entertain.* If you were giving an informative speech on computer viruses, for example, you might express your specific purpose as "to inform my audience about the methods of transmission of computer viruses." This purpose, however, is somewhat vague. More specifically, you might express it as "to have my audience be able to explain in their own words the ways a computer virus can be transmitted." Because this specific purpose includes a way of measuring your results—the audience should be able to describe how the virus is transmitted—it will point you toward a specified goal. The level of their understanding should be realistic—one speech cannot make them computer experts, but they should know how to protect themselves against viruses.

On the same topic, you might have as a persuasive specific purpose "to convince my audience to purchase a virus-detection program for their personal computer." Thus, a successful speech given this goal would lead to a number of audience members eventually purchasing the program. Some persuasive speeches are part of a longer process or campaign. For example, at the end of the first term a president gives an annual State of the Union speech in January. The ultimate purpose is to get votes in November, but this is just one step toward that goal. As a consequence, he or she might express the specific purpose for such a speech in more limited terms. For example, the president might have as the specific purpose "to persuade voters that I have a positive agenda for the next four years."

Speeches to entertain have the advantage of instantaneous feedback. Speakers know by the audience laughter or applause whether or not they have succeeded. So, a speaker might express a specific entertainment purpose as "to entertain my audience with the story of my worst computer nightmares." It is not necessary to state how you will measure this goal because success or failure is immediately evident.

Focusing on Your Thesis Statement

Recall from Chapter 2 that a thesis statement focuses your audience's attention on the central point of your speech. Just as a photographer must clearly focus on the primary subject of a photo, you as a speaker must bring the principal thrust of your speech into clear focus for your audience. Your analysis of the audience may determine when and how you present your thesis statement.

Normally, the thesis statement comes early in the speech, right after the opening. It is frustrating to an audience not to know the central point of a speech early. However, there may be times when presenting the thesis statement early is not the best strategy. For example, a hostile audience may tune you out as soon as they hear your position on a controversial issue. In that case, you may want to hold off stating your position until the end of the speech and instead begin with common ground. Again, audience-focused organization is a key to successful speech making.

Your thesis statement should help the audience understand what response you seek from them. As a case in point, you might be opposed to a tuition increase at your university or college. Assuming you are speaking to a group of student colleagues, you may wish to focus your speech on what they can do to fight the tuition increase. Thus, your thesis statement might be "we need to lobby the board of trustees of the university to stop this unjustified and harmful tuition increase." Notice that the thesis statement here is directly related to the specific purpose of your speech. In this instance, your specific purpose is "to convince other students to lobby the board of trustees to stop the proposed tuition increase." The thesis statement, if accepted and acted upon by the audience, will fulfill your specific purpose. While the specific purpose expresses your goal for the audience's response to the speech, the thesis statement expresses the essential message that is designed to fulfill that purpose.

Although the specific purpose is not normally stated explicitly to the audience, the thesis statement should be sufficiently related to that purpose to allow the audience to know what the speaker wants to accomplish. Sometimes the thesis statement may be less specific than the specific purpose. For example, if you are dealing with a hostile audience, rather than saying, "Today I am going to convince you that condoms should be distributed at your child's school," you might say, "Today I am going to offer some positive steps we can take to prevent the spread of AIDS to your children." You must be sensitive to your audience's attitudes, beliefs, and values in formulating a thesis statement that will both express the essence of your speech and allow the audience to give your views a fair hearing.

Even a speech to entertain should have a clear thesis. Obviously, there's no easier way to turn off an audience than to say, "Today I'm going to make you laugh." But it would be logical to say, "First dates are often a disaster, and mine was no different." Unlike a David Letterman monologue, which is often just a string of jokes, a speech to entertain should have a clear purpose, thesis, and structure.

Once you know your specific purpose and have formulated your thesis statement, it is time to organize the body of your speech. Although you might think that the introduction should be written first, this is rarely the case. Until you have constructed the body of the speech, it is difficult to find an appropriate introduction. Also, in sifting through your ideas and the research you've done for the body of the speech, you might find something that strikes you as ideally suited to a strong introduction.

ORGANIZING THE BODY OF THE SPEECH

As Plato suggested, every speech needs parts that are "composed in such a way that they suit both each other and the whole." Thus, your speech needs not only a strong introduction and conclusion but also a well-organized body to support your thesis statement and achieve your purpose. Carefully thought-out main points, subpoints, and supporting points will provide that organization.

Main Points

Main points are the key ideas that support the thesis statement of a speech. They should fully develop the thesis statement. As a result of understanding these points, your audience should be informed, persuaded, or entertained in accordance with your specific purpose. In developing your main points, keep five guidelines in mind. They are listed below and then described in more detail.

Guidelines for Developing Your Main Points

- **Limit the number of main points.**
- **Focus each main point on one main idea.**
- **Construct main points so that they are parallel in structure.**
- **State main points as simply as the subject will allow.**
- **Give all main points equal treatment.**

Number   Every speech needs to be anchored around two or more main points. (If there is only one main point, then that is, in effect, the same as your thesis statement, and what you think are subpoints are in fact the main points.) In our experience, more than five main points is too much for an audience to absorb. Three main points seems to be ideal. The audience (not to mention the speaker) usually can easily grasp three key ideas, especially if they are organized in a memorable fashion. As the number of points increases, each main idea tends to be devalued and the chances of you or your audience forgetting one or more ideas tend to increase. Obviously, there can be no rule in this regard, as some topics do not fit into three neat pigeon-holes. But if you find yourself with six, seven, or eight main points, your speech is likely to suffer because either you are trying to cover too much in your speech or what you really have are six to eight subpoints, which could be organized into fewer main points, each with two or three subpoints.

Focus   The main points should clearly relate to the thesis statement. They should fully develop the thesis statement, while not going beyond the focus of the speech. For example, if you are speaking on the structure of the federal government, your thesis statement might be "the federal government consists of three separate branches of government that check and balance one another." An obvious division of this focus into three main points would be

    I. The legislative branch is found in the Congress.

    II. The executive branch includes the president and the Cabinet.

    III. The judicial branch includes the Supreme Court and the lower courts.

Imagine, however, that your speech on the branches of the federal government excluded the judicial branch. Clearly, your thesis statement would have to account for the fact. If it didn't, you would most likely leave your audience wondering why you left out such a significant part of your speech. Or, on the other hand, suppose you decided to add another main point to the body of your speech, for example,

    IV. Corruption in government is a serious problem.

Although this point is certainly related to the federal government, it is out of the focus suggested by the thesis statement. Thus, you need to reformulate your thesis statement, or rethink the specific purpose, or drop the out-of-focus point.

Think of the thesis statement as limiting the territory covered by your speech. As you construct the body of the speech, include only those items that directly support your thesis statement. At the same time, do not allow your thesis statement to be incompletely supported. By the end of your speech, you should have fulfilled the promise of your thesis statement—no more, no less.

Each main point should be focused on one main idea. For example, consider the potential confusion of this main point:

    I. Corruption exists in Congress, and laws begin in Congress as bills.

The first part of the main point deals with the problem of members of Congress failing their public trust. The second part deals with the formal process by which our laws are passed. These two ideas should be expressed as separate main points:

I. Laws begin in Congress as bills.

II. Corruption exists in Congress.

Using two separate points does not mean that they are unrelated. Obviously, the method by which a bill becomes law, such as the role of key congressional committees in the process, may help explain why Congress is susceptible to corruption. But the two ideas are clearly different.

Parallel Structure Your main points form the essence of your speech, so they should be clear, concise, and memorable. One technique to help achieve this is to construct main points in parallel fashion. For example, which of the following is the more memorable way to phrase main points?

I. Congress is corrupt.

II. There are some corrupt members in the executive branch.

III. Some judges take bribes.

or:

I. Corruption corrodes Congress.

II. Corruption corrodes the White House.

III. Corruption corrodes the bench.

Obviously, the second example is easier to remember. The repetition of the phrase "corruption corrodes" in all three main points stresses the focus of this speech—that all three branches experience corruption.

Simplicity versus Complexity Whereas a reader can reread anything that is complex or confusing, the audience of a speech has only a limited opportunity to process information. If you phrase your main points as complex sentences, you may lose your audience. Concise and simple language will help make the structure of your speech clear. Again, compare two examples of main points:

I. AIDS is transmitted through unprotected sexual relations, including homosexual and heterosexual encounters.

II. AIDS is transmitted when drug users, often desperate for their next fix, share dirty needles.

III. AIDS is transmitted by the exchange of blood, such as in a transfusion or between a mother and her unborn child.

or

I. AIDS is transmitted through unprotected sex.

II. AIDS is transmitted through sharing of needles.

III. AIDS is transmitted by blood.

Which of the two sets of main points do you think the audience will remember? Although you will develop these main points in much more detail as you give the speech, statement of the main points should be as simple as the subject will allow.

Balance   You should aim for balance among the main points of your speech. For example, if one main point comprises two thirds of the speech, audience members may become confused and wonder what they missed. Perhaps they will wonder why you think that one point is so much more important than the other. Or they may suspect that there is another main point you forgot to mention.

Subpoints

Subpoints are to the main points what main points are to the thesis statement. A **subpoint** is an idea that supports a main point. Each main point should have at least two and no more than five subpoints. Consider, for example, our speech on the structure of the federal government:

   I. The legislative branch makes the laws.   [main point]
      A. The House of Representatives is based on population.   [subpoint]
      B. The Senate provides each state with equal representation.   [subpoint]

  II. The executive branch enforces the laws.
      A. The president is the chief executive officer.
      B. The Cabinet consists of the heads of the executive departments.

 III. The judicial branc]h interprets the laws.
      A. The Supreme Court is the final arbitrator of the law.
      B. Lower courts must follow the Supreme Court's rulings.

It makes no sense to have only one subpoint under a main point. For example:

   I. The legislative branch makes the laws.

      A. The House of Representatives is based on population.

If you wished to talk only about the House of Representatives, then that would be your main point. But if a main point is not subject to division into at least two subpoints, it probably is not of sufficient merit to be a main point. Rather, it is likely to be a potential subpoint under another point. Like main points, subpoints should be parallel in structure, simply stated, and given equal treatment.

Supporting Points

Sometimes the subpoints within your speech require further support and subdivision. Thus, you might choose supporting points for each subpoint. A **supporting point** is an idea that supports a subpoint. Returning to our example of the federal government, the body of a speech might be organized as follows:

[main point]   I. The legislative branch makes the laws.

[subpoint]   A. The House of Representatives is defined in the Constitution.
[supporting point]   1. Qualifications for office are specified in the Constitution.
[supporting point]   2. The powers of the House are specified in the Constitution.

Obviously, one could further subdivide each of these supporting points. However, such a detailed substructure probably would lose the audience. What's more, for a normal classroom speech, it is unlikely that you will ever have the time to develop most points beyond this level. If a speech seems to lend itself to further substructure, ask yourself if some of your supporting points are really subpoints, as well as whether some of the subpoints might be better phrased as main points or whether you should narrow your topic further.

If you must further subdivide a supporting point, use lowercase letters in your outline as follows:

[main point]   I. The legislative branch makes the laws.

[subpoint]   A. The House of Representatives is defined in the Constitution.
[supporting point]   1. The qualifications for office are specified in the Constitution:
[further support]   a. At least 25 years of age
[further support]   b. Citizen of the U.S. for at least 7 years
[further support]   c. Resident of the state represented

Patterns of Organization

There are a number of different patterns you can use to organize the body of your speech. In Chapter 2, we introduced four of those patterns. We now will add four patterns of organization, for a total of eight: time, extended narrative, spatial, categorical, problem–solution, refutational, causal, and Monroe's motivated sequence.

Time   Many topics lend themselves naturally to a temporal sequence. A **time pattern** is a pattern of organization based on chronology or a sequence of events. Topics of a historical nature are likely to follow a time sequence. Suppose you were speaking about the history of the U.S. space program, as did Tom Wolfe in his book *The Right Stuff.* You might divide it into the following main points:

I. The race begins in the 1950s with the launch of *Sputnik.*

II. The U.S.S.R. puts the first men into space in the 1960s.

III. The U.S. sets the goal to land on the moon by the end of the 1960s.

IV. Neil Armstrong is the first human to land on the moon in July 1969.

Topics that deal with a process, such as "how to" speeches, can frequently be ordered by a time sequence as well. You might sequence a speech on learning to ski in these terms:

I. Select the right equipment.

II. Invest in lessons.

III. Practice!

Extended Narrative   An **extended narrative** is a pattern of organization in which the entire body of the speech is the telling of a story. In Chapter 7, we introduced narrative as a form of support for a speech. As support, one main point of a speech might be a narrative, but the other main points might be in the form of statistics, expert opinions, facts, and the like. However, an extended narrative means the whole speech is one story. In this case you tell a story in sequence, with a climactic point at the end of the speech. This organizational pattern is often very useful, for example, in speeches to entertain. Thus, if you were to tell the story of your first blind date, you might pattern your speech after the following:

I. I am asked to go out with a blind date.

II. I meet the date.

III. Disaster follows.

Sometimes a persuasive speech can also be built around an extended narrative of some incident that dramatizes the problem you are addressing in your speech. An example of an extended narrative in a persuasive speech might be the following:

I. Jim had too much to drink at a fraternity party.

II. His frat brothers dared him to hop a moving freight train.

III. Jim attempted to jump on the moving train.

IV. He lost his balance and fell under the train; both of his legs were severed.

V. Jim lived and has dedicated his life to fighting alcohol abuse.

Notice that a story needs not only a plot line but also characters, including a central character with whom the audience can identify. In this particular story, the speaker would seek to create a sympathetic portrayal of Jim, who becomes the protagonist. Of course, each point would be developed in detail, and the audience should be held in suspense as the story unfolds. The moral of the story should not have to be stated explicitly but should be apparent to the audience. This is one of those speeches in which stating the thesis at the beginning would actually undermine the effectiveness of the speech. By the end of the speech, however, no one would doubt the speaker's central idea.

Spatial   A **spatial pattern** is a pattern of organization based on physical space or geography. Some topics lend themselves to a spatial or geographic order. Suppose you want to discuss weather patterns in the United States. You might divide your topic geographically into the east, south, north, and west. If you were trying to explain how a ship is constructed, you might do so in terms of fore, midship, and aft. Or if you were giving a tour of your hometown, your points might look something like this:

I. The east side is mostly residential.

II. The central part of town is the business district.

III. The west side is largely industrial.

Categorical   A **categorical pattern** is a pattern of organization based on natural divisions in the subject matter. Many topics naturally fall into categories. The federal government, as we've shown, can be naturally divided into the legislative, executive, and judicial branches. Communication messages are naturally divided into verbal and nonverbal categories. The essential principle is that you divide your topic along its natural boundaries. Thus, a speech advocating solar energy might be organized as follows:

I. Fossil fuels pollute the atmosphere.

II. Nuclear energy creates radioactive wastes.

III. Solar energy is nonpolluting.

When using this pattern, however, be careful that you don't create false categories. Although it may be categorically convenient to cast people into some specific groups, for example, it also can be highly misleading or even offensive. Much social and ethnic prejudice is rooted in the stereotyping of people into arbitrary categories.

Problem–Solution   Sometimes we speak to propose a solution to an ongoing problem. This is frequently the case when we speak persuasively. One way to approach this type of speech is to use the **problem–solution pattern,** a pattern of organization that analyzes a problem in terms of the stock issues of (1) harm, (2) significance, and (3) cause and proposes a solution that is (1) described, (2) feasible, and (3) advantageous. A specific

TV meteorologists often use a spatial pattern to explain the weather.

example of this pattern might be a speech about the need for better health care. In this case, you might organize the speech the following way:

I. (Problem) Millions of Americans are denied access to adequate health care.

   A. (Harm) People suffer and die without this care.

   B. (Significance) Over 37 million Americans lack basic health insurance.

   C. (Cause) There is a gap between government-sponsored health care (Medicaid and Medicare) and private insurance.

II. (Solution) We need a program of national health insurance to fill the gap.

   A. (Description) All businesses will be taxed to provide national health insurance.

   B. (Feasibility) Similar programs exist in almost every other industrialized country in the world.

   C. (Advantages) No longer will people be denied access to medical care simply because they cannot pay.

The relationship between harm and significance is important. Harm has to do with the bad consequences of the problem, in this case potential suffering and death. Significance has to do with the extent of the problem. If 100 people in a nation of 250 million were at risk of suffering or death because of an inadequate health-care system, this would be unfortunate, but it would not be a significant problem relative to the population of the nation. If millions were at risk, then the problem would be significant.

You also need to recognize that there can be numerous different solutions to the same problem. Thus, it is important to stress both the feasibility and the advantages of the solution you propose, if you hope to have it adopted by your audience.

Refutational   Sometimes you are in a position to answer the arguments of another speaker. Perhaps you are involved in a debate. Alternatively, you may read or hear something with which you disagree. The **refutational pattern** is a pattern of organization that involves the following steps:

   I. State the argument you seek to refute.

   II. State your objection to the argument.

   III. Prove your objection to the argument.

   IV. Present the impact of your refutation.

For example, if you wanted to refute the proposed national health insurance in the previous illustration of the problem–solution method, you might proceed with the following points:

   I. The proponents of national health care say the government should control health care. [States the argument you seek to refute.]

   II. Government bureaucrats, not physicians or patients, will control medical choices. [States your objection to the argument.]

   III. People from Canada, which has national health insurance, often have to come to the United States for medical care they are denied by their government-run program. [Presents proof for your objection.]

   IV. The quality of American health care will decline in a program run by government bureaucrats. [Presents the impact of your objection.]

Causal   The **causal pattern** is a pattern of organization that moves from cause to effect or from effect to cause. In cause-to-effect speeches, you are dealing with some known activity and showing your audience that it will produce certain effects. If these were desirable effects, you would be endorsing the activity. If they were undesirable, you would be suggesting that your audience avoid the activity. To illustrate this organizational pattern, suppose that you wanted to convince your audience to quit smoking:

   I. (Cause) Cigarette smoking contains a number of harmful chemicals.

      A. Carbon monoxide reduces the body's ability to absorb oxygen.

      B. Nicotine is an addictive substance.

    C. Tar is made up of thousands of chemicals.

  II. (Effect) Cigarette smoking leads to significant health problems.

    A. Carbon monoxide has been linked to low-birth-weight babies.

    B. Nicotine makes quitting smoking difficult.

    C. Tar is the principal source of cancer-causing chemicals in tobacco.

On the other hand, if you wanted to convince your audience of the need to reduce the power of special interests in Washington, you might argue from various effects back to finding the cause:

  I. (Effect) The country is in economic trouble.

    A. Real wages are declining.

    B. Many industries are moving overseas.

    C. Our deficit is growing.

  II. (Cause) We have a system of government that is too tied to special interests.

    A. Lobbyists influence Congress to make bad economic decisions.

    B. Politicians are more interested in getting reelected than solving problems.

    C. Only by breaking the power of special interests can we get our economy back on track.

Whether you move from cause to effect or from effect to cause, you need to provide proof of the causal links asserted in your speech. Simply because two things occur one after the other does not prove one caused the other. For example, just because a car breaks down doesn't mean the last person to drive it is responsible for the breakdown.

Monroe's Motivated Sequence **Monroe's motivated sequence** is a five-step organizational scheme, developed by speech professor Alan Monroe.[1] These five steps overlap somewhat with the introduction and conclusion of a speech, as well as the body. They are as follows:

    I. *Attention:* Gain your audience's attention.   [Introduction]

    II. *Need:* Show the audience that a need exists that affects them.   [Body]

    III. *Satisfaction:* Present the solution to the need.   [Body]

    IV. *Visualization:* Help the audience imagine how their need will be met in the future.   [Body]

    V. *Action:* State what actions must be taken to fulfill the need.   [Conclusion]

To see how this motivated sequence might work, consider the earlier example concerning national health insurance:

I. *Attention:* A child dies because her parents couldn't afford to take her to the doctor.

II. *Need:* You could become one of millions of uninsured Americans who face financial ruin if they become seriously ill.

III. *Satisfaction:* National health insurance would guarantee all Americans the right to health care, regardless of their income.

IV. *Visualization:* The United States would join nations like Canada, where no one fears seeing a doctor because of the cost.

V. *Action:* Write your senator and representative today, urging the passage of national health insurance.

Obviously, the motivated-sequence pattern is most directly suited to persuasive presentations. However, an informative presentation could use at least some of these steps, since informative speaking typically is the first step in a persuasive campaign. In an informative presentation, it is important to show your audience why they need to learn the information you have presented and, of course, to satisfy that need. Helping an audience visualize how they will use the information is also valuable. And often you will then want them to put what they have learned into action.

In constructing the body of your speech, choose one of the basic patterns of organization. As a reminder, we list them here.

Patterns of Speech Organization

Time

Extended narrative

Spatial

Categorical

Problem–solution

Refutational

Causal

Monroe's motivated sequence

Try to avoid mixing types of patterns. It is confusing to an audience to begin listening to a time sequence and then find themselves in the middle of a problem–solution speech.

After organizing the body of the speech, you can begin to construct your introduction and conclusion.

INTRODUCING YOUR SPEECH

You may recall from Chapter 2 that an introduction should do three things: open with impact, focus on the thesis statement, and connect with the audience. Let's look at each of these functions in turn.

Open with Impact

A speech should immediately grab the audience's attention. Within a few seconds, we begin forming impressions of others who come into our view. When you are speaking, your audience will form an immediate impression of you. One way to control this impression is to open your speech with impact. Of the numerous ways to do this, some of the most common are a story; a quotation; a startling statement; a reference to the audience, the occasion, or a current event; appropriate humor; a personal experience; or a thought-provoking question.

Story A brief story, real or hypothetical, is often a good way to begin your speech. For example, a student in one of our classes began her speech by describing the strange behavior of a person who was staggering and incoherent, and who finally collapsed. The quick conclusion most of her audience drew as she was describing the person was that he was drunk. Not only was this conclusion wrong, the truth startled the class. The person had diabetes and was suffering from insulin shock. Needless to say, the class became far more interested in hearing the speech about diabetes than if the speaker had simply begun: "Today I'm going to tell you about diabetes."

Quotation As we pointed out in Chapter 7, there are numerous anthologies of quotations, usually organized by topic. If you are having trouble deciding how to begin your speech, consider looking for a quotation that will captivate your audience and reinforce your main ideas.

Startling Statement Humans are attracted naturally to surprising, startling, and unusual events. If you can tie the introduction of your speech to a surprising or startling statement, you will be assured of your audience's undivided attention. For example, we recall a student in class who began her speech by announcing that her sister had died of toxic shock syndrome, which was the subject of the speech. Needless to say, her audience was startled and paid rapt attention to the speech that followed.

Reference to the Audience, Occasion, or Current Events Politicians often tailor their speeches to a specific audience and situation, saying such things as "I'm so happy to be here at (fill in the blank) college" or "I join with you in praising your football team's come-from-behind victory last night."

VIDEO FILE

If you have access to the videotape that accompanies this book, view segment 6, which includes examples of introductions and conclusions to several speeches.

Another possibility is to refer to a previous speaker. We recall an instance in one class when two students chose to speak on gun control, each taking the opposite side of the topic. The second speaker wisely incorporated reference to the prior speech into her introduction. To ignore a speech on the same topic, particularly one at odds with your own speech, is likely to turn off an audience. Without attempting to refute the other speaker, she acknowledged those opposing views but also stated that she would present the other side of the issue.

Finally, current events often spark interest and controversy. If you are speaking on a topic of current interest, it is often a good idea to lead off with the most recent happenings. If you are speaking on terrorism, and a hostage has just been released from captivity, that would be a good place to begin your speech.

Appropriate Humor   A classic *Far Side* cartoon showed Abraham Lincoln delivering the Gettysburg Address. His speech, however, begins with a joke, "And so the bartender says, "Hey! That's not a duck!" After a pause for laughter, Lincoln continues, "Fourscore and seven years ago. . . ."

Obviously, one would not begin a serious speech such as the Gettysburg Address with a joke. Humor, if not used properly, can backfire. It is best used on occasions when the audience will find it appropriate. An after-dinner speech, for example, is frequently an opportunity to employ humor.

However you use it, though, humor should be tied to the substance of your speech. Telling an irrelevant joke can detract from the main idea of your speech, rather than enhance it. It can also make you look foolish.

Finally, you need to be sensitive with regard to humor. Ethnic, sexist, and off-color jokes, for example, can get a speaker into justifiable trouble. The careers of Cabinet officials James Watt and Earl Butz both ended when inappropriate ethnic jokes they had told were reported in the press. Speakers need to err on the side of caution when they treat sensitive subjects with humor.

Writing humor is not as easy as it seems. We asked for the advice of a professional comedy writer for shows such as *Murphy Brown* and *Cybill*. His advice is in the box "On Writing Comedy: Russ Woody" on pages 240–241.

Personal Experience   Often there is no other more compelling testimony on a topic than your own personal experience. Not only can a personal experience draw in your audience and get their attention, it also can serve to build your own credibility. For example, the speaker on diabetes referred to earlier had a brother who was diabetic. However, she did not mention this fact until she had finished her speech. Had she begun with her own experiences with a diabetic brother, she would have enhanced her credibility for the remainder of the speech.

Thought-Provoking Question   Sometimes you can use a question to open your speech. A **rhetorical question** is one that the audience isn't expected to answer out loud. For example, a speech on secondhand smoke began: "How many of you have ever returned home smelling as though you were a stand-in for the Marlboro Man?"[2] Because of the attention-getting language, this worked well. However, a question can be an ineffective technique if it is not thought-provoking. For example, beginning a speech with "How many of you would like to learn to snow ski?" isn't likely to have much impact on your audience. Also, with rhetorical questions, audiences are sometimes unsure as to whether or not the question is meant to be answered out loud. On the other hand, we have seen speakers who effectively begin their speeches by asking audience members to respond to a series of questions by a show of hands. Questions, rhetorical or real, should be used only if they add impact to the opening of the speech.

Focus on the Thesis Statement

The central idea you want to convey to an audience should be captured by your thesis statement. Although you should have developed a thesis statement before writing the body of the speech, now is a good time to reflect on its phrasing. Have you really focused on the essential theme of your speech? Be sure your thesis statement is broad enough to incorporate all of your main points. At the same time, do not make your thesis statement so broad that your speech seems to leave something out.

As noted earlier, there may be situations, such as with a hostile audience, where you will not be ready to explicitly state your thesis early in the speech. In the introduction in these situations, indicate the general topic area of the speech, focusing on an area of common agreement, rather than the thesis, if it might provoke a defensive or hostile reaction from the audience. The thesis would therefore emerge toward the end of the speech, after you had made your case.

Connect with Your Audience

No speech should be constructed without asking yourself, "What's in it for the audience? What needs or desires will be fulfilled by listening to my speech?" The introduction is an opportunity to make the link between your speech topic and their lives. If you make this link in your introduction, you are much more likely to gain your audience's collective ear.

The introduction is also another opportunity to build your own credibility. You should link your topic not only to your audience but to yourself as well, stressing your similarity to the audience. The student who spoke on

On Writing Comedy: Russ Woody

As a college student, Russ Woody excelled in an event called "Speech to Entertain." Not only was humor Russ's hobby, it became his profession. Russ began his writing career at MTM productions, where he wrote episodes for shows such as *Newhart, St. Elsewhere,* and *Hill Street Blues.* For two years he was a producer and writer for *Murphy Brown,* for which he received an Emmy in 1990. He is currently the co-executive producer of *Cybill,* and he continues to write several scripts a year. We asked Russ to do the impossible—explain writing humor in 250 words or less. Here is the result.

Writing Humor?

by Russ Woody

Two-hundred fifty words on how to write humor? Gee, can't I just whack myself in the forehead with a ball peen hammer? Trying to explain humor is a little like trying to wrest a ripe banana from an immense and bitter gorilla. If not handled correctly, you can end up looking rather foolish.

With that in mind, "Hello, Mr. Gorilla . . ."

The fact of the matter is, humor is more difficult to write than drama. Because, while both humor and drama rely heavily on emotional content, humor is much more difficult to break down mechanically. Therefore it's more difficult to construct initially. It's relatively easy to figure out what makes a person sad or angry or uneasy or embarrassed or happy. Yet it is, for the most part, difficult to say why a person laughs.

So I guess the first thing you've got to do is figure out what type of humor appeals most to you. Monty Python, Andrew "Dice" Clay, The Naked Gun, Murphy Brown, Full House, Spy Magazine, Mad Magazine, Saturday Night Live. Whichever it is, find it. Then—study it. Watch it, read it, take it apart, figure out how it's constructed, how it's set up, how it pays off—figure out the dynamics of humor. (Which will make it terribly unfunny when you do, but that's the perpetual hell comedy writers live in.)

For instance—one of my favorite jokes of all time is in one of the Pink Panther movies where Peter Sellers goes into a hotel and approaches a man at the desk who has a dog

toxic shock syndrome used her family's tragedy to stress that the same thing could happen to any woman in the class. She not only made a connection to her classmates, she also established her personal credibility by virtue of her experience and her subsequent research on the topic.

Although connecting with the audience is an important part of the introduction to your speech, the connection should not be made only once. In fact, throughout your speech you should draw a connection between your message and your audience whenever possible.

sitting beside him. Sellers says, "Does your dog bite?" The guy says no. So Sellers reaches over to pat the little pooch, and it tries to rip his arm off. Sellers then looks to the guy and says, "I thought you said your dog didn't bite?" The guy says, "It's not my dog."

I love that joke because every element of it is real, and nobody involved thinks it's funny. The man was quite correct in his literal interpretation of Sellers's question. Sellers is more than a little annoyed at the man for misunderstanding what seemed to be a logical and straightforward question. And the dog is just pissed off. In a more general sense, one person becomes a victim because the other is a stickler for precise wording. It is extreme focus on one character's part and vulnerability on the other character's part. In a way, it's like the movie The In-Laws, with Peter Falk and Alan Arkin. Falk is intensely focused on his job with the government, which, in turn makes Arkin's life a living hell. (If you've seen the movie, you know what I'm talking about—if you haven't, go see it, because I'm coming up on two-fifty pretty fast here, so I can't get into it.)

When you've taken enough jokes and stories apart, you may start to get an idea of how to construct your own. That's when it gets really tough. Just be sure you always remember the one, underlying key to writing humor—oops, outta time.

CONCLUDING YOUR SPEECH

The conclusion of the speech should be brief and memorable. The last thing an audience wants to hear after "In conclusion . . ." is a 10-minute dissertation on some new aspect of the topic. When you say those magic words "in conclusion" or "to wrap up," be prepared to conclude. Avoid introducing points that were not covered in the body of the speech. If you have another main point to cover, then it belongs in the body of the speech, not the conclusion. There are, consequently, only two basic things to do in concluding your speech: to summarize and to close with impact.

Summarize

Tell the audience, very briefly, what you have told them in the speech. This is where clear, concisely developed main points pay off. Going back to an earlier example, you might conclude the speech on corruption in the federal government with "We have seen, therefore, that all three branches of government—the Congress, the executive, and the judicial—are vulnerable to the corrupting influence of money." Sometimes you may wish to explicitly number the main points in your summary—for example, "There are three types of bikes you'll see on campus. First, there are cruisers; second, there are mountain bikes; and third, there are touring bikes."

Close with Impact

The final words of your speech should be memorable. The close is your last chance to have an impact on your audience. As with the opening, it should be relevant to the main thesis of your speech. A few of the common techniques for closing are a short, memorable quotation, an anecdote or brief story, a direct appeal to action, and a return to your opening theme. If you have delayed presenting your thesis statement for strategic reasons, it should be incorporated just prior to this point (right after the summary). If you stated it earlier, it should be reiterated here.

Quotation   The same principles apply to a closing quotation as to an opening one. You want to capture the essence of your talk in a few words. If someone has said it better than you, then it is perfectly appropriate to quote that person. In the conclusion, it probably is best to state who you are quoting and then state the quotation. For example, it is less effective to say, "'I have a dream,' said Martin Luther King, Jr.," than to say, "As Martin Luther King, Jr., once stated, 'I have a dream.'"

Anecdote   The key in the closing is to be brief and to the point. A long, drawn-out story will undermine the effectiveness of the rest of your speech. A concluding anecdote should highlight your main focus, not detract from it. As with opening stories, such anecdotes can be real or hypothetical but should be clearly identified as such to your audience.

Direct Appeal to Action   This kind of conclusion is typical of a persuasive speech and is an explicit part of the motivated sequence. It involves telling your audience members specifically what they can do to fulfill their needs

or solve a problem—for example, sign a petition, write to Congress, or change their own behavior. A direct appeal to your audience is often the most appropriate way to conclude a persuasive presentation.

Jesse Jackson utilizes a direct appeal to action when seeking to register new voters.

Return to Opening   One of the most effective ways to close a speech is to return to where you began. Not only does this remind the audience of your introduction, it also gives your speech a sense of closure. It takes both you and your audience full circle. For example, the speech that began by describing a person suffering from insulin shock ended by telling the audience that now they would know how to recognize when someone was in insulin shock and would be able to get that person the help he or she needed. If you can find a way to tie your opening and closing together, you can intensify the impact of both.

Once you have constructed the body, introduction, and conclusion to your speech, you are ready for the next step: developing a preview and signposts for the body of the speech.

USING PREVIEWS AND SIGNPOSTS

As instructors we frequently have had the experience of being lost while listening to a speech, only to discover upon reading the outline that the speaker had a clear organizational pattern. The problem was not in the way the student organized the ideas of the speech, but in the way he or she communicated the organization to the audience.

Two ways to effectively communicate organization to an audience are through previews and through signposts. Although no one knows who first said, "Tell 'em what you're going to tell 'em; tell 'em; and then tell 'em what you told 'em," it is a saying with more than a grain of truth. As we noted in Chapter 2, a *preview* is a forecast of the main points of a speech. It simply tells your audience members what they are going to hear. In many ways, it is a summary before the fact. As Chapter 2 explained, *signposts* are transitional statements that bridge your main points. They tell your audience where you have been and where you are going in your speech.

Both previews and signposts provide clarity and emphasis to your speech. In addition, they help capture and hold your audience's attention. By cueing audience members about what will follow, a preview helps them put your statements into a coherent frame of reference. By telling listeners where you are in the speech, signposts help those who have become lost or inattentive pick up the thread of your speech.

Previews

The way to preview a speech is rather simple: Cue the audience to the fact that you are previewing the main points of your speech, and then state the points in the same sequence they will be presented. A brief preview might be "In today's speech, I would like to share the definition, transmission, and prevention of computer viruses." Or you may want to enumerate your main points, saying, "Today, I want to first define computer viruses; second, explain how they are transmitted; and third, offer a way to prevent them from infecting your own computer."

It is not always necessary, however, to be so explicit. There are often subtler ways of previewing your speech. For example, "All computer owners need to know what computer viruses are, how they are transmitted, and how to detect and prevent them."

Signposts

In the next chapter, transitional statements are discussed in more detail. For now, you should be aware of five basic transitional techniques.

Techniques for Signposting

- *Refer to preceding and upcoming ideas.* For example, "Now that you know what computer viruses are, I'll discuss how to prevent their spread to your computer."

- *Enumerate key points.* If you number your points in the preview, stick with that numbering plan in the signposts. For example: "First, never assume that a program from a friend or computer bulletin board is virus free."

- *Give nonverbal reinforcement.* Frequently, you can emphasize your verbal signposts nonverbally. Changes in vocal inflection signal a change is coming. Movement can signal a signpost. For example, some speakers physically move from one place to another while speaking in order to emphasize that they are moving from one point to the next. Others hold up fingers to indicate number of points.

- *Use visual aids to reinforce signposts.* Moving to a new page on your flip chart or putting up a new slide or transparency clearly signals to your audience that you are moving on. It's also a way to help you remember the sequence of your speech.

- *Use words that cue your audience that you are changing points.* Words like the following suggest a signpost: *next, another, number, moving on, finally, therefore, in summary.* Don't be afraid to be explicit about signposts. More speeches suffer from a lack of clear signposts than from being overly signposted.

PREPARING THE FORMAL OUTLINE

Once you have a rough structure of your speech, including the body, introduction, conclusion, preview, and signposts, it's time to prepare a formal outline of the speech if it is recommended or required by your instructor. A **formal outline** is a detailed outline used in speech preparation but not, in most cases, used in the actual presentation. Usually, such an outline should be typed or prepared on a computer, depending on your instructor's requirements. Such outlines help you put your ideas down in a clear and organized fashion. If submitted in advance of a speech, it also allows instructors to give you feedback and make suggestions.

There are two basic types of outlines. *Phrase or key word* outlines are meaningful to the speaker but probably would not make a lot of sense to anyone else. For example, a speaker might prepare the following outline for her own use:

Intro: Tell story

   I. Rock music

  II. Volume

 III. Deafness

Conclusion: Same story 10 years later

Because this outline probably would make sense only to the speaker, beginning speakers are frequently expected to prepare a *full-sentence outline*. In this type of outline, you include a full statement indicating what each main point and subpoint cover. All the parts of a speech are included, even signposts. Generally, a formal outline should include the following:

- Your specific purpose, phrased as an infinitive phrase (to . . .), describing exactly what you want your speech to accomplish.
- Three sections—labeled introduction, body, and conclusion—each separately outlined and beginning with the roman numeral "I."
- The introduction, including your opening, focus on thesis statement, and connection with the audience.
- A preview (in parentheses) of the main points of the speech.
- The body, including main points, subpoints, supporting points, and further support.
- Signposts (in parentheses) between the main points.
- The conclusion, including a summary and a close.
- A list of references used in constructing the speech. Specific quotations or facts drawn from a source, as discussed in Chapter 7, should also be cited in the main outline. Of course, you should check with your instructor about the specific outlining requirements, if any, for your class. Some instructors prefer a different source citation system, for example, than the one discussed in Chapter 7.

Outlines typically use a standard outline notation, which indicates the levels of subordination of points:

   I. Main point

     A. Subpoint

       1. Supporting point

         a. Further support

Any subdivision should include at least two matching points. Thus, if you have an "A" subpoint under a main point, there should also be at least a "B." Supporting point "1" should be matched by at least a "2," and further support "a" should be followed by at least a "b."

Many instructors prefer that outlines be written in complete sentences, at least through the level of subpoints. This provides a clearer idea to both you and your instructor of what you are going to say. Use only one sentence per point and divide separate ideas into different sentences. If you outline using paragraph form, what you really have is an essay with outline notation scattered throughout. Thus, the following is not really in outline form:

I. The first men on the moon were Americans. Neil Armstrong stepped out first. He was followed by Buzz Aldrin. At the same time, Michael Collins orbited the moon.

This paragraph could be turned into the following outline:

I. The first men on the moon were Americans.
  A. Neil Armstrong stepped out first.
  B. He was followed by Buzz Aldrin.
  C. At the same time, Michael Collins orbited the moon.

Notice how each sentence is placed in a separate point. The more general statement is the main point, and the specific instances are subpoints.

Some aspects of an outline do not need to be in complete-sentence form. For example, a speaker who wants to list the components of a larger whole, such as ingredients or tools, could use an outline like this:

1. Cigarette smoke has three components:
   a. carbon monoxide
   b. nicotine
   c. tar

You need to use judgment, therefore, when you are asked to write a complete-sentence outline. Use complete sentences for your main points and subpoints and anywhere the meaning would not be clear if not expressed in complete-sentence form.

The box "Sample Speech Outline: The Right to Breathe, by Deidra Dukes" follows the suggested format. Remember, however, to check with your instructor for specific requirements in your class.

PREPARING SPEAKER'S NOTES

Of course the outline is a preparation tool. We recommend that you use **speaker's notes,** which are brief notes with key words, usually written on cards, used when you are presenting a speech. Your final notes should be meaningful to you as a speaker, but not necessarily to anyone else. However,

Sample Speech Outline

Title of speech.

The Right to Breathe
by Deidra Dukes

This is the goal the speaker seeks to accomplish.

Specific purpose: To persuade the audience that cigarette smoking should be banned from public places.

Introduction

Speech is divided into introduction, body, and conclusion.

Introduction opens with impact, focuses on the thesis statement, and connects with the audience.

  I. **Open with impact:** How many of you have ever returned home smelling as though you were a stand-in for the Marlboro Man?
 II. **Focus on thesis statement:** Smoking should be banned in public places.
III. **Connect with audience:** Smokers are depriving us of the clean air we deserve to breathe.
  - A. Former Surgeon General C. Everett Koop said: "The right of smokers to smoke ends where their behavior affects the health and well-being of others" (Koop, 1986, p. xii).
  - B. <u>Newsweek</u> reports an estimated 50,000 people will die this year as a result of second-hand smoke (Cowle, 1990, p. 59).

Body

Previews are indicated by parentheses.

(**Preview:** Let me share with you three important ideas: First, second-hand smoke contains harmful chemicals; second, it threatens public health; and third, it should be banned in public places.)

First main point begins with I, not IV.

  I. **Main point:** First, consider the three harmful components of cigarette smoke:
  - A. Carbon monoxide is the same substance that can cause death from automobile exhaust.
  - B. Nicotine is the addictive drug in cigarette smoke.
  - C. Tar consists of some 4,000 chemicals, 43 of which cause cancer (Department of Health and Human Services, 1989, p. 15).

Sources are cited within parentheses in APA style; see Chapter 7.

(**Signpost:** These harmful substances don't just enter the smoker's lungs, which brings me to my second point.)

II. **Main point:** Second-hand smoke is a health threat to the public.
   A. According to the Environmental Protection Agency, second-hand smoke causes 3,800 lung cancer deaths each year (Cowle, 1990, p. 59).
   B. Dr. Stanton Glantz has concluded that 30,000 to 40,000 heart disease deaths occur each year from second-hand smoke (Cowle, 1990, p. 59).
   C. Overall, Dr. Glantz concludes that 50,000 deaths occur each year from second-hand smoke (Cowle, 1990, p. 59).
      1. For every eight people who will die this year from the direct effects of smoking, 1 nonsmoker will die (Cowle, 1990, p. 59).
      2. Today 137 innocent bystanders will die from the effect of other people's smoke.

(**Signpost:** We cannot ignore this public-health problem when a solution is available, as I explain in my third point.)

Signposts are indicated by parentheses.

III. **Main point:** Smoking should be banned in public places.
   A. Airlines have already banned smoking on all domestic flights of 6 hours or less (Sharn & Walmer, 1990, p. 1A).
   B. Workplaces should be smoke-free.
   C. Restaurants and public buildings should be smoke-free.

(**Signpost:** to summarize . . .)

Conclusion

I. **Summarize:** Today I have shared three main ideas with you.
   A. The chemicals in cigarette smoke make it a health hazard.
   B. Second-hand smoke is a major cause of lung cancer and heart disease.
   C. Banning smoking in public places would save thousands of lives a year.
II. **Close with impact:** If people choose to smoke, that's their business, but when they choose to ignore the dictates of common decency it becomes my problem.

Conclusion begins with I, includes a summary, and closes with impact.

(continued) ➤

IN THEIR OWN WORDS

Sample Speech Outline (continued)

    A. Smokers are constantly crying about their rights.
    B. Smoking in closed, public spaces is not an issue of rights, it's an issue of health.
    C. And the last thing in the mind of the American tobacco industry is my health and yours.

References

References are listed alphabetically by author, using APA style, explained in Chapter 7.

Cowle, G. (1990, June 11). Second-hand smoke: Some grim news. Newsweek, 115 p. 59.

Koop, C. E. (1986). Preface. The health consequences of involuntary smoking: A report of the Surgeon General. Rockville, MD: U.S. Department of Health and Human Services (pp. ix-xii).

Sharn, L., and Walmer, T. (1990, February 21). Smoking grounded in USA. USA Today, p. 1A.

U.S. Department of Health and Human Services. (1989, October). Smoking tobacco and health: A fact book. DHHS Publication No. (CDC) 87-8397.

you should rehearse until you don't need to look at the note cards frequently. It is especially important to know your introduction and conclusion very well. The best open or close to a speech can be undone by a speaker who reads it from cards, rather than making direct eye contact with the audience.

Cards about 4 by 6 inches in size seem to work best. Larger cards are too obtrusive; smaller cards require you to strain to see your notes and to constantly be shuffling cards. The following are some helpful hints for preparing note cards.

Tips for Preparing Note Cards

- *Use bright colors and large, bold lettering.* This will make your notes easier to see.

- *Use no more than five or six lines per note card.* If you cram too much on one card, you'll end up confusing yourself.

- *Put each part of a speech on a separate card.* For example, your introduction might go on one card, the body on another, and the conclusion on a third. That way you won't have trouble finding your main points after you complete your introduction nor will you confuse your conclusion with a main point.

- *Number your cards.* It is easy to lose track of your place while speaking. One way to help prevent this from happening is to number each card. That way, even if you inadvertently get your cards out of order, you can quickly recover.

- *Write on only one side of a card.* If you try to write on both sides, you compound the chances of losing your place.

- *Highlight main ideas.* Just as you highlight key passages in books, highlight the points you wish to emphasize.

- *Use note cards to make comments to yourself.* It is perfectly appropriate, for example, to write prompts to yourself on your notes.

Speaker's notes should be easy to read and may include comments to yourself.

For example, you might write "O.H." to remind yourself to show an overhead at that point of your speech.

- *Don't try to write your speech out word for word.* This will only encourage you to read your speech, rather than present it in a conversational manner. The only exception to this rule would be exact quotations, facts, or statistics, which obviously you need to write out. It is best to keep lengthy quotations to a minimum in speeches, however, as they inevitably will lead to loss of eye contact with your audience.

Speaker's notes contain all the same ideas as the complete outline, but the words are designed to cue you to what comes next. Only with practice can you speak from these notes and still be assured of covering all the ideas in the original outline. And this is the final point we wish to make: Successful speakers practice prior to an actual presentation. No matter how good your organization seems, it is only as good as your ability to deliver it. That takes practice. And practice doesn't mean running through your speech the night before or, even worse, the morning of your presentation. It means devoting significant amounts of time to practicing your speech until you have internalized its basic organization.

SUMMARY

Organization is vital to effective public speaking. As with all aspects of speech making, you should focus on your audience when organizing your speech. A well-organized speech refines the specific purpose, which describes what you want to accomplish in your speech. Next, you must create a clear thesis statement, which captures the essence of your speech.

Organize the body of the speech before tackling the introduction or conclusion. Two to five focused main points should fully develop the thesis statement. Use parallel structure, simplicity, and balance to help your audience remember your main points. Develop main points by using subpoints, supporting points, and further support. Organize the speech body in one of several patterns: time, extended narrative, spatial, categorical, problem–solution, refutational, causal, or motivated sequence.

The introduction to a speech should have impact, should focus on the thesis statement, and should connect with the audience. Effective openings may include a brief story; quotation; startling statement; reference to the audience, the occasion, or a current event; appropriate humor; personal experience; or a thought-provoking question.

The conclusion to a speech should summarize the main points of the speech and close with impact. Ways to close include a quotation, a brief anecdote, a direct appeal to action, or a return to the opening theme.

You must effectively communicate the organization of a speech to the audience. A preview of the main points and effective signposts between points help the audience follow the organization.

A formal outline is sometimes required of beginning speakers. Many instructors prefer students to use standard outline notation and write a complete-sentence outline. Speaker's notes, usually placed on small cards, can be used when presenting the speech.

Check Your Understanding: Exercises and Activities

1. Consider the following speech introductions. Rewrite them to fit the model of open, focus, and connect suggested in this chapter.

   Today, I'm going to talk to you about pit bulls. I got attacked last week by a pit bull, and I think they are really dangerous. Something's got to be done!

   Have any of you ever thought about going snow boarding? I really like to snow board and that's what my speech is going to be about.

   I think capital punishment is wrong. What if somebody who was innocent got killed? I'm going to persuade all of you that life without parole is a better way to go.

2. View a speech on videotape (either the tape that accompanies this text or a tape of a well-known public speaker). If no tape is available, consult an audiotape or a printed transcript of a speech. Using the format described in this chapter, construct a complete-sentence outline of the speech. How closely did the speech seem to follow the steps indicated in the chapter? Was the speech easy to outline? If not, how could the speaker have made the organization clearer?

3. Analyze a print ad in a magazine or newspaper, to see whether it uses a problem–solution, causal, or motivated sequence. If so, explain how each step is fulfilled. If not, discuss how the ad might be modified to fit one of these organizational patterns.

4. On the following pages is an outline of a speech, followed by a list of points in scrambled order. Your task is to match up the appropriate sentence from the scrambled list with the points in the outline. This may be done as an individual or group exercise, depending on your instructor's preference.

Specific purpose: _____

Introduction

  I. Open with impact: _____

  II. Focus: _____

  III. Connect with your audience: _____

Body

(Preview:) _____

  I. Main point: _____

    A. _____

    B. _____

    C. _____

(Signpost:) _____

  II. Main point: _____

    A. _____

    B. _____

    C. _____

(Signpost:) _____

  III. Main point: _____

    A. _____

    B. _____

    C. _____

Conclusion

  I. Summarize: _____

    A. _____

    B. _____

    C. _____

  II. Close with impact: _____

Scrambled list:

1. Use fresh bread, preferably whole-grain.
2. Use a quality jelly or jam, made without artificial additives.
3. Use either plain or chunky peanut butter.
4. You must have the necessary ingredients.
5. Fold the wax paper neatly around the sandwich.
6. Place the sandwich in a paper bag.
7. Use biodegradable wrappers, such as wax paper, rather than plastic wrap.
8. You need to package the sandwich to take to school.
9. Put the two slices together.
10. Spread the first slice with peanut butter.
11. Spread the other slice with jelly or jam.
12. You need to assemble the sandwich.
13. To inform the class how to make a peanut butter and jelly sandwich.
14. First make sure you have the necessary ingredients.
15. Finally, wrap the sandwich.
16. Second, assemble the sandwich.
17. Enjoy your lunch and go to a movie with the money you've saved.
18. You can save money and eat better.
19. Today you will learn how to make the perfect peanut butter and jelly sandwich.
20. Are you tired of spending five dollars for a greasy hamburger and fries?
21. Making a peanut butter and jelly sandwich involves three basic steps: having the ingredients, assembling the sandwich, and packaging the sandwich.
22. After you have the ingredients, you need to make the sandwich.
23. Unless you are eating it immediately, the sandwich must be wrapped to stay fresh.
24. To review, there are three steps:

Notes

1. Alan Monroe, *Principles and Types of Speech* (New York: Scott, Foresman, 1935). See also the most recent edition: Bruce E. Gronbeck, Raymie E. McKerrow, Douglas Ehninger, and Alan H. Monroe, *Principles and Types of Speech Communication*, 12th ed. (New York: HarperCollins, 1994).

2. Deidra Dukes, "The Right to Breathe," speech delivered at California State University, Chico, 1992.

Coolio's Grammy award-winning song, "Gangstas in Paradise," was, contrary to its title, anti-gang and anti-violence.

9

Language
Making Verbal Sense of Your Message

How can I tell what I
think until I see what
I say?
—Edward Morgan
Forster[1]

OBJECTIVES

After reading this chapter, you should be able to:

- Construct examples that illustrate the relationship between language and thought.
- Describe the role language plays in relating to cultural, demographic, and individual diversity.
- Describe the "different voice" that characterizes women's and men's speech.
- Differentiate between denotative and connotative meaning.
- Use rhetorical devices such as metaphor and simile to vary language intensity in your speeches.
- Use concrete language, as well as contrast and action, to reduce uncertainty on the part of your audience.
- Use verbal immediacy and transitional devices in your speeches.
- Avoid marginalizing and totalizing language, using inclusive language instead.
- Avoid sexist and stereotypic language.

KEY CONCEPTS

competence-enhancing language
connotative meaning
denotative meaning
inclusive language
language intensity
linguistic relativity hypothesis

marginalizing language
sexist language
totalizing language
verbal immediacy
verbal qualifiers

257

Mary Shapiro and Thomas Donovan have always had a rocky relationship. Shapiro is chief of the Commodities Future Trading Commission, the federal agency that polices the volatile commodities market. Donovan is president of the Chicago Board of Trade, which promotes the busiest commodities exchange in the United States. When Shapiro learned that Donovan had told his board members during a closed-door meeting that he wouldn't be "intimidated by some blond, 5-foot 2-inch little girl," their relationship took a turn for the worse.[2]

To suggest that Shapiro was displeased about the content of Donovan's speech would be an understatement. She quickly let the financial press know that she wouldn't be bullied by people "lobbing verbal grenades through the window."[3] For the record, Shapiro added that she was also 5-feet, 5-inches tall and, at age 39, no longer a little girl.

This example points to an incontrovertible fact: Language is not neutral. The words we choose to express ourselves and to describe others can elicit the full range of human emotions. This chapter is about language and its role in giving meaning and impact to our ideas. It is also about the power of words and how they affect the way we think about ourselves, our experiences, and the people with whom we come into contact.

On one level, our goal in this chapter is to assist you in appreciating the larger role language plays in our lives. On another level, our goal is to show you how you can use your appreciation of language to construct messages that will be appropriate to both your speech's purpose and the audience with whom you share it. We'll explore the relationship between words and the objects they are meant to represent, how language influences experiences, how language relates to audience diversity, and how you can use language to enhance how you and your speech are perceived by your audience.

LANGUAGE, PERCEPTION, AND EXPERIENCE

Just as a map is not the territory it represents, a word is not the object it is intended to describe. Words are simply spoken sounds or written characters that symbolize or communicate meaning. People use them to refer to the persons, places, and things with which they come into contact. Their meaning depends on the set of experiences people associate with the words when they use, see, or hear them. This fact that meaning depends on experience applies to the members of your audience.

Words have a dramatic impact on the process of perception. When we are told something is "good" or "bad" before we see or experience it, we are likely to rate it the same way. In experiments where subjects have been shown pictures of people described as popular, the subjects rate them as highly attractive. Subjects who are told the same people are unpopular rate

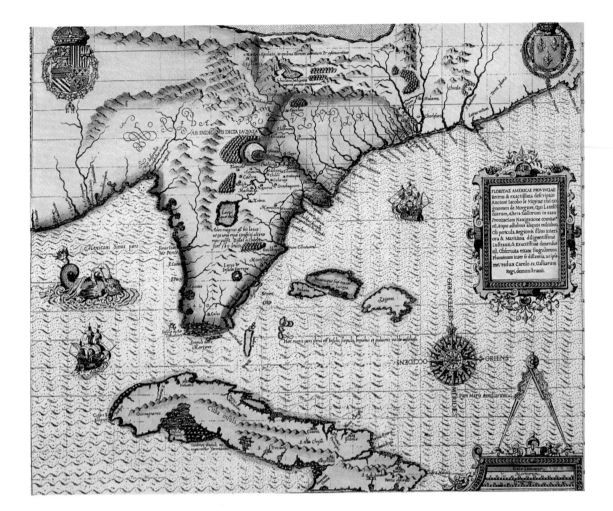

them as significantly less attractive. Thus, the words you choose when you speak will influence how your audience perceives your message.

What is true of individual words is even more true of the language one speaks. Whether you speak English, French, Spanish, or Russian makes a difference in how you experience the world. Just as perception influences the meaning assigned to words, language influences the meaning people assign to everything they experience. According to the **linguistic relativity hypothesis,** introduced over 40 years ago by cultural anthropologist Benjamin Whorf, what we perceive is limited by the language in which we think and speak. Different languages lead to different patterns of thought.[4]

Whorf formulated this hypothesis while studying the Native American language of the Hopi. He discovered there are no words in their language

A map represents a territory, but it is not always accurate as this sixteenth-century map shows.

Last year, people skied

on champagne powder,

windblown pack, groomed,

corn snow, cold smoke, frozen

granular, firm, good crud,

bottomless powder, sugar,

machine tilled, crust, hero

powder, buffed snow, man

made, corduroy, ball bearings,

velvet, cut up powder, spring

snow, ballroom, and acre

after acre of virgin powder.

[*Eskimos may have more words*

for snow, but we have more lifts.]

THE ASPENS
SNOWMASS • BUTTERMILK
ASPEN MOUNTAIN

Aspen Central Reservations 1·800·262·7736 Snowmass Central Reservations 1·800·332·3245.
The Aspen Skiing Company Hotels: The Little Nell, The Snowmass Club 1·800·525·6200.

This ad uses terms for snow that are meaningful to skiers and snow boarders. The language is unique to their sports and enhances the images that come to mind when they think about the cold white stuff that is simply "snow" to the rest of us.

for the concept of incremental time: no seconds, no minutes, and no hours. Thus, it would never occur to the Hopi that someone could be half an hour early or late for a visit, because they have no words for the concept.

Each language has certain concepts that cannot be easily expressed in other languages. Thus, the expression "something was lost in the translation" doesn't mean part of a statement was literally lost as it was translated from one language to another. It means an equivalent idea couldn't be found in the second language, so part of the statement's original meaning was diminished. In constructing a speech, the first thing you'll want to do is choose words and sentences that you believe will lead people to perceive and think about your speech as it is intended.

LANGUAGE AND AUDIENCE DIVERSITY

Having seen that words and language color our perception and experience, we now can examine the relationship between language and the three types

of diversity (cultural, demographic, and individual) introduced in Chapter 5. Understanding the connections between language and diversity is crucial to effective speaking, since today's audience is more diverse than ever.

Language and Cultural Diversity

When choosing language to construct your speech, you need to consider the *cultural diversity* in your audience. How you refer to people from a culture other than your own can either facilitate or undermine how you and your speech are perceived. Consider an informative speech given by an international student, Amin Nazur.

Amin called his speech "There's No Such Thing as an Arab." Amin wanted to show how people inaccurately used the word *Arab* in referring to Middle Easterners. "We are not Arabs," Amin pointed out, "but Jordanians, Kuwaitis, Palestinians, and Saudis. While we share much in common culturally," Amin went on to say, "there is no single, all-encompassing Arab culture. Arab culture is a creation of the Europeans." Amin was sharing a

Edward James Olmos' recent film, My Family, Mi Familia did an excellent job of showing how people who share the same culture use language differently depending on their generation.

lesson from which we can all learn. The fact that a word is commonly used in reference to a culture doesn't make it accurate. We need to go out of our way to ensure that we understand the cultural diversity so characteristic of today's speech transactions. At a minimum, this understanding means doing research on culturally appropriate language.

Language and Demographic Diversity

You will recall from Chapter 5 that *demographic diversity* is reflected in the groups to which people belong and with which they identify. This includes such characteristics as nationality, race and ethnicity, gender, and religion. Demographic diversity also includes social and economic class, the region of the country that people call home, and the generation to which people belong.

Demographic diversity, while always an important consideration of a speaker's audience analysis, has become even more so. Today's college classroom is likely to be populated by people with a variety of different demographic backgrounds. Race and ethnicity, as cases in point, are often an important part of today's audience diversity.

How you refer to a specific racial or ethnic group can have a strong impact on the individual members of that group in your audience. For example, when Anglos speak to a gathering of English-speaking people of Mexican descent, they need to choose the appropriate language in referring to the audience. Scholars Mario Garcia and Rodolfo Alvarez suggest that people of Mexican descent in the United States constitute several rather than a single demographic group.[5] Two such reference groups are Mexican Americans and Chicanos/Chicanas. The Mexican American group comprises people who immigrated from Mexico to border states, such as California and Texas, following World War II. According to Garcia and Alvarez people who consider themselves Mexican Americans are generally older and more conservative than those who identify themselves as Chicanos or Chicanas, who are generally younger and more militant.

Chicanos and Chicanas came of age in the 1960s and gained some attention in the 1970s. They perceived Mexican immigrants who wanted to assimilate with the predominant Anglo culture as sell-outs. To distinguish themselves from the Mexican American group, Chicanos and Chicanas adopted specific patterns of behaving, including their own code words. The list of code words included *vendido* (sell out) and *socios* (the old boy network). Today, members of this demographic group sometimes refer to each other as *veteranos* (veterans). Thus, referring to Chicanos/Chicanas as Mexican Americans in a speech would be inappropriate. As a speaker, you need to learn as much as possible about the language preferences of your audiences. Otherwise, you may inadvertently offend at least some of them.

The varied preferences of Spanish-speaking people are also true for many other demographic groups as well. Some African Americans prefer being referred to as black. And though they may be too polite to tell you so, the Chinese, Hmong, Japanese, Korean, Laotian, Taiwanese, and Vietnamese prefer being referred to by their nationality rather than being categorized as Asian.

As a speaker, you cannot afford to overlook the demography of your audience in choosing language. How you refer to people who identify themselves with specific demographic groups and the words you use in talking about the demographic groups themselves not only will influence how the content of your speech is received but audience perceptions of your credibility as well.

Language and Individual Diversity

Choosing appropriate language for a speech doesn't stop with a consideration of cultural and demographic diversity. You also must consider and evaluate *individual diversity*, which reflects such factors as personal views on the meaning of gender, sexual orientation, and religious beliefs. The fact that one is Catholic, Jewish, Muslim, Hindu, or Protestant, for example, doesn't tell you much about the diversity of beliefs held by people who consider themselves a member of one of these religions. Moreover, religious affiliation is only one element of the individual diversity of your audience. Consequently, before choosing the language with which you'll construct your speech, you also will have to explore the individual beliefs, attitudes, and values of the people in your audience.

As a case in point, think about an audience of people who describe themselves as Christians. Such people are extraordinarily diverse in what they believe individually. Some think the Bible is to be taken literally as the word of God; others believe the Bible should be interpreted metaphorically. Knowing this kind of information in advance is essential for speakers who want the language of their speech to be audience appropriate.

Remember, the words and sentences with which you construct your speech will influence the meaning of your speech in the minds of the audience members. You want to control this process as much as possible. Thus, doing your homework about the relationship between language and diversity as it reflects your speech transaction is a matter of common sense.

USING LANGUAGE EFFECTIVELY

Let's assume that you have thoroughly analyzed the speech situation, including how audience diversity should be reflected in your choice of words to construct your speech. You are now ready to begin writing the outline of your speech with language that will enhance your credibility with your audience and create a high degree of mutual understanding. There are a number of guidelines you will want to follow in this process. The first rule concerns choosing language that makes every member of your audience feel included in your message. This is known as inclusive language, as opposed to marginalizing or totalizing language, concepts we will explain shortly. The second rule concerns choosing language that will enhance rather than undermine audience perceptions of your competence as a speaker.[6] Finally, the third rule concerns using language to its fullest potential to involve your audience in your speech.

Use Inclusive Language

The first rule in choosing the words of your speech is to use language that is inclusive. **Inclusive language** helps people believe that they not only have a stake in matters of societal importance, but also have power in this regard. Inclusive language doesn't leave people out of the picture because of their gender, race, ethnicity, age, religion, sexual orientation, or ability. At the same time, however, it avoids defining people on the basis of such characteristics.

Remember the example with which we opened this chapter? Thomas Donovan, president of the Chicago Board of Trade, referred to Mary Shapiro, chief of the Commodities Future Trading Commission, as a "5-foot 2-inch little girl." Are his words an example of inclusive language? Of course not. His statement illustrates two types of language you'll want to avoid in constructing your speech. The first type is called *marginalizing*. The second type is called *totalizing*.

Marginalizing language diminishes people's importance and makes them appear to be less powerful, less significant, and less worthwhile than they are. Marginalizing language also appeals to biases audience members may hold consciously or subconsciously. When Thomas Donovan called Mary Shapiro a little girl, for example, his language was more than sexist or politically incorrect. He was using language to make Mary Shapiro appear a powerless child incapable of directing powerful adults like himself.

Totalizing language defines people on the basis of a single attribute, such as race, ethnicity, biological sex, or ability. In a speech, the following statements would exemplify totalizing:

"The disabled in this audience . . ."

"As a woman, you've got to learn to assert yourself."

"As a victim of racism . . ."

"Because you are Latino . . ."

"This is really a guy book."

"We, the People": Barbara Jordan

The late Congresswoman and scholar Barbara Jordan was one of the most impressive and eloquent speakers of the second half of the 20th century. Not only did she possess a powerful voice and impeccable diction, she used language in a way that few could match. Many compared her speeches to those of Winston Churchill and Franklin Roosevelt. Here is a brief excerpt of her statements during the debate on the impeachment of President Nixon in 1974:

We, the people. It is a very eloquent beginning. But when that document was completed on the 17th of September in 1787, I was not included in that "We, the people." I felt somehow for many years that George Washington and Alexander Hamilton just left me out by mistake. But through the process of amendment, interpretation and court decision I have finally been included in "We, the people."[1]

Two decades later, Jordan was asked to head the United States Commission on Immigration Reform. Testifying before

the very committee of which she was once a member, Jordan echoed her words from long ago:

I would be the last person to claim that our nation is perfect. But we have a kind of perfection in us because our founding principle is universal—that we are all created equal regardless of race, religion or national ancestry. When the Declaration of Independence was written, when the Constitution was adopted, when the Bill of Rights was added to it, they all applied almost exclusively to white men of Anglo-Saxon descent who owned property on the East Coast. They did not apply to me. I am female. I am black. But these self-evident principles apply to me now as they apply to everyone in this room.[2]

[1] "Barbara Jordan: A Passionate Voice," *Sacramento Bee*, 18 January 1996, A16.
[2] Jerelyn Eddings, "The Voice of Eloquent Thunder," *U.S. News and World Report*, 29 January 1996, 16.

Each of these statements could be well-meaning and intended to demonstrate the speaker's sensitivity to people with disabilities, women, Latinos, and men. Yet, what each statement does in reality is call attention to a single attribute among audience members and treat the attribute as if it were the only thing about audience members that truly counted. Disabled people are more than their disability, women and men are more than their biological sex, and people discriminated against by racists are more than simply victims. Speakers need to use language that acknowledges that people are complex individuals. The late Barbara Jordan spoke eloquently of the need to include *all* people in our vision of America (see the box "'We, the People': Barbara Jordan").

Use Competence-Enhancing Language

A number of researchers have documented that there is a difference between "powerful" and "powerless" speech.[7] Powerless speech is characterized by the use of language such as hedges (I *kind of* agree with you), qualifiers (I *could* be wrong), hesitations (uhs and ums) and tag questions (That's right, *isn't it?*). On the other hand, powerful speech is fluent and direct and avoids these types of phrases. Messages containing a significant amount of powerless language produce lower ratings of communicator power, attractiveness, and competence, whereas powerful speech produces higher ratings on these dimensions.

Therefore, the second rule to follow in constructing the text of your speech is to use powerful, **competence-enhancing language,** words that emphasize rather than undermine audience perceptions of your competence. Language that enhances perceptions of competence avoids verbal qualifiers.[8] **Verbal qualifiers** erode the impact of what you say in a speech.

Beginning speakers often use verbal qualifiers without thinking of them as such. They say, for example:

"It's just my opinion, but . . ."

"You'll probably disagree, but . . ."

"This is my belief, but you may think otherwise."

"I'm pretty sure, though I could be wrong in stating . . ."

"Of course, your opinion counts at least as much as mine."

Competence-enhancing language emphasizes the significance of what you say in a speech. Whether giving an informative, persuasive, or testimonial speech you should be the expert on the subject or person. Not only does this require that you do your homework, it also requires you to choose language that illustrates the fact. Using language such as the following is one way of accomplishing this without appearing to be a "know-it-all" to your audience.

"Ten years of research demonstrates that . . ."

"For the past four summers, I've been involved with . . ."

"As a lifelong member in the United States, . . ."

"Scholars tell us . . ."

Each of these statements begins with a phrase that emphasizes the speaker's competence. They imply that through either research or experience, the speaker knows his or her subject well. You should not exaggerate your claims beyond what you know to be true, but you should take full credit for the facts as you know them.

Use Language to Its Fullest Potential

The third and final rule is to use language to its fullest potential in your speeches. There are many ways to do this. The ones we encourage you to use involve denotative and connotative meaning, grammar, pronunciation, uncertainty reduction, immediacy, and expressiveness.

Denotative and Connotative Meaning Words have two general types of meaning.[9] The first is **denotative meaning,** which is the generally agreed upon meaning for a word that you find in a dictionary. The second is **connotative meaning,** which is a secondary meaning, usually carrying an attitudinal or emotional component. This meaning will depend on the speech situation and the composition of your audience. Under most circumstances a speech will include words with both types of meaning. On occasion, though, a speaker may choose to emphasize words he or she believes are high in one or the other types of meaning.

In a speech before a group of people who speak English as a second language, for example, speakers will want to use words in a manner consistent with their denotative meaning. This is because the audience probably will translate words literally rather than figuratively. Imagine the difficulty non-native speakers of American-style English would have in translating a statement such as "How many of you have lived with a roommate who bogarts the phone?" Their only reference for the word *bogart* (hoard or fail to share) might be Humphrey Bogart, the star of classic films such as *Casablanca* and *The African Queen.*

On occasion, however, speakers may want to use words that have special meaning to the context in which the speech will take place and to the audience members who will share in the transaction. In a creative writing class, for instance, the instructor wants to encourage people to think about how they can evoke multiple images in the minds of readers. Thus, the teacher might ask class members to rewrite the sentence "The sky is blue" so that it will stimulate the readers' imagination. As a result, students might write, "The azure sky on a cloudless day" or "The sky had turned to the color of blue ice."

The point is that as a speaker, you need to think in advance about the denotative and connotative meanings of the words with which you construct your speech. Don't leave the issue to chance or assume that your audience will "know what you mean" when you use a word.

Grammar In the effort to use language to its fullest potential, speakers need to consider the rules of grammar. Some common mistakes are double negatives, incorrect subject–verb agreement, and inappropriate slang.

A double negative occurs when someone uses a negative to modify another negative. As in mathematics, a negative times a negative is actually a

Common Irritants Grate on the Ears

DEAR READERS:

I recently wrote a column on the misuse of words, grammatical goofs and assorted speech irritants, and invited my readers to send me their pet peeves concerning same. Well, here's Collection No. 2:

The most annoying speech irritant is still all those "you knows?" and a close second is beginning every sentence with "basically." People who say, "I could care less" mean to convey that they care so little they could *not* care less—which is what they should have said in the first place.

Most people, even those in the jewelry business, pronounce "jewelry" as "jool-ree" instead of "jool-uh-ree."

And many people in the real estate business pronounce "Realtor" as "reel-a-tor"; it's "reel-tor," really it is.

If you think "epitome" means the ultimate, the tops or the height of—go stand in the corner. "Epitome" means a person or thing that is typical of, or possesses to a high degree the features of a whole class.

The word "arthritis" is correctly pronounced "arth-right-us" (three syllables); so why do so many people insist on pronouncing it "arthur-ri-tis"? The same for the word "athlete"—not "ath-a-leet."

My pet peeve is the lawyer or journalist who uses the word "gentleman" as follows: "According to the police report, a masked gentleman knocked the elderly woman to the ground and fled with her purse." (Some gentleman!)

The word "nauseous" is often misused, even by well-educated professionals, instead of the word "nauseated." Here's a way to remember the distinction: If you are nauseated, you are sick. If you are nauseous, you make other people sick.

Regardless of what you read in the ads, "Where it's at" is incorrect. "Where it is" is correct. Forget "at."

positive. Thus, "No one never works around here" really means that there is no person who "never works." That suggests people really do work, the opposite of what the speaker intended.

Incorrect subject–verb agreement occurs when a plural subject is matched with a singular verb or vice versa. Thus, you want to avoid such sentences as, "We is going to the movies."

Finally, unless they are essential to the speech, certain expressions common in everyday conversation are inappropriate in a speech. Many speech teachers object in particular to the overuse of "you know" and "like." It is irritating to hear, "You know, like, I really mean it."

This is far from a complete list of grammatical pitfalls for the speaker. And speech is not as formal as written English. Although you are not supposed to end a sentence with a preposition, it is not uncommon to hear

Do you know what an asterisk is? Of course you do. It's the little starlike symbol used in print to indicate the omission of letters or words. But why do most people pronounce it "ass-trick"?

The confusion with "lie" and "lay" is still baffling to many. I explained that people lie down and chickens lay eggs. A reader now informs me, "People lay money on the counter, dogs lie by the fire, and magazines are found lying on the table. All last summer, I lay in my hammock and didn't produce a single egg."

Prominent newscasters have said "most unique" and "partially destroyed." "Unique" and "destroyed" are absolute terms and cannot be qualified, any more than "pregnant" or "dead."

Please do not confuse "momento" and "memento." A momento is a unit of time (Spanish: "uno momento"). A memento is a souvenir, a memory.

Finally, the misplaced "only" is a common gaffe. For example, the one-time popular song, "I Only Have Eyes for You" is meant to say, "I have eyes for you only." For a lover to croon, "I only have eyes for you," is to say: "I have no lips, no arms or anything else—only eyes—for you," which would be a grave disappointment for both of them.

Never say, "It's a true fact." If it's a fact, it's true. Also forget "old antique." If it's an antique—it's old.

In closing, for heaven's sake—never say, "for heaven's sakes." Some people do, so for heaven's sake, watch your language. And if you have a pet peeve I haven't mentioned, please send it to me.

someone in a speech say, "I know what it's all about." The best advice we can give is that if you are in doubt about any grammatical issues, consult someone who is knowledgeable and ask his or her advice or check a grammar handbook, such as Strunk and White's *Elements of Style*.

Pronunciation   Anyone who thinks pronunciation doesn't count is sorely mistaken. Every time we hear someone say "nukular" instead of "nuclear" or "ex-scape" instead of "escape" we grit our teeth. And as the box "Common Irritants Grate on the Ears," a reprint of a Dear Abby column, so well illustrates, we aren't the only ones who react negatively to mispronounced words. However, even Dear Abby can get it wrong. She suggests that *jewelry* should be pronounced "jool-uh-ree." If you check your dictionary, you'll discover that she has misplaced the "l." The proper pronunciation is "joo-uhl-ree." Perhaps that's worth 10 lashes with a wet noodle.

Mispronunciation of words can lead to a number of problems. Two of the most significant involve meaning and how you are perceived. Frequently, for example, people say "assure" when they mean "ensure." Assuring your child that she is safe is not the same as ensuring the safety of your child. *Assure* and *ensure* mean two different things. Mispronouncing words may also lead audience members to form an unfavorable impression of you. Although saying "I'd like to go wid' chew" may be acceptable in conversations with friends, it won't enhance your credibility in the eyes of most audience members.

Uncertainty Reduction   You'll also want to choose language for your speeches that reduces feelings of uncertainty among audience members. Uncertainty-reducing language is concrete rather than relative and ambiguous, varies in its level of intensity, invites contrasts and makes use of words that suggest action, and makes effective use of signposts. Although there are exceptions, people prefer messages that reduce rather than increase uncertainty, whether the message is meant to inform people about a problem-solving strategy, teach them about principles of accounting, or alleviate their fears about catching a deadly disease.[10]

Concrete Language   Language that is concrete is less likely to increase audience uncertainty than language that is ambiguous or relative. The more concrete language is, the less the listener has to mentally stretch to understand it. The word *cat*, for example, is less concrete than the phrase "blue-eyed, long-haired Persian cat." The word *cat* requires us to come up with our own image of a cat. The phrase supplies us, at the least, with a specific kind of cat with which to build a mental image.

Ambiguous words generally are abstract. As a result, how audience members interpret them depends largely on their individual experience. Consider the word *pornography.* As we know all too well, what one person considers a work of art another person may dismiss as filth. To simply describe something as a piece of pornography, then, takes control of the meaning of the word out of the hands of a speaker and puts it in the hands of individual audience members. Relative words, such as *pure* and *a lot* suffer from the same problem. What is pure to you may not be pure to us. And while one person may think 10 is "a lot," another may think it's "a little." The more ambiguous or relative your language is, the more likely your speech will have an effect other than what you intended. Use concrete language as much as possible.

Language Intensity   A second suggestion for reducing uncertainty is to vary the intensity of your language as you speak. **Language intensity** is the degree to which words and phrases deviate from neutral. The intensity of the words we use varies along a continuum ranging from relatively neutral to highly intense. For example, "savory and delicious" is more intense than "tastes good." By the same token, a phrase such as "I find you attractive" is not nearly as intense as a phrase such as "I wanna rock your world."

Care needs to be exercised to avoid words so intense they may cause people to react negatively—to turn off to what we are trying to say in a speech. Language that is threatening or highly fear arousing, for example, tends to turn people off. So does language generally regarded as obscene or off-color.

Contrast and Action A third way you can reduce uncertainty is to use contrasting phrases and words that suggest action. In discussing the irrationality that often grips the minds of people when going to war, German philosopher Friedrich Nietzsche wrote, "How good . . . bad music and bad reasons sound when we march against the enemy."[11] Nietzsche's simple contrast between good and bad is much more effective in making war seem illogical than any extended discussion would have been. And this would have been especially true had Nietzsche delivered the line in a speech.

As you know from your own experience, public speaking is ill suited to extended and convoluted language. The simpler and more active your language, the better. Thus, when Bill Clinton's 1992 campaign slogan was "The economy, stupid," everyone understood what he meant. On the other hand, when First Lady Hillary Rodham Clinton tried to explain her health-care reform proposal, the ideas were so complex that few people understood what she meant.

Try to use words that are exciting and action-oriented. For example, which do you find more involving, "The speech was well received" or "The speech was a 10"? What about "He got mad" versus "He went ballistic"? To hear examples of action words, listen to sportscaster John Madden. His speech is liberally sprinkled with action words such as "whack," "annihilate," and "wham."

Signposts The fourth and final technique you can use to reduce audience uncertainty is to make effective use of signposts, which we introduced in Chapter 8. We've repeatedly emphasized how important it is to let your audience know where you are going with your speech. You know from your own experience taking lecture notes that it's much easier to follow an instructor who uses verbal signposts that alert you to changes in direction or clearly link one thought to another. You need to do the same for the members of your audience.

Signposts are transitional words and phrases, such as those listed in Table 9.1 on page 273, that tell your audience you are about to make or already have made a shift in direction. Signposts also serve to verbally link

John Madden's use of action words has made him a fixture as a sports announcer.

your thoughts as you speak. It's always a good idea to let your audience know that there is a sequence to your message—"Let's consider three important issues"—and then to remind your audience where you are in that sequence—"Having covered the first issue, let's now look at the second."

It's also a good idea to let your audience know that your speech is close to the end by using transitional words and phrases such as "finally," "in sum," "in conclusion," and "to close." Far too many times we've watched audiences guess whether they're hearing the end of the speech; the sign of their uncertainty is premature clapping.

Immediacy A sage once said that speakers need to recognize that there's a fine line between teaching and preaching to an audience. When you teach, you involve your audience as co-participants in the transaction. Immediate language is more likely to encourage this feeling than is language that emphasizes "I'm up here and you're down there."

Verbal immediacy is the use of language that promotes the perception of closeness between speaker and audience. Words high in immediacy suggest closeness between people and imply that a speech is a transaction

TABLE 9.1 Transitional Words and Their Functions

Adding a point:	furthermore, besides, finally, in addition to
Emphasis:	above all, indeed, in fact, in other words, most important
Time:	then, afterwards, eventually, next, immediately, meanwhile, previously, already, often, since then, now, later, usually
Cause and effect:	consequently, as a result, therefore, thus
Examples:	for example, for instance
Progression:	first, second, third, furthermore
Contrast:	but, however, in contrast, instead, nevertheless, on the contrary, on the other hand, though, still, unfortunately
Conclusions:	therefore, to sum up, in brief, in general, in short, for these reasons, in retrospect, finally, in conclusion

SOURCE: E. Hughes, J. Silverman, and D. R. Wienbroer, *Rules of Thumb* (New York: McGraw-Hill, 1990), 99. Reprinted with permission of McGraw-Hill.

between one person and many people, rather than a one-sided event in which one speaks *to* people.[12]

Some evidence suggests that women are more inclined to use immediate language than are men. Psychology professor Carol Gilligan suggests in her ground-breaking book, *In a Different Voice,* that women tend to think in terms of "we" whereas men tend to think in terms of "me."[13] The words women typically choose to express themselves reflect their more immediate, "we" orientation. The words men often choose, on the other hand, reflect their less immediate orientation, creating unnecessary and not always desirable distance between themselves and their audience. As a general rule of thumb, speakers should try not only to think in terms of "we" but also to avoid using the pronoun "I."

Another way speakers can increase immediacy is to phrase assertions in the form of questions. For example, instead of saying, "I think," it's more immediate to say, "Wouldn't you agree?" Along the same lines, instead of saying, "I'm going to tell you," it's much more immediate to say, "Let's look at . . ." Table 9.2 on page 274 compares less and more immediate ways of using language.

Expressiveness Finally, good speaking demands expressive language that keeps an audience involved with the transaction. This kind of language includes traditional rhetorical devices, such as metaphor, simile, alliteration, parallel structure, and repetition.

Metaphor is one of the most powerful sources of expressive language. A metaphor is a figure of speech in which a word or phrase literally denoting one kind of object or idea is used in place of another to *suggest* a likeness

TABLE 9.2 How to Say it More Immediately

Less immediate	More immediate
I Me You Them	We Us
I think It's my opinion I know	Wouldn't you agree? How many of us believe . . . ?
Tell Show Explain	Share Look at
Talk from	Talk between

or an analogy between them. It's one thing, for example, to say that a corporation is "polluting the environment." It's quite another to say that the same corporation is "raping virgin timberland." To say that "freedom is an open window" or that "music unshackles the mind and spirit" would be metaphorical. Metaphors provide an audience with a kind of linguistic break from the expected. Thus, just when audience members may be losing interest in a speech, a phrase or word can grab them by the lapels.

Simile is a form of figurative language that invites a direct comparison between two things that are quite different. A simile usually contains the words *like* or *as.* "Sharp as a tack," "tight as a snare drum," and "pointed as an ice pick" are examples of simile. Similes can be used effectively to vary the intensity of your speech.

Alliteration is the repetition of the same initial sound in a series of words. Jesse Jackson is famous for using alliteration to make his speeches more expressive and memorable. Instead of saying, "People need to be given a purpose," for example, Jackson might say, "Empower people with pride, and purpose is sure to follow."

Parallel structure is the use of the same structure for each main point of your speech. It provides a way to help your audience remember your key points and at the same time serves as a verbal cue that you are presenting a main point. For example, when John F. Kennedy ran for president, he used the phrase "I am not satisfied . . . we can do better" to highlight each of his major criticisms of the Republican administration.

Repetition is the use of the same words repeatedly in a speech to drive home a point. Martin Luther King, Jr., is perhaps best remembered for his

"I Have a Dream" speech. The speech derives its name from the repetition of the phrase "I have a dream" throughout the speech.

Use Visual, Kinesthetic, and Auditory Involvement

Not all people process information in the same way. Research shows that some people need to see a lesson, others need only to hear it, and still others need to become immersed in the subject matter. These three styles of learning are technically called *visual, auditory,* and *kinesthetic.* The obvious way for a speaker to deal with these three is to augment a speech with visual aids, speak audibly and clearly, or involve the audience in demonstrations or other hands-on experiences. Yet, sometimes options one and three are impossible for a speaker.

To get around this fact, author and corporate trainer Loretta Malandro encourages her clients to connect metaphorically with the varied learning styles present in most audiences. Table 9.3 on page 276 gives a number of specific visual, auditory, and kinesthetic words that help your audience better process your speech.

Although you may not be able to literally "show" your audience members prejudice, you can connect with visual learners by

- asking them to envision a world free of hate,
- drawing a picture of racism or sketching out an example for them, or
- making a hazy concept such as affirmative action crystal clear so that they can see the problem.

Although you may not be able to let them literally "feel" your thoughts, you can connect with audience members who need to experience some things by asking them to imagine

- what racism feels like,
- a problem as a giant weight pressing down on them, or
- how oppressed people hunger for freedom.

And though you may not be able to literally produce the "sound" of abused children for your audience members, you can connect to auditory learners by asking them

- whether they hear what you're trying to say,
- to imagine what it's like to live in a world where people are silent about injustice, or
- to imagine the cacophonous sound of the competing voices in Congress.

TABLE 9.3 Words Linked to Vision, Hearing, and Touch

Visual words

Focus	Graphic	Watch	Colorful
Bright	Illustrate	Vision	Glimpse
Show	Color	Brilliant	Look
Pretty	See	Evident	Sight
Envision	Picture	Sketch	Shining
Draw	Hazy	Oversight	Hidden
View	Peek	Clearly	Notice
Clear	Imagine	Perspective	

Auditory words

Listen	Ringing	Compliment	Pardon
Hear	Resonate	Loud	Sound
Discuss	Yell	Silent	Request
Declare	Told	Shout	Whispering
Implore	Call	Talk	Quiet
Acclaim	Assert	Noisy	Ask
Harmony	Profess	Orchestrate	
Petition	Noise	Address	

Kinesthetic words

Feel	Terrified	Hunger	Contact
Pressure	Burdensome	Doubt	Nurture
Hurt	Firm	Shocking	Emotion
Get the point	Tense	Heavy	Graceful
Experience	Touchy	Touch	Sensual
Longing	Pushy	Concrete	Weighty
Wait	Shatter	Irritated	problem

SOURCE: Excerpted from: *Twentieth Century Selling.* © Dr. Loretta Malandro. Taught in her program "Speak With Impact," offered by Malandro Communication Inc., Scottsdale, Arizona.

The point is simple. Not everyone in your audience will respond in a like manner to the words you speak. Thus, to maximize audience members' receptivity to what you say, you must make every effort to use expressive words that reflect their different styles of information processing.

In this section we have discussed a number of guidelines for the effective use of language. They are summarized in the list that follows.

Guidelines for Using Language Effectively

- Use language that includes all members of your audience. Avoid language that marginalizes or excludes some people. Also avoid language that defines people by a single attribute, such as a disability.

- Use language that enhances your audience's perception of your competence. Avoid language that undermines their confidence in you.

- Take advantage of all the potential inherent in language. Choose words carefully, with your audience in mind. Use correct grammar and pronunciation. Make your audience comfortable—reduce their uncertainty—by using concrete words, by varying the intensity of the words you choose, by using contrasting and action-oriented words, and by using signposts to signal where you are in your speech. Use language that makes your audience feel closer to you, rather than more distant. Finally, involve your audience by using rhetorical devices to make your language more expressive.

- Connect with the different styles of processing information that the members of your audience may have. Use visual, auditory, and kinesthetic words to help them process your speech.

USING LANGUAGE APPROPRIATELY

We conclude this chapter with a discussion of two issues that are not so much a matter of right and wrong but, rather, of rhetorical sensitivity. The use of language appropriate to your rhetorical situation is not just a matter of effectiveness; it is also one of being ethically sensitive to the detrimental effects stereotypic and biased language can have on people. We look at two specific types of problems caused by inappropriate language; first, the use of language that stereotypes people; second, the use of language that stereotypes people on the basis of their biological sex.

Avoid Stereotypes

Do you see anything wrong with the following references?

"John's a victim of cystic fibrosis."

"Don't forget that Susan's wheelchair bound!"

"It's okay, Lupe, there's plenty of disabled seating in the new auditorium."

"The Howards' baby is physically challenged."

According to the Disabled Student Services on our campus, each of these statements is constructed with inappropriate language. If you're surprised, then please know that so were we. We've heard terms like *victim of* and *physically challenged* used by people in all walks of life, including student speakers.

The fact that we think we know what constitutes appropriate language doesn't excuse us from researching the subject. Language is dynamic and in a continuous process of change. What's more, words such as *victim* or terms such as *wheelchair bound* once were acceptable. Today, however, people with disabilities are defining their own terms on their own grounds. Further, in doing so, those with disabilities have said they prefer the following descriptors to the first set we listed for you.

"John has cystic fibrosis."

"Don't forget that Susan's in a wheelchair."

"It's okay, Lupe; there's plenty of seating in the new auditorium for people in wheelchairs."

"The Howards' baby has a disability."

Thus, we want to remind you of the old adage "It's better to remain silent and be thought a fool than to open your mouth and prove it." When in doubt about words and their consequences, consult an authority. If that's not possible, then when in doubt about a word leave it out.

Of course, it is not just people with disabilities who are stereotyped. People in different professions, of different ethnicities, and different sexual orientations, to name just a few categories, are frequently the subject of stereotypic language. The speaker who is sensitive to language avoids such stereotypes. One particular type of stereotype deserves discussion in its own right, sexist language.

Avoid Sexist Language

Sexist language is language that stereotypes gender roles, for example, *housewife* and *fireman*. Why is sexist language a problem? Because it conveys, intentionally or not, a stereotype of certain roles and functions, based on sex. When the head of an academic department is referred to as a chair-*man,* a member of the U.S. House of Representatives is called a Congress*man,* and a flight attendant on an airplane is known as a steward*ess,* it is clear which roles are held to be "male" and which ones "female. As a communication professor explains in the box "Sexist Language: Dr. Madeline Keaveney," these stereotypes have a damaging effect, particularly on women and girls. Thus, a sensitive public speaker needs to avoid sexist language.

One of the easiest ways to unintentionally convey sexism is to use singular pronouns in the masculine form. For years, speakers and writers ex-

Sexist Language: Dr. Madeline Keaveney

Dr. Madeline Keaveney regularly teaches a class on the subject of communication and gender and has written widely on the topic as well. Her comments here should further your understanding of the importance of the language you choose when you speak.

Sexism, which is discrimination based on biological sex, permeates our language. Pronoun usage, generic and occupational terms, even common metaphors suggest that men and men's experiences are valued more than women and women's experiences. Given that codification and standardization of our language occurred during an era when women were absent from the public sphere, such sexism in language should not be surprising. People took for granted that man was the norm or model for all humans, and few individuals were bothered by the fact that "man" paradoxically referred to both human males and all human beings.

So, why change sexist language practices? Because they damage girls and

women. Numerous studies have conclusively demonstrated that when girls think about policemen or read about prehistoric man, they do not see themselves. Girls and women see themselves only when the language used to describe their concerns or activities clearly includes them.

Just as girls and women were not validated by textbooks that excluded women's experiences and contributions, so, too, women and girls are not included when language substantively or linguistically ignores them. Publishers have attempted to redress textbook deficiencies by more directly addressing the experiences and concerns of both males and females. Changes in language usage can have the same positive benefits. Insisting on nonsexist language usage will add to advances made by girls and women in other aspects of society. If girls/boys and women/men are to be encouraged to reach their full potentials, they must see themselves fully and fairly reflected in the language we all use to communicate with one another.

cluded women from their examples involving a single person, saying such things as,

"If a person is strong, he will stand up for himself."

"When someone believes something, he shouldn't be afraid to say so."

"An individual should keep his promise."

If you have no other choice in constructing examples to illustrate your speech, you can do one of two things with regard to singular pronouns. First, you can say "he or she" in conjunction with a singular verb. Second, you can use "she" in some cases and "he" in others. Yet both of these alternatives are awkward, and neither is likely to please everyone in your audience. Thus, we suggest a third alternative: Use plural nouns and pronouns when constructing examples to make your speech more vivid, involving, and inclusive. Instead of saying, "If a person is strong, he will stand up for himself," say "Strong people stand up for themselves." Instead of saying, "When someone believes something, he shouldn't be afraid to say so," try, "When people believe something, they shouldn't be afraid to say so." And instead of saying, "An individual should keep his promise," simply say, "People should keep their promises."

SUMMARY

Language is central to effective speaking. The words that make up language are symbols of the objects they are meant to describe. Words influence the process of perception. Language not only influences perception but the process of thinking as well, as expressed in the linguistic relativity hypothesis. The language of a speech should reflect the cultural, demographic, and individual diversity characteristic of today's audiences. Consequently, the language of a speech should be inclusive rather than marginalizing or totalizing. Language should be appropriate and nonsexist.

To make full use of language, speakers should use competence-enhancing language, which means eliminating unnecessary verbal qualifiers. Using language effectively also involves differentiating between denotative and connotative meaning and using words that reduce uncertainty. To make their speech vivid, speakers should use rhetorical devices such as metaphor, simile, alliteration, parallel structure, and repetition. Effective speaking also demands sound grammar and correct pronunciation. In addition, the language of a speech should connect metaphorically with the varied learning styles present in most audiences. Finally, speakers should choose appropriate language. Special care should be taken to avoid stereotypic and sexist language.

Check Your Understanding: Exercises and Activities

1. Rewrite the following paragraph using inclusive language:

    When a speaker begins his speech, the first thing he must do is thank the chairman of the group for the opportunity to speak to his group. As we know, the quality that separates man from the animals is the ability to speak. Regardless of his job, a man must know how to speak clearly. Similarly, a woman must know how to impart language skills to her children. Thus, every speaker is urged to use language to the best of his ability.

2. Write five transitional statements (signposts) without using the following words:

   first (second, third, etc.)

   therefore

   next

   finally

   in conclusion

3. Company X has an internal policies manual that is written in marginalizing language. As an employee of the company, you find the language disturbing and believe the language in the manual should be changed. Write a letter to the head of the documents division explaining why you believe such changes are necessary and why you believe the changes will enhance the image of the company. (Thanks to Dr. Madeline Keaveney for suggesting this exercise.)

4. Exclusive language is marginalizing and biased. Provide an inclusive-language alternative for each of the following, or state under what conditions the term might be appropriately used in a speech. (Adapted from Rosalie Maggio, *The Bias-Free Word Finder: A Dictionary of Nondiscriminatory Language* (Boston: Beacon Press, 1991).)

   actress

   airline stewardess

   businessman

   craftsmanship

   doorman

   executrix

   goddess

   meter maid

   mother

   majorette

   Mrs. John Doe

   old wives' tale

   waitress

Notes

1. W. H. Auden and L. Kronenberger, *The Viking Book of Aphorisms* (New York: Dorsett Press, 1981), 238.

2. "This Boss Is No Girl, She's Just Stunned," The Sacramento Bee, 10 October 1995, C2.

3. "This Boss Is No Girl," C2.

4. Benjamin Lee Whorf, *Language, Thought, and Reality* (New York: Wiley, 1956).

5. Earl Shorris, *Latinos: A Biography of the People* (New York: Norton, 1992), 95–100.

6. Julia T. Wood, ed., *Gendered Relationships* (Mountain View, Calif.: Mayfield, 1996), 39–56.

7. See, for example: W. M. O'Barr, *Linguistic Evidence: Language, Power, and Strategy in the Courtroom* (New York: Academic Press, 1982); James J. Bradac and Anthony Mulac, "A Molecular View of Powerful and Powerless Speech Styles: Attributional Consequences of Specific Language Features and Communication Intentions," *Communication Monographs* 51 (1984): 307–19.

8. H. Giles and J. Wiemann, "Language, Social Comparison, and Power," in *Handbook of Communication Science*, ed. C. R. Berger and S. H. Chaffee, (Newbury Park, Calif.: Sage, 1987).

9. Tom McArthur, ed., *Oxford Companion to the English Language* (Oxford: Oxford University Press, 1992).

10. Charles R. Berger and R. J. Calabrese, "Some Explorations in Initial Interaction and Beyond: Toward a Developmental Theory of Interpersonal Communication," *Human Communication Research* 1 (1975): 99–112.

11. Auden and Kronenberger, *The Viking Book of Aphorisms*, 359.

12. L. A. Malandro, L. Barker, and D. A. Barker, *Nonverbal Communication*, 2nd ed. (New York: Random House, 1989).

13. Carol Gilligan, *In a Different Voice* (Cambridge, Mass.: Harvard University Press, 1982).

How you say
something may be
as important as
what you say.

10

Delivery

Engaging Your Audience Nonverbally

OBJECTIVES

After reading this chapter, you should be able to:

- Define nonverbal behavior and distinguish between verbal and nonverbal behavior.
- Describe the relationship between delivery and the eight basic dimensions of the nonverbal system.
- Display nonverbal behaviors characteristic of effective delivery, including control of the speaking environment, proper attire, eye contact and expressive facial cues, vocal variation in pitch, range, rhythm, and tempo, clear and distinct vocal articulation, and gestures and movements that serve as emblems, illustrators, and regulators.
- Control distracting self-adaptive behaviors.
- Use time to enhance your credibility and communicate urgency, drama, humor, and the like during your speech.
- Explain the guidelines for developing a proactive, rather than reactive, delivery.
- Display nonverbal examples of complementing, contradicting, and repeating the message; substituting for a verbal cue; increasing the perception of immediacy; exciting the audience; and delivering a powerful speech.

KEY CONCEPTS

delivery

emblem

environment

illustrators

nonverbal behavior

proactive delivery

regulators

self-adapting behaviors

zone of interaction

285

People often pre-sume much about a person based on nonverbal behavior, even though they shouldn't.

Diana Griego Erwin is a syndicated newspaper columnist who writes about everyday experiences, including lessons she's learned from her day-to-day encounters with people. In a recent column, Erwin related a lesson about the degree to which you can read a person based on nonverbal behavior. She recounts how a teenage boy boarded the commuter train on which she and her young daughter were riding:

> He looked nervous, and that is what scared me. . . . If a director needed a jit-tery type for a movie such as "Speed," this is the guy they would cast. By the time he sat down, beads of sweat had popped up on his nose and brow, and he pulled at one side of the black and red woolen cap he wore. He'd look over his shoulder, then look outside. In the space of about 30 seconds, he adjusted his coat twice.[2]

Erwin continues in this vein and tells the reader that she not only was frightened by the boy's appearance and "suspicious" behavior but also was prepared to protect herself should the boy move on her and her daughter.

Then Erwin reveals the rest of the story. Just before the next stop, Erwin says,

> The boy-man looked frantically outside. Just before [the train] stopped, he looked at me; made eye contact. "Will you save these seats?" he asked.
>
> He hurried to the doorway where a bent, aging woman struggled to climb the stairs.... He took her arm to help her. "Grandma," he said, "I worried the whole time we split up. I never should have let you talk me into leaving you there like that."[3]

All of us are at least a little like columnist Diana Griego Erwin. We presume much about a person based on nonverbal behavior, even though we probably shouldn't. The same also is true of speakers and audiences encountering each other for the first time.

This chapter focuses on the relationship between nonverbal behavior and delivery of a speech. The chapter is designed to complement the previous chapter's discussion of the role language plays in constructing your message. Audiences will arrive at conclusions, both right and wrong, about you on the basis of your nonverbal delivery. Our goal is to show you how you can shape nonverbal behavior to your advantage. We begin by looking at ways of focusing your delivery on your audience and the rhetorical situation you face. We next focus on the differences between verbal behavior, or the content component of your message, and nonverbal behavior, which is the relational component of your message. Then we discuss the interdependent dimensions that define the overall nonverbal system, and demonstrate the functional role these dimensions play collectively in the effective delivery of your speech.

VIDEO FILE

If you have access to the videotape that accompanies this book, view segment 7, which shows the ways nonverbal communication can function in the delivery of a speech.

FOCUSING YOUR DELIVERY ON YOUR AUDIENCE

Never forget that public speaking is a transaction between you and your audience. Just as the language you choose for your message should reflect the nature of your audience, so too should your delivery. As a result, we begin our discussion with some audience-related factors you will want to consider while thinking about the delivery of your message. Specifically, we discuss choosing an appropriate method of delivery, adapting to diverse audiences, and adapting delivery to the speech occasion.

Choosing an Appropriate Method of Delivery

Recall from Chapter 2 that there is more than one way to deliver a speech. We discussed four different methods of delivery. As you review your analysis of your audience and rhetorical situation, one of your most important decisions will be an appropriate method of speech delivery.

Manuscript Delivery   As you'll recall from Chapter 2, manuscript delivery involves writing out the speech completely and reading it to the audience. This method may be the best choice when your audience requires precise information from you. When you are speaking about highly technical matters before a group of engineers, for example, the precision with which you deliver the information may be extremely important. Similarly, if you expect your words to be quoted by others, having a manuscript of your speech helps ensure accuracy.

Anytime you use a manuscript, however, the dynamics of delivery are restricted. As we show later in this chapter, eye contact, movement, and gesture are important dimensions of nonverbal behavior that may enhance your delivery. Tying yourself to a manuscript interferes with each of these. Manuscript speaking also impedes spontaneity between you and your audience because the manuscript restricts opportunities to survey and creatively respond to audience feedback. Further, a manuscript demands a lectern, which can stand as a barrier between a speaker and the audience. Finally, this method of delivery can sound stilted and artificial because the language of a written message generally is more formal than spoken language.

If you must utilize a manuscript, therefore, learn it well. Practice repeatedly so that you do not have to look down often. Mark up your manuscript with notes to yourself and underline main ideas. Also, be sure pages are numbered so that they will not get out of order. Use a large typeface and double or even triple spacing. Manuscript speaking is far more difficult than most people realize. Its success depends on practice and skill in converting words on a page into a living speech.

Memorized Delivery   A speaker using memorized delivery writes out the speech and commits it to memory before presenting it to the audience without the use of notes. Most audiences don't expect a memorized speech, unless they are watching a professional speaker who is highly paid, an actor delivering a soliloquy in a play, or a student competing in a speech tournament. In fact, in a typical speech class, an obviously memorized speech would probably strike most students and the instructor as odd. Although memorization allows you to concentrate on eye contact, movement, and gesture, it does so at a price. You may forget parts of your speech and it requires a greater investment of time than any other method.

When writing a speech to be memorized, keep the organization simple so that you will not confuse one point with another. A good rule of thumb is to memorize it in small chunks. Learn a paragraph, then move on to the next one, and so on. Practice reciting your speech from the beginning through as far as you have it memorized. The repetition of earlier parts will help fix them in your mind. Finally, don't panic if you forget a part of the speech. Try to ad-lib for a bit and often the next section will come to mind.

Impromptu Delivery   Impromptu delivery is a spontaneous, unrehearsed method of presenting a speech. Usually, these short speeches are given in response to someone who asks you to say a few words, make a toast, or respond to an inquiry. Although an audience is always appreciative of an eloquent impromptu speech, an organized and confidently spoken message is normally enough to fulfill any audience's expectations.

Impromptu speaking frees you from any impediments to using the full range of nonverbal behaviors available to speakers, but you are most likely so busy concentrating on what you are going to say that you ignore delivery. Thus, impromptu delivery is not as effective as the next method we will discuss in using the full range of nonverbal behaviors available to you as a speaker. If you are likely to be called on to speak in an impromptu fashion, consult Chapter 15 where we discuss this type of speech in more detail.

Extemporaneous Delivery   For most students who are still learning to give a speech, extemporaneous speaking remains their best choice of delivery method. Recall from Chapter 2 that extemporaneous delivery combines careful preparation with spontaneous speaking. The speaker generally uses brief notes rather than a manuscript or an outline. Extemporaneous speaking enables you to maintain eye contact, move, gesture, and spontaneously adapt to audience feedback. You may choose not to use a lectern, depending on how extensive your notes are and how comfortable you are moving freely before the audience.

Today's audiences are more likely to expect and appreciate the extemporaneously delivered speech than other methods of delivery. Just as it allows the speaker to remain in contact with the audience, so does it allow the audience to remain connected to the speaker. Audiences not only can give feedback to someone speaking extemporaneously but also can assess the degree with which their feedback registers with the speaker.

This doesn't mean that extemporaneous speaking is without drawbacks. Note cards can restrict the range of gestures used when you refer to them, and they can also be distracting when waved about while you're speaking. Finally, you can get carried away with note cards, writing down so many of your thoughts that the note cards become almost a manuscript.

Delivering Speeches to Diverse Audiences

Both the method and style of delivery should reflect the diversity of your audience. Throughout this chapter we offer numerous specific examples of cases in which a particular nonverbal behavior means one thing to one culture and something entirely different to another. For example, consider how three different audiences might respond to the same speech. As you speak, a North American audience returns your eye contact and nods in agreement with you. A British audience also returns your eye contact, but heads remain motionless. And a West African audience avoids making direct eye contact with you altogether. What should you make of their feedback in each condition? Before you decide, perhaps it would help to know this: When the British agree with a speaker, they sometimes blink rather than nod their head. Further, the more direct the eye contact of West Africans, the less they respect the person to whom it is directed. Knowing the typical patterns of nonverbal behavior in a given culture is essential if you are to accurately interpret the nonverbal behaviors of your audience members.

Another example of differences among culturally diverse audiences concerns your voice. Almost from birth, the norm for the North American culture is "to speak up and let yourself be heard." What is normative here, however, may be loud in Japan or among the upper class in Great Britain. And much as we may want to be heard, we don't want to be perceived as loudmouths.

Adapting Delivery to the Speech Occasion

Last, how you present your speech depends on the specific rhetorical situation you face and the kind of delivery your audience is likely to expect. A speech commemorating or honoring a person calls for a formal and dignified delivery. Other speech situations call for an energetic, dynamic delivery. A motivational speaker, for example, usually dispenses with the lectern and moves about the stage, perhaps even into the audience. A lively style is expected and rewarded. Then there are situations that call for a lighthearted, comic style of delivery. For example, "roasts" honoring someone often are punctuated with good-natured joking at the honoree's expense. Unlike a commemorative speech, a delivery at a "roast" should be informal and lively. The key is to understand what the audience expects in a given situation and match your delivery style to those expectations.

CHARACTERISTICS OF NONVERBAL BEHAVIOR

Delivery involves the nonverbal behaviors by which a speaker conveys his or her message to an audience. Delivery is what brings mere words to life in the public speaking transaction. **Nonverbal behavior** is a wordless system of communicating. What makes a behavior nonverbal as opposed to verbal? Is it the absence of sound? That cannot be the case, since sign language is considered a form of verbal communication, with signs merely substituting for written or spoken language. Although scholars argue about the exact definition of nonverbal behavior, most agree that it is distinct from verbal behavior in at least three ways: It is continuous, uses multiple channels simultaneously, and is spontaneous.

The Continuous Nature of Nonverbal Behavior

Verbal behavior, composed of words, is discrete. This means verbal behavior can be divided into distinct elements, as was the case when you first began to learn about nouns, verbs, and adjectives. These elements of composition are governed by complex rules, dictating how they should be combined in your speech to form phrases, clauses, and sentences. Each word has a denotative meaning that can be found in the dictionary. Words must be arranged in a precise manner to convey the intended meaning. For example, the words "I am happy" must be arranged in that order to convey the intended meaning. To say, "Am I happy" changes the statement to a question. To say "Happy am I" seems odd to English speakers. When words with agreed-on meaning are used in a specified order, the meaning of the verbal behavior is apparent as in this example. This is not so with nonverbal behavior, which is continuous rather than divisible.[4]

Consider the expression of happiness as you speak. What the audience sees is a complex message that involves the entire face. The muscles of the face contract, affecting the eyebrows, the corners of the mouth, and the corners of the eyes. Unlike verbal behavior, these involuntary movements cannot be broken down into compositional elements. The eyes, for example, do not convey "I," while the eyebrows say "am" and the mouth represents "happy." You cannot rearrange the components to convey a different meaning, as you can with "I," "am," and "happy." There are no rules of grammar to explain the meaning conveyed by these facial expressions. Only the total, continuous combination of these elements can constitute the nonverbal expression of happiness.

The Simultaneous Use of Multiple Channels

Returning to the example of expressing happiness, nonverbal behavior also involves the simultaneous use of multiple channels.[5] For example, try conveying an emotional expression, such as happiness, anger, sorrow, or bewilderment, through a single channel of communication, for example, your mouth or eyes or hands. You'll soon see that it is difficult if not impossible. At the same time, you'll recognize that we use these multiple channels simultaneously rather than sequentially. When happy, we express the emotion all over our face, not with our eyes first, mouth second, eyebrows and forehead third and fourth.

The Spontaneous Nature of Nonverbal Behavior

As each of the preceding characteristics might lead you to believe, the final distinguishing characteristic is that nonverbal behavior is spontaneous. With the possible exception of so-called Freudian slips, when people unintentionally say what they really mean, verbal behavior is planned behavior.[6] We consciously think about the words we speak and write, though we do so with such speed it may not occur to us.

Smiles, gestures, and body language occur at a subconscious level. This doesn't mean that people never plan or orchestrate gestures when they speak. Sometimes they do, and their nonverbal behavior is likely to look phony. Most of us learn to distinguish between authentic and phony nonverbal behaviors by the time we reach our teens. Unless nonverbal behavior is rehearsed to the point it becomes habit, therefore, planned gestures especially will be recognized as insincere. This is a major reason for people putting so much stock in the meaning they infer from nonverbal behavior.

THE NONVERBAL COMMUNICATION SYSTEM

A system is a collection of interdependent and interrelated components. A change in one component will produce changes in them all. The nonverbal system has as its components several interdependent dimensions of behavior that profoundly affect the delivery of a speech. The specific dimensions we discuss in this section are the environment, appearance, the face and eyes, the voice, gestures and movement, posture, touch, and time. As a speaker intent on delivering a message effectively, you need to approach these dimensions systematically. Further, the verbal language with which you construct your speech should take into account what you've learned from your systematic assessment of the nonverbal dimensions.

The Environment

For our purposes, **environment** refers to our physical surroundings as we speak and the physical distance separating us from our audience. Both our surroundings and our physical space have an undeniable impact not only on our delivery but also on how the speech is perceived by our audience.

The physical characteristics of the room in which you speak—for example, lighting, temperature, comfort, and aesthetics—will influence both you and your audience physically and psychologically.[7] A bright, aesthetically neutral room, which is neither sterile nor plushly decorated, and in which the temperature is 68 degrees will have a much different overall impact on the speech transaction than a room that is dimly lit, richly furnished, and 75 degrees. Whereas in the first both you and your audience are likely to be alert and attentive, the second might prove so comfortable that neither you nor your audience are sufficiently aroused for your transaction. Thus, you would have to plan your delivery accordingly. Whereas your "normal" pattern of delivery probably would be appropriate in the

Informal situations such as this one invite a conversational delivery style.

first environment, you probably would need to put extra energy and enthusiasm into the delivery to succeed in the second.

A second environmental consideration is the physical layout of the room. We have been in situations where student presentations were hindered by pillars supporting the roof, by the width and length of the room, and by immovable objects such as tables. Sometimes you have no alternative but to do the best you can in such situations. As a result, you move more than you had planned as you speak, abandon visual aids that would prove impossible for your entire audience to see, or make gestures larger and more exaggerated than is customary for you.

At other times, however, you will have the opportunity to physically arrange the room in which you will speak. This may include the position of a lectern, elevation of a stage, and configuration of an audience. Given this opportunity, experienced speakers will arrange the environment in concert with their style of delivery. Speakers who have a traditional style of delivery may prefer a lectern, perhaps an overhead projector immediately to their side, and an elevated stage from which to speak. Speakers who are much less formal in their style of delivery may want the room to be arranged so that they can move from side to side or even up and down its length.

Both the traditional and informal styles of delivery can be equally effective. However, the room layout consistent with the traditional style is more restrictive than its counterpart in two ways. The first way concerns

FIGURE 10.1
Zone of interaction in the traditional room setting. Where people are seated in rows and the speaker is stationary, eye contact between speaker and audience is limited to the shaded area.

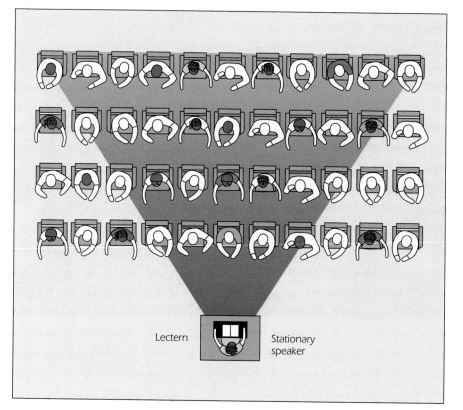

Lectern   Stationary speaker

the **zone of interaction,** the area in which speakers can easily make eye contact with audience members (Figure 10.1). The second way concerns the amount of space physically separating speakers from their audience.

The zone of interaction is limited to the range of your peripheral vision. The immediate zone of interaction between speakers and their audience diminishes as a room gets larger. To compensate for this fact, speakers have two choices. Either they can shift the zone of interaction by looking from side to side or they can physically move from one point to another when they deliver their speeches. This latter choice is illustrated in Figure 10.2. Obviously, in a very large room the traditional style of delivery limits you to looking from side to side in the attempt to shift the zone of interaction. This means that you cannot help but ignore part of your audience part of the time.

The traditional style of delivery allows less flexibility in manipulating the physical distance separating speakers from their audiences. Whereas a speaker who moves about the room can reduce or increase distance physically as well as psychologically, a relatively stationary speaker is restricted

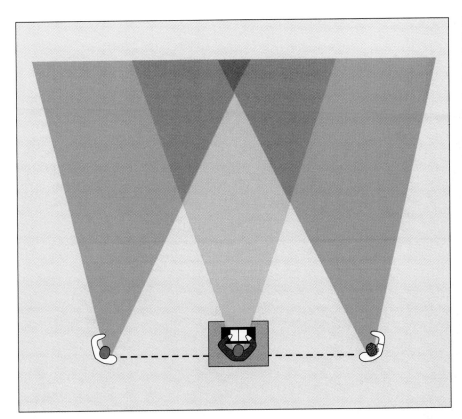

FIGURE 10.2
Shifting the zone of interaction with movement. Changing positions can increase the perception of inclusiveness as well as add energy to your speech.

to the latter. Thus, for those who prefer this style of delivery, eye contact becomes their primary agent for managing how immediate they are perceived to be by their audience, a point which we discuss shortly.

To summarize: The relationship of the speaking environment to delivery is a significant one. Not only does it influence your style of delivery, it also influences how you are perceived by your audience. Experienced public speakers try to plan the delivery of their speeches accordingly. When faced with a "tough room," for example, they know that the arousal level of their delivery will need to increase if they are to reach their audience. Inexperienced speakers, on the other hand, all too often play "victim" to their speaking environment. Instead of surveying and planning for the environment, they simply deliver their speech as if the environment were of no consequence to them. As a student of public speaking, you know what's good and bad about the layout of the classroom in which you must speak. Thus, you too should plan your delivery accordingly. The box "Seating Arrangements" on page 296 discusses another factor you should consider when planning your delivery.

SPEAKING OF . . .

Seating Arrangements

Can the physical seating arrangement have an impact on both your speech and the manner in which it is perceived? A very dramatic one. As a result, you should think about your goals as a speaker and the physical layout of the room in which you speak. Traditional rows will focus attention exclusively on you. A horseshoe arrangement, however, allows audience members to make eye contact with each other. And speaking at the head of a conference table not only narrows the zone of interaction but also puts a physical barrier between you and your audience. Which of these arrangements do you think would most likely encourage audience feedback and participation? Why?

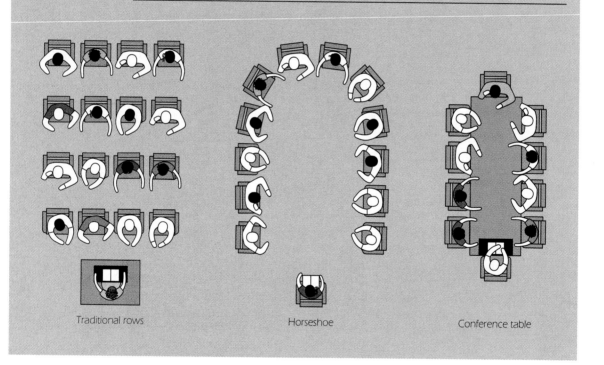

Traditional rows   Horseshoe   Conference table

Appearance

Appearance often has a disproportionately significant effect on audience perceptions of a speaker's message and delivery.[8] Speakers never get a second chance to make a first impression with an audience. First impressions largely are based on appearance, including body type and height, skin and hair color, and clothing and accessories.

The significance of appearance to public speaking can be measured in at least two ways. The first involves audience members' first impressions. The second involves how people perceive themselves as a result of their appearance and the impact this perception has on their self-confidence and delivery.

According to communication expert Dale Leathers, "Our visible self functions to communicate a constellation of meanings which define who we are and what we are apt to become in the eyes of others."[9] These "others" are the people with whom we come into contact, including the members of our audiences.

Audience members use appearance to initially make judgments about a speaker's level of attractiveness. The consequences of this judgment are far-reaching for speakers. Research tells us that speakers perceived as attractive by audience members also are perceived as smart, successful, sociable, and self-confident. As a result, speakers who fall into this category enjoy an audience whose initial impression of them is favorable.

Yet appearance influences more than an audience's initial impression of a speaker. Appearance also can have a very real effect on a speaker's self-confidence. Research tells us that speakers who feel they appear attractive report greater self-confidence than those reporting otherwise.[10]

Although some facets of your appearance and their impact on audience perception are outside your control—for example, body type and height—there is one facet you can easily control: your dress. Simply said, your dress should be appropriate to the situation. Obvious as this advice may seem, it is frequently ignored by students in public speaking classes. All too often they show up to speak dressed as if they had thought little about the appropriateness of their attire. Their attitude, as reflected in their dress, seems to be saying, "It's just a speech class."

Consider an analogy. Good students know what the research suggests about the relationship between the appearance of a term paper and the mark it receives. Frequently, it's the difference between a minus or a plus in their grade. Good students, therefore, go to some length to make sure that their papers not only conform to the requirements but "look" impressive as well.

The same relationship may exist between appearance and the marks students receive on their speeches. Although an Armani suit may not turn a mediocre speech into an outstanding one, it certainly won't cause the speaker to lose points. Although inappropriate attire or careless grooming will never add points to a speech, moreover, there is a chance they will unnecessarily detract from such things as the speaker's perceived competence.

The Face and Eyes

In the previous chapter, we advised that in your speeches you use immediate language, that is, language that promotes the perception of "closeness" between you and your audience. We pointed out that immediate language can reduce the undesirable feelings of distance sometimes separating speakers from audiences. Immediate language also can lead people to regard you as friendly and approachable, stimulating, open to dialogue, and personable. What is true of immediate language is even more true of nonverbal behavior. The face and eyes are very useful in communicating friendliness to an audience and reducing undesirable feelings of distance between the speaker and audience.

Yet making the delivery of your speech more immediate is only one of the roles the face and eyes play in enhancing your delivery. The face and eyes, for example, can communicate happiness, surprise, fear, anger, disgust, contempt, sadness, and interest. The face and eyes also can modify the intensity of any of these nonverbal expressions of emotion.[11]

Just as we can use rhetorical devices such as metaphor to manipulate language intensity, we can use the face and eyes to intensify our delivery. In most cases, we intensify what we say in this manner with little or no conscious thought. As we grow angry, for example, the muscles in our face tense and our eyes narrow spontaneously. The purveyor of bad news can make things even worse by accentuating it with the face and eyes.

You also can use your face and eyes to neutralize the message you deliver. Based on an analysis of your rhetorical situation, you may know that at least some members of the audience will disagree with your views. Suppose you are in a class situation that requires you to deliver a persuasive speech. If your topic is a truly controversial one, you can reasonably predict that not everyone in your audience will agree with everything you say. Although you may not be able to win them over, you also don't want to alienate them. As a result, you may want to use your face and eyes to neutralize some of the more contentious and evocative points you wish to make.

In a sense, what we give an audience in our face and eyes will determine what we can expect to get back from our audience. Thus, an intensely worded argument accompanied by the delivery of an equally intense message in the face and eyes invites the same from those who differ with us. On the other hand, using the face and eyes to neutralize the message improves your chance of a more favorable response from your audience.

This brings us to eye contact, specifically. In the North American culture, eye contact is perceived as a specific message. Speakers who are respectful, trustworthy, friendly, and interested in our well-being make eye contact with us. What's more, the best speakers don't simply make eye contact with the audience, but with individual members of the audience as they deliver their speech. This makes it appear to the audience member that he or she is engaged in dialogue with the speaker.

Remember, though, this kind of eye contact is a North American norm, not a universal one. In many cultures, the focus and sustained eye contact North Americans expect would be frowned upon. Such eye contact is viewed

Can you identify the meaning of these different facial expressions?

by members of many Asian cultures, for example, as rude and even hostile. As both a speaker and an audience member, you should keep this in mind. As a speaker, recognize that when international students appear uncomfortable with or don't return your attempts to make eye contact, it may be the result of their culture. As an audience member, realize that your expectancies about eye contact may be at odds with the norms of the international student who is speaking.[12]

The Voice

Try reading out loud this familiar nursery rhyme under three different conditions. In the first condition, your goal is to make your audience sad. In the second, your goal is to make your audience happy. And in the third, your goal is to make your audience anxious about the well-being of the characters.

> Mary had a little lamb,
> Its fleece was white as snow;
> And everywhere that Mary went,
> The lamb was sure to go.

Much of the emotional impact of your delivery is conveyed in your voice.[13] Consider an emotion such as excitement. We've heard many speakers unconvincingly tell an audience that they were excited about both their topic and the opportunity to speak. What betrayed their true feelings was not their language, but the absence of appropriate emotion in their voice.

To suggest that we can use our voices in a number of ways to enhance the delivery of our speeches would be an understatement. Drama, irony, sarcasm, and urgency are but a few of the emotions we can convey vocally.

To gain maximal control of your voice you need to know two things: the mechanics of the voice, and the importance of finding your own voice rather than imitating the voice of someone else.

Vocal Production   The production of sound in the voice is fairly straightforward. We take in air and expel the air through the trachea across our vocal cords, which are contained in the larynx, and then across our teeth, tongue, and lips (Figure 10.3). Variations in the amount of air expelled, the positioning of the vocal cords, or the placement of the teeth and tongue and position of lips will result in variations in the sounds we produce. Shallow breathing and the rapid expulsion of air across the vocal cords, for example, will produce a much different sound than breathing deeply and then slowly expelling the air. In the first case, your voice is likely to be described as feminine and in the second masculine, even though neither is necessarily true. The placement of tongue and shape of lips affect how sounds are articulated. The mechanical operation of the voice is not as important to our purpose as are the mechanical characteristics of the voice. These include volume, pitch, range, rhythm, tempo, and articulation.

Volume   Volume is how loudly you project your voice. It is a consequence of both the amount of air you expel when speaking and the force with which you expel it. Some examples of people with "big" voices, capable of speaking with great volume, are singer Bette Midler, conservative broadcaster Rush Limbaugh, actor James Earl Jones, and the late congresswoman

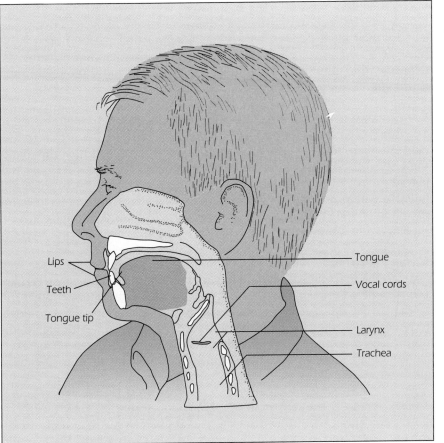

FIGURE 10.3
Physiology of the
voice.

and distinguished professor Barbara Jordan. Some people, on the other hand, are naturally soft-spoken.

As a public speaker, you need to have enough volume to be heard by your audience. Too soft a voice will simply not be heard. On the other hand, shouting at the top of your lungs can turn off your audience. The key is to speak loudly enough to be heard, while not speaking too loudly for the room. Of course, if you have the use of a microphone, you can be heard even if you speak relatively softly. It is also useful to vary your volume during the speech, using either an increase or decrease in volume as a means of emphasis. If the entire speech is delivered at the same volume, nothing will stand out as most important.

Pitch Pitch refers to the degree our voices are high or low. A person who sings bass has a low pitch, whereas a person who sings soprano has a high pitch. The pitch of blues singer B. B. King's voice is low, whereas the pitch of heavy-metal rock star Axl Rose's voice is relatively high. Effective speakers vary their pitch during their speech. One must be careful, however, because an excitable voice can often assume a higher-than-normal pitch. At the same time, one should not attempt to artificially alter the pitch, since it will appear unnatural and may strain the voice.

Range   Range is the extent of the pitch, from low to high, that lies within a person's vocal capacity. Just as a piano, for example, has a tremendous range in pitch, some speakers have a great vocal range. On the other hand, some speakers are like an electric bass guitar, which no matter how well played, does not have much range. As a speaker, you need to make the fullest use of your normal conversational vocal range. Raising or lowering the pitch of your voice can emphasize a particular word or phrase in your speech. Avoid a monotone delivery, which can lull your audience to sleep.

Rhythm   Rhythm is extremely important to the delivery of your speech. It involves the characteristic pattern of your volume, pitch, and range. Perhaps you have heard someone describe a speaker's voice as "singsong." What this means is that the speaker's voice is consistently going up and then down in pitch in a predictable and sometimes irritating pattern. Although variation in the rhythm of your voice is certainly to be encouraged, the exact pattern of variation shouldn't be completely predictable as your speech begins to unfold.

Tempo   Tempo is the rate at which you produce sounds. How quickly or slowly you speak will influence how you are perceived. Tempo also tends to vary across and even within cultures. In the Deep South, for example, tempo is relatively slow. In the East, tempo is accelerated. This is readily apparent if you compare the tempo of Southern actress Holly Hunter's delivery with that of Eastern actress Marisa Tomei.

Because tempo varies, you have to use good judgment in terms of how quickly or slowly you speak. Doing either to the extreme can turn off your audience. An excessively rapid pace can be perceived as a sign of nervousness. An excessively slow pace may suggest a speaker is not well prepared. Researchers have found that moderate to fast rates of speaking tend to be associated with increased perceptions of a speaker's competence on the part of the audience.[14] Other researchers have noted a ceiling to that effect, however, meaning that too fast a rate of speaking can backfire.[15] In addition, when audiences perceive speech rates as similar to their own, they are more likely to find the speaker socially attractive and to comply with his or her requests.[16] The best advice, therefore, is to moderately vary your tempo. Not only will this accommodate the different preferences of individuals in your audience, it also will enhance the overall effect of your message.

Your tempo is also affected by pauses. Sometimes a brief moment of silence can convey a lot to an audience. Pausing just before delivering the crucial word or phrase helps grab the audience's attention. Pausing after you've made an important point gives it time to sink in. Don't be afraid to use pauses when appropriate. It is better to pause a moment than to fill the air with "ums," "uhs," and "you knows," which are really "vocalized pauses."

Articulation   Articulation refers to the distinctness with which we make individual sounds. We've all experienced the frustration of listening to someone who sounds "mushy," failing to distinctly vocalize sounds. A common articulation problem comes from either running together differing sounds or dropping parts of a word: "goin' " instead of "going," "wanna" instead of "want to," or "whatcha doin'?" in place of "what are you doing?" If you expect an audience to understand what you are saying, you need clear articulation. A good way to test your articulation is to tape-record your speech and listen critically to yourself. If you find a consistent articulation problem or set of problems, you may want to find out if your college or university offers a course in voice and articulation. Sometimes drama or theatre departments have courses in voice for performers that can also be of assistance. Severe articulation problems are often best treated by a speech pathologist. But for most students in public speaking classes, exercising care, practicing, and slowing down are the keys to being understood by the audience.

In the final analysis, judgments about the relationship between the qualities of your voice and the quality of your delivery will depend on the preceding characteristics operating in concert. Important as pitch or tempo may be on their own, it is their collective impact with range and rhythm that most counts.

Finding Your Own Voice   With this in mind, let's now turn to your voice specifically. Are you pleased with the way it sounds and complements your overall delivery? No matter how you answered this question, it is just as important for you to find your own voice as a speaker as it is for authors to find their own voice when they write. We mention this need to find your own voice with good reason. When public speaking students are advised to make better use of their voice in their delivery, all too often they take this to mean they must change their voice to some ideal. The ideal, moreover, is usually thought to be the voice of a television or radio personality.

We don't encourage you to imitate the vocal delivery of someone who hosts a game show, reads the news, or introduces music videos. Instead, we encourage you to experiment with your voice; for example, record your attempts to convey varying emotions in your voice, listen to yourself, and then repeat the process. This kind of exercise will let you hear what your vocal strengths and weaknesses are. In the process, be realistic but not un-fairly harsh about how you think you sound. Chances are, what you think you hear is much different than what others hear.

Finally, recognize that important as it is, your voice is but a single non-verbal component of your overall delivery. Not all good speakers have tremendous "pipes." For example, Ricki Lake's and Geraldo Rivera's voices may be interesting, but they would hardly be described as rich in timbre. Further, if you were to listen to a number of paid speakers, you would see that this is the case. All of us tend to underutilize the full potential of our voices. What ultimately counts, then, is whether we're willing to do the hard work necessary to rectify this fact. If you think something about your voice needs to be changed, see the box "Tips for Improving Your Voice."

Gestures and Movement

You've heard the expression "different strokes for different folks?" Nowhere is it more applicable than it is to the subject of gestures and movement rel-ative to delivery. Although Ronald Reagan neither moved nor gestured very much when he spoke, he was a consummate public speaker. And though you practically have to nail the Reverend Jesse Jackson's feet to the floor to keep him from moving, he too is a public speaker of notable achievement. Thus, before we say a single word about how much or how little you should gesture or move as you speak, we want to say this: Your gestures and your movements as you grow as a public speaker should be a refined reflection of what you do naturally.

As is the case with the face and eyes, gestures and movements also can be used to intensify or lessen the emotional impact of our verbal messages. Many gestures, for instance, serve as affect displays; that is, they visibly communicate feelings. Placing both hands near the heart at the same time we explain how important a subject is to us is an example. So too are clenched fists, open palms held face up, or lightly slapping the side of the face.

Given the preceding caveat, gesturing and moving can complement your delivery in several ways.[17] These include making your delivery more emblematic, making your delivery more illustrative, and regulating the speech transaction.

Emblems   The speeches of the best public speakers are usually rich in em-blems. An **emblem** is a nonverbal behavior that can be directly translated into words and phrases and may replace them.[18] For example, Winston Churchill's "V" was an emblem for victory. Thus, emblems must meet the following criteria:

1. The emblem means something specific to the audience members.

SPEAKING OF . . .

Tips for Improving Your Voice

Like it or not, people will make judgments about you on the basis of the way you sound. George Bush, for example, was criticized for sounding "shrill" near the end of the presidential campaign in 1992. Evidently, this meant he was beginning to sound desperate—which is not the way an incumbent president wants to be perceived. On the other hand, Bill Clinton so overused his voice that it became hoarse and raspy. Near the end of the campaign, Hillary Rodham Clinton was forced to speak for her husband, because he had completely lost his voice.

Although we want you to be comfortable with your voice, the following tips may help you if you think something about your voice needs to be changed.

- *Relaxation:* More than one problem with voice can be solved by monitoring tension in your vocal apparatus. Nasality, shrillness, or screeching, and excessive rate of speech

often are a consequence of tension/stress. The same relaxation techniques discussed in Chapter 3 can therefore be used to alleviate the impact of tension/stress on your voice.

- *Vocal variation:* Tape-record yourself or have someone tape you when you speak. If you find as a result of monitoring your audiotape that greater vocal variation is needed, pick out someone whose vocal characteristics you admire and repeatedly listen to the person. Then try to model the vocal variation in which the person engages. Repeat this process while using a tape recorder.

- *Being heard:* Have a friend monitor your speaking volume. When you speak too softly, tell your friend to raise an index finger within your view. Use this signal to increase the volume of your voice. The goal is to be easily heard, even in the back of the room.

---

2. The emblem is used intentionally by the speaker to stimulate meaning.

3. The emblem can be easily translated into a few words.

Gestures are defined by the culture in which they are learned. As a case in point, when Richard Nixon was vice president to Dwight Eisenhower, Nixon incited an embarrassing protest while deplaning at a South American airport. He greeted the crowd with arms outstretched above his head, the thumb and first finger of each hand joined together in what North Americans take to mean "A-OK." In many South American countries, however, this nonverbal emblem was then synonymous with what we call "giving the finger" or "flipping someone off."

Late-night talk show host Jay Leno uses a gesture to illustrate his verbal message.

Illustrators **Illustrators** are nonverbal behaviors that accompany speech and "show" what is being talked about. Although a lot like emblems, they are more general and seldom translate into a few words. The most common way we nonverbally illustrate is with our hands. Verbal directions or descriptions beg for the use of our hands. Try giving someone directions or describing an object—say, a spiral staircase—without using your hands.

At the beginning of the semester, we usually ask a student to describe the shapes in Figure 10.4 to other students without showing them or using their hands to illustrate the shapes. Students listening attempt to reproduce the shapes on paper. Not only do both groups find the task next to impossible, most also consider it frustrating.

Regulators **Regulators** are gestures that influence the amount and type of feedback received from the audience. If you hold up your hand when asking audience members whether they've ever felt frustrated waiting in line, for example, you are much more likely to prompt them to raise their hands as well. If you are stationary throughout a speech, your audience will give you much different feedback than if you were to move and periodically change the zone of interaction. Using gestures and movement to regulate feedback, however, requires planning and rehearsal. An unplanned or inappropriate gesture or specific movement may elicit a response from the audience that you hadn't expected.

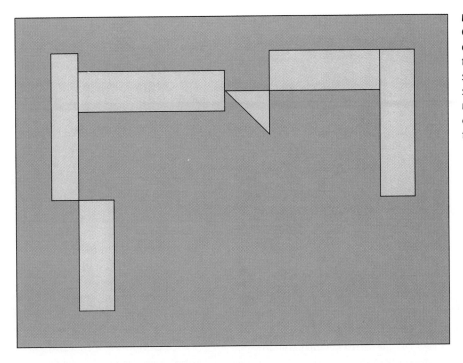

FIGURE 10.4
Can you instruct a classmate on how to draw an identical set of geometric shapes without using nonverbal expressions or referring back to the figure itself?

Regulating audience feedback is particularly important when a speaker answers audience questions. Without regulation, such question-and-answer sessions can turn ugly. The box "Handling the Q&A" on pages 308–309 provides some practical advice on how to handle audience questions.

Posture

This dimension is obviously related to movement, gestures, and your overall appearance. Posture is very important to your delivery and the manner in which it is received. People make all kinds of attributions about speakers on the basis of their posture, ranging from how confident a speaker is to how seriously the speaker takes the topic and the situation. At the least, consequently, you will want to guard against an audience making an incorrect attribution about you because you slouched, folded your arms across your chest, stood with one hand on your hip, or put your hands in your pockets.

Because the norms governing appropriate posture vary across cultures, there are no hard and fast rules for speakers to follow. Still, given what we know generally about the culture of the beginning public speaking class, there are some steps you can follow to achieve a good posture for delivering your speeches. Remember that the more you slouch and shrink posturally, the less powerful you are likely to be perceived.

SPEAKING OF . . .

Handling the Q & A

Frequently after a speech, you will be expected to take questions from the audience. You should not be fearful of this situation, as it is actually an opportunity to gain important feedback from your audience as well as to clarify points that may not have been completely understood. Successfully answering questions, even hostile ones, can add to your credibility as a speaker. The key is to regulate that feedback in a constructive manner. Some basic guidelines for handling the question-and-answer period following a speech are given below.[1]

- *Announce at the outset that you will take questions at the end of your speech.* Under no circumstances take questions during the speech, as it will cause you to lose control of the situation. When audience members know they will have the opportunity to ask questions at the end of the speech, they will be able to think about them as you speak.

[1] Some of these guidelines are based on a pamphlet by Robert Haakensan, *How to Handle the Q&A* (Philadelphia: Smith Kline & French Laboratories, Department of Public Relations, n.d.).

- *Overprepare for your speech.* You need to know more than you cover in the speech if you are to take questions. If you expect a hostile audience, it is a good idea to anticipate their toughest questions and prepare answers in advance.

- *Restate questions if they cannot be heard by all.* If you are speaking with a microphone, someone asking a question from the audience probably cannot be heard. Restating the question not only allows everyone to hear what was asked, it also allows you time to think of an answer. If a question is wordy, hostile, or imprecise, try to rephrase it in a way that neutralizes some of the problems with the question.

- *Answer questions directly with facts to back up your answers.* This requires you to be fully prepared. However, if you don't know the answer, just say so. You can always promise to obtain the facts and get back to the questioner at a later date. It is better to admit you don't know an answer than to be proved wrong because

Guidelines for Posture While Delivering a Speech

- **Find your center of balance. Usually this means standing with your feet apart at about shoulder width.**
- **Pull your shoulders back, sticking your chest out and holding your stomach in.**
- **Keep your chin up and off your chest.**

you tried to bluff your way through an answer.

- *Take questions from different audience members.* Don't let yourself get into a debate or an argument with one audience member. Insist that everyone who has a question gets a chance to ask it before you return to a previous questioner. Choose questioners from different parts of the room as well so that everyone feels they will get their chance.

- *Be brief.* Answer questions as succinctly as possible and move on to the next question. Overly long answers bore the audience and frustrate others who want to ask questions.

- *Announce when you are near the end of the Q&A.* When you sense the audience growing restless, the questions have become repetitive, or you are near the end of your allotted time, simply announce that you can take only one or two more questions.

- *At the end of the Q&A, restate the focus of your speech and summarize its essential points.* This is your chance to get in the last word and remind the audience of the basic theme of your speech. Depending on the situation, you may want to make yourself available for informal discussion after the speech.

Retired General Colin Powell uses gestures to regulate audience questioning.

- **Initially let your arms rest at your side with palms open, which will allow you to gesture easily as you speak.**

Touch

Touch, which is by far the most intimate and reinforcing of the nonverbal dimensions, can affect your delivery in at least two ways.[19] The first involves **self-adapting behaviors,** which are distracting touching be-haviors that speakers engage in unconsciously.

Frequently in arousing situations, we touch our face, hair, or clothes without realizing it. Just as frequently we touch some convenient object. We may squeeze the arm of a chair, roll our fingers on a tabletop, trace the outside edge of a glass with our fingertip, or mistake the top of a lectern for a conga drum. We do these things unconsciously.

Because public speaking is arousing, it too can provoke these self-adaptive forms of touch. Further, they can needlessly detract from your delivery. Tugging at an earlobe, rubbing the outside of your upper arm, or jingling the change in your pocket won't help your delivery. Neither will pounding on the lectern with the palms of your hands or rocking it from side to side.

The second way touch can affect your delivery concerns people. At some point, it's likely your presentations will involve other people. Corporate trainers spend much of their lives giving informative presenta-tions that involve audience participation. The same can be said for sales managers, teachers, attorneys, and practitioners of public relations. Touch very often comes into play in these scenarios. Sometimes it's as simple but as important as shaking a person's hand. At other times, however, it may involve guiding someone by the hand, patting someone on the back, or even giving a more demonstrative tactile sign of approval. At the same time, one must avoid touch that can be interpreted as inappropriate. For example, there have been several widely reported cases of schoolteachers ac-cused of inappropriately touching students. Unwelcome touching can, in fact, be grounds for accusations of sexual harassment.

Time

The final nonverbal dimension to think about relative to delivery is time. As journalist Michael Ventura writes,

> Time is the medium in which we live. There is inner time—our personal sense of the rhythms of time experienced differently by each of us; and there is im-posed time—the regimented time by which society organizes itself, the time of schedules and deadlines, time structured largely by work and commerce.[20]

First, time varies from one individual to the next. Research confirms what you no doubt long ago suspected. The internal body clock each of us has regulates not only when we sleep but also peak performance when we're awake. Some people perform best from early to mid morning, some during the middle of the day, and others late at night. What is true of per-formance in general, moreover, is true of public speaking specifically. During our time awake, there are periods when our speaking abilities peak, de-pending on our individual body clock. Most of us know from our own experience that we either are or are not very alert in the early morning or late afternoon. To the extent that one can arrange speaking times, attempt to schedule a time when you know your mind and body will be alert.

Time affects our delivery in other ways as well. For example, the time limits you face as a speaker can have an impact on your delivery. As a result of attempting to cover too much material, for example, time limits may cause you to "hurry" your delivery. Conversely, if you find that you're about to finish your speech under the minimum time requirement of an assignment, you may slow down the delivery of your speech in the attempt to meet the time requirement.

The audience's perception of your delivery also will be affected by your "timing," a term frequently used in reference to actors and comics. Just as their timing of a joke or dramatic monologue can spell the difference between success and failure, so too can your timing. Rushing a punch line or dramatic anecdote, for instance, may negate its intended effect. Telling a story too slowly may do likewise.

Because the norms that govern the use of time vary across cultures, how fast or how slowly you deliver your speech may be a consideration. Whereas a relatively speedy style of delivery may be well received in New York City, it may be received as evidence of the "little time" you have for an audience in parts of the South and Southwest. Conversely, a slow rate of speech, which some mistakenly confuse with the speed at which a person thinks, may prove irritating to audience members whose culture is fast paced.

Finally, whether you are "on time" or late not only for a speech but just in general, affects your credibility in our North American culture. People who are on time are perceived as efficient and courteous, both of which affect perceptions of competence and trustworthiness. People who are routinely late give the impression they are disorganized and not especially considerate of the time needs of an audience. This is very true of both your classmates and your instructor.

THE FUNCTION OF NONVERBAL BEHAVIOR IN DELIVERY

The eight dimensions of nonverbal behavior we've been talking about perform a number of important functions in speech delivery.[21] As we've discussed, these dimensions interact to make our speeches more emblematic and illustrative. They also can help us regulate audience feedback and intensify or lessen the emotional impact of what we say during a speech. Other ways that nonverbal dimensions such as the face, eyes, and voice function to facilitate the delivery of our messages include complementing, contradicting, and repeating the message; substituting for a verbal cue;

increasing the perception of immediacy; exciting the audience; and delivering a powerful speech.

Complementing Your Message

A complementary nonverbal cue serves to reinforce what you verbally share with your audience. A genuine smile on your face as you thank your audience for the opportunity to speak, for example, carries more weight than either message standing on its own. There are many ways to complement the delivery of your message nonverbally. Changing the expression on your face, raising the pitch of your voice, or even breaking off eye contact are just a few of them.

Contradicting Your Message

Often, people contradict themselves nonverbally while communicating interpersonally. Forcing a smile and saying, "I had a great time," is a classic example. While the smile may have covered up how they really felt, chances are it only served to contradict what they said but didn't mean.

Usually we try to keep the preceding from happening. In the case of public speaking, however, we can use contradiction to enhance our delivery, for example, by rolling our eyes, shrugging our shoulders, or having a sarcastic expression. Certainly, Shakespeare knew that contradiction could enhance delivery. He frequently wrote speeches for his characters that invited actors to contradict their verbal statements with nonverbal cues. For example, in Marc Antony's eulogy of Julius Caesar, the line "But Brutus was an honorable man" is usually delivered by an actor in a sarcastic voice that says exactly the opposite. Because it is an attention-getting device, this kind of antithesis in a speech can enhance the impact with which the verbal message is delivered.

Repeating Your Message

Repetition is one of the most common ways speakers manipulate their message nonverbally. It's also one of the easiest ways to do this as well. Raising three fingers as you say you have three points to make doesn't require the oratorical skill of a Colin Powell.

Repetition differs from complementing in a significant way. Whereas a complementary nonverbal cue reinforces the message, a repetitious one serves to make it redundant. The classic example is when *Star Trek*'s Mr. Spock makes the Vulcan V sign while saying "Live Long and Prosper." Other examples include nodding your head up and down while communicating agreement and shaking your head from side to side when communicating disagreement.

Substituting for a Verbal Cue

Have you ever seen entertainers and politicians raise their hands and motion in the attempt to stop an audience's continued applause? They are using a nonverbal cue as a substitute for a verbal one. In many circumstances, such a nonverbal cue is both more appropriate and more effective than a verbal one. An icy stare shot in the direction of someone talking as you speak is likely to be less disruptive, for example, than politely asking the person to be quiet. Shrugging your shoulders, reaching out with open palms, and raising your eyebrows, moreover, may more clearly communicate your bewilderment than to actually say you're puzzled by something.

Increasing the Perception of Immediacy

As we said in the discussion of the face and eyes, nonverbal behavior can also increase the perception of immediacy between you and your audience. Again, immediacy concerns how psychologically close or distant people perceive each other, as well as the degree to which they perceive each other as approachable.[22]

Generally, the perception of immediacy between people is desirable. This is because people who are perceived as immediate are also perceived as friendly and approachable, stimulating, open to dialogue, and interpersonally warm.

Because public speaking normally takes place in a setting that arbitrarily puts physical distance between speakers and their audiences, speakers usually have to reduce this physical distance psychologically. We can do this in at least two ways. The first, which we discussed at length in Chapter 9, involves the use of immediate language. The second is to make our delivery more nonverbally immediate.

The easiest and most effective way to make the delivery more immediate is through nonverbal channels. Eye contact is the perfect case in point. Even when people are separated by substantial physical distance, eye contact enables them to bridge this distance in a psychological sense. The best public speakers, for example, are often the ones who seem to be speaking to us with their eyes as well as their voices.

Eye contact is not the only medium, however, through which we can achieve greater immediacy with our audience. It also can be achieved with facial expressions such as a smile, with a conversational rather than condescending tone of voice, and by standing beside the lectern instead of appearing to hide behind it.

Exciting the Audience

One way we gauge the effectiveness of a speech is the degree to which it stimulated us. The best speakers are the ones who make us think, provoke us to laugh, or motivate us to act. Although it is possible for speakers who are unexciting themselves to excite an audience, it is not probable. Generally, an audience's degree of excitement can be traced to the degree of excitement the audience senses in the speaker.

The level of excitement of public speakers is most noticeable in their nonverbal behavior. This includes rate of speech, volume of speech, and vocal as well as facial expressions. Excited speakers, the research tells us, speak faster and louder than speakers unaroused by their topic or by the transaction between them and their audience. Excited speakers, the research also tells us, reveal more of themselves as they speak through changes in facial expressions as well as changes in the pitch of their voice.

Does this mean that someone who simply is excited also is a good speaker? Of course not. Too much excitement can be as distracting as too little excitement can be boring. The idea, then, is to moderate your excitement for your topic or audience rather than to inappropriately exaggerate it with your delivery.

Delivering a Powerful Speech

When it comes to public speaking, the power of words depends mightily on the manner in which they are delivered. No doubt many speech writers have suffered as the power of the words they so carefully crafted was wiped out by the person delivering them. This shouldn't and needn't be the case. With care and practice, you can capitalize on the varying dimensions of nonverbal behavior to make the delivery of your speech powerful. Some of the ways you can do this are obvious; others are more subtle.

Posture is an obvious way you can control the power of delivery. Standing tall and self-assured, in and of itself, communicates power. When combined with movement away from the lectern, this is even more the case.

You also can enhance the power of your delivery with your eyes, with your voice, and through movement and gestures. In North America, at least, powerful speakers make eye contact, speak in a controlled and confident tone of voice, reduce the distance between themselves and their audience by moving closer to it, and gesture as a natural extension of their spoken message. In stark contrast, speakers whose delivery lacks power avoid eye contact, fail to speak up, and usually try to tie up their hands by sticking them in pockets, gripping the side of the lectern, or hiding them behind their back.

TAKING A PROACTIVE APPROACH

Knowing something about the nature and functions of nonverbal behavior should assist you in making your speech delivery proactive rather than reactive. To engage in **proactive delivery** means that the speaker takes the initiative and anticipates and controls for as many variables as possible, rather than merely reacting to them. Reactive delivery is like the boxer who only counter-punches. This wait-and-see attitude is rarely the mark of a championship boxer, and it can be disastrous for even the most seasoned public speaker. The guidelines that follow should assist you in making sure that your nonverbal behavior enhances—rather than detracts from—the delivery of your speech.

Guidelines for Proactive Speech Delivery

1. *Familiarize yourself with your speaking environment.* This is important because it will influence the quality of your delivery. Know well in advance and plan for such things as seating arrangement, availability and location of lectern, availability and location of overhead screen and projector or easel for displaying poster boards or charts, and lighting.

2. *Take control of your appearance.* Dressing appropriately is one of the easiest ways to enhance initial impressions of you as the medium of your message. Think about the possible effects of apparel, such as the baseball cap that seems to be attached to your scalp, the baggy shorts you prefer, or the saying on your favorite T-shirt.

3. *Increase your nonverbal immediacy.* Practice using your face and eyes to increase immediacy with your audience. Specifically, practice making eye contact with individual members of the audience. If possible, videotape your practice session and review the tape for immediate facial expressions. On the day of your speech, smile at your audience and establish eye contact before speaking.

4. *Use natural gestures.* Review your practice tape to check on your gestures. Do they appear natural and complement your delivery, or do they appear forced and detract from your spoken message?

5. *Work to improve your voice.* Review the box "Tips for Improving Your Voice." Don't be afraid to experiment with your voice. At the same time, remember to be true to your own voice.

6. *Time your Speech.* Do this more than once and on videotape if you can. Note your timing and the degree to which the rate at which you speak facilitates the mood you want to communicate to your audience. Also, remind yourself that your practice time probably will be longer than when you actually speak before your audience.

7. *Avoid self-adapting behaviors.* **During practice, watch out for self-adapting behaviors such as playing with your hair, tugging on a finger, cracking knuckles, licking your lips, and hiding your hands. Self-adapters such as these will call attention to themselves and undermine perceptions of your power and self-confidence.**

8. *Work on posture.* **Check out your posture and what it conveys about your comfort and level of confidence. Remember, good delivery is next to impossible without good posture.**

SUMMARY

Effective speech delivery begins by focusing on your audience. Choosing among manuscript, memorized, impromptu, and extemporaneous delivery methods depends on the audience and the rhetorical situation you face. Nonverbal behaviors may carry different meanings depending on the cultural, demographic, and individual diversity of an audience. The appropriate style of delivery depends also on the speech occasion.

Unlike language, nonverbal behavior is a wordless system of communicating. Nonverbal behavior is continuous, uses multiple channels simultaneously, and is spontaneous.

The system of nonverbal behavior is composed of eight interdependent dimensions: the environment, appearance, the face and eyes, the voice, gestures and movement, posture, touch, and time. The environment includes such things as the seating arrangement, physical layout of the room, temperature, and lighting. Appearance includes how you dress and what your attire communicates to your audience. The face and eyes are very expressive, communicating emotional states such as joy, anger, and sadness. The voice also influences audience emotions through such characteristics as volume, pitch, range, rhythm, tempo, and articulation. Gestures and movement, including emblems, illustrators, and regulators, complement verbal behavior and regulate the speech transaction, including the kind of feedback you receive from an audience. Good posture is important to effective delivery and can affect your audience's perception of you. Touch is often used to compensate for nervousness when you speak and includes distracting self-adaptive behaviors such as slapping the top of the lectern. Time is important to public speaking in terms of how your audience perceives you and in terms of the "timing" of your speech.

The eight dimensions of nonverbal behavior function to enhance the delivery of speeches. These functions include complementing, contradicting, and repeating the message; substituting for verbal cues; increasing the perception of immediacy; exciting the audience; and delivering a powerful speech. Guidelines for proactive delivery include familiarizing yourself with your speaking environment, taking control of your appearance, increasing your nonverbal immediacy, using natural gestures, working to improve

your voice, timing your speech, avoiding self-adapting behaviors, and working on posture.

Check Your Understanding: Exercises and Activities

1. Observe a speaker outside of your class. Keep track of the number of
times the speaker (1) changes the zone of interaction, (2) moves away
from the lectern, and (3) gestures. On a scale of 1 to 10, with 10 being the high end, rate the speaker in each of these areas. Compare
and discuss your observation and ratings with those of other students.
See if a pattern emerges.

2. Differences in nonverbal norms, as well as differences in communication styles and patterns, are common across cultures. Choose two or
three North American norms for nonverbal behavior—for example,
eye contact, gesturing, and time. Interview a student or faculty member from a culture different than North American about how these
communication behaviors differ in his or her culture. Write a short
paper summarizing your findings.

3. Explain why sign language is a *verbal* behavior whereas vocal variation in pitch, rate, tempo, and the like are *nonverbal*, even though
sign language is not vocalized and vocal variation is.

4. Explain why nonverbal behavior is continuous, uses multiple channels simultaneously, and is spontaneous and how these characteristics
distinguish it from verbal behavior.

5. Review the eight guidelines for proactive delivery. Before your next
speech, develop a plan to use at least four of these guidelines to improve your delivery skills in that speech.

6. Ask a classmate to apply Exercise 1 to your next speech. Talk with the
classmate afterward about the relationship between his or her observations and the overall effectiveness of your delivery.

Notes

1. Edward T. Hall, *The Silent Language* (Greenwich, Conn.: Fawcett Publications,
1959), 15.

2. Diana Griego Erwin, "Signs Were There; Facts Were Missing," *Sacramento Bee,*
17 December 1995, A2.

3. Erwin, "Signs Were There; Facts Were Missing," A2.

4. J. Burgoon, D. W. Buller, and W. G. Woodhall, *Nonverbal Communication: The
Unspoken Dialogue,* 2nd ed. (New York: Harper and Row, 1989). See also
M. Knapp and J. A. Hall, *Nonverbal Communication in Human Interaction,* 3rd
ed. (Fort Worth, Tex.: Harcourt, Brace, and Jovanovich, 1992).

5. L. A. Malandro, L. Barker, and D. A. Barker, *Nonverbal Communication,* 2nd ed. (New York: Random House, 1989).

6. V. P. Richmond and J. C. McCroskey, *Nonverbal Behavior in Interpersonal Relationships* (Englewood Cliffs, N.J.: Prentice-Hall, 1991).

7. R. Sommer, "Man's Proximate Environment," *Journal of Social Issues* 22 (1966): 60.

8. Ellen Berscheid and Elaine Walster, "Beauty and the Best," *Psychology Today* 5, no. 10 (1972): 42–46.

9. D. Leathers, *Successful Nonverbal Communication: Principles and Practices* (New York: Macmillan, 1986).

10. Malandro, Barker, and Barker, *Nonverbal Communication.*

11. P. Ekman and W. V. Friesen, *Unmasking the Face: A Guide to Recognizing Emotions from Facial Expression* (Englewood Cliffs, N.J.: Prentice-Hall, 1975). See also P. Ekman, W. V. Friesen, and S. Ancoli, "Facial Signs of Emotional Expression," *Journal of Personality and Social Psychology* 39 (1980): 1125–34.

12. P. Ekman, *Telling Lies* (New York: Norton, 1985). See also Bella M. DePaulo, Miron Zuckerman, and Robert Rosenthal, "Humans as Lie Detectors," *Journal of Communication* 30 (1980): 129–39; R. E. Kraut, "Verbal and Nonverbal Cues in the Perception of Lying," *Journal of Personality and Social Psychology* 36 (1978): 380–91.

13. K. R. Scherer, H. London, and J. J. Wolf, "The Voice of Confidence: Para-linguistic Cues and Audience Evaluation," *Journal of Research in Personality* 7 (1973): 31–44; J. Thakerar and H. Giles, "They Are—So They Spoke: Non-Content Speech Stereotypes," *Language and Communication* 3 (1981): 255–61.

14. George B. Ray, "Vocally Cued Personality Prototypes: An Implicit Personality Theory Approach," *Communication Monographs* 53 (1986): 266–76.

15. Richard L. Street and Robert M. Brady, "Evaluative Responses to Com-municators as a Function of Evaluative Domain, Listener Speech Rate, and Communication Context," *Communication Monographs* 49 (1982): 290–308.

16. David B. Buller and R. Kelly Aune, "The Effects of Speech Rate Similarity on Compliance: An Application of Communication Accommodation Theory," *Western Journal of Speech Communication* 56 (1992): 37–53.

17. Judee Burgoon, "Nonverbal Communication Research in the 1970s: An Overview," in *Communication Yearbook 4,* ed. D. Nimmo. (New Brunswick, N.J.: Transaction Books, 1980), 179–97.

18. Joseph A. Devito, *The Communication Handbook: A Dictionary* (New York: Harper & Row, 1986), 105.

19. Stephen Thayer, "Close Encounters," *Psychology Today* 22, no. 3 (1988): 31–36. See also A. Montague, *Touching: The Significance of the Skin* (New York: Harper & Row, 1971).

20. Michael Ventura, "Trapped in a Time Machine With No Exits," *Sacramento Bee,* 26 February 1995, C1.

21. Burgoon, Buller, and Woodhall, *Nonverbal Communication: The Unspoken Dialogue.* E. T. Hall, "System for the Notation of Proxemic Behavior," *American Anthropologist* 65 (1963): 1003–26.

22. Malandro, Barker, and Barker, *Nonverbal Communication.*

The use of visual aids can enhance most presentations.

11

Presentational Aids

OBJECTIVES

After reading this chapter, you should be able to:

- Explain the advantages of using presentational aids in your speeches.
- Select the types of presentational aids that are appropriate to the purpose of your speech.
- Select the appropriate materials for constructing your presentational aids.
- Use the principles of simplicity, visibility, layout, and color in constructing and using visual aids.
- Practice setting up and using your presentational aids before your speech.
- Effectively use presentational aids in your speech.

KEY CONCEPTS

audio aids
audiovisual aids
bar chart
flip charts
flow chart
line graph

organizational chart
overhead
transparency
pie chart
presentational aids
visual aids

VIDEO FILE

If you have access
to the videotape
that accompanies
this book, view
segment 8.

It shows how a
number of visual
aids can be used
to enhance your
speech.

Presentational aids are visual, audio, and audiovisual devices that can add an important dimension to a speech. To understand the difference a presentational aid can make, just think about trying to give a friend directions to your home. Which is clearer—to explain it verbally or to both draw a map and explain it? Which is the more effective advertising—a radio ad or a full-color television commercial that can be seen as well as heard? Which is more interesting to listen to for a 50-minute class session—an instructor who lectures the entire time or one who uses a variety of visual media to supplement the lecture?

In each case you probably chose the second alternative. Adding visual or even audio information to any presentation is likely to help your audience comprehend, remember, accept, and act on your ideas. An effective opinion leader uses all the means at his or her disposal to influence others. A study conducted by the University of Minnesota for 3M found that people who saw a presentation with visual support were more likely to be persuaded, had an improved perception of the speaker, as well as greater comprehension and a higher attention level, and were more likely to agree with the verbal material of the presentation than people who saw the same presentation but without visual support.[1]

ADAPTING PRESENTATIONAL AIDS TO YOUR AUDIENCE

Whether you should use visual aids depends on the rhetorical situation, particularly on the audience and their goals and expectations. For example, visual aids would usually seem out of place in a sermon or eulogy. On the other hand, a teacher who never used any kind of presentational aid would be unusual. Classrooms are designed with chalkboards and sometimes overhead projectors and video monitors for a reason.

Always keep in mind how your audience will process the presentational aids you use in your speech. For example, how large will charts, posters, and objects need to be in order to be seen from the back of the room? If you are using sound, will you be able to amplify it sufficiently for the audience to hear? If you must darken the room for slides, will this present a problem for audience members who need to take notes? As with all other aspects of public speaking, if you design your presentational aids with the audience's needs in mind, you are much more likely to achieve your purpose.

TYPES OF VISUAL AIDS

Visual aids are presentational aids that convey a message visually. There are numerous types of visual aids that you may want to consider for your

speech. Five basic types are objects; models; photographs; diagrams and illustrations; and charts, graphs, and maps. Let's consider each type of visual aid in turn.

This speaker's use of a map enhances his speech on geography.

Objects

In some cases, the object you are discussing in your speech is perfectly suited to your needs. A speech about the bagpipe might call for you to demonstrate on the instrument itself. A demonstration of karate or judo almost demands that you use people to show how the moves are done; in this case, people are your presentational aids.

The keys to using objects are to make sure they are easily visible to your audience and that they are appropriate to the situation. A speech on auto repair could not use a real car, because it would be too big for most classrooms. A small but visible part from an automobile could be used to illustrate how to repair it. Inappropriate objects can also create problems. For

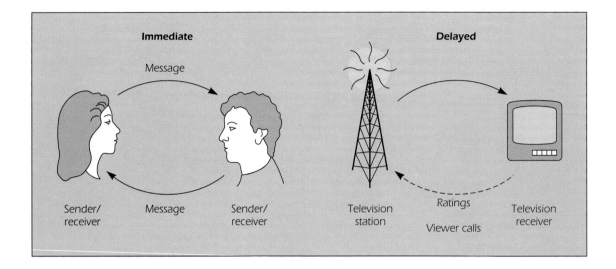

Immediate

Message

Sender/
receiver   Message   Sender/
receiver

Delayed

Television
station

Ratings

Viewer calls

Television
receiver

FIGURE 11.1
Diagrams can be
used to illustrate ab-
stract concepts, such
as communication
feedback.

example, almost every semester we have students who wish to do speeches on some aspect of firearms. However, firearms are prohibited on our campus (except for those of campus security officers) for obvious reasons. Wine tasting is another popular topic we must veto, because alcohol is also prohibited on our campus. Thus, before you plan a speech using actual objects, be sure to ask your instructor what is appropriate and permissible on your particular campus.

Models

Often a three-dimensional model of an object can be used when it is impractical to use the actual object. We recall a speech on the common American cockroach. Bringing live cockroaches to the classroom would have been disconcerting, to say the least. However, the student cleverly constructed a large-scale model of a cockroach that she kept hidden in a box until just the right instant, when she revealed the topic of her speech. Not only was her speech informative and entertaining, it also was enhanced by her ability to explain her subject vividly with her model.

Photographs

A photograph of your object can be a very useful visual aid, as long as it is clearly visible to everyone in the audience. Thus, you must either enlarge the photo to poster size or show it through a slide or overhead projector. For example, a speech on art history would be greatly enhanced by slides or enlargements of photographs of various periods and styles of paintings.

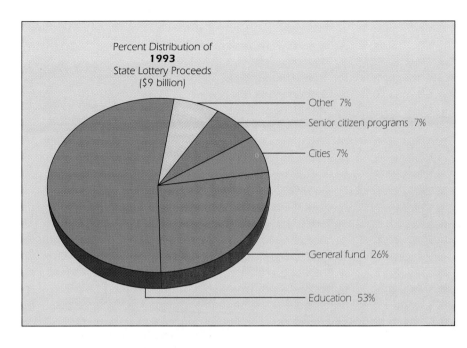

Percent Distribution of
1993
State Lottery Proceeds
($9 billion)

Other 7%

Senior citizen programs 7%

Cities 7%

General fund 26%

Education 53%

FIGURE 11.2
Pie Chart
Percent Distribution
of 1993 State Lottery
Proceeds (Source: U.S.
Bureau of the Census,
*Statistical Abstract of the
United States: 1995,*
115th edition.
[Washington, D.C.,
1995], 298.)

Diagrams and Illustrations

Sometimes an illustration or a drawing will serve your purpose better than a photograph. Diagrams are a good way to represent the parts of an object. For example, a cutaway drawing of a firearm can be used to explain its function, and the diagram—unlike a real gun—is neither illegal nor dangerous. Figure 11.1 illustrates a more abstract concept, communication feedback, through use of a diagram.

Charts, Graphs, and Maps

Often a speech calls for a particular kind of visual representation of numbers and statistics through charts or graphs. Three of the following types of charts and graphs are particularly useful for depicting statistical information: pie charts, line graphs, and bar charts.

Pie Charts   A **pie chart** is a circular chart that divides a whole into several parts, each represented by a slice of the circle proportional to its share of the whole. Figure 11.2 shows a typical pie chart that represents the percentage distribution of state lottery proceeds in 1993. The advantage of pie charts is that they simplify and dramatically illustrate the relative proportions of parts of a whole. Pie charts are not of much use, however, in demonstrating trends over time, since several pie charts would need to be

FIGURE 11.3
Line Graph
Media Usage by
Consumers: 1984 to
1998 (Source: U.S.
Bureau of the Census,
*Statistical Abstract of the
United States: 1995,*
115th edition.
[Washington, D.C.,
1995], 568.)

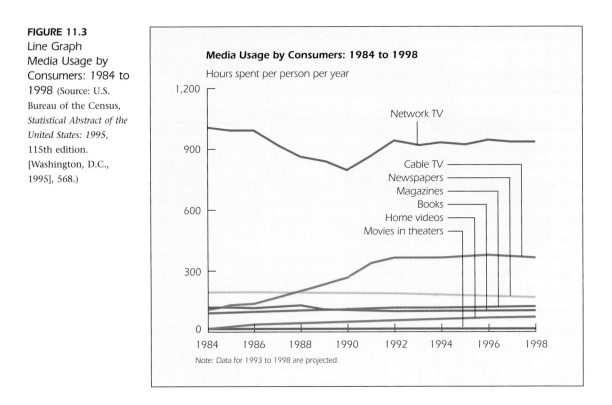

displayed simultaneously, one for each unit of time. That would make each chart smaller and more difficult to see.

Line Graphs   A **line graph** shows numerical data as a series of points connected by a line. It is well suited to showing changes over time, such as changes in media usage by consumers over a 15-year period, as in Figure 11.3. By using more than one line (each can be in a different color), you can show how two or more things compare across the same time period. Thus, if you wanted to compare spending on schools with spending on defense over the past 10 years, a line chart with two lines would work well.

Bar Charts   A **bar chart** uses filled in vertical or horizontal bars to represent various quantities, as shown in Figure 11.4. By grouping two or more bars or by color-coding them, you can compare two or more categories. For example, the first bar chart in Figure 11.4 compares the participation of men and women in the 10 most popular sports in 1993. The other chart shows how per capita food consumption has changed over the period of 1970 to 1993. You can readily see that consumption of beef has declined, while chicken and turkey has increased.

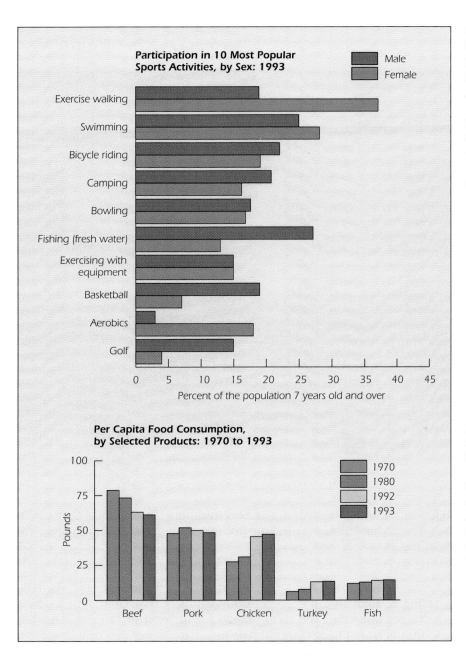

FIGURE 11.4
Bar Charts

Participation in 10 Most Popular Sports Activities, by Sex: 1993 (Source: U.S. Bureau of the Census, *Statistical Abstract of the United States: 1995*, 115th edition. [Washington, D.C., 1995], 250.)

Per Capita Food Consumption by Selected Products: 1970 to 1993 (Source: U.S. Bureau of the Census, *Statistical Abstract of the United States: 1995*, 115th edition. [Washington, D.C., 1995], 106.)

Organizational Charts   An **organizational chart** represents the structure of an organization, using boxes and lines to convey hierarchy and lines of authority. Figure 11.5 on page 328 is an example. Such charts are useful in

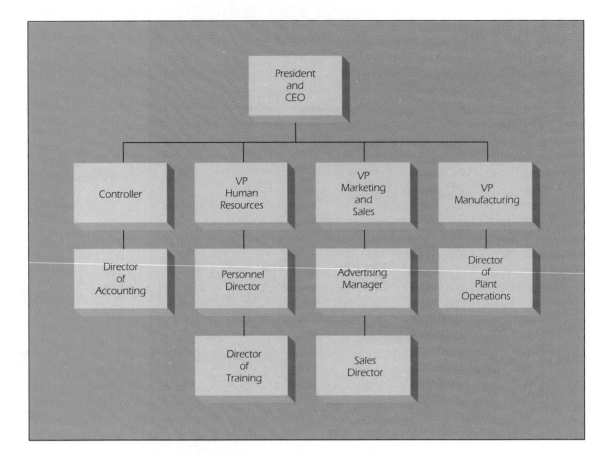

FIGURE 11.5
Organizational Chart

business, industry, or governmental organizations. For example, they can il-lustrate the organization's structure for new employees or be part of an an-nual report to shareholders.

Flow Chart   A **flow chart** uses boxes and arrows to represent the rela-tionship of steps in a process. In other words, a flow chart shows how a process is carried out. For example, you might construct a flow chart, like the one in Figure 11.6, to illustrate the steps necessary in preparing a speech.

Text-Only Charts   Sometimes a visual aid will consist exclusively of text. For example, a speaker might list on a visual aid textual material such as main points of a speech, the steps involved in a process, or important informa-tion for audience members to remember. For example, Sally Garber's "Dieting and Physical Activity," which was outlined in Chapter 2, used a

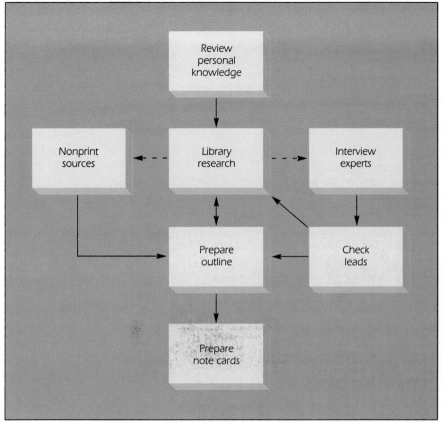

FIGURE 11.6
Flow chart illustrating the steps necessary in preparing a speech.

visual aid that listed four guidelines to a healthy life: make a lifetime commitment, take pleasure in eating, make wise food choices, and exercise.

Maps   Maps are useful for speeches describing the spatial layout of an area, whether a dangerous intersection in your hometown or the disputed border between hostile nations. Maps can also be used to describe a dynamic process, such as a battle. At the site of the historic battle of Gettysburg, for example, numerous maps display various stages of the battle. One large-scale map uses embedded lights to show the daily progress of the battle.

MATERIALS FOR VISUAL AIDS

Visual aids can be made from a number of different materials. The same concept, say, a pie chart, might be expressed on a poster, a transparency, or a slide. Typical media for visual aids include poster board, flip charts, overhead transparencies, slides, handouts, and chalkboards.

Poster Board

Poster board is one of the most common materials used by students for their visual aids. You can draw illustrations, diagrams, or charts on it with colored marking pens. Or you can paste enlarged pictures on it or emphasize key words with rub-on letters or other prepared materials. Colored poster board may be visually more interesting than white board, as long as it contrasts with the lettering.

Use a pencil to lightly sketch in the words or diagram, and then use felt-tip markers in various colors to finish the poster. Permanent markers are preferable, because posters prepared with water-based marking pens can be easily ruined by rain or a clumsy roommate. Use poster board that is thick enough to stand up without folding over. During the presentation, put the poster on an easel. Otherwise, you will have to either hold it while talking or lean it up against the wall or lectern. This makes for a hard-to-see and wobbly visual aid.

If you are using a series of posters, prepare and place them in the order you will need them in the speech. Use a blank poster to cover posters that are not in use. As you begin talking about each poster, remove the blank and place it behind the poster you are discussing. When you are finished talking about that poster, remove it, revealing the blank poster. When you are ready to talk about the next poster, move the blank sheet behind it, and so on, until you get to the last poster.

Flip Charts

Flip charts are a series of drawings, charts, or graphs, usually attached at the top by a binding and supported on an easel. Speakers use flip charts to present a series of visual aids in a predetermined order. As with poster board, rough out your visual aid in light pencil and then fill in the sketch with permanent marking pens. Be sure that the ink does not bleed through to the next sheet of paper. Leave blank sheets between visual aids if you will not be using one immediately after another.

Overhead Transparencies

An **overhead transparency** is a plastic sheet that can be drawn on or used in a photocopier and then projected on a screen for an audience to see. Overhead transparencies are a popular visual aid in business and classroom presentations. They have the advantage of low cost and ease of preparation, and they can be used without dimming the lights too much. Many

It is important to support posters and flip charts on an easel.

classrooms and business conference rooms have overhead projectors, but you should always check in advance to make sure a projector is available. Also be sure to check out the equipment in advance, since machines operate differently.

Anything you can put on a poster or flip chart you can also put on an overhead transparency. You can write or draw directly on the transparency with a special pen, or you can use a computer to create text or graphics and then transfer that to a transparency using a photocopier. When creating the transparency, use lettering at least one-quarter inch high.[2]

One easy way to make a transparency is to take a chart or graph from a book or magazine, enlarge it on a photocopier, and then copy the enlarged version onto the transparency. It may take you several tries to get exactly the image you want, so don't try to enlarge directly onto the plastic sheet. Enlarge on plain paper and then copy your final version onto the transparency. When using a photocopier, be sure to use transparency stock designed for plain-paper copiers; otherwise, the transparency can melt inside the copier!

It is also possible to print text or graphics directly onto a transparency with some computer printers. Again, be sure to use the transparency stock designed for your printer.

For color transparencies, you can take a black-on-clear transparency and color it with water-based pens. If you are artistic, you can write or draw directly on the transparency with colored marking pens. If you have a color printer, you may be able to directly print a color transparency. Or you can print a color version on paper and then copy it on a color photocopier. Finally, you can use a color photocopier to copy a color original from a magazine or book.

The following guidelines should help you with your overheads.

Guidelines for Creating and Using Overheads

- Make the text large enough to be seen when projected on a screen. A simple rule of thumb is that the smallest image on the screen must be at least 1 inch high for every 30 feet of viewing distance. To check for size, stand 10 feet away from your transparency and read the text unprojected with the naked eye. If your vision is normal and you can't read it from that distance, it is too small and needs to be enlarged before it is copied onto a transparency.[3] Most photocopiers have an enlargement feature.

- Place the projection screen high enough for those in the back of the room to see clearly, with the bottom at least 48 inches from the floor. To avoid a keystone effect, where the top of the image is wider than the bottom, angle the screen so that the bottom is pulled back toward the wall. Ideally, the screen should be to the right of a right-handed presenter so that the speaker can write on the transparency without blocking the light.[4] Be sure to consider the audience's line of sight. Depending on where you are standing, you may be blocking the view of some of the audience members. Move away from the machine at times to give all of your audience members a clear view. Don't hesitate to ask if everyone can see.

- When using the overhead projector, don't turn your back on the audience to point to something on the screen. Instead, use a pointer or a pencil to point to the plastic sheet on the projector. This technique enables you to maintain eye contact with your audience and yet point to things on the overhead.

- Consider using special water-based marking pens to underline or otherwise highlight points on overheads as you go along. For example, a black-on-clear overhead could be livened up by using a red pen to underline key words. You can also use colored pens in advance to add color to black-on-clear outlines on charts or graphs.

- Just as you cover a poster board or flip chart when not in use, turn off the overhead projector when you are not using it. Don't leave an old overhead up on the screen, and never just project a bright light with no content on the screen. On the other hand, make sure you leave the overhead on long enough for the audience to read it and, if necessary, copy down pertinent information. The amount of time will vary with the amount of material on the overhead.

- Use a piece of paper to cover the parts of the overhead you haven't discussed yet.[5] Covering part of an overhead and revealing points as you go along—a technique known as revelation—keeps your audience on track with you. It also allows you to control the pace of your presentation and prevents audience members from reading ahead.

- Keep a printed copy of each transparency on the lectern so that you can refer to it without having to stare into the glare of the projector's light or turn your back on your audience to read the screen.

Slides

Slides are a useful way to project a picture or other image onto a screen to ensure that everyone in the audience can see. However, because slides require a darkened room, it's best to present them all together, since you don't want to speak in the dark between segments of your speech that use slides.

Be sure to organize your slides in advance. You probably will be using a carousel projector, a round tray with slots for slides. Make sure you load the slides properly, usually upside down, so that you're not embarrassed by an upside-down or reversed slide during your speech. Having to right an improperly loaded slide will disrupt your entire presentation.

Most slide projectors have a remote control so that the speaker can control the pace of the slides. If this is not the case, someone must sit at the slide projector and advance the slides for you. Be warned, however, that it is distracting to have a speech interrupted by constant calls for "next slide, please."

If you plan to use slides, rehearse their use carefully. If you must use a colleague to advance the slides, work with that person so that he or she knows roughly when to expect slide changes.

Although a slide presentation can be highly effective when done professionally, most beginning speakers should stick to simpler visual aids. Photographs that can be enlarged and placed on poster board, for example, often work just as well as slides and do not require any special equipment.

Handouts

Handouts create special problems for speakers. If they are distributed prior to the speech, your audience is likely to be reading the handout, not listening to what you say. Distributing them during the speech will disrupt the flow of your presentation and take up valuable time. If you wait until after the speech to distribute them, they cannot be an integral part of the speech.

The major use of handouts is to give your audience something to take with them from the speech. Perhaps you want your audience to write letters to members of Congress, so it is appropriate to give them addresses to take away from your speech. If you do not plan to directly use the handouts in the speech, by all means pass them out after you are finished speaking. If you have a recipe or formula that you want to distribute to the audience, you could put it on an overhead transparency or poster board and leave it on display long enough for it to be copied, or you could announce in advance that you will distribute copies after the speech.

Sometimes, however, you have a handout that should be used during the speech. Perhaps there is a self-administered questionnaire that your audience is expected to fill out and refer to during the speech. In cases where you do need to use a handout during the speech, distribute it at the beginning of the speech and ask your audience to turn it over and not look at it until you call on them to do so. Of course not everyone will comply, but at least you will minimize the number who are looking at the handout rather than listening to you.

In general, use handouts only when no other type of visual aid will serve your purpose. Handouts create a distraction and allow the audience, not the speaker, to control the focus of attention. In all cases, avoid passing a single handout around the audience while you are speaking. This is the worst possible situation, as every member of the audience will see it at a different time, and there will be a distraction from your speech every time the handout moves to the next person.

Chalkboards

Chalkboards or erasable marker boards are sometimes useful for putting up brief information. For example, a phone number, an address, or a few key words can be quickly placed on a chalkboard. However, using a chalkboard as your sole or major visual means of support is not wise. For one thing, you have to turn your back on the audience in order to use the board. Anything more extensive than a few words will take longer to write than you would need for a prepared visual aid, such as an overhead transparency.

Even classroom teachers should consider alternatives to the chalkboard. Overhead projectors with a roll of acetate film can be used by math teachers, for example, to work through sample problems. Rather than turning their back on the class, teachers can do the problems while still facing their class.

In short, the chalkboard is of limited use to most speakers. Erasable marker boards have one advantage: Their white background and the availability of multicolored markers make them more interesting to use than the traditional black or green chalkboard. However, you still have to turn your back on the audience in order to use these boards effectively.

GUIDELINES FOR CREATING AND USING VISUAL AIDS

Once you have decided on your visual aids, there are four basic guidelines you need to keep in mind: simplicity, visibility, layout, and color.[6] Let's consider each of these in turn.

Simplicity

There is a common tendency to try to put too much information on any one visual aid. We have seen people simply take a page from a magazine and copy it onto an overhead transparency. Some students try to save a few dollars by putting two or three ideas on one poster. These tendencies undermine the effectiveness of visual aids. The best advice we can give you is to keep it simple![7]

Tips for Simplicity

- Limit yourself to one idea per visual aid.
- Use no more than six or seven words per line.
- Use no more than six or seven lines per visual aid.
- Use short, familiar words and round numbers.
- Keep charts and graphs simple enough to be sketched easily by your audience.

Visibility

Any visual aid is only as good as it is visible to your audience.[8] If they can't see it easily, it will hinder your presentation as your audience members strain or ask a neighbor what's on the screen.

Tips for Visibility

- Make your images at least 1 inch high for every 30 feet of viewing distance.
- Create transparencies that are readable by the naked eye at 10 feet. Use type no smaller than one-quarter inch, which is known as

18-POINT TYPE.

- Make sure you do not block your audience's view of your visual aid as you show it during the speech.

Layout

An organized, consistent, and uncluttered layout is necessary for an effective visual aid.[9]

Tips for Layout

- Place images near the top of your visual aid to ensure maximum visibility.
- Accentuate key points with bold type, underlining, or color.
- Write horizontally, not vertically. Vertical writing is hard to read.
- Leave generous margins, larger on top than bottom and equal on the sides.
- Present information from left to right and from top to bottom. For example, a chart showing progression over time should have the oldest year on the left and the most recent year on the right, not vice versa. If the information is presented vertically, the oldest should be at the top and the most recent on the bottom.

Color

Research has shown that the proper use of color helps your audience pay attention, comprehend, and remember your visuals.[10]

Tips for Color

- Use primary colors, such as red, blue, and yellow, which have been shown to create the strongest impact.

- Use sufficient contrast for your audience to see clearly. Yellow lettering on a white background, for example, is almost invisible.
- Use colored backgrounds, as long as the color is not so dark that the message is hard to see. Colored backgrounds are more visually soothing.
- Don't use clashing or confusing colors. For example, don't use red to show profits and black to show losses.

AUDIO AND AUDIOVISUAL AIDS

Although most people think only of visual aids, there are other ways to enhance a presentation. Some presentational aids add only sound, whereas others combine sound and pictures.

Audio aids are presentational aids that use sound only, such as tape recordings. Some speeches cry out for sound, such as one on different styles of music. A speech discussing different dialects obviously would be enhanced by samples of speech from different regions. A speech on old-time radio shows might use a few snippets from Abbott and Costello.

The most obvious way to prepare audio aids is with a tape recorder. Because you are unlikely to have time in a five- or ten-minute speech to completely present a song, let alone a symphony, you will want to edit your tape to include only the brief portion of the sounds you need. You can do this on any recording equipment that permits you to dub from tape to tape or from CD to tape. One could also use sophisticated and expensive recording equipment, but for most student speeches, a simple tape deck will do the job.

Audiovisual aids are presentational aids that combine sound and sight, such as films, videotapes, filmstrips, and slide/tape presentations. Films and videotape offer sound and motion, whereas filmstrips and slide/tape presentations combine still photos with sound.

Videotape has several advantages over film. Unlike film, videotape does not require a darkened room. Also, you can much more easily search a videotape for a particular segment. With two VCRs and audio and video cables to connect the machines, you can even edit videotape presentations. Usually, however, speakers have their videotapes cued to the points they plan to use. For example, we recall a student who was speaking against the colorization of old black-and-white movies. She brought in two versions of Frank Capra's classic, *It's a Wonderful Life*. In about a minute, she was able to compare a scene originally shot in black and white with the colorized version of the same scene. Her audience could clearly see for themselves the differences colorization had made.

With either film or videotape, the big danger is that you will cease to be a speaker and become merely a projectionist or button pusher. Any use

Computer-assisted presentations can still fall prey to human error.

of video or film should be brief (no more than a minute or so for a 10-minute speech) and central to the speech. With video, also consider the use of slow motion or freeze frame to emphasize your point. For example, a speaker explaining gymnastic scoring might want to freeze the tape or use slow motion to call attention to mistakes that warrant a deduction in points.

Filmstrips or slide/tape presentations basically involve prerecording the speech, which is then presented in coordination with still photos projected on a screen. For most speech classes, this is not an appropriate method, because it replaces your speech with the mediated presentation. However, the slide/tape technology is often useful for sales presentations, as a teaching device, and in situations where a speaker will follow up with a speech. Because the time limits for most speech classes do not allow for this technology, we will not go into it in detail here. Suffice it to say that, with the right equipment, one can prepare an effective slide/tape presentation at a reasonable cost.

COMPUTER-ASSISTED PRESENTATIONAL AIDS

One of the most exciting developments in presentational aids has been the use of computers to create and present visual and audiovisual aids.[11] At a minimum, computers enable you to create charts, graphs, illustrations, and other visual depictions that can be transferred to slides, overheads, or posters. With a color printer, you can create attractive graphics rather easily. Special transparency sheets can be printed on directly by a laser or ink-jet printer.

Because of the wide variety of software and hardware available, we will not specifically discuss any one program or computer. However, among the leading software packages you may have the opportunity to deal with are Adobe Persuasion or Microsoft Powerpoint. Whether you are using an IBM-

Computers not only help speakers create visual aids, they may also be used to show them.

compatible PC or a Macintosh, you will find a wide range of programs that can assist you in preparing visual aids for your speeches.

The advantage of using software designed specifically for presentation graphics is that many programs will create appropriate charts or graphs once you enter your information. Also, there are usually prepared templates that you can use in preparing your own graphics. Clip-art images are typically part of the package, allowing you to pick and choose images that fit your needs. A scanner will allow you to directly store pictures in your computer for use in graphics. In short, the computer can help you in the creative process of producing graphics to be displayed on the traditional media of visual aids.

Because the screen on a computer is too small to be seen by an audience, you need a way to project your visual aids on a large flat screen, just as you would an overhead transparency or slide. There are thin, transparent display units, called liquid crystal display pads, made for this purpose. The pad is placed on top of an overhead projector and connected by a cable directly to your computer. At the same time an image is displayed on your computer screen, the pad on the overhead displays the image on a thin panel through which the light from the overhead projector can pass. This projects the image on the screen for your audience to see. Even animation and sound are possible with the right hardware and software.

Of course, the downside to this technology is that the speaker risks becoming secondary to the equipment. And if you do not know how to

Murphy's Law

Murphy's law is the well-known adage "If anything can go wrong, it will." Unfortunately it applies as much to the use of presentational aids in public speaking as to your car battery on a cold morning. Although you can prepare your visual aids thoroughly, there is no way to be completely prepared for the "unexpected." The best defense is to anticipate problems and prepare alternatives. Here are a few of the things that can go wrong that you need to prepare for (at one time or another, they have all happened to the authors of this book).

Problem: The battery in your equipment (tape recorder, microphone, or whatever) is dead.

What to do: Test the equipment the morning of your speech and carry a spare battery.

Problem: There is no overhead projector, even though you reserved one.

What to do: Make sure you call to confirm your reservation on the morning of your speech. Physically check out the projector if possible.

Problem: The overhead projector's light bulb is burned out.

What to do: Most overheads have a spare light bulb. Make sure you know where it is beforehand.

Problem: The slide projector (film projector, VCR, etc.) does not work.

What to do: Again, check it out in advance if possible. If it unexpectedly fails, you will need to verbally describe what is on your slides. We recall one case where a person simply stood in front of a blank screen,

correctly operate the computer, or if there is an equipment failure, you risk embarrassment. Thus, for beginning students, we recommend computers primarily for the creation of more traditional visual aids. However, the range of computer-assisted presentations is ever increasing and will likely become increasingly common throughout your lifetime.

Hints for Using Presentational Aids

Before Your Speech

- Check the room and your equipment.
- Practice, if possible, with the same equipment in the same room where you will give your speech.
- Double-check your presentational aids immediately before the

pretended to show slides, and described them in elaborate detail as he went along ("As you can clearly see from this slide . . ."). It turned a frustrating situation into a humorous one.

Problem: Your visual aids are out of order or upside down, or some are missing.

What to do: An ounce of prevention is worth a pound of cure. Check and double-check them before the speech. If you run into this problem, try not to get flustered. Make a joke while you look for the missing visual; if you can't find it, verbally describe the visual or skip a part of the speech.

Problem: There's no chalk for the chalkboard or no dry erase markers for the white board.

What to do: Bring extra chalk or dry erase markers with you.

Problem: It takes a lot longer than you thought to demonstrate a process using your visual aids.

What to do: First, always practice with your visuals so that you know how long it will take. Second, if you are demonstrating a multistep process, have various steps along the way already prepared.

Remember, nothing can happen to you that hasn't already happened to someone else. Most audiences are sympathetic to speakers who are obviously prepared and yet encounter technical difficulties beyond their control. At the same time, audiences have little sympathy when Murphy's law strikes someone who is just winging it. And keep in mind, "Murphy was an optimist."

speech. For example, make sure posters, overheads, or slides are in proper order, right-side up, and ready to go.

- Allow ample time for setup and takedown.

During the Speech

- Avoid distractions—cover or remove visual aids and turn off projectors when not in use.
- Do not block the audience's view.
- Allow the audience enough time to process the information—then remove the aid.
- Talk to your audience, not to the visual aid.

No matter how much you plan, things can still go wrong. For some tips on how to cope with the unexpected, see the box "Murphy's Law."

SUMMARY

Presentational aids can make the difference between a successful speech and a failure. People learn more, remember longer, and are more likely to be persuaded by speeches with effective presentational aids.

As with all other aspects of your speech, begin by analyzing the rhetorical situation and the audience in deciding whether to use presentational aids and which ones to use. Be sure that visual aids will be visible to the audience and appropriate to the occasion.

Basic types of visual aids are objects; models; photographs; diagrams and illustrations; and charts, graphs, and maps. The media commonly used for visual aids include poster board, flip charts, overhead transparencies, slides, handouts, and chalkboards. Other presentational aids include audio aids, such as tape recorders, and audiovisual aids, such as films, videotapes, filmstrips, and slide/tape presentations.

Computer-assisted graphics enable you to prepare professional-looking charts, graphs, and visual depictions that can be directly printed on overhead transparencies or paper. These graphics can be converted into everything from slides to posters. Computers can also be used during a presentation, although there is a danger of letting the computer steal the show from the speaker.

Four basic guidelines for creating and using visual aids are simplicity, visibility, well-planned layout, and effective use of color. Before your presentation, check your equipment and presentational aids. Rehearse if possible with the exact equipment you will be using. Allow time for setup and takedown. During the speech, avoid distractions, do not block your audience's view, allow the audience time to process the information, and talk to your audience, not your visual aids.

Check Your Understanding: Exercises and Activities

1. Check at your college or at local copying shops to find out where you can have the following made: black-on-clear overhead transparencies, color overhead transparencies, enlarged photographs, slides, videotapes.

2. Find out where on campus you can obtain an overhead projector, and find out who can answer questions about its operation. Learn how to turn it on and off, how to focus it, and what to do if the bulb is burned out.

3. Find an example of a bar chart, a pie chart, a line graph, and a map in *USA Today* or your local newspaper, and describe whether each one would make a suitable visual aid for a speech. Evaluate them in terms of *simplicity, visibility, layout,* and *color.*

4. Contact the computer center at your college or university. What, if any, services are available to help you prepare computer graphics for your speeches? If you own or have access to a computer, go to a computer dealer or consult a software catalog, and find at least three presentation graphics programs available for your computer.

5. Consider the following speech situations: an informative speech on the impressionist movement in art; an informative speech on the Persian Gulf War; a persuasive speech about health insurance in the United States; a speech to entertain on the topic of traveling by train, plane, or automobile. What types of visual aids would be most appropriate for each speech situation, and why?

Notes

1. Donald R. Vogel, Gary W. Dickson, and John A. Lehman, "Persuasion and the Role of Visual Presentation Support: The UM/3M Study," commissioned by Visual Systems Division of 3M, 1986, cited in John J. Makay, *Public Speaking: Theory into Practice* (Fort Worth, Tex.: Harcourt Brace Jovanovich, 1992), 172–73.

2. Minnesota Western, *Visual Presentation Systems* (Oakland, Calif.: Minnesota Western, 1988–89), 180.

3. Minnesota Western, *Visual Presentation Systems,* 180.

4. Minnesota Western, *Visual Presentation Systems,* 170–71.

5. Minnesota Western, *Visual Presentation Systems,* 177.

6. Minnesota Western, *Visual Presentation Systems,* 180–81.

7. Minnesota Western, *Visual Presentation Systems,* 180.

8. Minnesota Western, *Visual Presentation Systems,* 180.

9. Minnesota Western, *Visual Presentation Systems,* 181.

10. Minnesota Western, *Visual Presentation Systems,* 181.

11. Margaret Y. Rabb, ed., *The Presentation Design Book: Projecting a Good Image with Your Desktop Computer* (Chapel Hill, N.C.: Ventana Press, 1990).

PART FOUR

Contexts for
Public Speaking

Jaime Escalante
motivated his students
to achieve through
the power of ganas,
the desire to succeed.

12

Informative Speaking

Determination plus
hard work plus con-
centration equals suc-
cess, which equals
ganas.
—Jaime Escalante[1]

OBJECTIVES

After reading this chapter, you should be able to:

- Explain how to adapt your informative speech to audiences with diverse learning styles.
- Explain the concept of informative speaking in terms of its cognitive, affective, and behavioral components.
- Discuss the relationship between informative speaking, opinion leadership, and persuasion.
- Use the message attributes—novelty, compatibility, comprehensibility, relative advantage, observability, and trialability—in your informative speeches.
- Prepare informative speeches that explain, instruct, demonstrate, or describe.
- Illustrate how informative speaking can be used in your other classes, at work, and in your community.

KEY CONCEPTS

affect	informative speaking
behavior	learning
cognition	novelty
compatibility	observability
comprehensibility	relative advantage
ganas	trialability

Jaime Escalante, whose picture you see in the opening photograph, is not simply a gifted teacher. He is a remarkable person. He immigrated to the United States from Bolivia in 1969, where he had taught mathematics and physics. He spoke not a single word of English. But Escalante had what he called *ganas*—that is, a desire to succeed regardless of the odds against it. Thus, at age 30, he re-entered school to work toward his teaching credential, even though it meant subjecting his out-of-shape body to a required course in P.E.

The rest of the story, of course, is probably well known to you. Escalante's life became the subject of the critically acclaimed film *Stand and Deliver.* In the movie, actor Edward James Olmos portrays Escalante, who took East Los Angeles barrio students who could barely do simple math and, in two years of intensive work, prepared them for the Advanced Placement Test in Calculus. His students were so successful that all 18 who attempted the test in 1982 passed, the most from any high school in Southern California. Each year, more students passed; by 1987, 87 of his students passed the exam. Remember, these were students who were not expected to attend college, let alone receive college credit for calculus while still in high school. But as Escalante says, "Students will rise to the level of expectations." When students wanted to quit, Escalante would challenge them by saying, "Do you have the *ganas?* Do you have the desire?"[2]

Although there are many reasons that Escalante was able to overcome odds others would have perceived as insurmountable, we think his success in life as well as in the classroom can be found in that word of his: *ganas.* Not only did Escalante have it when he needed it, but also his life is testimony to the fact that he has instilled it in many of his students. As a result, they too have succeeded.

In a sense, this chapter is about *ganas.* Like Jaime Escalante, the best informative speakers do more than simply pass on information to an audience. With their words and actions, they create a desire in their audience to put the information to constructive use. In the case of Escalante, the desire involved a subject that many students prefer to avoid: mathematics. In yours, it may involve anything from how we treat our environment to the kind of foods we eat.

Informative speaking is the process by which an audience gains new information from a speaker. Put another way, the goal of informative speaking is audience learning. In order for you to be an effective informative speaker, you need to master several skills, which we will look at in this chapter. These skills include

- focusing on your audience and appealing to their various styles of learning;
- understanding the cognitive, affective, and behavioral components of informative speaking;

- recognizing the relationship between informative speaking, opinion leadership, and persuasion;
- learning to utilize various attributes of messages in informative speaking;
- putting theory into practice in speeches that explain, instruct, demonstrate, or describe; and
- understanding the differences and similarities among the forums in which you are likely to give informative presentations, namely, the classroom, the workplace, and the community.

Teaching kids to play basketball is an opportunity for an informative presentation.

FOCUSING ON YOUR AUDIENCE: ADAPTING TO DIFFERENT STYLES OF LEARNING

Consider the following scenarios. In the first, the president of the United States goes on national TV to explain a foreign-policy situation that could lead to the commitment of our armed forces. In the second, a police officer visits a local elementary school to instruct children about bicycle safety. In the third, an NBA pro at a basketball camp demonstrates to high school students the proper techniques for accurate free-throw shooting. And in the fourth a NASA spokesperson describes findings from the latest Hubble space telescope transmissions.

Each of these scenarios can be viewed as a speaking situation. Further, each involves a speaker publicly *informing* an audience. In each case, the speaker must focus on relating the information to the needs and goals of the audience members. Jaime Escalante had to first reach out to and connect with his students before he could really begin to teach them calculus. So too must every informative speaker reach out to and connect with his or her audience before presenting them with information.

Informative Speaking and Styles of Learning

One important consideration in focusing on your audience is recognizing that not everyone has the same style of learning. Not everybody thinks in a linear or "logical" fashion. Some people can simply read a book and absorb the information, whereas others need to hear and see to learn. Still others learn best by doing. Good public speakers recognize these differences and appeal to as many styles as possible. Here is one listing of diverse learning styles:[3]

- *Auditory linguistic:* Learning by hearing the spoken word.
- *Visual linguistic:* Learning by seeing the printed word.
- *Auditory numerical:* Learning by hearing numbers.
- *Visual numerical:* Learning by seeing numbers.
- *Audio–visual–kinesthetic combination:* Learning by hearing, seeing, and doing in combination.
- *Individual:* Learning when by oneself.
- *Group:* Learning in collaboration with other people.
- *Oral expressive:* Learning by telling others orally.
- *Written expressive:* Learning by writing.

At first, such a long list of diverse learning styles may be intimidating. How in the world can one speech or even a series of speeches adapt to all of these different ways of learning? Of course, you cannot be all things to all people. But teachers confront this variety of learning styles every day. Many teachers use a combination of methods—individual and group work, written and oral assignments, print and visual materials—in an effort to adapt to the variety of learning styles in their classrooms.

Rather than trying to guess which one style of learning is most widespread in an audience and focusing on that, it is better to use multiple channels and modes of learning. That way, you are likely to reach most of your audience members with something that suits their style of learning. In any given audience, there are likely to be individual learners as well as group learners, those who respond best to oral instruction and those who need to read it, and so on. Using visual aids, for example, is an excellent way to reinforce visually what you say orally. Distributing a handout after a speech can help visual learners retain what was said. Provide your audience with an opportunity to use as many senses as possible to process your message. If parts of your presentation can be seen, heard, and even touched, you will increase the odds that your message will sink in.

One speech we heard, for example, was about using acupressure to relieve stress. By instructing the class to press on certain points on their bodies, the speaker allowed the audience to use their sense of touch to understand what was being said. Other speakers appeal to the sense of taste. We frequently have international students speak about a food unique to their culture and bring samples for the audience to try. Further, the active involvement of some audience members will help reach those who need group reinforcement to learn. Audience involvement is a technique used by Jonathan Studebaker, who we introduced in Chapter 2. He frequently talks to children at elementary schools about dealing with disabilities and tries to involve them by asking them questions and responding to their answers. A speech by Jonathan is not a one-way transmission, but a true transaction between him and the audience.

The Components of Learning

Learning is the acquisition of new information. But it is more than just mentally absorbing the knowledge. Learning has three components: cognitive, affective, and behavioral.[4] **Cognition** is the purely mental component of learning. For example, when schoolchildren memorize the Pledge of Allegiance to the flag, they have learned a series of words and phrases. **Affect** is the emotional/attitudinal component of learning, the way you *feel about* having to learn something and your attitude toward the subject matter. The attitude of patriotism and reverence toward the American flag represents the affective component of the Pledge of Allegiance. **Behavior** is the skill component of learning, the ability to do something with the knowledge acquired. Reciting the Pledge of Allegiance is an overt behavior.

Mathematics provides another good example of these three components of learning. Jaime Escalante was not satisfied if his students merely memorized calculus formulas. That would be a purely mental, or cognitive, process. He changed his students' affect, or attitude, toward math. If you have seen the movie based on his life, you know that at first his students didn't believe they could learn calculus. He had to help them have faith in themselves and their ability to achieve in math. Finally, Escalante had to

FIGURE 12.1

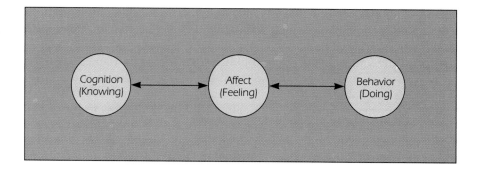

influence his students' behavior. Not only did they need to know the rules of calculus, they had to perform on the Advanced Placement Test. Notice that no one component of learning stands alone. All three components are linked to each other, as Figure 12.1 indicates.

Your goal in an informative speech is to facilitate learning: to provide information on your topic, to influence your audience's attitude toward your topic, and to affect their behavior in relation to your topic.

Informative Speaking and Opinion Leadership

Informative speaking plays a dual role in the process of opinion leadership. Recall from Chapter 1 that an opinion leader influences others to adopt innovative ideas, products, or processes. Because learning involves adopting *new* ideas, it is in one sense a *result* of the opinion leadership process. At the same time, informative speaking is part of the larger process of opinion leadership. The *first* stage in the process of opinion leadership is providing information about your topic. The *second* step is persuading the audience that the information should be used in a way consistent with your goals. Jaime Escalante didn't just give his students the facts about how to do calculus; he persuaded them to use that information to gain college credit and improve their lives. Information that is compelling enough for you to share with your audience should be made compelling enough for them to listen. Any chance of leading audience opinion in a specific direction, moreover, rests with this crucial and necessary informative step.[5]

Successful opinion leaders are also people who are perceived by their audience as credible sources, who are moderately similar to them. In Chapter 13 we will discuss the concept of source credibility at greater length, but it is important that you realize now that, in any speaking situation, your ability to influence your audience is a function of your perceived credibility, that is, your believability. This is based on perceptions of competence and trustworthiness. Obviously, Escalante's success as a teacher was largely a result of his credibility with students, particularly since they perceived him as moderately similar in many respects to themselves. Recall from Chapter 5 that source credibility is the modern-day equivalent of what Aristotle called "ethos."

Although academics may be fond of "knowledge for knowledge's sake," most students seek and remember knowledge they find personally and professionally useful. Over the course of a semester or quarter, therefore, part of a teacher's job is to ensure that students understand the usefulness and relevance of the knowledge they acquire. The first step in teaching information to students usually involves some type of informative presentation, most commonly a lecture. In a sense, a good lecture is an effective informative speech. It should provide students with information that is stimulating and potentially useful. At the lecture's end, moreover, it should leave students feeling that the experience was a positive one and that the information shared is relevant to them. The same is true when you deliver an informative speech.

The Informative–Persuasive Continuum

Students often ask when a speech is merely informative and when it is both informative and persuasive. Some people argue that a speech can be exclusively informative, with no purpose other than passing information along to an audience. Others argue that the distinction between an informative speech and a persuasive speech is blurred.

We are in the second camp. We believe that an informative speech is not worth giving unless it is designed to stay with the audience and influence their lives in some way. What good, for example, is an informative speech about the proper equipment for safe roller blading if it doesn't increase the probability that the audience will seriously consider the information? By the same token, what good is an informative speech on preventive health practices, such as using a condom, if it has no motivational value for an audience?

Instead of looking at the relationship between informative and persuasive speeches as a dichotomy, therefore, think about them in terms of a continuum (shown in Figure 12.2). On one end of the continuum is knowledge, on the other end is behavior. Given the poles of this continuum, behavior change is seldom the result of a singularly persuasive speech delivered by a singularly credible and charismatic speaker. More typically, persuasion is a process, composed of a series of interdependent messages over time. In the so-called real world, this process—this campaign—begins with someone or some agency providing people with information designed to stimulate them. The information is then used as a base from which to build a more explicitly persuasive campaign to influence people's behavior.

We encourage you to view your informative speeches from the perspective of this continuum. Although a single speech may be predominantly directed toward the informative end of the continuum, it may also contribute to the process of persuading at least some audience members to change at some point in the future. In order to gain experience in the kind of informative speaking you're likely to do in your professional life, try to select a topic that is reasonably serious and relevant to people's real concerns. Talking about a frivolous topic because you think your goal is simply to provide information is generally a waste of time, both yours and your audience's.

SIX ATTRIBUTES OF EFFECTIVE INFORMATIVE SPEAKING

What makes one speaker's presentation so informative and stimulating that you want to learn more about what you initially thought was a boring topic? And why does another speaker's presentation leave you cold from the beginning to end? Is the reason (a) the speaker, (b) the topic, (c) the message, (d) your perceptions, or (e) all of the above? Because the public speaking transaction is an interdependent system, the answer, of course, is (e) all of the above.

However, if an informative speech is seen as personally or professionally relevant, it can be successful in spite of being delivered by a marginally skilled public speaker. The reverse, moreover, is not always true; that is, we may not find an entertaining speaker personally or professionally informative.

Research over the past two decades suggests that the likelihood of an audience perceiving information as relevant depends significantly on six message attributes: novelty, compatibility, comprehensibility, relative advantage, observability, and trialability.[6] These attributes represent the criteria people use to decide whether a speaker's information is worth the time and effort necessary to pay attention and actively process it.

Novelty

Novelty is the quality of being new and stimulating. Just as plants are heliotropic, we human beings are stimulitropic. In other words, plants continuously orient themselves to the sun to activate the process of photosynthesis, while we continually orient ourselves to new and unique sources of stimulation.

Although novelty alone is not enough to sustain an informative speech, it certainly can make your speech more effective. Research has time and again documented the fact that the perception of novelty heightens selective exposure, selective attention, and selective retention of information. In other words, people are likely to seek out, pay attention to, and remember novel information. The most obvious way to get the benefit of novelty in

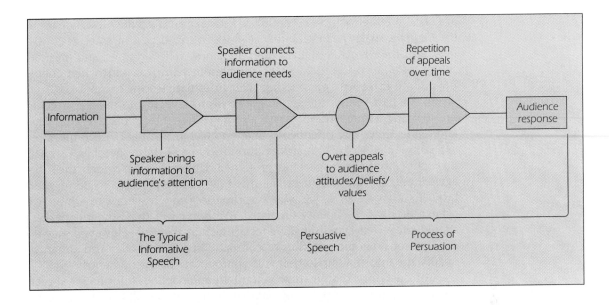

FIGURE 12.2
Continuum of
informative to
persuasive speaking.

an informative speech is to choose a topic that is novel for your audience. You're much more likely to initially captivate the attention of audience members with the unfamiliar than with the mundane. Novelty, however, shouldn't be confused with the obscure. For example, whereas computer software for accountancy probably would be an obscure topic for most audiences, the fact that the software could save you money on your taxes might be a novel topic.

Another way to use novelty to your advantage is in the construction of your message. Even though the rule of thumb is to structure your speech so that the audience can predict what comes next, this is not an unbending rule. Sometimes it is to your advantage to violate the expectancies of an audience. Writers, for example, sometimes begin with a story's end and then backtrack. Similarly, a skilled speaker could start a speech with what normally would be considered its conclusion and build backward.

Finally, novelty in your delivery can work to your advantage when speaking informatively. Audiences, for instance, generally are accustomed to speakers who are relatively stationary. Movement may add needed novelty to your presentation. In addition, if you review some of our suggestions about the nonverbal dynamics of delivery, you'll find other ways to introduce novelty to your presentation.

Compatibility

Early in this book we said that communication is perceptual and that the process of perception is selective. Basically, people perceive what they choose to perceive. In the effort to reach your audience with an informative speech, a second message attribute you'll need to take into account is compatibility. **Compatibility** is the audience's perception that a message is consistent with their belief systems—their attitudes, beliefs, values, and lifestyle. All too often, speakers fail to take compatibility into account when choosing a topic and then constructing their informative speech.

In the past year, for example, we've heard several informative speeches on AIDS and its prevention. We've also had students approach us after class and tell us they were offended or made to feel unjustifiably uncomfortable as a consequence of (1) the information in some of these speeches, (2) their perception that these speeches promoted a lifestyle with which they disagreed, and (3) the use of visual aids they didn't perceive to be in good taste. To a large degree, we were surprised by these reactions to a topic we believe needs to be openly discussed. We don't feel that student speakers should altogether avoid sensitive topics such as this one. However, they do need to consider the question of compatibility so that they can soften or qualify the information so that it is appropriate for the audience.

Consider, for example, how you might approach an informative speech on the constitutional rights of accused felons for two different audiences. The first audience is composed of law school students. The second is a group of veteran police officers. Both audiences need the information you have. Would you give an identical speech to both of them? Probably not. For the police officers, you most likely would have to qualify the information in your speech with such statements as

> "I realize some of you take exception with the courts' rulings on the rights of the accused."
>
> "Putting our personal feelings aside, the Constitution is clear . . ."
>
> "Before I begin, I want you to put the shoe on the other foot; assume that you are the accused."

The point is that information that is potentially incompatible with audience members can be made palatable if it is presented in a way that acknowledges the audience's point of view.

Comprehensibility

No matter how simple or complex your topic, your audience should perceive it as something they can understand. **Comprehensibility** is the perception that a message is not too difficult or complex to understand. Research tells us that one of the quickest ways to turn off an audience is to complicate a topic. You don't have to avoid complex topics for your informative speeches. In fact, they are likely to be both novel for your audience and interesting for you to research. The goal is to make complex topics comprehensible and compelling.

Jaime Escalante's calculus classes in *Stand and Deliver* are models of the presentation of complex information. He broke the lessons into easy-to-digest bits, what he called "step by step." In fact, he would say to his students, "This is easy." It's not so much the complexity of the topic as the complexity of a speaker's explanation that makes a topic difficult for an audience to understand.

An excellent way to reduce the complexity of a speech is through analogies or comparisons. Explain a complex process, for example, by comparing it with a common process based on the same principle. One speech we heard explained nuclear power plants by using an analogy to the steam produced by heating water in a tea kettle.

Visual aids can also be helpful in reducing complexity. For example, we recall a speech about a complex carbon molecule in which the speaker used a "tinkertoy" model to show what the molecule looked like. The speaker also used an analogy, calling the molecule a "soot ball," to help the audience visualize what it would be like.

Relative Advantage

When we introduced the tools you need to get started on your first speech, we talked about the importance of connecting with your audience. Audience members need to know explicitly why it is in their interest to listen to what you have to say.

When we connect with our audience, we are in effect saying, "My topic and message hold some relative advantage for you." The **relative advantage,** or the audience's perception that a message will benefit them, can be a more informed view on some topic or an improved way of behaving. Don't think that just because you have a good idea, people will necessarily see the advantage in adopting it. History is replete with good ideas, the proverbial better mousetrap, that are collecting dust for want of the public's attention. Consider two examples from Everett M. Rogers's classic work, *The Diffusion of Innovations.*[7]

If you have studied the history of science, you may recall that the disease scurvy, caused by a deficiency of vitamin C, was a serious problem for sailors on long voyages. As early as 1601, it was found that sources of vitamin C effectively inhibited scurvy. Yet it took almost 200 years for the British navy to put this finding to use on its ships, and almost 75 years more for sources of vitamin C to be made available on commercial ships.

The second example concerns the arrangement of the keyboard on typewriters and personal computers. If you have ever thought the keys were illogically arranged, you are not alone. A far better method of arrangement of keys has been available since 1932. The Dvorak method is more efficient than the system almost everybody uses and is more easily mastered. So why weren't you taught the Dvorak method in the beginning? Because the one you use was invented in 1873 and has been designed into almost all keyboards ever since. One of the reasons for staying with the less-logical keyboard was that the metal keys of early typewriters stuck when the typist worked too quickly. Thus, the keyboard we use today on computers and electric typewriters was originally invented to *slow down* typists on mechanical typewriters.

You can probably think of other good ideas that people have failed to adopt. Macintosh users were amused at the hype over Windows '95, pointing out that the same simplicity of use has been available on the Mac for a decade. Yet 90 percent of all personal computers are IBM-compatibles, not Macs. And despite its demise as a format for video recording, Sony's betamax was technically superior to VHS. The list of great ideas that haven't been adopted is endless. And the key to getting your ideas accepted is to show the audience the relative advantage inherent in adopting them.

All too often, speakers assume that audience members will recognize they have something to personally or professionally gain from a speech. What may be perfectly obvious to the speaker, however, may be just the opposite for the audience. Consider a case with which you already have some experience—college classes. Regardless of the subject matter of their classes, most college professors believe that the information they have to share is absolutely essential to every student's intellectual well-being. So secure are they in this belief, in fact, some seldom spend any time convincing students that there are "good reasons" for their being in the professor's class.

Occasionally, this oversight doesn't much matter—for example, when students are taking a course in their major. Students listen because they know they "have to learn" what is being taught, regardless of how well it's being taught. This is seldom the case, though, when they find themselves in a required course outside their major. "Why do I need a course in art history?" complains the computer science major, while the chemistry major asks, "Why do I need a class in public speaking?" To motivate students in math classes, Jaime Escalante put together a video called *Who Needs Math?* starring people like Bill Cosby.

Just as teachers have an obligation to connect their course to the professional aspirations of students, so do speakers have the same kind of obligation to their audiences. It's not enough that their information is perceived as novel or compatible by their audience. Their information—their speech—also must be readily perceived as something that will benefit their audience.

Observability

Seeing is believing, or so the saying goes. Information that can be made observable for your audience can work to your advantage. **Observability** is the degree to which information can be seen. For example, in and of themselves, statistics such as gross national product, median income, the consumer price index, and the rate of inflation can ring very hollow in the ears of an audience. Yet such information very often is the stuff of which informative speeches are made. One way to breathe life into statistics is to augment the speech with creative visual aids, such as those discussed in Chapter 11. In fact, this kind of augmentation may be what makes your audience nod in understanding instead of staring back at you with blank expressions.

The need for observability is not limited to statistical information. A working model of an internal combustion engine certainly would help a mechanically disinclined audience understand an informative presentation on automotive engineering; a detailed cross section of the human eye would help a group of biology students understand the role of the cornea; and even a visually appealing list of the daily diet of the American teenager might help a group of nursing students relate to an informative speech on nutrition.

Although visual aids may be the most obvious way to give pictorial life to your informative speech, you also can provide word pictures for your audience. For example, in the effort to assist your audience in visualizing your information you can ask the audience to imagine a situation; use examples for which the audience is likely to have a visual referent, such as the Statue of Liberty, a landmark at your school, or a national park; and use descriptive adjectives, action words, and visual metaphors. Regardless of how you give visual life to your informative speech, however, the objective is the same: You want your audience to "see" what it is you are talking about.

Trialability

The final message attribute we want to share with you is most relevant to informative presentations that require some demonstration. **Trialability** is the opportunity to experiment with an idea, a product, or a practice without penalty. Simply put, people prefer to "try something on for size" before deciding on its personal or professional worth.

In the business world, for instance, when the PC began to replace the typewriter, and the fax and e-mail began to replace letters, trialability was essential to informative presentations on the uses of these new technologies. One of the lessons learned in the process of computerizing the workplace was that people were quicker to respond favorably to innovations when provided with an opportunity to try them out in a nonthreatening environment.

Of course, it is often not realistic to have an entire audience "try out" something as you speak. Sometimes the solution is to provide the audience with information on where they can go to try out what you have discussed in your speech. For example, a speech on CPR should include specific information on where to get hands-on training. On other occasions, you can invite a few audience members to the front of the room and have them try out the process in front of everyone else, showing how it can be done. Then you can urge audience members to try it out on their own. In any case, if some kind of trial experience can be incorporated into a speech, it will enhance the audience's understanding of the subject matter.

At some point in either your educational or professional life, you can reasonably expect to provide some demonstration for an audience. It may be something as simple as explaining your job, or it may be assisting people in the solution of a complex problem. Whether simple or complex, the best demonstrations are those that involve the people with whom you are speaking. After all, it's much easier to relate to information with which we have hands-on experience than to relate to information that has been conveyed passively.

PUTTING THEORY INTO PRACTICE

Now that you know some of the principles related to conveying information to an audience, it's time to plan your own informative speech. This section offers some practical suggestions for how to give an informative speech. We discuss four ways to inform an audience: explanation, instruction, demonstration, and description. Informative speeches may employ more than one of these modes of informing. And the list is not exhaustive. Nevertheless, these four categories should be a useful way of thinking of how to translate the principles of informative speaking into an actual speech.

Speeches That Explain

One of the primary functions you may wish to accomplish in an informative speech is to explain some process, object, or concept to an audience. Your political science teacher may explain the *process* of democratization of the Eastern European nations. Your astronomy teacher may explain the composition of a star, an *object*. Your communication teacher may explain how verbal and nonverbal messages differ, a *concept*.

In selecting a topic for a speech that explains something, keep in mind that the topic should be relevant to the audience, something they are capable of understanding, and something you can explain in the time allotted. Although the theory of relativity is highly relevant, explaining it in a 5- to 10-minute speech is a tall order.

The message attribute of comprehensibility is particularly important in speeches that explain. Recall that one way to reduce complexity for an audience is to use an analogy. Consider the use of analogy in this excerpt from a speech by Jonathan Studebaker, explaining a disease he has:

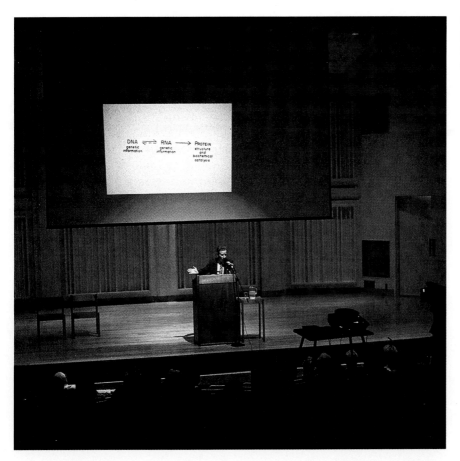

Observability is an important attribute of speeches that explain.

> Like I said, I'm a nice person. I'm cheerful, I'm energetic. Okay, so I have a disability. I was born with osteogenesis imperfecta, a disease which causes my bones to be fragile. Have you ever accidentally dropped a glass on the floor? What happens? It breaks. Well, my bones kinda break like glass, which is why I tell people, when you carry me, treat me like your best crystal.[8]

The use of a simple analogy of bones to glass helps the audience understand a disease most of us cannot even pronounce. For Jonathan's purposes, which are to introduce himself and explain his disability, that is the extent of the technical information his audience needs to know.

A second attribute that is important in speeches that explain is observability. One of the best ways to make something observable is with visual aids. They can make an abstract concept concrete and thus easier to understand.

During your college career, you will undoubtedly be called on to explain something to an audience, if not in your public speaking class, then in another setting. Similarly, in the professional world, it is common for people to be called on to explain everything from a new product idea to why the last quarter's sales were so bad. Using the principles of comprehensibility and observability can help you enhance your explanations.

Speeches That Instruct

Informative speaking can also be used to instruct an audience. The key to instruction is to provide new information the audience can put to use. Modern educational theory emphasizes observable behavioral objectives; that is, after receiving instruction, the student should be able to show that he or she has mastered the subject, either by answering questions or by engaging in some activity.

The message attributes of novelty and relative advantage are particularly relevant to speeches that provide instruction. First, consider novelty. Unless the information in your speech presents *new* information to your audience, all you have done is bore them with what they already know. For example, speeches on how to ride a bike or how to pack your suitcase are unlikely to provide anything new to an audience. However, some new topics can be perceived as irrelevant or of no relative advantage by large portions of an audience. For example, a speech on how to wax your skis is old news to experienced skiers, but irrelevant to nonskiers in the class.

So, the key to speeches that instruct is to provide new yet relevant information to your audience. That means using the novelty of your topic to gain interest while pointing out the relative advantage of learning the information to at least the majority of listeners.

Speeches That Demonstrate

Speeches that demonstrate are closely related to those that provide instruction, but they use the message attributes of observability and trialability. In a speech that demonstrates, the speaker actually shows the audience how to do something. Further, a good demonstration will allow the audience to try out what is being demonstrated, if not during the speech itself, then later on their own. A good example of speeches that demonstrate are the late-night infomercials. From food dehydrators to onion slicers, the product is demonstrated for the audience. The use of the product is clearly observable to the viewers at home and in the studio. Audience members are often given a chance to try the product. Viewers are urged to order the product and try it at home, with a no-risk, money-back guarantee. The combination of observability and trialability has made infomercials highly successful.

Whatever a speaker is demonstrating, he or she needs to provide audience members with enough information to do the activity on their own, or with information on where to obtain further instruction, so that they can try out the activity. For example, although no one can master karate from

a single speech, or even a series of speeches, a demonstration of karate moves can spur an audience member to seek out individual instruction in the martial arts. In fact, many martial arts studios make a practice of giving demonstrations in schools and at public events as a way of recruiting new students.

Topics for speeches that demonstrate need to be chosen with care. A complex, difficult task cannot be adequately demonstrated in a few minutes. There can even be the danger of making people think they know how to do something based on a speech when in fact they do not. Few of us could do CPR, for example, based on simply watching a speaker demonstrate the activity. We need the opportunity to try it out (perhaps on a life-size doll) before we can know whether we can do it. On the other hand, another lifesaving technique, the Heimlich maneuver, is often the subject of demonstration and can be learned in a reasonably short time.

Clothing designer Diane von Furstenberg uses the principle of observability on QVC as she wears the shirt she is selling on the air. Like other on-air salespeople, she also employs the principle of trialability by offering a money-back guarantee.

Failure to properly prepare for a demonstration is the hallmark of Tim Allen's comedy on Home Improvement, but it can lead to disaster in an informative speech.

The key to making your demonstration effective is careful planning. For example, if you have ever watched the show *Home Improvement,* you know that Tim (The Tool Man) Taylor rarely has practiced what he is doing. If you plan to demonstrate a process in your speech, rehearse it carefully. Also, it is sometimes useful to prepare various steps of the process in advance. Watch any cooking show demonstration on TV. The onions are already chopped, the flour is already sifted and measured, and so on. You don't want the audience drifting off as you measure ingredients or sift the flour. Providing a written recipe in a handout or as a visual aid will save you a lot of time and let the audience focus on watching your demonstration. In short, a demonstration requires extra preparation.

In addition, be sure that the demonstration is an accurate re-creation. If you misinform an audience, you have done more harm than good. Depending on what you are demonstrating, you might even be inviting injury to the audience member or someone else. Make certain, therefore, that you can accurately demonstrate the process in the time allowed.

Finally, make sure the demonstration is visible to the audience. We recall a student who was an expert fisherman and wanted to demonstrate the art of fly tying. Since fishing line is almost invisible and a fish hook is very difficult to see, he used a large-scale fish hook (made from a coat hanger) and colored yarn to tie his fly. Only by enlarging the actual objects was he able to give the audience a meaningful demonstration.

Speeches That Describe

Another function of informative speeches is description. Observability is the key to descriptive speech. Not only can visual aids be useful; you may also want to provide a word picture of your subject. Consider the following description of a familiar character, Mickey Mouse, provided by student speaker Jennie Rees:

> They designed him using a circle for his head and oblong circles for his nose and snout. They also drew circles for his ears and drew them in such a way that they appeared to look the same any way Mickey turned his head. They gave him a pear-shaped body with pipe-stem legs, and stuffed them in big, oversized shoes, making him look like a little kid wearing his father's shoes.[9]

Can't you almost picture Mickey from that description? Visual language is key to effective description.

Description can be used not only for physical objects but also for scenes or events. Consider the briefings given by General Norman Schwarzkopf during the Persian Gulf War. He used a variety of maps and charts to explain every move. He used terms from football and other sports, calling the American troop movements a "Hail Mary pass." Further, rather than merely telling the audience about the success of U.S. smart bombs, he used a video to show the accuracy with which targets were destroyed. In one memorable incident, he pointed to a vehicle passing through the cross hairs of the bomber just before the target was hit. He called the driver, "the luckiest man in Iraq."

Putting It All Together

Whether your speech is primarily explanation, instruction, demonstration, or description, it is important that you incorporate as many of the six attributes of effective informative speaking as possible. Regardless of the type of speech, keep in mind that compatibility is a important factor. If your audience sees the topic as incompatible with their needs, beliefs, attitudes, or values, they will view your speech as a hostile persuasive attempt, rather than an informative speech.

What, then, does an effective informative speech look like? For one example, see the box "Sample Informative Speech: Eating Disorders and Their Warning Signs, by Kelli Wells" on pages 366–367. This speech and the accompanying annotations should help you put together the concepts discussed in this chapter as you plan and prepare your own informative speech.

VIDEO FILE

If you have access to the videotape that accompanies this text, view segment 9. It shows Kelli Wells's informative speech "Eating Disorders and Their Warning Signs."

Sample Informative Speech

Eating Disorders and Their Warning Signs, by Kelli Wells

This speech was prepared and delivered by Kelli Wells, a student in a speech class. It is reprinted here with her permission. The following text was prepared based on a transcript of Kelli's speech. Because extemporaneous speaking frequently leads to unintentional errors, we have edited the speech for you to read.

Notice how Kelli uses a vivid description to capture the audience's attention.

Also, because it is a personal experience, her credibility on the topic is established.

Kelli stresses the relative advantage of learning about eating disorders—you may save a life.

Kelli's preview is clear and direct.

Kelli uses clear language to explain a complex topic in terms everyone can understand.

The difference between the two disorders is clearly explained.

I knew my best friend had a problem. Didn't she know what she was doing to herself? Her weight and food consumption had become an obsession with her. I could see how it was controlling her. But in her mind, it was all she could control. She couldn't eat anything without quickly running to the bathroom. I had to hear daily how fat she was and how her life would be so much better if she was thinner. As she got deeper and deeper into an eating disorder, bulimia nervosa, she was no longer the person I used to know. I know the signs of an eating disorder, and I was able to confront her about her problem. She was able to get help and now she's doing much better.

I've seen firsthand how an eating disorder can affect someone. That's why it's important that we all know about them and the warning signs of an eating disorder. You may be able to save a life. Knowing more about eating disorders will enable you to be more aware of what may be going on in the mind of even a friend or a family member.

Tonight, you will be informed of the main types of eating disorders, who are the most likely candidates, and the signs to look for.

The two main types of eating disorders are anorexia and bulimia nervosa. The fear of obesity and the pursuit of thinness represent the driving force in both these mental disorders.

In anorexia nervosa this fear is expressed through a number of symptoms, including the desire to maintain a very low body weight, body-image disturbance, and avoiding food altogether. There is intense fear of getting fat and an obsession with being thin. These are the two most cognitive features of anorexia.

Anorexic individuals also struggle with body-image disturbance. They have a distorted view in which they perceive their body to be fat, in spite of its thin appearance. They also suffer extreme dissatisfaction with the size or the shape of the body. Food avoidance is another problem. Anorexics will avoid food altogether and obtain only small amounts of diet food, such as salads or fruits.

Young women with bulimia nervosa share many of the same symptoms as anorexics. Most bulimic women are dissatisfied with their current body weight. Bulimics, however, are not as effective in dieting and usually weigh within the normal range. So they are able to avoid treatment for many years. But actually what they are doing to their bodies is completely destroying their systems. Bulimics binge-eat, which means they eat large amounts of food uncontrollably, and then force themselves to purge the calories consumed to avoid weight gain. For many bulimic individuals the act of eating is associated with the feeling of being out of control. They're able to regain control by purging.

Now that you are informed of the two main types of eating disorders, anorexia and bulimia nervosa, it's important to know who the most likely candidates are for having these disorders.

The most widespread group of people that are affected by these disorders are young women. Our society today believes that the thinner you are, the better your life will be. Young women begin to measure their self-esteem on their dieting success. They believe that eating is the cause and result of many of their problems. So they become trapped in a vicious cycle of rigid behavior focused on food. We're continually confronted in newspapers, magazines, and television, with ads imploring and encouraging us to eat and prepare all kinds of food. At the same time, young women are encouraged and pressured to be thin and maintain perfect figures by fashion designers. This paradox is hard to manage and for most young women results in an eating disorder.

In doing my research, I found statistics for college populations from the book Eating Disorders: Assessment and Treatment, by Scholtz and Johnson. In 22 studies done across college campuses, an average of 7.6 percent of college women suffer from some type of eating disorder. As we can see, this is a problem that shouldn't be forgotten.

Now that I have informed you that young women are the most affected by these disorders, it is crucial to know the warning signs. In bulimia nervosa, the warning signs are dehydration, digestive disorders, severe dental problems, and muscle weaknesses. In anorexia, the symptoms are dry skin and hair, cold hands and feet, general weakness, and most importantly extreme weight loss.

In conclusion, let me summarize the three main points I informed you about tonight. First, the two main types of eating disorders are bulimia and anorexia nervosa. Second, young women are the most likely candidates for having these disorders. And thirdly, the symptoms which I shared with you are important to know in helping a friend or even a family member.

My best friend felt what many women feel everywhere, that to be thin equals happiness. Eating disorders are vicious traps that, once you get into, are very hard to get out of. Hopefully now, by knowing more about them, you can help someone you care about.

Notice the clear use of signposts in the speech to indicate transitions between points.

By citing statistics on college-age women, Kelli connects with her college-age audience.

Observable symptoms of the disorders are presented. (Would a visual aid have been helpful here?)

Summary is clear and accurate.

Conclusion ties back to introduction. Audience members are urged to use the information in the speech.

FORUMS FOR INFORMATIVE SPEAKING

Informative speaking is probably the form of public speaking you're most likely to be called on to do at some point in your life. One of the chief reasons is that informative speaking is used in so many settings, including the classroom, the workplace, and the community.

Informative Speaking in the Classroom

Two time-honored traditions in the college classroom are the term paper and oral report. Although most students have at least passing familiarity with the elements of a good term paper, many students don't make the connection between the elements of a good oral report and the process of informative speaking.

Undergraduate speech majors are usually pleased to see that an oral report is required in a course outside their major. They know that an oral report basically is an informative speech. Thus, by putting to use what they know about informative speaking, they usually are able to give oral reports that are both substantively and stylistically more effective than those of their classmates.

Viewing the oral report as an opportunity to speak informatively has several advantages. First, it provides you with an organizational framework for constructing your report. Second, it reminds you that you have an audience for your report whose background and perceptual reality must be taken into account. Finally, it forces you to think about how relevant the information in your report is to both your instructor and student colleagues.

Informative Speaking in the Workplace

All the people we have profiled in this book realize now what they didn't necessarily realize as undergraduates: Regardless of major or career, the ability to stand up and speak publicly is a skill both admired and rewarded in the real world.

No matter what you plan on doing to make a living, the odds are great that you will need to make informative presentations. Although you won't necessarily have to speak informatively to large numbers of people, you can reasonably expect to speak informatively to your immediate co-workers, perhaps your entire department, or in a meeting with people to whom you're subordinate. It is common in the workplace to make informative presentations before groups. For some presentations you will have to stand and speak; other presentations may be delivered from your seat.

Although the different situations require adjustments in your style of delivery, the substantive elements of your informative presentation are the same. You will still need to follow a cohesive organizational sequence, analyze your audience carefully, and consider the message attributes described earlier in this chapter.

All too often, speakers get trapped into thinking that the smaller their audience, the more informal their delivery and content can be. Instead, they need to make the relational features of the message more interpersonal without sacrificing the content of the message. They can increase nonverbal immediacy, for example, while protecting the formal structure of the speech.

Informative Speaking in the Community

You can reasonably expect to speak informatively with members of your community in at least one of two capacities: as a representative of your employer or as a concerned citizen. Private, as well as public, enterprises are justifiably concerned about their image within their local community. Opinion poll after opinion poll shows that the public is increasingly suspicious of the motives of private enterprise and increasingly dissatisfied with the performance of public agencies in particular. It's not uncommon, therefore, for these organizations to make themselves available to service groups, such as Rotary International, the general public, or a citizens' group organized around a specific cause.

Some businesses have a person whose job is company spokesperson; large corporations may even have whole departments dedicated to public relations. Many organizations, however, have come to expect anyone in management to serve as an informative speaker to the community. In fact, private corporations, such as IBM, and public agencies, such as the police or fire department, may actually write such community service into their managers' job descriptions. Thus, just because you currently perceive your intended career as low profile, that doesn't necessarily make it so.

Finally, remote as the possibility may seem to you now, you may one day want or need to speak informatively as a private citizen. If you live in a community where cable television is available, your city council meetings probably are televised on your community access channel. If you tune in, you will see ordinary citizens making informative presentations at these meetings. Topics can range from the environmental impact of a new housing development to excessive noise from student housing. If you watch several of these presentations, you probably will conclude that very few of the speakers have much training in public speaking; people who do have training are easy to spot.

Your days as a public speaker will not be over once you've completed this class. Given what we've said here, in fact, you should now realize they are just beginning.

SUMMARY

To be successful, informative speakers must do as Jaime Escalante did, instill *ganas,* the desire and the motivation to succeed, into their audiences. Speakers must also adapt their informative speeches to audiences with diverse learning styles. One way to do so is to incorporate multiple methods and channels of learning into their speeches.

Informative speaking is the process by which an audience gains new information from a speaker. Learning is the acquisition of new information by a person, and it involves three interrelated components: cognition, the purely mental aspects of learning; affect, the emotional/attitudinal component; and behavior, the skill component. Informative speaking is related to opinion leadership and persuasion by virtue of being the first step in the process of influencing people to adopt new ideas, products, and processes. Informative and persuasive speaking are best viewed as ends of a continuum, rather than totally unrelated types of speaking.

Informative speakers should use the message attributes novelty, compatibility, comprehensibility, relative advantage, observability, and trialability in their informative speeches. Informative speeches may explain, instruct, demonstrate, and/or describe. Each of these types of speeches employs one or more of the six attributes of effective informative speaking.

Informative speaking is by far the most common type of public speaking and routinely occurs in the classroom, the workplace, and the community.

Check Your Understanding: Exercises and Activities

1. Develop an outline for a one- to two-minute speech in which you inform an audience about a topic with which you are personally very familiar. Then show how you would adapt that speech to at least three different learning styles: auditory linguistic, visual linguistic, and audio–visual–kinesthetic.

2. On a topic of your choice, explain how you would prepare an informative speech so that it would have an impact on the listeners' cognitive, affective, and behavioral learning.

3. On a topic of your choice, explain how you would prepare an informative speech that would play a role in the process of opinion leadership on that topic. How would your speech play this role?

4. Come up with at least two possible topics each for speeches that explain, instruct, demonstrate, and describe. Do some topics seem to fall naturally into one category? Are there other topics that might be used for more than one type of speech?

5. Reread Kelli Wells's speech "Eating Disorders and Their Warning Signs," presented earlier in the chapter. (If you have access to the videotape that accompanies this book, you may also view the speech in segment 9.) To what extent does this speech incorporate the attributes of novelty, compatibility, comprehensibility, relative advantage, observability, and trialability discussed in this chapter? To what extent would the speech benefit from further use of any of these message attributes? After reading and/or viewing the speech, construct an outline of the speech, identifying the opening, connection with the audience, focus, main points, summary, and close.

Notes

1. Jay Mathews, *Escalante: The Best Teacher in America* (New York: Henry Holt, 1988), 191.

2. *Stand and Deliver,* director Tom Menendez, with Edward James Olmos, Lou Diamond Phillips, Rosana De Soto, and Andy Garcia, An American Playhouse Theatrical Film, A Menendez/Musca & Olmos Production, Warner Bros., 1988.

3. P. Friedman and R. Alley, "Learning/Teaching Styles: Applying the Principles," *Theory into Practice* 23 (1984): 77–81. Based on R. Dunn and K. Dunn, *Teaching Students Through Their Individual Learning Styles: A Practical Approach* (Reston, Va.: Reston Publishing, 1978).

4. Michael D. Scott and L. R. Wheeless, "Instructional Communication Theory and Research: An Overview," in *Communication Yearbook I,* ed. Brent D. Ruben (New Brunswick, N.J.: Transaction Books, 1977), 495–511.

5. Everett M. Rogers and R. Adhikarya, "Diffusion of Innovation: An Up-to-Date Review and Commentary," in *Communication Yearbook III,* ed. Dan Nimmo (New Brunswick, N.J.: Transaction Books, 1979), 67–81.

6. Michael D. Scott and Scott Elliot, "Innovation in the Classroom: Toward a Reconceptualization of Instructional Communication" (paper presented at the annual meeting of the International Communication Association, Dallas, Texas, 1983).

7. Everett M. Rogers, *Diffusion of Innovations* (New York: Free Press, 1983).

8. Jonathan Studebaker, "Speech of Self-Introduction: Who Am I?" The full text appears in Appendix A.

9. Jennie Rees, "Informative Speech: Mickey: A Changing Image." The full text appears in Appendix A.

Sarah and Jim Brady appealed to opinion leaders in Congress, such as Senator Bob Dole, in their successful effort to pass the "Brady Bill" to enforce a waiting period for the purchase of handguns.

13

Persuasive Speaking

Character may almost be called the most effective means of persuasion.
—Aristotle[1]

OBJECTIVES

After reading this chapter, you should be able to:

- Describe how your assessment of the rhetorical situation is important to persuasive speaking.
- Describe the four goals persuasive speeches are designed to achieve.
- Define ethos, logos, and pathos.
- Describe the process of elaborated thinking in relationship to persuasion.
- Demonstrate how to use Toulmin's model of argument to create a persuasive message.
- Demonstrate how to use first-, second-, and third-order data as evidence in a persuasive speech.
- Explain the rationale for presenting a two-sided persuasive message, and construct a two-sided persuasive message.
- Demonstrate how certain types of persuasive appeals are linked to audience members' emotions and primitive beliefs.

KEY CONCEPTS

backing	logos
claim	pathos
elaboration likelihood model	qualifier
ethos	rebuttal
first-, second-, and third-order data	source credibility
grounds	warrant

The first week in April 1981 was a good time to be a Republican. Ronald Reagan had just been sworn in as president that January, after defeating Democrat Jimmy Carter. It was even better if you happened to hold an important post in the Reagan White House, as did Press Secretary James P. Brady. As a result, Brady was feeling good about himself and his boss, who had just delivered a speech to 3,500 labor leaders.

As usual, a throng of reporters and tourists awaited President Reagan and his entourage as they emerged from the building. As usual, the reporters present immediately began to shout, "Mr. President, Mr. President." And, as usual, Press Secretary Brady stepped ahead of the president to field the questions the reporters were yelling.

What happened in the next two seconds was horrifying. John Hinckley, a disturbed young man, fired six shots from a .22 caliber automatic pistol in the direction of President Reagan, hitting the president, Secret Service Agent Tim McCarthy, and Brady. Reagan and McCarthy recovered completely. Brady, wounded in the head, was permanently disabled and would never completely recover his considerable talents as a communicator.

Fast-forward 12 years. Sarah Brady is testifying before Congress about the merits of a handgun-control bill that bears her husband's name. In a short time, the Brady Bill will become law, the culmination for Sarah and Jim Brady of a decade-long campaign to control the purchase of guns like the one that had been used by John Hinckley. In the course of that campaign, Sarah Brady not only became the founder of Handgun Control, Inc., a nationwide lobbying group dedicated to changing handgun laws, but she also became a public speaker of unquestionable persuasive skills.[2]

Although you may never find yourself thrust into the national limelight like Sarah Brady, you can still count on preparing and delivering at least a few persuasive speeches over the course of your life. What's more, you can learn a lot about this process from Sarah Brady's example. In this chapter we use the case of Sarah Brady to illustrate the process of preparing and delivering an effective, persuasive speech. The topics covered in this chapter include

- the relationship between persuasive speaking and the rhetorical situation;

- factors to take into account in your attempts to reinforce what an audience believes, to inoculate an audience against counterpersuasive speeches, to change audience attitudes, and to prompt an audience to act;

- the relationship of persuasive speaking to the concepts of ethos, pathos, and logos; and

- how you can use these three concepts to construct an effective persuasive speech.

Schoolchildren are frequently the target of persuasive efforts aimed at inoculating them against peer pressure to use illegal drugs.

FOCUSING ON YOUR AUDIENCE: ASSESSING THE RHETORICAL SITUATION

Audience-focused persuasive speaking begins with an assessment of the rhetorical situation, which we first talked about in Chapter 5. You will need a clear understanding of your goals as a speaker, knowledge about your audience, and an assessment of the constraints facing you, including the ethical boundaries you must respect.

The Four Goals of Persuasive Speaking

There are four common, and sometimes interdependent, goals we can achieve through persuasive speaking. The first is to *reinforce* the attitudes, beliefs, and values an audience already holds. Keynote speeches at national political conventions, for example, are usually designed to bolster the common core of beliefs, attitudes, and values to which members of a political party subscribe.

The second goal of persuasive speaking is to *inoculate* an audience against counterpersuasion, that is, persuasive messages opposed to your views. Although it is possible to bolster an audience member's attitudes, beliefs, and values through straight reinforcement, it takes more to make them truly resistant to counterpersuasion. Anti–drug use messages aimed at children, for instance, are most effective when they give sound reasons not to use drugs, rather than telling kids to "just say no." Children can then use these reasons to defend their anti–drug use behavior when confronted with peer pressure to experiment with illegal substances.

The third goal of persuasive speaking is to *change attitudes*. This is a difficult task, because the audience is usually one that disagrees with or is even hostile to your position. For example, a speaker calling for the legalization of marijuana needs to realize that most audiences will not share that point of view. Changing people's attitudes requires incremental change over time. Taking small steps, such as first convincing an audience that marijuana should be legalized for medical purposes, is more likely to achieve success than trying to change people from total opposition to total support in a short time.

The fourth goal of persuasive speaking is to prompt an audience to *act*. This is the most difficult goal to achieve. People are seldom moved to act as a result of a single persuasive speech. A foundation must first be laid that will make the audience likely to act. That takes time and repetition of the message. When it appears that people are responding to a single message, the persuasive speech usually is the most recent in a long line of catalysts that have been building momentum for action. Consider the people who respond to an evangelist's call to get out of their seats, move to the stage, and orally proclaim their faith. The fact that these people voluntarily chose to be in the audience means they probably were predisposed to act. Thus, the evangelist's persuasive sermon was a catalyst rather than the sole cause of their action.

Which of these four goals you will pursue in a given speech depends largely on the audience you are addressing. If they already share your attitudes and values, then a speech of reinforcement is called for. On the other hand, if they are likely to be the subjects of counterpersuasion, or if their commitment to your point of view is shaky, then inoculation is likely to be your goal. If you face an audience opposed to your views, you will need to attempt to change their attitudes, usually a time-consuming incremental process. Finally, if the audience is primed by prior persuasive messages to behave in accordance with your goals, then prompting them to action may be your best approach. Although these goals are related, any given persuasive speech is likely to focus primarily on one outcome.

Analyzing Audience Diversity

The realization of any of these goals depends on how well you have analyzed your audience. Audience analysis starts with an assessment of the relationship between the audience and the goal you hope to achieve. Recall from Chapter 5 that not all audiences are capable of acting to help you achieve your goals, even if they desire to do so. For example, people who are not U.S. citizens or who are under age 18 cannot vote in elections. The candidate who directs a persuasive campaign to either of these groups is just wasting time and money. To prepare and deliver a persuasive speech intended to induce action, therefore, makes sense only if a group is capable of acting.

Once you are sure your goal makes sense in relation to your audience, the next step is to analyze audience diversity. Remember that there are three levels of audience diversity you'll need to consider: cultural, demographic, and individual. Cultural diversity concerns collective ways of thinking and acting. Demographic diversity reflects the attributes according to which people can be grouped, for example, the generation to which people belong. Finally, individual diversity is revealed in people's most deep-seated beliefs, attitudes, and values.

Simply put, the more you know about audience diversity, the better you will be able to predict how the audience is likely to respond to issues and the people associated with the issues. A persuasive speech about product safety delivered to the National Association of Manufacturers, for example, would be quite different from one delivered to a group of personal-injury attorneys. In either case you would have to construct your persuasive message on the basis of what you knew about each demographic group.

Ethical Constraints

Finally, audience-focused persuasive speaking is bound by ethical constraints. The realization of your persuasive goal, for example, shouldn't come at the expense of your audience. Selling worthless swampland may help the speaker achieve the goal of making money, but only at the expense of gullible audience members who may lose their savings. The end you hope to achieve must reflect not only your interests but those of your audience as well. Along the same lines, you need to thoroughly think through the persuasive means you plan on using to achieve your goal. Noble ends do not justify ignoble means. As a case in point, we happen to believe that the remaining stands of giant sequoias should be protected from logging. We also would be happy to assist someone in preparing and delivering a speech that suggests reasonable means to achieve this end. This doesn't mean, however, we would help someone who, as a part of his or her persuasive message, plans to advocate tree spiking, placing metal spikes in trees to prevent them being cut down. Such activity can lead to serious injury or even death of the loggers.

Sarah Brady's Rhetorical Situation

Sarah Brady's course of persuasive speaking had one ultimate goal: action. To get there, however, she had to first reinforce the attitudes of those who shared her beliefs and convince them to join her campaign. Brady also had to inoculate sympathetic Republicans in Congress, who knew from the outset that they would come under intense pressure to oppose her efforts. She had to give these members of the House and Senate evidence they could use to counter the arguments of the powerful pro-gun lobby.

Sarah Brady's most significant audience was Ronald Reagan. She knew that if she could win him over to her side, she might convince other opinion leaders in the Republican party to either support or at least not stand in the way of the legislation proposed by Handgun Control, Inc. By appealing to the former president based on his own near brush with death and the sacrifice made by her husband, Brady eventually did win the support of Reagan, who initially opposed the bill. This considerably expanded the audience of people willing to hear her persuasive message.

One of the things Sarah Brady didn't do was build a persuasive campaign based solely on emotion, which she could have easily done. Although emotional appeal was certainly a part of her message, it was balanced with evidence and reasoning. She avoided the temptation to exploit her husband and other victims of gun violence as objects of pity. Instead, she took the ethical high road, going beyond her husband's injury to demonstrate there was overwhelming evidence to support handgun control. She demonstrated the need for a federally mandated waiting period between the purchase and delivery of handguns. In doing so, Brady stayed within the boundaries of ethical speech.

ARISTOTELIAN ROOTS OF PERSUASIVE SPEAKING

Most contemporary theory and research about persuasive speaking follows in the footsteps of Aristotle. Not only did Aristotle define rhetoric as "the faculty of observing in any given case the available means of persuasion,"[3] he identified three means of persuasion—ethos, logos, and pathos—which were briefly introduced in Chapter 5. These three means of persuasion parallel the three basic elements in any persuasive speech situation: speaker, message, and audience.

Ethos: The Credibility of the Speaker

Aristotle believed that to be persuasive a speaker must be not only competent but also a person of substantial character. Aristotle described this combination of competence and character as **ethos.** He believed that ethos was a personal attribute and was essential to a speaker's chances of persuading an audience. In fact, as the opening quotation in this chapter suggests, he viewed ethos as the most important aspect of a speaker's persuasiveness.

THE BORN LOSER reprinted by permission of Newspaper Enterprise Association, Inc.

Modern communication researchers have substantiated Aristotle's thinking about the importance of ethos. Today's scholars use the term **source credibility,** which is the audience's perception of the believability of the speaker.[4] It is a quality your audience gives to you rather than one with which you are born. Thus, a speaker might be truly competent in a particular subject matter, but if the audience does not know this, the speaker's expertise will not increase his or her credibility. Similarly, a speaker may be of good character, but if the audience does not believe it, the speaker will suffer low credibility.

If the concept of source credibility reminds you of opinion leadership, that should be no surprise. You may recall from Chapter 1 that an opinion leader is a person who influences others to adopt innovative ideas, products, or processes. This is, of course, exactly what a persuasive speaker is trying to do. The more a speaker is perceived as a credible source, the more likely it is that he or she will function as an opinion leader.

Logos: The Message

Aristotle also recognized the power of words (*logos* is Greek for "word") in the process of persuasion. As a result, he spent considerable time theorizing about both the nature of words and the manner in which they were arranged to form a message. **Logos** is the proof a speaker offers to an audience through the words of his or her message. Aristotle believed speakers should use logical proof. Consider two examples. In the first, the speaker claims without any proof that Socrates is mortal. In the second, the speaker makes the same point in the form of syllogism, that is, a conclusion plus the premises supporting it. Specifically, the speaker tells the audience, "All men are mortal. Socrates is a man. Therefore, Socrates is mortal." In this case, the speaker not only has stated a conclusion the audience can either accept or reject but also has communicated proof in support of the conclusion.

Aristotle believed that there are several ways to prove a point. A syllogism follows the rules of formal logic, and Aristotle claimed that rhetoricians actually use an abbreviated syllogism (called an enthymeme) in speaking. He also believed that speakers could prove their case through the use of examples and signs. As they did for ethos, modern researchers also have found considerable support for Aristotle's claims about logos. In another section of this chapter, we will encourage you to use different types of logical proof in much the same way Aristotle suggested over two thousand years ago.

Pathos: Motivating Your Audience

Finally, Aristotle recognized the role of the audience's emotions in the process of persuasion. He reasoned what modern researchers have demonstrated again and again: People are persuaded not simply by cold logic but also by emotional appeals. **Pathos** refers to the emotional states in an audience that a speaker can arouse and use to achieve persuasive goals. These methods are not inherently unethical, but they can be abused by unscrupulous persuaders.

Aristotle cataloged the many emotions a speaker can evoke in the attempt to persuade people. Specific emotions he mentions in his writings about persuasion include anger, fear, kindness, shame, pity, and envy.[5] Although contemporary researchers have studied each of these emotions in relation to persuasion, fear, which we will discuss later in this chapter, has been of particular interest.

Up to this point, we have said that effective persuasive speaking begins with analysis of the rhetorical situation, including the goal or goals you hope to achieve, the audience you will address, and the ethical constraints by which you must abide. We also have said that effective persuasive speaking should reflect the thinking of Aristotle and the contemporary research that has validated his thinking. Here, we want to shift our focus to the practice of persuasive speaking. We follow Aristotle and contemporary researchers in looking at the three basic means of persuasion: establishing speaker credibility, constructing a logically convincing message, and appealing to audience members' emotions.

THE SPEAKER: PERSUASION THROUGH ETHOS

As we noted earlier, credibility is rooted in audience perceptions of believability. Contemporary communication research shows that this perception is composed of two parts: competence and character.[6] Although both are necessary to sustain the perception of ethos, neither is sufficient in itself to do so. To perceive you as credible, your audience must believe that you are not only competent about your topic but also a person of character who can be trusted.

Credibility is dynamic and changeable. The fact that a speaker is perceived as credible going into a persuasive speech doesn't guarantee that he or she will still be perceived as credible afterward. Similarly, the speaker who begins with little credibility can build credibility in the process of speaking. One of your goals is to build and maintain your credibility as you speak. You want it to be at least as high when you conclude as it was when you began.

Credibility Before the Speech

Often, speakers' reputations precede their appearance before an audience. In fact, their reputation may be what prompts the audience to attend, especially when the speaker has unique qualifications to speak about the topic. For example, because Sarah Brady was personally touched by the destructive force of a handgun, her audiences had reason to believe she was uniquely qualified to speak about handgun control.

Of course, most of us are not experts, and may not even be known to our audience. One way to build your credibility before you speak is to have someone introduce you to the audience. In Chapter 15, we will talk about how to present a speech of introduction that will enhance an audience's perception of the speaker's credibility. If you do not have an introduction, you will have to establish your credibility by what you say in your speech and how you say it.

Credibility During the Speech

The level of credibility at the outset of the speech is insufficient to sustain the perception of believability. Credibility by way of reputation can be negated as a result of the speaker's appearance, message, and delivery. Often little-known political candidates begin with high credibility which vanishes once the public learns more about them. Ross Perot, for example, once led the public opinion polls in his independent run for the presidency in 1992. But as people learned more about him, and after he temporarily withdrew from the race, his credibility suffered. Although he did garner considerable support in the election, he never regained his original level of credibility with voters.

On the other hand, even speakers with little initial credibility can build their ethos during their speech. As a case in point, students in an introductory public speaking course may have little initial credibility with each other because they don't know each other and don't know each other's qualifications to speak on various topics. Practically speaking, then, these students begin to build their credibility with their first speeches. Their appearance, the care with which they've prepared their message, and their delivery can begin to establish their competence and character with their fellow students and their instructor.

To make certain you are perceived as a credible speaker in a persuasive transaction, though, you'll need to provide your audience with proof of your credibility through the logos of your message. The reasoning and evidence you present in your persuasive speech should not only support the arguments you make but also support the audience's perception that you are competent and a person of high character. Also, if you have special expertise or credentials that are relevant to your topic, you'll want to share the fact with your audience.

Credibility After the Speech

Speakers whose persuasive message bolstered their credibility with an audience cannot rest on their laurels. Just as initial credibility can suffer from a poor speech, the credibility you've established during your speech can be negated as well. No one knows this better than former President George Bush. Following his acceptance speech at the 1988 Republican convention, in which he proclaimed "Read my lips. No new taxes," his credibility soared in the eyes of the public. He was, subsequently, elected by a landslide.

During his term of office, however, Bush reneged on his no-new-taxes pledge. Not only did he lose credibility with the public as a result, but his going back on his word became a major issue in the 1992 presidential election. Even though Bush told the public he had been wrong in going along with the congressionally approved tax increase, he was never able to recapture public confidence.

Never lose sight of the fact that perceived credibility is dynamic. Once gained, credibility continues to need nourishment. The following list provides some reminders and tips for maintaining credibility.

Tips for Speaker Credibility

- **Ask yourself about the degree to which your audience already perceives you as credible. Also ask yourself whether your classroom behavior could have lowered your credibility in the eyes of the other students. For example, coming to class late and interrupting a speaker, not being ready to speak when it was your turn, or delivering speeches that were hastily put together tells other students about your competence and character. If this is the case, you'll need to work harder to establish your credibility.**

- **Dress appropriately for the occasion. Persuasion is serious business and should be approached seriously.**

- Incorporate any special expertise or experience you have with your topic into the body of your speech. This information will enhance the audience's perception of your competence.

- Use evidence to support the claims you make. The logos of your speech will help enhance your ethos.

- Engage your audience nonverbally, using the characteristics of effective delivery described in Chapter 10.

- Use powerful language (which research suggests is linked to persuasive effects), as described in Chapter 9.

- Use inclusive language, discussed in Chapter 9, to make certain all audience members believe they have a stake in the topic of your persuasive speech.

Using Similarity and Dissimilarity

The perception of moderate similarities between communicators and their audiences can augment the persuasive effects of credibility. People can be very suspicious initially of people they perceive to be dissimilar. Conversely, people can be very trusting initially of people they perceive as similar.

Like credibility, similarity is a perception and it is composed of several parts. Chief among them are appearance, background, and belief system. We perceive people whose appearance is a reflection of our culture or group to be similar to us. We then use this surface cue to infer similarities in background and belief system.[7]

If you are a traditional 18–21-year-old student at a traditional four-year college or university, chances are that you are highly similar to the audience you will be speaking to in class. If you can couple similarity with proof that you have competence on your topic beyond that of audience members, you will be able to capitalize on your similarity. Should you be unable to demonstrate special competence, however, similarity may undermine your credibility. It's a case of the audience saying, "What does that person know that we don't know? He or she is no different than any of us."

If you are not similar to your audience, don't worry. You also can make the dissimilarity work to your advantage. For an example, see the box "Sample Persuasive Speech: Fear Is Real Among Freshman Students, by Ryland G. Hill, Jr." on pages 384–386. If you are a reentry student, a parent, or a part-time student with a full-time job, you can use your experience to bolster audience perception of your credibility. After all, you have real-world experience that the traditional 18–21-year-old undergraduate probably lacks. If you can combine this dissimilar experience with some common ground you do share with your audience, it will enhance your credibility and increase your persuasive effects.

VIDEO FILE

If you have access to the videotape that accompanies this text, view segment 10. It shows Ryland G. Hill, Jr.'s, persuasive speech "Fear Is Real Among Freshman Students."

Sample Persuasive Speech

Fear Is Real Among Freshman Students, by Ryland G. Hill, Jr.

After retiring from the navy, Ryland Hill, Jr., decided to go back to school at age "thirty something." Currently, he's majoring in early childhood education. That's right, the former chief petty officer wants to be an elementary school teacher. The following text was prepared based on a transcript of a persuasive speech Ryland delivered in his class. Because extemporaneous speaking frequently leads to unintentional errors, we have edited the speech for you to read. Although Ryland is in many respects dissimilar from his classmates, he focused his speech on something he believes he shared in common with all undergraduates—fear.

Ryland begins his speech with a quotation from a respected source, Eleanor Roosevelt.

Eleanor Roosevelt once quoted an unknown author by saying, "You gain strength, courage and confidence by every experience in which you . . . stop to look fear in the face. . . . You must do the thing you think you cannot do."

Today, in the '90s, incoming college freshmen often report becoming anxious before entering college. The transition from high school to college brings fears to the surface. Likewise, students who return to college after many years of absence report similar fears.

Ryland establishes a connection with the audience despite dissimilarity in age.

College freshmen find it difficult to identify exactly where the problem lies. As a reentry student myself, I have experienced the same difficulty and would like to persuade you that it's essential to be aware of the subtle effect that fear has on each and every one of us in each class that we take.

Ryland clearly previews the points he will make.

Today we'll look at some reasons why the fear of failure, the fear of the unknown, and self-fulfilling prophecies have paralyzed freshman students from achieving their full potential. And finally we'll discuss three solutions that can eliminate harmful effects that fear can produce.

Freshman students develop fears that create doubt. A common fear is the fear of failure. Some students doubt their ability to succeed at a college level. These students have often received negative feedback throughout their elementary and high school years. They suffer from low self-esteem and are insecure about their new academic experience.

Note the use of authority to support his point about students learning from their mistakes.

Students in their first year have potential to do well in school, but usually they underachieve and they may be afraid of making mistakes. But in the counseling center at Berkeley's Writer's College, students are told that making mistakes is important. It is a way of learning about our strengths, and what works well for us, and what does not work. It's only when we do not learn from our mistakes and refuse to correct them that they become failures. People don't reach their full potential because of important challenges in life, as Robert Steinberg writes in 1986. It is also easier for students to spend a lot of energy and time dodging the system and their work as assigned due to the fear of failure.

Now that we understand why the fear of failure has such a crippling effect on students in their first year, let's examine another reason why fear plays such a pivotal role in the lack of a freshman's success.

Instead of high school counselors making students see that they have the potential to achieve, they make predictions which students feel are like a prophet predicting their very future. Well-meaning counselors sometimes steer students away from attending college. They advise the students to consider the work force instead. In today's economy, jobs today call for more than just a high school diploma. The students receive a "can't do" message, further lowering their self-esteem. Often this leads to a cycle of low grades and low achievements, fulfilling the prophecy of failure.

Robert Steinberg's book Intelligence Applied *explains why intelligent people may fail. Steinberg has identified stumbling blocks that get in the way of even the brightest and the sharpest of freshman students, and prevent them from becoming academically successful. "It scarcely matters what talents people have if they are not motivated to use them," he writes.*

First-semester students rely on the correctness of their college professors. Students are still immature and rely on others for their external rewards. But a lot of students say that immaturity has nothing to do with their grades here at Chico State University. Steinberg states: "A lack of self-confidence gnaws away at a person's ability to get things done and this becomes a self-fulfilling prophecy." It's all in your mind.

Now that we understand how self-fulfilling prophecies can create fear in freshman students, let's take a brief look at the fear of the unknown and see how it can be a deterrent to our success as first-year students.

Any new experience that one knows little about can be real scary. On holidays and birthdays, for instance, we receive unknown gifts that are new and different, yet, we don't fear those types of gifts, do we? Yet maybe it all lies in the way one packages things. An attractive package that we are expecting is the one that we look forward to receiving. College officials here at Chico State University should let freshman students know that there is a beauty and a joy in the gift called a college education.

Now that we can see how fear of the unknown can disguise itself as a problem, let's look at three solutions that can be very helpful in battling fears that we face on our college campuses.

First is to identify some traits that define a successful student. Successful students tend to be risk takers. Just enrolling in college is a risk to some. Yet they do it, and they take the first step toward success. Successful students also learn from their mistakes. Remember, it's

Note the signpost that reminds us of the point just made and prepares us for the next.

Quotations from authority are used to bolster Ryland's point and also his own credibility.

Notice use of analogies to make the point that we don't always fear the future.

Ryland uses a problem–solution format and presents three solutions to the problem of freshman fears.

(continued) ➤

IN THEIR OWN WORDS

Sample Persuasive Speech (continued)

not a failure if you're willing to correct your mistake and learn from it. They need to recognize their successes and overcome their failures as Professor Johnson, 1990, says.

Note use of signposts to enumerate points.

The second solution is that we must look at college life as a challenge. When we view college life as a roller coaster with its ups and its downs, as long as we believe that life is going to return to the top again, we can rise to the challenge and we can persevere.

And lastly, we can envision our future. We must see ourselves as successful people. And even when things become blurry, and even when we're losing our focus, we can maintain the ability to fine-tune our lives and become even more goal-directed.

We must have faith in ourselves and stay persistent, and stay willing to keep trying. When we don't succeed the first time, we can search for solutions until we are successful. It is difficult for many students to appreciate their own success. I'm going to repeat that. It is difficult for many college students to appreciate their own success. Successful students have learned to celebrate their victories, but most importantly, they have learned to overcome their college fears.

Hill summarizes his main points.

To summarize, today we have discussed reasons why fear is real among college freshmen, and we gave practical solutions to overcoming it. Successful freshman students are confident enough to believe in themselves. But most importantly, they expect their classmates to appreciate their abilities.

Conclusion ties back to opening by again using the quotation from Eleanor Roosevelt.

As Eleanor Roosevelt reminds us, while thinking about overcoming our college fears, "You gain strength, courage, and confidence by every experience in which you . . . stop to look fear in the face. . . . You must do the thing you think you cannot do. You must do the thing you think you cannot do." Thank you.

Think about Sarah Brady and her audience. She had access to circles of influence not open to the traditional supporters of handgun-control legislation because of similarity. She was one of the Republican Party's elite by virtue of her husband's position. Opinion leaders in the Republican Party also saw her as sharing a background and belief system with them.

At the same time, Sarah Brady was dissimilar from fellow Republicans in at least three respects. First, she and her family had been personally victimized by a man who had had no problem purchasing a handgun despite the fact that he had been diagnosed with schizophrenia. Second, as a result of what had happened to Jim Brady, she became an expert on the subject of handguns. Finally, as a woman, she was dissimilar in gender to the vast majority of the Republican members of Congress.

How Similar or Dissimilar Are You and Your Audience?

Fill out this form prior to your first persuasive speech. Compare your appearance to that of your audience. In what ways are you similar and in what ways dissimilar? Do the same for your cultural, demographic, and individual factors. In what ways can you use your similarities to build your credibility? How can you overcome or even positively utilize your dissimilarities?

Factors to Assess Prior To Persuasive Speech	*Similar to Audience*	*Dissimilar from Audience*
Appearance		
Cultural Factors		
Demographic Factors		
Age		
Socioeconomic status		
Geographic origin		
Ethnicity		
Gender		
Religion		
Language		
Factors Relating to Your Speech Topic		
Attitudes [toward it]		
Beliefs [about it]		
Values [regarding it]		
Behavioral intentions [toward it]		
Other Factors		

To sum up, then, you can use similarity and dissimilarity to augment audience perceptions of your credibility. You simply need to inventory how you may be similar to or dissimilar from your audience, and think through how you can use the similarities and dissimilarities to your advantage. To conduct your inventory, refer to the box "How Similar or Dissimilar Are You and Your Audience?"

THE MESSAGE: PERSUASION THROUGH LOGOS

Assuming that you have controlled for such things as appearance and the degree to which your classroom behavior has affected audience perceptions of you, it is your message and its delivery that most influences audience perceptions of your credibility. What you put into your persuasive message and the manner in which you configure it are crucial to your success in re-inforcing, inoculating, changing attitudes, or prompting people in your audience to act.[8]

Although the level of goodwill between Sarah Brady and her audience was high from the beginning, it was what she did once she had her audience's attention that changed minds and stirred action. Sarah Brady had a persuasive message that her audience could not ignore, as you can see in the box "Sample Persuasive Message: Firearms: . . . And the Case Against Them, by Sarah Brady." Had this not been the case, her credibility on the issue of gun control would have been short-lived.

To build a persuasive message like Sarah Brady's, you need at least four things. First, you need to know something about the way in which people in an audience respond to persuasive messages. Second, you need a model of argument you can use as a template for your persuasive message. Third, you need to know how to flesh out this model with evidence and reasoning. Finally, you need to know the extent to which you should include both sides of a controversial issue in your message.

The Elaboration Likelihood Model and Persuasion

Like any speech transaction, the persuasive transaction involves active participation by both the speaker and the audience. In some persuasive transactions, the audience engages actively in thinking critically about a complex topic. In other situations, the audience responds almost without thinking. Social psychologists Richard Petty and John Cacioppo present the **elaboration likelihood model** of persuasion to explain why audience members will use an elaborated thinking process in some situations and not in others.[9]

To illustrate these differences in how a message is processed, consider the topic of gun control. The causes of violence in America, the statistics on whether guns are more likely to kill the gun owner or the criminal, and the correct interpretation of the Second Amendment are all complex issues. Fully developed arguments on the topic of gun control invite the audience to engage in what Petty and Cacioppo call *elaboration* of the message, or "central route processing." On the other hand, some messages about gun control do not provoke much thinking. "When guns are outlawed, only outlaws will have guns" and "Stop the violence—ban handguns" are both

IN THEIR OWN WORDS

Sample Persuasive Message

Firearms: . . . And the Case Against Them, by Sarah Brady

Note the claims made in this persuasive message, the type of evidence offered in support of these claims, and the warrants, implied or stated, that link the grounds with the claims.

As America enters the next decade, it does so with an appalling legacy of gun violence. The 1980s were tragic years that saw nearly a quarter of a million Americans die from handguns—four times as many as were killed in the Viet Nam War. We began the decade by witnessing yet another President, Ronald Reagan, become a victim of a would-be assassin's bullet. That day my husband Jim, his press secretary, also became a statistic in America's handgun war.

> Grounds: Statistics, examples

Gun violence is an epidemic in this country. In too many cities, the news each night reports another death by a gun. As dealers push out in search of new addicts, Smalltown, U.S.A., is introduced to the mindless gun violence fostered by the drug trade.

> Warrant: Drug trade causes gun violence

And we are killing our future. Every day a child in this country loses his or her life to a handgun. Hundreds more are permanently injured, often because a careless adult left within easy reach a loaded handgun purchased for self-defense.

> Warrant: Guns purchased for self-defense kill children

Despite the carnage, America stands poised to face an even greater escalation of bloodshed. The growing popularity of military-style assault weapons could turn our streets into combat zones. Assault weapons, designed solely to mow down human beings, are turning up at an alarming rate in the hands of those most prone to violence—drug dealers, gang members, hate groups and the mentally ill.

> Claim: Assault weapons could turn streets into combat zones
> Grounds: Rate up among violence-prone

The Stockton, Calif., massacre of little children was a warning to our policymakers. But Congress lacked the courage to do anything. During the year of inaction on Capitol Hill, we have seen too many other tragedies brought about by assault weapons. In Louisville an ex-employee of a printing plant went on a shooting spree with a Chinese-made semiautomatic version of the AK-47, gunning down 21 people, killing eight and himself. Two Colorado women were murdered and several others injured by a junkie using a stolen MAC-11 semiautomatic pistol. And Congress votes itself a pay raise.

> Grounds: Examples of Stockton, Louisville, Colorado

The National Rifle Association, meanwhile, breathes a sigh of relief, gratified that your attention is now elsewhere. The only cooling-off period the N.R.A. favors is a postponement of legislative action. It counts on public anger to fade before such outrage can be directed at legislators. The N.R.A. runs feel-good ads saying guns are not the problem and there is nothing we can do to prevent criminals from getting guns. In fact, it has said that guns in the wrong hands are the "price we pay for freedom." I guess I'm just not willing to hand the

> Rebuttal to NRA

(continued) ➤

IN THEIR OWN WORDS

Sample Persuasive Message (continued)

next John Hinckley a deadly handgun. Neither is the nation's law-enforcement community, the men and women who put their lives on the line for the rest of us every day.

Two pieces of federal legislation can make a difference right now. First, we must require a national waiting period before the purchase of a handgun, to allow for a criminal-records check. Police know that waiting periods work. In the 20 years that New Jersey has required a background check, authorities have stopped more than 10,000 convicted felons from purchasing handguns.

We must also stop the sale and domestic production of semiautomatic assault weapons. These killing machines clearly have no legitimate sporting purpose, as President Bush recognized when he permanently banned their importation.

These public-safety measures are supported by the vast majority of Americans—including gun owners. In fact, these measures are so sensible that I never realized the campaign to pass them into law would be such an uphill battle. But it can be done.

Jim Brady knows the importance of a waiting period. He knows the living hell of a gunshot wound. Jim and I are not afraid to take on the N.R.A. leaders, and we will fight them everywhere we can. As Jim said in his congressional testimony, "I don't question the rights of responsible gun owners. That's not the issue. The issue is whether the John Hinckleys of the world should be able to walk into gun stores and purchase handguns instantly. Are you willing and ready to cast a vote for a commonsense public-safety bill endorsed by experts—law enforcement?"

Are we as a nation going to accept America's bloodshed, or are we ready to stand up and do what is right? When are we going to say "Enough"? We can change the direction in which America is headed. We can prevent the 1990s from being bloodier than the past ten years. If each of you picks up a pen and writes to your Senators and Representative tonight, you would be surprised at how quickly we could collect the votes we need to win the war for a safer America.

Let us enter a new decade committed to finding solutions to the problem of gun violence. Let your legislators know that voting with the gun lobby—and against public safety—is no longer acceptable. Let us send a signal to lawmakers that we demand action, not excuses.

Margin annotations:

Claim: Waiting period needed

Grounds: N.J. example

Claim: Must stop assault weapons

Claim: Vast majority support. But where is the evidence? No grounds.
Grounds: Testimony, personal experience

Refutes counter-argument of "responsible gun owners"

Claim: Call for action

---

examples of messages that are designed to avoid an elaborated thinking process. Petty and Cacioppo term this "peripheral route processing."

The questions for a public speaker are (1) what factors are likely to lead an audience to engage in either central or peripheral message processing and (2) which of these processes is most likely to lead to the achievement of speaker goals?

The second question is the easiest to answer. In most situations, the speaker wants the audience to use the elaborated, or central processing, route. The reason is that if the argument presented by the speaker is accepted by audience members, they are more likely to undergo long-term attitude change. The audience member who thinks through the various arguments about violence in America, the likelihood of a gun killing the owner rather than the criminal, and the purposes of the constitutional right to bear arms is likely to form a strongly held attitude on gun control. Those who later seek to change that attitude will face a difficult task. On the other hand, the audience member who reaches an opinion through the peripheral route, based on slogans such as "Guns don't kill people; people kill people," is likely to be easily persuaded to another position by subsequent persuasion. Thus, the public speaker who wants his or her message to "stick" needs to provoke audience members into an elaborated method of thinking using the central processing route.

To return to the first question: What factors affect the likelihood of elaboration on the part of an audience member? If audience members are motivated and able to understand a message, they are more likely to engage in elaborated thinking. On the other hand, if they find a message irrelevant or are unwilling or unable to understand the message, they are more likely to follow the peripheral route. Some factors are beyond the speaker's control. For example, individual listeners differ in their "need for cognition," that is, their need to process information centrally.[10] There's not much a speaker can do to make people who don't like to think about messages do so. On the other hand, a speaker can take steps to make the topic relevant to the audience and to provide understandable and strong arguments that will be persuasive to those who are motivated to process the message centrally.

The elaboration likelihood model is depicted in Figure 13.1 on page 393. Let's walk through this figure to further explain the model. As you can see from the route on the left side of the model, an audience member must be *motivated* and *able* to process your message to engage in the central processing route of elaborated thinking. Depending on their *initial attitude,* the *quality of your argument,* and similar factors, an audience member may have either *favorable* or *unfavorable* thoughts about the topic. If the message isn't sufficient to stimulate such thoughts, audience members won't engage in elaborated thinking. If new ideas are *adopted* and *stored in memory,* and these are more *salient* (relevant) than what the audience member previously thought, then *attitude change* (favorable or unfavorable) will occur and be relatively enduring. These attitudes are also more likely to *predict future behavior.*

On the other hand, if the peripheral route is followed because audience members are *not motivated* to engage in elaborated thinking, *cannot understand* the message, or find the message *ineffective,* then attitude shifts are relatively *temporary* and *susceptible to further persuasive* efforts for the other side. Future *behavior is not predictable* from such attitude shifts.

FIGURE 13.1
(Opposite page)
Model of elaboration
likelihood (From
Richard E. Petty and
John T. Cacioppo, "The
Elaboration Likelihood
Model of Persuasion," in
*Advances in Experimental
Social Psychology, Vol. 19,*
ed. Leonard Berkowitz
[New York: Academic
Press, 1986]. Reprinted
by permission.)

The first step in applying the elaboration likelihood model to your own persuasive speech is selecting an appropriate topic. We have repeatedly emphasized the importance of this deceptively simple step because your audience must be motivated to pay attention to your topic. Not only must you choose a topic that your research tells you the audience should find stimulating, but you also must connect the topic to the personal and professional needs of your audience. For example, a speech on the Americans with Disabilities Act might not be directly linked to the needs of an audience without disabilities. But pointing out that each of us is only one accident or serious illness away from disability can make the connection clear.

The second step is making your topic and message comprehensible for your audience. As discussed in Chapter 12, audiences tend to turn off to messages perceived as too complex for their information-processing abilities. An audience whose nonverbal feedback says "Huh?" is not likely to favorably evaluate your persuasive message.

Now comes the hard part. The third step has to do with the audience's initial position regarding your message. Even if your topic is stimulating and your message is comprehensible, there is no guarantee people will respond favorably to it. Members of your audience may disagree with the position(s) taken in your message. The degree to which they disagree is likely to vary as well. Whereas a group of businesspersons may be very receptive to the argument that environmental regulations are too restrictive, costing jobs and economic growth, the local Sierra Club chapter may have an opposite reaction that they hold passionately. This fact reemphasizes, then, just how important it is to learn as much as possible about your audience prior to constructing your persuasive message. Simply put, if you craft a persuasive message without sufficient knowledge of what your audience already believes regarding your topic, the message is destined to fail. Audience members will incorporate their own preexisting knowledge and attitudes into their processing of your message, overwhelming the arguments you have provided them. A persuasive message is not simply a narrative that reflects its author's point of view. A persuasive message is based on factors known to affect audience beliefs, attitudes, and occasionally values.

To summarize: Elaboration likelihood clearly suggests an active role on the part of the audience you hope to persuade. This active role includes (1) seeing your topic as relevant to their needs, (2) understanding and comprehending your message, and (3) centrally processing the nature and quality of the information offered in terms of the audience's preexisting knowledge and beliefs.

The Toulmin Model of Argument

One way to increase the likelihood of central route processing is to use philosopher Stephen Toulmin's model of argument, depicted in Figure 13.2 on page 394. Toulmin's model makes an excellent template to use in con-

VIDEO FILE

If you have access to the videotape that accompanies this text, view Segment 11, that shows reasoning in action using the Toulmin model.

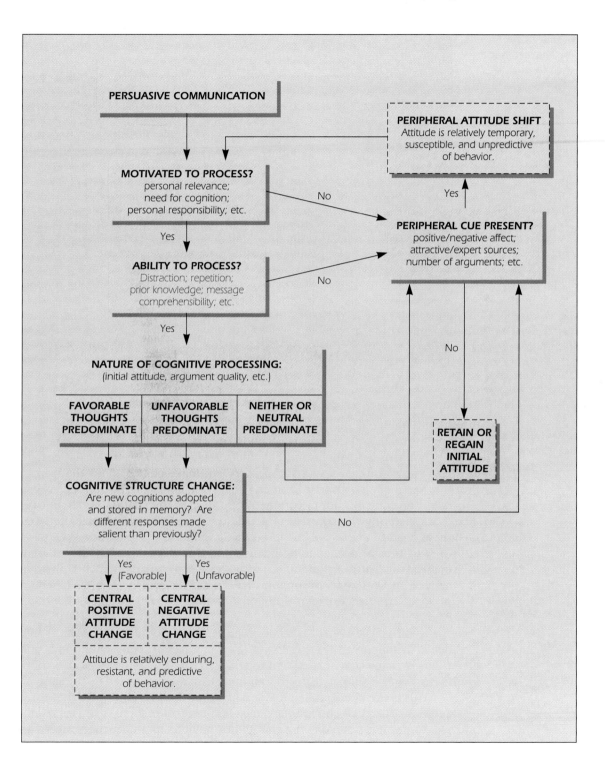

FIGURE 13.2

The Toulmin model of argument. *(An Introduction to Reasoning,* Second Edition, by Stephen Toulmin, Richard Rieke, and Allan Janik. Copyright ©1984. Adapted by permission of Prentice-Hall, Inc. Upper Saddle River, NJ.)

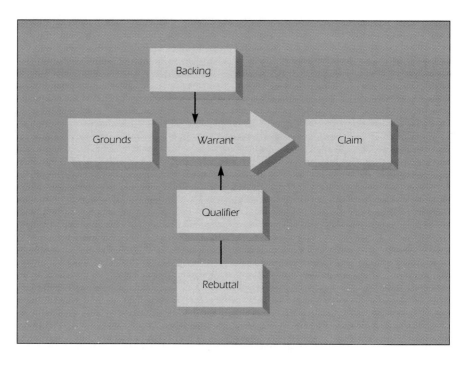

structing the arguments in a persuasive speech. According to Toulmin, a sound argument involves *at least* a claim, grounds for making the claim, and a warrant that connects grounds and claim.[11]

A **claim** is a conclusion that a persuasive speaker wants an audience to reach as a result of a speech. Speakers can make claims about the facts as they see them, about basic human values, and about public policies. As you might imagine, it's not uncommon for a speaker to make claims about each of these during the course of a persuasive speech. The differences between these types of claims are discussed in Chapter 14.

Just because someone asserts a claim, that doesn't constitute an argument for its truth. An argument also requires **grounds,** which is the evidence a speaker offers in support of a claim. This evidence can be based on personal experience, expert testimony, established fact, or statistics or other data.

Good persuasive speakers also connect the grounds they offer as evidence in support of their claims. Such a connection between grounds and claim is called a **warrant.** Although warrants can be implied, we think these connections between grounds and claim are best stated by the speaker.

This is not the complete model, however. Toulmin indicates that three additional parts of an argument *may* be present. In some cases, for example, the warrant may be one that is not obvious to audience members. In that case, a fourth element of Toulmin's model comes into play, backing. **Backing** is support for the warrant. If an audience does not already believe in the warrant, the speaker will need to build additional argument and evidence to support it before attempting to convince the audience of the soundness of the whole argument. Knowing what warrants an audience will accept and which ones require additional backing is essential to effective persuasion.

An additional component is the **rebuttal,** which represents an exception to or a refutation of the argument. It is usually preceded by the word "unless," indicating that the claim is true except when conditions stated in the rebuttal are present. As we will discuss later in this chapter, it is important in presenting a two-sided message to let the audience know if they may encounter exceptions or refutations of your argument. Finally, unless an argument is 100 percent certain, it will need to have a **qualifier,** which is an indication of the level of probability of the claim.[12] Qualifiers may be a single word, such as "probably," a brief phrase, such as "very likely," or even a probability expressed as a percentage. In human affairs, it is rare to deal with absolute certainty. Acknowledging to an audience your degree of certainty helps you avoid appearing to take an extreme or unreasonable position.

How does this model of argument apply in actual practice? Let's begin with a simple case. Suppose you glance out the window and the sky is filled with clouds. You think to yourself, "It's going to rain," and you grab your umbrella. Although you may not realize it, your reasoning can be analyzed as an argument using Toulmin's model. Figure 13.3 on page 396 shows how this analysis would look. Based on the *grounds* of a cloudy sky, you reason using the *warrant,* cloudy skies are a sign of rain, which is based on the *backing* of your past experience, that there is a 75 percent chance (*qualifier*) of the truth of the *claim* that it is going to rain, unless (*rebuttal*) the clouds have a low moisture content.

Now that you understand this basic version of Toulmin's model, let's look at the relationships among claims, grounds, and warrants in a more complicated situation. If you've read Sarah Brady's persuasive message, note that the first claim she makes is that "gun violence is an epidemic in this country." To support this claim of fact, Brady offers grounds in the form of two and possibly three different types of evidence. Technically, these three types of evidence are called first-, second-, and third-order data.[13]

First-order data is evidence based on personal experience. As mentioned earlier, the life experience of people can be quite persuasive. Certainly this is true in the case of Sarah Brady. She states in the opening paragraph of her message that the attempted assassination of President Reagan led to her husband becoming "a statistic in America's handgun war." She also offers first-order data in the tenth paragraph of her message to support a policy claim that comes later.

FIGURE 13.3
Analysis of an argument using Toulmin's model.

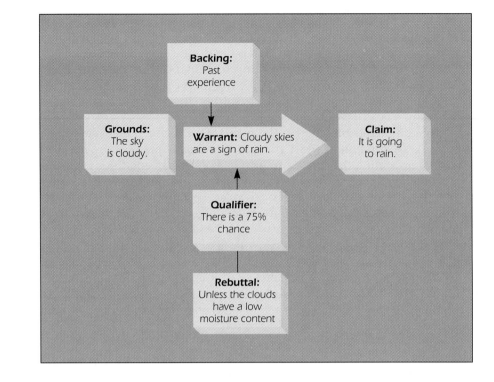

Second-order data is evidence based on expert testimony. Although this kind of evidence is commonly used as grounds in support of a claim, it is missing in its truest form from Sarah Brady's message, unless you look upon Brady as an expert herself. In that case, the entire message constitutes a form of second-order data. To add second-order data to her message, she might have quoted police chiefs or legal experts supporting gun control.

Third-order data is evidence based on fact and statistics. Sarah Brady's message contains numerous examples of third-order data. These examples include her description of the Stockton, California, school massacre, the ex-employee incident in Louisville, Kentucky, and the Colorado incident in which two women were murdered by a junkie. These are indisputable facts and a good use of third-order data to support the claim that "gun violence is epidemic in this country."

Most of the warrants in Sarah Brady's persuasive message are implied rather than stated specifically. The unstated generalization she wants us to make as a result of her persuasion is that gun control legislation is both needed and warranted. Whether she has made the case that such legislation is warranted, however, is for you to decide.

Obviously, we think that using Toulmin as a template for your own persuasive messages will help you considerably. The model forces you to think about your message critically. At a minimum, for example, the model requires you to ask and answer questions that not only will make your message logical, but also increase the likelihood of elaboration in the minds of audience members. The following is a list of the kinds of questions the model encourages you to ask and answer as you construct your persuasive speech.

Questions to Ask When Constructing a Persuasive Speech

1. **What is the nature of the claim or claims I plan on making?**

2. **What kind of evidence do I need to offer in support of my claim? First-, second-, or third-order data? All three? How will the evidence I offer influence perceptions of my credibility?**

3. **What can I do to make certain that my audience will make the connection between the claim and the evidence I offer as grounds in support of it? Is the warrant really so obvious I don't need to make it explicit for my audience?**

4. **Will the warrant need additional support in the form of backing to be acceptable to the audience?**

The Importance of a Two-Sided Message

You also need to think about both the order of argument in your persuasive message and the inclusion of a qualifier and a rebuttal. Whereas the research once was equivocal in this regard, it now shows that whenever possible, you'll want to make sure your persuasive speech is two-sided rather than one-sided.[14]

Whereas a one-sided persuasive speech only offers evidence in support of your claim, a two-sided persuasive speech makes use of what Toulmin called the qualifier and the rebuttal. Let's say, for example, that you want to persuade your audience to support the claim that the war on drugs is a failure. In a standard, one-sided persuasive speech you would ground the claim with evidence and appeals you believe will prove effective with your audience.

In a two-sided speech, you would do all of this and more. After making the claim, giving grounds, and connecting the grounds to the claim with a warrant, you also would include a qualifier in your message and then indicate what rebuttals one might expect to hear to the argument. Of course, this does not mean you abandon your claim. Rather, this means you acknowledge counterarguments to it. You would then go on in your speech to point out either the weaknesses in the rebuttal or reasons the rebuttal is not sufficient to set aside your overall claim. We've modeled this for you in Figure 13.4 on page 398. Based on the *grounds* that drug use is up among

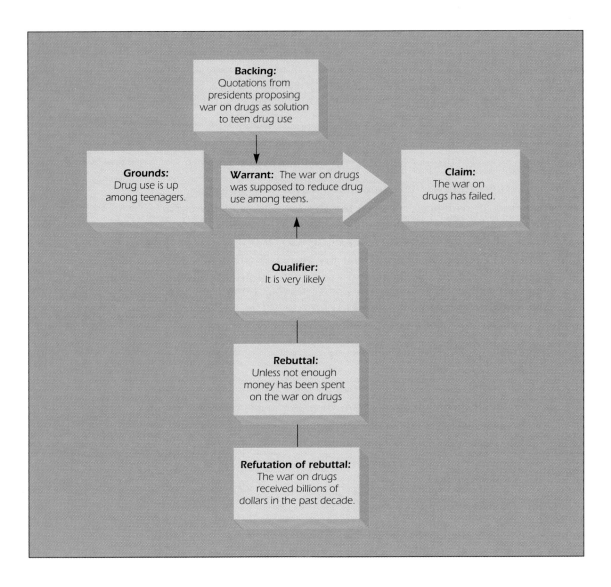

FIGURE 13.4
Example using
Toulmin's model of
argument.

teenagers and then using the *warrant* that the war on drugs was supposed to reduce drug use among teens, which is based on the *backing* of quotations from former presidents, you find it very likely (*qualifier*) that the *claim,* the war on drugs has failed, is true. You would acknowledge the other side's *rebuttal* that the claim would be untrue if not enough money had been spent on the war on drugs. You would then *refute* that rebuttal by pointing out the billions of dollars spent on the war on drugs during the past decade.

As you can see, the rebuttal represents the other side of the message. It simply tells the audience that there are reasonable people who don't sup-

port your claim, and then gives the audience an example of the kind of evidence these reasonable people have given for not supporting your claim. You then refute this example with a further argument or show that in spite of the rebuttal, your overall claim is still strong.

Sarah Brady didn't present a two-sided message. When she mentions those who oppose her view, such as officials of the National Rifle Association (NRA), she is negative in tone. This one-sidedness unnecessarily undermines her message. Brady would have been better off to (1) suggest that there are reasonable people in the NRA, (2) mention that many of these people believe the control of handguns will open the gates to more repressive forms of control, and (3) then show how this belief is really based on a logical fallacy known as the slippery slope, which will be discussed in Chapter 14.

Not only is a two-sided message more persuasive than a one-sided message, but research suggests at least two other benefits from its use. First, a two-sided message enhances the audience's perceptions of the speaker's credibility. Second, because it gives audience members arguments to rebut those arguments most commonly associated with the opposing view, a two-

Animal-rights groups often base their persuasive messages on strong appeals to their audience's emotions.

sided message also makes audience members more resistant to counter-persuasion.

THE AUDIENCE: PERSUASION THROUGH PATHOS

To this point, we've been talking about arguments that appeal to reason. Logical argument, however, is neither the only kind of appeal open to you nor always the most effective. Sometimes the belief systems of people are so closed that logical appeals have little chance of succeeding. As a result, the speaker may choose to appeal to audience members' emotions or primitive beliefs with messages people have been conditioned to respond to in specific ways. Whereas logical proofs are designed to induce elaborated thinking on the part of the audience, the appeals which follow are designed to provoke audience members to respond without the benefit of such elaborated thought. These appeals are linked to emotions such as anger, fear, kindness, calmness, confidence, unkindness, friendship, shame, pity, enmity, shamelessness, and envy.[15] To illustrate the way appeals to the emotion operate, we will review one of the best-researched emotional appeals, fear.

Appealing to Emotions: Motivating Through Fear

Common sense tells us that we sometimes do things as a result of fear; for example, we obey the law because we are afraid of the penalties we could suffer should we break it. Yet the research suggests that when it comes to persuasive speaking, fear has its limits. Whether your goal is to encourage the use of shoulder and lap belts while driving, demonstrate how flossing your teeth can prevent gum disease, or convince people everyone needs a gun for self-protection, the research is clear: Persuasive messages that arouse moderate levels of fear in audience members are much more effective than those using high levels of fear. This fact is especially true, moreover, when the speaker gives audience members a set of clear-cut steps they can take to reduce the fear the speaker has aroused.[16]

As you can see in Figure 13.5, the relationship between fear and persuasive effects is like the relationship between speech anxiety and performance, explained in Chapter 3. As the level of fear aroused in an audience begins to increase, so do persuasive effects. Too much fear, however, diminishes persuasive effects because it tends to elicit denial from audience members. In a sense, audience members respond to the high level of fear the speaker has aroused in them by saying, "That could never happen to me."

If employed in moderation, however, fear has its uses. Many public service campaigns use moderate levels of fear to encourage positive behaviors

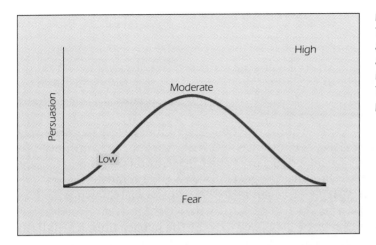

FIGURE 13.5
The relationship between fear appeals and persuasion. As the level of fear aroused in an audience begins to increase, so do persuasive effects. Too much fear, however, diminishes persuasive effects.

such as not smoking, practicing safe sex, and taking advantage of medications that control high blood pressure. The slogan "If not for yourself, then do it for the ones you love" is a good example. Produced by the American Heart Association, this persuasive message tells people with high blood pressure that they need to think about the feelings of the people they would leave behind if they failed to control their high blood pressure. This message involves a mild but effective level of fear. Fear isn't an inherently unethical form of persuasion. Used moderately to achieve an ethical end, it is but one of the choices you have in deciding on how to appeal to your audience.

Appealing to Primitive Beliefs

Emotional appeals frequently are combined with appeals to primitive beliefs. Primitive beliefs are basic beliefs instilled since childhood about how people should relate to one another. Research shows that the use of appeals that connect with primitive beliefs about reciprocity, liking, authority, social support, scarcity, and commitment is both widespread and effective in persuasive communication.[17]

Reciprocity   A reciprocity-based appeal can work in one of two ways in a persuasive speech. Candidates for political office often promise to give something in return for a person's vote. They may promise to reciprocate by proposing legislation, supporting a specific bill, or voicing a concern of their constituency.

Another common way reciprocity is used in a persuasive speech is when the speaker calls on the audience to reciprocate. During homecoming week, as a case in point, the school president may appeal to alumni for financial support. The appeal is usually couched in terms of "giving something back to the institution that gave you so much."

The reason reciprocity is so effective is because people are conditioned from an early age to return favors, gifts, and services. Reciprocity is a norm. Thus, when people receive a promise or are asked to return something received, the conditioned response is to reciprocate in kind.

Liking   Liking is another primitive belief commonly used in persuasive campaigns. Politicians, for instance, enlist stars from film and music to speak persuasively on the politician's behalf. The assumption is that if a star is well liked, the feeling may be generalized to the candidate the star endorses. Liking is a staple of advertisers who employ well-known people as spokespersons for a product. It's not that the celebrity is an expert about the product, but that he or she is well liked by the public. Thus, if well-liked figure Michael Jordan eats Wheaties, or Candice Bergen talks up Sprint's long-distance service, the hope is that the public will also like the product being pitched.

Authority   Authority-based appeals tap into another primitive belief. Research shows that some people are predisposed to comply with the requests of individuals and institutions perceived as authoritative. Examples of these authoritative sources range from members of law enforcement and the clergy to agencies such as the military and the Internal Revenue Service. Thus, a speaker attempting to encourage a group of Catholics to voice their opposition to abortion might use the words of the pope as an appeal. Similarly, an IRS agent speaking before a group of accountants at a convention might use a written statement from the IRS as part of an appeal.

Social Support   An appeal based on social support is nothing more than an appeal based on numbers. There's a tendency among people to think that if enough folks say something is so, then it must be so. In her persuasive message supporting gun control, for example, Sarah Brady doesn't say, "People support gun control." Instead, Brady says, "These public safety measures are supported by the *vast majority of Americans*—including gun owners." Research shows that when people are confronted with an appeal supported by large numbers, they are much more likely to be persuaded by the appeal. In a sense, they accept social support as a form of grounds for the argument.

Scarcity   The appeal to scarcity is based on the law of supply and demand. It is a maxim in economics that when demand exceeds supply, the value of the commodity increases. Thus, an appeal based on scarcity is also one based on relative value. As was the case with reciprocity, authority, and social support, people are conditioned to believe that something which is

The use of a celebrity such as Candice Bergen to promote Sprint relies on her being likable.

scarce is valuable enough to demand their attention. Persuasive speeches about the environment frequently use scarcity as the basis of appeal. For instance, the ecological benefit of the rain forests is made even more valuable when the speaker tells the audience that the world's rain forests are disappearing at an alarming rate.

Commitment   Commitment is one of the most powerful methods of persuasion. Notice that Sarah Brady's persuasive message closes with an appeal for commitment from her audience. When people make even small commitments as a result of a persuasive message, the principle of psychological consistency comes into play. This principle tells us that we all feel pressure to keep our attitudes, beliefs, and values consistent with our commitments. Thus, if an appeal to commitment leads a person to write a letter, or volunteer to serve, or even sign a petition, it increases the chances of the person's attitudes, beliefs, and values reflecting the commitment. Thus, in some cases action may actually precede changes in attitude, reversing the normal order of persuasive goals.

To reiterate, the appeals you make in your persuasive message should reflect your goal and your audience. Not all audiences jump on hearing an authority-based appeal. There also are people who will steadfastly refuse to get on a bandwagon, no matter how many other people have already done so. Choosing the right form of appeal or appeals to flesh out your persuasive message, therefore, is part science and part art.

PERSUASIVE SPEAKING IN PRACTICE

The final topic we deal with is some practical suggestions about how to prepare your persuasive speech. We will look at adapting your goals to your audience, speech organization, and balancing the means of persuasion.

Adapting Your Goals to Your Audience

Speeches to reinforce or inoculate an audience presume that your audience members are either already supportive of your point of view or uninformed about the topic. These are friendly or neutral audiences. In this case, you can expect your views to receive a fair hearing. You will want to build a strong case, of course, but you need not fear your audience will reject you out of hand.

A speech to change attitudes, by definition, means your audience disagrees with you. This is termed a hostile audience. Although they may not be overtly hostile (booing and hissing), they are unlikely to be open to your point of view without a lot of work on your part. Such a speech requires you to begin with a common ground on which you and your audience can agree. After doing so, it is realistic only to move them slightly toward your position on the topic. Speaking to a group of gun owners about the need for gun control is a difficult task. You might begin by indicating you agree with the Second Amendment and do not seek to infringe on their right to bear arms. Rather, you want to see control of those kinds of weapons that are primarily used by gangs against law-abiding citizens. Perhaps you would simply argue for banning Teflon-coated bullets that can pierce police body armor. In any case, do not expect a massive conversion from this type of audience.

Finally, speeches that seek to prompt people to act presume that your audience is prepared by prior messages to take action or that your topic is not inherently controversial. For example, prompting people to floss their

Evangelist Billy Graham uses public commitment as a way of gaining religious converts.

teeth is not a topic that people are hostile to, though they may be uninformed about the benefits of acting. Such a speech needs to focus on the tangible benefits of action. In the case of an audience already primed by previous messages, your main task is to motivate them to act. People have heard for years about the benefits of wearing seat belts, yet a significant number of people still fail to do so. Rehashing arguments they have already heard is of little use. You need to tell them something new that will get them to finally act. A dramatic story, for example, about how your own life was saved by wearing a seat belt might be the key ingredient in such a speech.

Organizing Your Persuasive Speech

In Chapter 8 we introduced a number of ways to organize a speech. Two organizational patterns described there are particularly suited to persuasive efforts. The first is the problem–solution pattern, sometimes called stock issues. This pattern of organization analyzes a problem in terms of harm, significance, and cause and proposes a solution that is described, feasible, and advantageous. Many persuasive topics are about problems we face individually or as a society. By beginning with a discussion of the problem, the speaker heightens the audience's interest but avoids turning off a hostile audience with a solution they might initially reject. A speech on gun control that begins with a discussion of the growing gang problem is far more likely to receive a hearing from a pro-gun group than a speech that begins by calling for gun control. Even individual problems are susceptible to this pattern of organization. If you examine Ryland Hill, Jr.'s, speech, you'll see that this is his basic approach.

The second useful pattern for persuasive speaking is Monroe's motivated sequence, a five-step organizational scheme, including attention, need, satisfaction, visualization, and action. Because the final step is action, this pattern is particularly well suited to speeches calling for your audience to act. As should all good speeches, this type begins by capturing the audience's attention. Like the problem–solution pattern, this speech focuses on a problem (called a need) before proposing its solution (satisfaction). But this pattern goes further by asking the audience to visualize the satisfaction of the need and then calling on them to act.

Regardless of the organizational pattern you choose, there are some principles of organization you should follow. First, always put your best arguments and support either early or late in the speech. Do not hide them in the middle. Over the years, research has shown that in some cases people best remember what they hear first whereas in other cases, what comes last is most memorable. Either way, the middle of the speech is not the place for your best material.

Second, with hostile or indifferent audiences, it is particularly important to have some of your best material early in the speech. Otherwise, they will tune you out before you get to the critical points.

Balancing the Means of Persuasion

Finally, although it might sometimes seem like we have treated ethos, logos, and pathos as separate means of persuasion, this is not really the case in practice. Your ethos will affect how your audience perceives the logos of your speech. If you have high credibility, the audience is more likely to accept your arguments. Similarly, if you have strong evidence and arguments in your speech, your credibility will grow in the audience's mind. And unless you touch the audience with pathos, it is unlikely that they will be motivated to act or believe in what they have heard. While Sarah Brady certainly had credibility and used strong logic in her speech, were it not for the emotional appeal associated with her husband's gun-inflicted injuries, it is unlikely she would have prevailed in getting the Brady Bill passed. In short, a good persuasive speech relies on all three factors—speaker, message, and audience—for its success.

SUMMARY

As Sarah Brady's example illustrates, persuasive speaking begins with an assessment of the rhetorical situation, which includes the goal(s) the persuasive speech is designed to achieve. Four common goals of a persuasive speech are to reinforce existing beliefs and attitudes, to inoculate against counterpersuasion, to change attitudes, and to prompt the audience to act. The probability of a persuasive speech achieving these goals requires a thorough understanding of the audience's cultural, demographic, and individual diversity. Finally, an assessment of the rhetorical situation demands that speakers examine the constraints they face, including ethical boundaries.

Aristotle proposed a three-part model of persuasion comprising ethos, logos, and pathos. Ethos, or perceived credibility, is essential if a speaker hopes to persuade an audience. Logos, or the words of the speech in the form of logical proof, also has been shown to affect a persuasive speaker's success. Pathos, or the emotions a speaker stirs in the audience, interacts with ethos and logos in the process of persuasion.

Two contemporary models that can assist speakers in putting Aristotle's thinking into practice are elaboration likelihood and Toulmin's template of argument. Elaboration likelihood shows speakers the two potential paths an audience can take in response to a persuasive message. One is complex and requires critical thinking; the other is more simplistic and involves conditioned responses to certain kinds of appeals.

Toulmin's template of argument is useful in the construction of a speech designed to provoke an elaborated response from an audience. The template consists of a claim, grounds, and a warrant. The claim is the conclusion the speaker wants the audience to reach. Grounds are evidence a speaker offers in support of a claim. The warrant is the connection between the grounds and the claim. In addition, the speaker may need to provide backing, or further support for the warrant. A qualifier indicates the degree of certainty of the claim. And a rebuttal indicates an exception or refutation of the claim.

Three types of grounds (evidence) commonly used to support a claim are personal experience or first-order data, expert testimony or second-order data, and facts and statistics or third-order data.

A two-sided message includes a qualifier and a rebuttal in addition to a claim, grounds, and a warrant. Two-sided persuasive speeches are generally more effective than one-sided speeches. Two sided-messages also confer greater credibility on a speaker and can be used to inoculate an audience against counterpersuasion.

Sometimes grounds take the form of appeals that are designed to produce conditioned rather than elaborated responses from an audience. These appeals are meant to trigger basic emotions such as fear and rely on primitive beliefs about such things as reciprocity, liking, authority, social support, scarcity, and commitment. Such appeals can be both effective and ethically used by a person constructing a persuasive speech.

Check Your Understanding: Exercises and Activities

1. Suppose you are giving a speech on the topic of gun control. How would you change your persuasive message to achieve each of the four persuasive goals: reinforcement, inoculation, attitude change, and action? Using the concept of the rhetorical situation, how would these goals differ depending on possible audiences for this topic and the constraints you would face in each situation?

2. On a topic of your choosing, construct examples of appeals based on the six primitive beliefs discussed in the chapter (reciprocity, liking, etc.).

3. Consider the following list of topics: (1) preventing AIDS, (2) preventing tooth decay, (3), the importance of wearing seat belts. Construct a brief message based on a moderate-level "fear" appeal for each of these topics. At what level—low, moderate, or high—do you think your fear appeal would diminish the persuasive effects, causing audience members to reject your message? At what point do you think arguments based on fear on these topics would become unethical?

4. Find a recent speech by a public figure, such as the president. These can be found, for example, in the publication *Vital Speeches.* Or use one of the speeches in the appendixes of this book. Reread the analysis of Sarah Brady's persuasive message in this chapter. Use this analysis as a guide in identifying the claims, grounds, and warrants in the speech you have chosen.

5. Follow up on the list of tips we gave for assessing and enhancing perceptions of your credibility. List the specific factors you believe make you credible about the topic of your persuasive speech. Then describe how you plan on using these specific factors so that they will sustain the perception of credibility as you deliver your speech.

6. Newspaper editorials constitute a persuasive message. To improve your ability in recognizing the types of appeals being used, select a recent column from a nationally syndicated writer such as George Will, William Safire, Molly Ivins, or Ellen Goodman. Mark what you consider to be appeals the columnist is using. Note whether these appeals are intended to affect your emotions or your primitive beliefs. Finally, label the emotion or belief the appeal is targeted at arousing.

Notes

1. Aristotle, *Rhetoric,* trans. W. Rhys Roberts (New York: Modern Library, 1954), 25.

2. Sarah Brady, "Firearms: . . . And the Case Against Them," *Time,* 29 January 1990, 23–24.

3. Aristotle, *Rhetoric,* 25.

4. Sarah Trenholm, *Persuasion and Social Influence* (Englewood Cliffs, N.J.: Prentice-Hall, 1989).

5. Aristotle, *Rhetoric.*

6. James C. McCroskey, *An Introduction to Rhetorical Communication,* 5th ed. (Englewood Cliffs, N.J.: Prentice-Hall, 1986).

7. D. J. O'Keefe, *Persuasion: Theory and Research* (Newbury Park, Calif.: Sage, 1990).

8. O'Keefe, *Persuasion: Theory and Research.* See also John C. Reinard, "The Empirical Study of the Persuasive Effects of Evidence: The Status After Fifty Years of Research," *Human Communication Research* 15 (1988): 3–59.

9. Richard E. Petty and John T. Cacioppo, *Communication and Persuasion: Central and Peripheral Routes to Attitude Changes* (New York: Springer-Verlag, 1986).

10. Irvin A. Horowitz and Kenneth S. Bordons, *Social Psychology* (Mountain View, Calif.: Mayfield, 1995), 287–288.

11. Stephen Toulmin, Richard Rieke, and Allan Janik, *An Introduction to Reasoning,* 2nd ed. (New York: Macmillan, 1984).

12. Toulmin originally termed this the *qualifier* but added the term *modality* in his later works. We prefer the simpler term, *qualifier,* which is what we will use in this book.

13. James C. McCroskey, *An Introduction to Rhetorical Communication.*

14. Mike Allen, "Meta-Analysis Comparing the Persuasiveness of One-Sided and Two-Sided Messages," *Western Journal of Communication* 55 (1991): 390–404.

15. Aristotle, *Rhetoric.*

16. Irving Janis, "Effects of Fear-Arousal on Attitude Change: Recent Developments in Theory and Experimental Research," in *Advances in Experimental and Social Psychology,* vol. 3, ed. L. Berkowitz (New York: Academic Press, 1967), 166–224.

17. Robert Cialdini, *Influence: Science and Practice,* 2nd ed. (New York: HarperCollins, 1988).

Political debates
require voters to think
critically about what
is being said

14

Thinking and Speaking Critically

OBJECTIVES

After reading this chapter, you should be able to:

- Explain the difference between argumentativeness and verbal aggressiveness.
- Analyze, construct, and evaluate arguments using the Toulmin model of reasoning.
- Differentiate among patterns of reasoning.
- Identify and refute common fallacies of argument.

KEY CONCEPTS

argumentativeness
authority warrant
causal warrant
comparison (analogy) warrant
critical thinking
fallacy

generalization warrant
inference
pseudoreasoning
sign warrant
verbal aggressiveness

In the previous chapter, we introduced Sarah Brady, wife of Reagan press secretary James Brady and president of Handgun Control, Inc. As we noted, after over a decade of campaigning for the Brady Bill, Sarah Brady saw her efforts come to fruition with the signing of the legislation by President Clinton. However, that is not the end of the story. With the shift to a more conservative Congress in 1994, calls to repeal the Brady Bill and the ban on semiautomatic assault weapons began to be given serious attention.

As with so many controversial issues, there are two sides to this argument. In the box "The Case for Firearms," J. Warren Cassidy, the executive vice-president of the National Rifle Association, attempts to refute the case for gun control. As we examine the nature of critical thinking and constructive argument in this chapter, we will refer back to both Brady's and Cassidy's messages on gun control. Thus, you should read the case for firearms now as well as review Brady's message in Chapter 13.

CRITICAL THINKING AND PUBLIC SPEAKING

Critical thinking is the process of making sound inferences based on accurate evidence and valid reasoning. Understanding how to think critically about arguments is the first step to constructing and communicating those arguments to an audience. As noted in Chapter 13, logical proof is an important part of any persuasive message. To successfully persuade others of your side of a controversial issue, it is important to have well-constructed, sound arguments for your side. As the elaboration likelihood model introduced in the preceding chapter shows, you are more likely to induce a permanent change in attitude if you use sound evidence and reasoning.

Pseudoreasoning and Fallacies

As pointed out in Chapter 4, we spend more of our time listening to others than actually speaking. Understanding critical thinking is essential to differentiating messages that are logical from those that are not. Frequently, something sounds good on first hearing but proves to be illogical. **Pseudoreasoning** refers to an argument that appears sound at first glance but contains a fallacy of reasoning that renders it unsound. A **fallacy** is "an argument in which the reasons advanced for a claim fail to warrant the acceptance of that claim."[1] Thus, one of the goals of this chapter is to help you recognize fallacies that are a sign of pseudoreasoning. Even if you agree with the conclusion of a speaker, you ought to do so based on sound logic, not just because he or she sounds good.

It is important to distinguish here between intentional and unintentional fallacies. Certainly not everyone who makes an error in reasoning is

Sample Persuasive Rebuttal Message

The Case For Firearms, by J. Warren Cassidy

J. Warren Cassidy is executive vice-president of the N.R.A.

The American people have a right "to keep and bear arms." This right is protected by the Second Amendment to the Constitution, just as the right to publish editorial comment in this magazine is protected by the First Amendment. Americans remain committed to the constitutional right to free speech even when their most powerful oracles have, at times, abused the First Amendment's inherent powers. Obviously the American people believe no democracy can survive without a free voice.

In the same light, the authors of the Bill of Rights knew that a democratic republic has a right—indeed, a need—to keep and bear arms. Millions of American citizens just as adamantly believe the Second Amendment is crucial to the maintenance of the democratic process. Many express this belief through membership in the National Rifle Association of America.

Our cause is neither trendy nor fashionable, but a basic American belief that spans generations. The N.R.A.'s strength has never originated in Washington but instead has reached outward and upward from Biloxi, Albuquerque, Concord, Tampa, Topeka—from every point on the compass and from communities large and small. Those who fail to grasp this widespread commitment will never understand the depth of political and philosophical dedication symbolized by the letters N.R.A.

Scholars who have devoted careers to the study of the Second Amendment agree in principle that the right to keep and bear arms is fundamental to our concept of democracy. No high-court decision has yet found grounds to challenge this basic freedom. Yet some who oppose this freedom want to waive the constitutionality of the "gun control" question for the sake of their particular—and sometimes peculiar—brand of social reform.

In doing so they seem ready, even eager, to disregard a constitutional right exercised by at least 70 million Americans who own firearms. Contrary to current antigun evangelism, these gun owners are not bad people. They are hardworking, law abiding, tax paying. They are safe, sane and courteous in their use of guns. They have never been, nor will they ever be, a threat to law-and-order.

Use of comparison of First and Second Amendments

Red herring: What does where N.R.A. supporters live have to do with the issue at hand?

Unsupported assertion: Which scholars?

Straw argument: gun-control advocates do not say gun owners are bad people

(continued) ➤

IN THEIR OWN WORDS

Sample Persuasive Rebuttal Message (continued)

History repeatedly warns us that human character cannot be scrubbed free of its defects through vain attempts to regulate inanimate objects such as guns. What has worked in the past, and what we see working now, are tough, N.R.A.-supported measures that punish the incorrigible minority who place themselves outside the law.

Rebuttal to Sarah Brady's claim of epidemic

As a result of such measures, violent crimes with firearms, like assault and robbery, have stabilized or are actually declining. We see proof that levels of firearm ownership cannot be associated with levels of criminal violence, except for their deterrent value. On the other hand, tough laws designed to incarcerate violent offenders offer something gun control cannot: swift, sure justice meted out with no accompanying erosion of individual liberty.

Negative examples: where gun control failed

Violent crime continues to rise in cities like New York and Washington even after severe firearm-control statutes were rushed into place. Criminals, understandably, have illegal ways of obtaining guns. Antigun laws—the waiting periods, background checks, handgun bans, et al.—only harass those who obey them. Why should an honest citizen be deprived of a firearm for sport or self-defense when, for a gangster, obtaining a gun is just a matter of showing up on the right street corner with enough money?

Stereotypes: Police administrators as out of touch with rank-and-file police
Effect-to-cause relationship questioned: Gun control would not have prevented crimes

Antigun opinion steadfastly ignores these realities known to rank-and-file police officers—men and women who face crime firsthand, not police administrators who face mayors and editors. These law-enforcement professionals tell us that expecting firearm restrictions to act as crime-prevention measures is wishful thinking. They point out that proposed gun laws would not have stopped heinous crimes committed by the likes of John Hinckley Jr., Patrick Purdy, Laurie Dann or mentally disturbed, usually addicted killers. How can such crimes be used as examples of what gun control could prevent?

There are better ways to advance our society than to excuse criminal behavior. The N.R.A. initiated the first hunter-safety program, which has trained millions of young hunters. We are the shooting sports' leading safety organization, with more than 26,000 certified instructors training 750,000 students and trainees last year alone. Through 1989 there were 9,818 N.R.A.-certified law-enforcement instructors teaching marksmanship to thousands of peace officers.

False dilemma: It's not either hunter safety or fighting gun control

Frankly, we would rather keep investing N.R.A. resources in such worthwhile efforts instead of spending our time and members' money debunking the failed and flawed promises of gun prohibitionists.

intending to deceive. On the other hand, someone who is seeking to "pull the wool over an audience's eyes" may indeed use fallacies intentionally. Either way, it is the consumer of communication—the audience—who must

BEWARE OF SPEAKERS BEARING GIFTS...

remain vigilant to avoid being misled, whether by accident or design, by pseudoreasoning.

Argumentativeness and Verbal Aggressiveness

In Chapter 6, we maintained that when listeners detect fallacious reasoning, they are ethically obligated to bring it to light. Simply remaining silent allows the speaker to mislead those who are not well trained in critical thinking. However, there is an important distinction between being argumentative and being verbally aggressive. In his book *Arguing Constructively*, Dominic A. Infante makes the distinction between these two personality traits.[2] **Argumentativeness** is the trait of arguing for and against the *positions* taken on controversial claims. For example, an argumentative person might say, "The idea of a flat tax sounds good, but it would lead to massive increases in the federal debt." **Verbal aggressiveness,** on the other hand, is the trait of *attacking* the self-concept of those with whom a person disagrees about controversial claims. A verbally aggressive person might say, "The flat tax sounds like something a bunch of rich freeloaders dreamed up while sailing their yachts." Argumentativeness is not only socially beneficial; it is the only way one can take the process of critical thinking into the public arena. Verbal aggressiveness, on the other hand, is a destructive and hostile trait that destroys personal relationships. Constructive argumentativeness is the best approach for the public speaker. Being able to disagree without being disagreeable fosters a positive communication transaction.

In the spirit of constructive argumentation, therefore, we will consider how to test arguments for their soundness. Using the Toulmin model introduced in the preceding chapter, we will suggest appropriate tests for the grounds, claims, warrants, backing, qualifiers, and rebuttals of various types of arguments. Further, we will show how the failure to meet these tests can result in fallacies, turning what could be sound arguments into pseudo-arguments.

FALLACIES ASSOCIATED WITH GROUNDS

All arguments are built on the grounds, or evidence, which the arguer points to in supporting the claim. If the grounds are either absent or defective, then the argument cannot be sound. In Chapter 7, we discussed various types of supporting material that might form the grounds of an argument, including examples, facts, statistics, expert opinion, explanations, descriptions, and narratives.

When you are examining the grounds of an argument, be sure that the examples are relevant, of sufficient quantity, and typical. Facts should come from a reliable source and be verifiable, recent, and consistent with other known facts. Statistics should be taken from a reliable and unbiased source, based on fair questions, and accurately collected. You should be told how the sample was selected to ensure that it was random and representative. Any differences should be greater than the margin of error, and the base of any percentages should be stated. Expert opinion depends on the source's expertise, reliability, and lack of bias. Explanations should be clear and accurate. Descriptions should be accurate and vivid. Narratives must have probability (coherence) and fidelity to the real world.

Grounds that fail one or more of these tests are likely to constitute a fallacy. In particular, there are four fallacies associated with grounds: unsupported assertion, distorted evidence, isolated examples, and misused statistics.

Unsupported Assertion

There are a number of ways in which the grounds, or evidence, in support of an argument can be defective. The most egregious case is the absence of any grounds to support a claim. The *unsupported assertion* is really the absence of any argument at all. Fans of the sitcom *Cheers* probably recognize this tendency in Cliff Claven, who is always spouting the most absurd facts as if they were gospel. An argument without grounds is no argument at all.

In his argument about firearms, J. Warren Cassidy claims, "Scholars who have devoted careers to the study of the Second Amendment agree in principle that the right to keep and bear arms is fundamental to our concept of democracy." What scholars? How many? The claim just sits there with no evidence to support it. This is not to say that it is untrue, merely that there are no grounds offered in the message to support it. Similarly, in her argument about handguns, Sarah Brady says, "These public-safety measures [meaning controls on guns] are supported by the vast majority of Americans—including gun owners." As with Cassidy's claim about scholars and the Second Amendment, there is no evidence to support Brady's claim; it is simply asserted.

Verbally aggressive people can destroy relationships by engaging in personal attacks.

Distorted Evidence

Less easily discovered is the argument that relies on distorted evidence to support its claim. *Distorted evidence* is significant omissions or changes in the grounds of an argument that alter its original intent.

A good example of distorted evidence is found on the movie advertisement page of your local newspaper. Frequently, a movie will tout itself as "daring," "enthralling," or "thumbs up" when a reading of the full review will reveal that these words were used in a different context. Perhaps the reviewers really said, "This movie was a daring attempt that missed the mark. The only thing that was enthralling about this movie was the credits that signaled it was ending. In deciding whether to rate this movie thumbs up or down, it took only about 10 minutes to see that this was thumbs way down!"

Isolated Examples

Another problem with grounds lies in the use of *isolated examples,* nontypical or nonrepresentative examples, to prove a general claim. Recall that to reason from examples requires that the instances be representative of the larger class—in a word, typical. It is almost always possible to find an isolated example to illustrate just about any claim. For example, we often hear about cases of welfare abuse. One radio commentator recently told the story of a man who reported to the police that his food stamps had been stolen from his car—a Mercedes. Of course, most people on welfare don't drive a Mercedes. Yet the image of welfare recipients living it up at the taxpayers' expense has been a staple of popular mythology for decades. The reality is that most people on welfare are actually children living in poverty. Isolated examples do not prove that everyone on welfare is lazy or abusing the system.

Misused Statistics

Statistics are often very helpful in giving us a general picture of a topic, something not provided by examples. However, to be useful, grounds must meet the basic tests outlined in Chapter 7. Let's now look at four of the most frequent cases of *misused statistics.*

Poor Sampling   Statistics based on self-selected or nonrandom samples are worse than useless—they're misleading. For instance, many television stations and newspapers now have call-in polls whereby you can express your opinion on the issues of the day by dialing one of two numbers, each representing one side of the issue. Of course, there is no guarantee that the station's audience represents the public at large or that members of the audience will call in proportion to their number in the general population.

Lack of Significant Differences   Often the difference between two candidates in a preference poll is less than the poll's margin of error. Thus, if candidate A leads B by three points, but the poll has a five-point margin of error, there

F.D.A. Commissioner David Kessler uses his critical thinking skills to refute tobacco company claims that cigarettes are not addictive.

is no statistical significance to that difference, a fact often ignored by political pundits.

Misuse of "Average"   There are three ways to compute an average. As an example, consider the differences between the mean, the median, and the mode of the same houses selling at a range of prices:

$$
\begin{aligned}
& \$100,000 \\
& \$100,000 \\
& \$150,000 \\
& \$250,000 \\
& \$1,000,000 \\
\text{Mean} = {}& \$320,000 \\
\text{Median} = {}& \$150,000 \\
\text{Mode} = {}& \$100,000
\end{aligned}
$$

The mean is simply the arithmetic average: Add all the selling prices, and divide the total by the number of houses sold. The median is the midpoint in a series of numbers. Half of the houses sold for more and half for less than the median. Finally, the mode is simply the most frequently occurring number or value. All of these terms are, of course, correctly termed "average." However, depending on your purposes, you could argue that you live in a high-, medium-, or low-cost neighborhood.

Misuse of Percentages   Percentages are meaningful only if you know the base on which they are computed. Consider the confusion often present in political and commercial advertising. For example, though it is true that while Bill Clinton was governor, Arkansas led the nation in job creation in the year prior to his election as president, it is also true that Arkansas had one of the lowest job bases to begin with. If you start out at a very low level, even large percentage increases may not be very large in real terms.

FALLACIES ASSOCIATED WITH CLAIMS

There are three types of claims a person can make. A *claim of fact* is one that can in principle be verified by objective means. For example, J. Warren Cassidy claims that "the American people have a right 'to keep and bear arms.' This right is protected by the Second Amendment to the Consti- tution." This claim is easily verified by looking up the Second Amend- ment. Even if a claim of fact is not currently known to be true or false, as long as it is theoretically verifiable, it is still a factual claim. We don't know for sure if there is life on other planets, but theoretically the question could be answered empirically, if we had the means to directly observe radio sig- nals from deep space, for example.

A *claim of value* makes judgments about good and bad, right and wrong. When Cassidy argues that "the Second Amendment is crucial to the main- tenance of the democratic process," he has gone beyond mere fact, to make a value judgment about the right to keep and bear arms.

A *claim of policy* offers a solution to some problem. Sarah Brady has a clear position on what should be done about gun violence: pass a handgun waiting period and stop the sale of semiautomatic assault weapons. To con- vincingly prove a claim of policy, one must prove the stock issues that (1) there is a need for the policy, (2) the proposed policy would fulfill that need, and (3) the benefits of the proposed policy outweigh the costs. It seems clear that Cassidy disagrees with Brady on all three points. He argues that there is no need for the legislation she proposes, because tougher penalties for using a gun in committing a crime have worked. He argues that gun-control won't work, using the examples of New York and Washington, cities with stiff gun-control laws and high crime rates. And he argues that to pass such laws would be unfair to law-abiding citizens.

Red Herring

Claims may be fallacious if they are irrelevant, the so-called *red herring*. Sometimes called a smoke screen, a red herring is an irrelevant issue introduced into a controversy to divert attention from the real controversy. Debates over public issues are well known for the use of red herrings to divert attention from the issues that concern most people. For example, Cassidy argues, "The N.R.A.'s strength has never originated in Washington but instead has reached outward and upward from Biloxi, Albuquerque, Concord, Tampa, Topeka—from every point on the compass and from communities large and small." Aside from taking advantage of the prevailing "anti-Washington" sentiment in the United States, what exactly does that have to do with whether or not we should pass the Brady Bill? It is a red herring, irrelevant to the issue at hand.

Arguing in a Circle

Another common fallacy is the use of a claim to prove its own truth, called *arguing in a circle*. Arguing in a circle, sometimes called *begging the question,* occurs when the argument actually proves nothing because the claim to be proved is used as the grounds or warrant for the argument. For example, consider the door-to-door evangelist who insists that you must believe in his or her version of the Bible. Why? you ask. The person immediately opens a Bible and quotes you scripture to support the claim. Basically the argument looks something like this:

Claim: My version of the Bible is the truth.

Grounds: Quotation from scripture

Warrant: My version of the Bible is the truth.

In other words, the claim is also the warrant.

Of course, such clear-cut expressions of question-begging are rare. But many arguments, when distilled to their essence, do in fact beg the question.

FALLACIES ASSOCIATED WITH WARRANTS AND BACKING

Grounds do not directly prove a claim. There is a connection between the grounds and the claim, whether stated or unstated. You may recall from Chapter 13 that Toulmin calls this link the warrant. The warrant is the license that authorizes an arguer to move from grounds to a claim. Thus, if one were to argue, as in the example in Chapter 13, that it's going to rain because it is cloudy, the observation about clouds only proves it will rain given the warrant that clouds are a sign of rain. The process of moving from grounds, via a warrant, to a claim is called an **inference.**

Sometimes people confuse observed grounds with claims based on inference. To see how well you can distinguish between inferences and observations, try reading the story and answering the questions in the "Uncritical Inference Test" box on pages 424–425. This test was devised by William V. Haney, a former business professor who now heads his own consulting firm.

To his basic model of grounds–warrant–claim, Toulmin adds backing, which is support for the warrant. In some cases a warrant is readily believed by an audience. In others, the warrant needs additional backing in the form of evidence before the audience will believe it is true. For example, suppose your audience is unaware that the Supreme Court has upheld numerous gun-control laws over the years. They assume that the Second Amendment guarantees unlimited rights to bear arms. If you presented a warrant, therefore, that gun control was permissible under the Constitution, they would not believe it. Thus, you would need to present *backing* for that warrant. You might quote the Second Amendment, which begins "A well regulated militia. . . ." Similarly, you might cite a number of Supreme Court cases that have permitted reasonable limits on gun ownership. Backing comes into play, therefore, when a warrant either is not known to the audience or is contrary to what they already believe.

Different types of warrants provide different ways of moving from grounds to claim and are associated with different patterns of reasoning. We introduce here the five most common types of warrants: generalization, comparison, causal, sign, and authority. In examining any argument, it is important to determine whether the warrant and its accompanying backing are sound. We look at each type of warrant and suggest some of the common fallacies peculiar to each type of argument.

Generalization Warrants

A **generalization warrant** is a statement that either establishes a general rule or principle or applies an established rule or principle to a specific case. Warrants involving generalizations are used in two ways. Some warrants take specific instances and use them to establish generalizations. For example, suppose we want to generalize about college students. Based on our experience with the students in our public speaking class, we might generalize that "most college students are politically uninvolved." Other warrants take already existing generalizations and apply them to specific instances. For example, suppose we know from a previously established generalization that all college students must be high school graduates. Thus, we can conclude that any specific student in a college class is a high school graduate.

The relationship between a generalization establishing arguments and a generalization applying arguments looks like the diagram in Figure 14.1.

Establishing Generalizations   A warrant that establishes a generalization uses specific instances, as represented in examples, statistics, narratives, and the

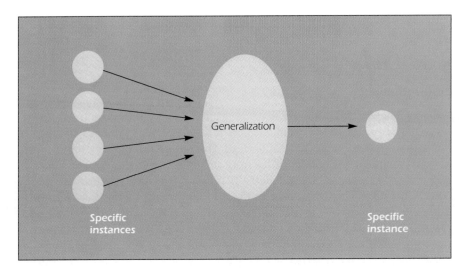

FIGURE 14.1
Generalizations are established based on a number of specific instances. Once accepted, generalizations are then applied to further specific instances.

like, to reach general conclusions. Consider Sarah Brady's argument. She uses specific examples and statistics to support her generalization that gun violence is an epidemic. She uses the examples of the Reagan assassination attempt, as well as the massacre of children on a schoolyard in Stockton, California, a Louisville shooting spree, and the murder of two Colorado women to support her generalization. She also cites statistics on the number of deaths from handgun violence. Warrants establishing generalizations are subject to tests of relevance, quantity, typicality, precision, and negative example. These tests can be expressed in the questions listed below.

Questions to Ask When Evaluating a Generalization

- Are the grounds relevant to the claim?
- Is there a sufficient quantity of grounds to establish the claim?
- Are the grounds typical of the larger population?
- Is overgeneralization avoided?
- Are there significant negative examples?

Let's apply these tests to Brady's generalization that gun violence is an epidemic. Clearly her examples are relevant. Is there a sufficient quantity of grounds to support the claim? She cites several examples, including her husband's wounds in the Reagan assassination attempt. In addition she cites statistics of 250,000 deaths from handguns in a decade. There seems to be plenty of evidence that a problem exists here.

Uncritical Inference Test

Instructions

Read the following story. Assume that all the information presented in it is definitely accurate and true. Read it carefully because it has ambiguous parts designed to lead you astray. No need to memorize it, though. You can refer to it whenever you wish.

Next read the statements about the story and indicate whether you consider each statement true, false, or "?". "T" means that the statement is *definitely true* on the basis of the information presented in the story. "F" means that it is *definitely false.* "?" means that it may be either true or false and that you cannot be certain which on the basis of the information presented in the story. If any part of a statement is doubtful, make it "?". *Answer each statement in turn, and do not go back to change any answer later, and don't reread any statements after you have answered them. This will distort your score.*

To start with, here is a sample story with correct answers.

Sample Story

You arrive home late one evening and see that the lights are on in your living room. There is only one car parked in front of your house, and the words "Harold R. Jones, M.D." are spelled in small gold letters across one of the car's doors.

Statements About Sample Story

1. The car parked in front of your house has lettering on one of its doors. Ⓣ F   ?
   (This is a "definitely true" statement because it is directly corroborated by the story.)

2. Someone in your family is sick.   T   F ⑦
   (This could be true, and then again it might not be. Perhaps Dr. Jones is paying a social call at your home, or perhaps he has gone to the house next door or across the street, or maybe someone else is using the car.)

3. No car is parked in front of your house.   T Ⓕ ?
   (A "definitely false" statement because the story directly contradicts it.)

4. The car parked in front of your house belongs to a woman named Johnson.   T   F ⑦
   (May seem very likely false, but can you be sure? Perhaps the car has just been sold.)

So much for the sample. It should warn you of some of the kinds of traps to look for. Now begin the actual test. Remember, mark each statement *in order*—don't skip around or change answers later.

The Story[1]

A businessman had just turned off the lights in the store when a man appeared and demanded money. The owner opened a cash register. The contents of the cash register were scooped up, and the man sped away. A member of the police force was notified promptly.

Statements About the Story

1. A man appeared after the owner had turned off his store lights.   T   F   ?

2. The robber was a *man*.   T   F   ?

3. The man who appeared did not demand money.   T   F   ?

4. The man who opened the cash register was the owner.   T   F   ?

5. The store owner scooped up the contents of the cash register and ran away.
   T   F   ?

6. Someone opened a cash register.   T   F   ?

7. After the man who demanded the money scooped up the contents of the cash register, he ran away.   T   F   ?

8. While the cash register contained money, the story does *not* state *how much*.   T   F   ?

9. The robber demanded money of the owner.   T   F   ?

10. A businessman had just turned off the lights when a man appeared in the store.
    T   F   ?

11. It was broad daylight when the man appeared.   T   F   ?

12. The man who appeared opened the cash register.   T   F   ?

13. No one demanded money.   T   F   ?

14. The story concerns a series of events in which only three persons are referred to: the owner of the store, a man who demanded money, and a member of the police force.   T   F   ?

15. The following events occurred: someone demanded money; a cash register was opened; its contents were scooped up; and a man dashed out of the store.
    T   F   ?

Answers appear on pages 446–447.

Source: Excerpted with special permission from William V. Haney, *Communication and Interpersonal Relations*, 6th ed. (Homewood, IL: R.D. Irwin, Inc., 1992), 231–33, 241.

[1]The story and statements are a portion of the "Uncritical Inference Test," copyrighted 1955 and 1983 by William V. Haney.

Are the grounds typical? Certainly her examples are not. An attempted presidential assassination and the Stockton, California, schoolyard shooting were newsworthy precisely because they were not typical. However, Brady bolsters her specific examples with statistics. Thus, combining examples and statistics ensures that her examples are not atypical.

Is overgeneralization avoided? Referring to gun violence as an "epidemic" suggests a level of urgency and danger on Brady's part. Is this really an epidemic, or is it a problem confined to certain areas of the country or certain populations? She never addresses that question.

Finally, are there negative examples? Brady claims that violence with firearms is widespread. But Cassidy presents evidence that violent crimes with firearms have stabilized or declined. These statistics constitute negative examples to refute Brady's claim of an epidemic.

The complete argument might look like the model in Figure 14.2. Based on the *grounds* of several examples, and using the *warrant* that these examples are typical of gun violence, which is supported by the *backing* of statistics showing 250,000 deaths from handguns in the 1980s, Brady makes the *unqualified claim* that gun violence is an epidemic, unless violent crime has stabilized or declined, as Cassidy argues in *rebuttal*.

Hasty Generalization The most common fallacy associated with warrants which generalize from specific instances to a general conclusion is known as *hasty generalization*. This occurs when there are too few instances to support a generalization or the instances are unrepresentative of the generalization. The key here is to limit generalizations to the extent justified by the grounds. For example, suppose you once purchased an American car. It gave you nothing but trouble. You decide American cars are unreliable and vow to purchase only foreign automobiles. You have engaged in hasty generalization. Maybe Fords are more reliable than Dodges. Perhaps American manufacturers have improved their product. To reach a generalization from one or even a handful of instances is to form a hasty generalization.

Applying Generalizations On the other hand, if we know a generalization is true, we can apply it to a specific instance and reach some valid conclusions about that specific instance. For example, we know that anyone born in the United States is, by definition, a U.S. citizen. Thus, if you show us your birth certificate, and it says you were born in Alaska, we know you are a U.S. citizen. Warrants applying generalizations are subject to tests of applicability to all cases, exceptions, backing, and classification.

Questions to Ask When Evaluating Applications of a Generalization

- **Does the generalization apply to all possible cases?**

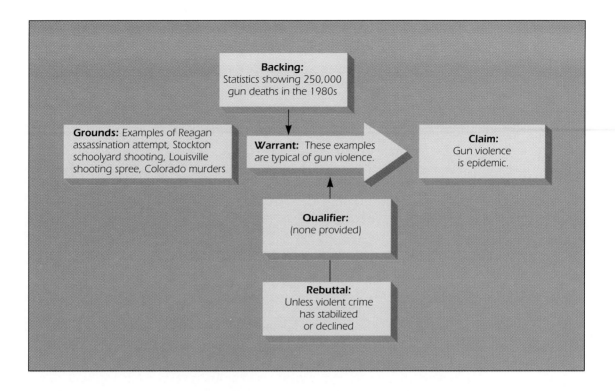

- **Are there exceptions to the generalization? If so, does the specific case fall within one of the exceptions?**
- **Is the generalization well backed?**
- **Does the specific instance fall clearly within the category specified by the generalization?**

FIGURE 14.2
Argument establishing a generalization.

Figure 14.3 on page 428 illustrates an argument applying a generalization. In this case, we know that the generalization *warrant,* all native-born Americans are citizens, is true because of the *backing* found in the U.S. laws and Constitution. Given the *grounds* that John is a native-born American, we can be almost certain (*qualifier*) that the *claim,* John is a U.S. citizen, is true. There is a possible *rebuttal,* however; the claim is true unless he has renounced his citizenship.

Stereotyping   The most common fallacy associated with warrants that apply established generalizations to specific instances is known as *stereotyping.* This fallacy assumes that what is considered to be true of a larger class is necessarily true of particular members of that class. Thus, while it may be true that professional basketball players are generally tall, you would be wrong to assume that Mugsy Bogues is tall just because he plays in the NBA.

FIGURE 14.3
An argument applying a generalization.

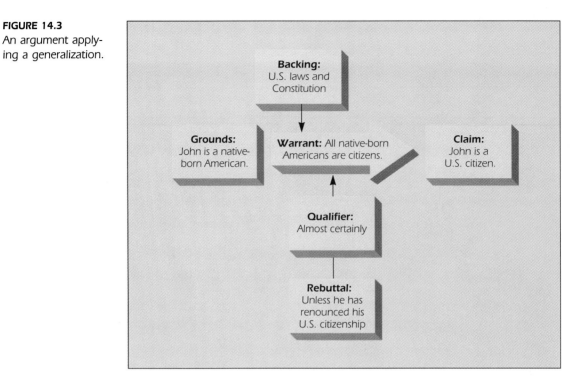

When you hear people talk about all people of any given race or group being the same, you can be fairly sure that they are guilty of the stereotyping fallacy. "Everybody on welfare is lazy," "All college students are liberals," and "All politicians are crooks" are examples of stereotyping.

We must be cautious about applying generalizations. One of the authors recalls a lecture in which he was discussing the impact of proposed tuition increases on minority students. He argued that such students would be disproportionately hurt by the increased fees. After the class, he was approached by an African American student who pointed out that not all minority students are from poor families and not all poor students are from minority groups. Indeed, the student was right. There is always a danger in dealing with generalizations that one will stereotype a whole group when there are notable exceptions to such generalizations.

False Dilemma   Another common fallacy associated with applying generalizations is the *false dilemma,* a generalization that implies there are only two choices when there are more than two. "America, love it or leave it," was a common false dilemma during the protests of the 1960s. Those who responded, "America, change it or lose it," were probably just as guilty of either-or thinking. Thus, a true dilemma requires proof that there really are only two choices. Consider the following telephone call to a newspaper.

Not all NBA players fit the stereotype of being tall, as Mugsy Bogues (Charlotte Hornets) proves.

They should fight child abuse

I'd like to talk to the pro-lifers about abortion. They want to stop abortion so bad and they take their time to do it. Why don't they take the same painstaking time to help fight children being killed by dads and moms when they get a very light sentence?[3]

Of course, one can be both pro-life (or anti-abortion) and against children being killed by their parents. The key to a real dilemma is that there are in fact only two choices and that they are mutually exclusive. In this case, one could support both of these values without contradiction, and thus no real dilemma exists.

Comparison (Analogy) Warrants

An argument based on a **comparison (analogy) warrant** claims that two cases that are similar in some known respects are also similar in some unknown respects. These arguments are called comparisons or, more commonly, analogies. They are subject to tests of literalness versus figurativeness, similarity, and relevance.

Questions to Ask When Evaluating Comparisons or Analogies

- **Are only literal analogies used for proof?**
- **Do the similarities outweigh the differences?**
- **Are the similarities more relevant than the differences to the claim being made?**

Let's begin with the difference between literal and figurative analogies. A literal analogy claims that two different instances are really similar. For example, prior to the war in the Persian Gulf, many proponents of using military force compared Saddam Hussein to Adolf Hitler. They argued that if Saddam's occupation of Kuwait was allowed to stand, he would continue to conquer his neighbors and expand his territory, just as Hitler had done in Europe. Opponents of military involvement, on the other hand, often argued that the Gulf War could become another Vietnam War, with the United States bogged down in a faraway foreign land, in a war that would be both unpopular at home and costly in terms of lives and money. Both sides were attempting to provide literal analogies to other wars in order to support their claims that the United States either should or should not fight in the Persian Gulf.

A figurative analogy, on the other hand, is a device of language that is used to enhance the persuasiveness of the speech. While a figurative analogy clearly seeks to establish some similarity between the two items being compared, no one could reasonably argue that they are really alike. For example, some people made the comparison of Saddam to a schoolyard bully. If the United States didn't stand up to him, he would be encouraged to become a bigger bully. No one believed, however, that Saddam was just a big bully using his fists to beat up little kids and steal their lunch money. A schoolyard bully might cost you a black eye and your lunch money. Saddam cost human lives and billions of dollars.

Although there is nothing wrong with figurative analogies as a persuasive device, if you rely on them to provide proof for a claim, you are on shaky ground. There is no logical force to such arguments.

Next, in a good analogy or comparison the similarities should outweigh the differences. If they do not, the analogy will not be very powerful. For example, when comparing Adolf Hitler and Saddam Hussein, there are clearly many similarities. Both were dictators, both had engaged in atrocities against their neighbors and their own people, and both invaded neighboring nations. There are also important differences. For example, Hitler commanded one of the most powerful military machines in history, whereas Saddam's army proved to be technologically backward. Further, there was no united front against Hitler; in fact, the Soviet Union had signed a pact with him. With very few exceptions, there was an array of nations opposing Saddam that was almost unparalleled in recent history.

Finally, the similarities, rather than the differences, should be most relevant to the claim being made. In the comparison of Saddam and Hitler, whereas Hitler and his allies had the military might to make war on the world, Saddam was unable to launch a meaningful attack on even his closest enemy, Israel.

Figure 14.4 on page 432 shows how the complete argument by comparison might evolve on this topic. Based on *grounds* that the failure to oppose Hitler led to his conquest of Europe, and using the *warrant* that what was true of Hitler is true of Saddam, probably (*qualifier*) the *claim* that the failure to oppose Saddam will lead to his conquest of the Middle East is true. *Backing* for the warrant comes from the common traits that both men are ruthless dictators with aggressive plans. The claim is true unless (*rebuttal*) Saddam's military strength has been exaggerated.

False Analogy The most common fallacy associated with comparison warrants is the *false analogy*. This occurs when two things that are not really comparable are compared as if they were essentially the same. For example, we recall a letter written to a newspaper by a reader angered with newly enacted laws requiring motorcyclists to wear helmets. This reader complained that the legislature had become another Saddam Hussein, acting like a dictator in passing a mandatory helmet law.

Of course, the differences in these two situations are dramatic. The legislature is an elected body. The law was passed based on safety concerns and is not unlike laws requiring motorists to wear seat belts. The key to the anal-

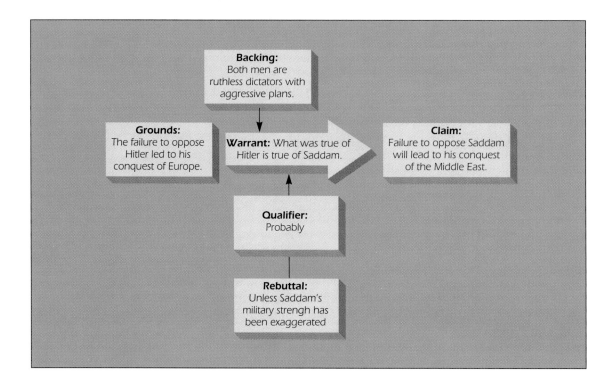

FIGURE 14.4
An argument by comparison.

ogy is whether or not the legislature and Saddam are both dictators. In the case of Iraq, the people have no way, short of a coup or revolution to remove the offending person, whereas the voters have an opportunity every two years to "throw the bums out."

Causal Warrants

Frequently we seek to determine either what has caused something or what effect a particular action will have. An argument based on a **causal warrant** claims that a cause will produce or has produced an effect. We can reason either from cause to effect or from effect to cause.

Reasoning from *cause to effect* involves predicting what will happen if some action is taken. For example, in recent years the ozone layer that protects the earth has developed "holes," or thin spots. Based on this fact, some experts predict that there will be many more deaths from skin cancer than if the ozone layer had not developed holes. Clearly this reasoning process moves from a cause (depletion of the ozone layer) to a predicted effect (skin cancer deaths) (Figure 14.5). Based on the *grounds* that the ozone hole al-

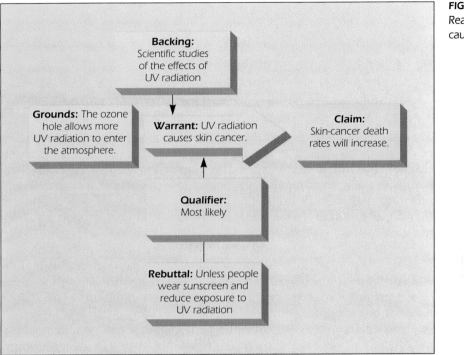

FIGURE 14.5
Reasoning from
cause to effect.

lows more UV radiation to enter the atmosphere, and using the *warrant,* UV radiation causes skin cancer, which has *backing* from scientific studies, most likely (*qualifier*) the *claim* is true that skin-cancer death rates will increase, unless (*rebuttal*) people wear sunscreen and reduce their exposure to UV radiation.

On the other hand, one might ask why the ozone layer has been depleted. According to some experts, chlorine-containing chemicals, called CFCs (chlorofluorocarbons), are the principal culprit in destroying the ozone. These chemicals are found in auto air conditioners, refrigerators, and the like. In this instance, one is reasoning from *effect* (depletion of the ozone layer) *to cause* (CFCs) (Figure 14.6 on page 435). This argument shows that based on the *grounds* that the ozone layer has a larger hole and CFCs have increased, using the *warrant* that CFCs are capable of destroying ozone, which has *backing* from scientific studies, most likely (*qualifier*) the *claim* is true that CFCs caused the depletion of the ozone layer, unless (*rebuttal*) there are other causes of ozone depletion.

Causal warrants are subject to tests of relatedness, other causes, other effects, and mistaking order in time for causality.

Questions to Ask When Evaluating Causal Reasoning

- **Is the cause related to the alleged effect?**
- **Are there other causes of the effect?**
- **Are there other effects from the same cause?**
- **Has time sequence been mistaken for cause (post hoc fallacy)?**

Let's apply these tests to the argument about CFCs and the depletion of the ozone layer. First, is the depletion *related* to CFCs? Based on a considerable body of scientific study, this connection seems well established. Further, is the ozone depletion related to the increase in skin cancer? Again, scientific studies have established that ultraviolet radiation is a cause of skin cancer and that the ozone layer screens out ultraviolet radiation from the sun.

Are there *other causes* of the effect? While CFCs cause ozone depletion, there are other causes as well. For example, the exhaust from shuttle rockets contributes to the breakdown of the ozone layer. Although this may not be the major cause of the problem, it means that eliminating CFCs alone may not be enough to end the problem.

How about *other effects* from the same cause? If CFCs are banned immediately, we may lose many of their benefits, such as air conditioning. Although some substitutes have been developed, they won't work in existing refrigeration units. So, while banning CFCs might seem like a simple solution, we need to consider other effects such a ban would cause.

Finally, we must be careful not to assume a causal relationship just because two events occur one after the other in *time*. We recall a letter to a local newspaper that attributed the end of the California drought to the prayers of particular ministers in a small foothill community. While it is true that the ministers prayed and the rains came, that does not mean one event caused the other. Similarly, although skin-cancer death rates are rising as the ozone is decreasing, that does not prove, in and of itself, that the ozone depletion is causing the death rates from skin cancer to rise. It might be the case, for example, that people are spending more time in the sun than they once did. One should always be particularly suspicious of claims of cause and effect based solely on time sequence.

Post Hoc Warrants dealing with effect-to-cause reasoning frequently commit the fallacy of assuming that because one event preceded another, the first event must be the cause of the second event. Technically, this is known as the *post hoc ergo propter hoc* fallacy ("after the fact, therefore because of the fact"). Cassidy argues that the passage of tough laws to punish those who use guns illegally has worked. "As a result of such measures, violent crimes with firearms, like assault and robbery, have stabilized or are actually declining." Of course, just because such laws were passed and crime

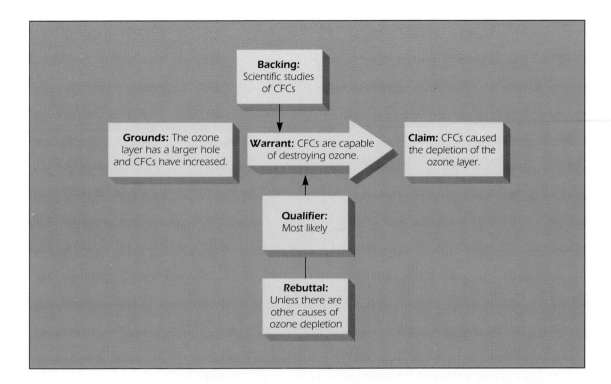

stabilized or declined does not mean one event caused the other. For example, many demographers attribute the recent decline in violent crime to the fact that there are relatively fewer people in the most crime-prone age group (late teens to early twenties). This is a result of the delay of baby boomers in starting families until they reached their late twenties or early thirties. As these children begin to enter adolescence, some demographers predict that we will see crime once again rise. Just because one event—gun laws—was followed by another—reduced crime—in no way proves that the first event caused the other.

Slippery Slope Warrants that reason from cause to effect are susceptible to the *slippery slope* fallacy. This fallacy involves assuming that just because one event occurs, it will automatically lead to a series of undesirable events, like a row of dominoes falling down automatically once you knock over the first one. In common language, this fallacy is sometimes expressed, "If you give them an inch they'll take a mile."

How many times have you heard someone argue that allowing abortions will lead to infanticide? Or perhaps you've been told that if you don't get a college degree you will end up homeless and broke. The slippery slope

FIGURE 14.6
Reasoning from effect to cause.

fallacy occurs when you assume that a series of events will result from one action without there being a relationship between the action and the projected events.

Sign Warrants

Perhaps you've heard someone say, "It's going to rain, I can feel it in my bones." Or you've read a newspaper article stating that the economy is in a recession, because the latest "leading economic indicators" are pointing downward. These are examples of reasoning from sign. A **sign warrant** is reasoning in which the presence of an observed phenomenon is used to indicate the presence of an unobserved phenomenon.

In sign reasoning, the warrant asserts that the grounds provide a reliable sign that the claim is true. Some signs are infallible; most are merely probable. The absence of brain waves is considered legally as an infallible sign of death. On the other hand, no one would claim that the rise or fall of stock prices is even close to an infallible sign of the state of the economy. Sign warrants are subject to tests of reliability and conflicting signs.

Questions to Ask When Evaluating Sign Reasoning

- **Are the signs reliable indicators of the claim?**
- **Are there conflicting signs?**

A detective examines a crime scene for signs of forced entry, struggle, and the like. Anyone who is a fan of Sherlock Holmes will recall that he often made a case based on the most obscure signs. One small sign would point him to the guilty subject every time.

Unfortunately, in real life, such reliable signs are harder to find. In testing sign reasoning, ask how reliable such signs have been in the past. For example, economists often make predictions about the future of the economy based on figures for unemployment, housing starts, and so on. A careful examination of their track record on making such predictions will suggest just how much confidence you should have in their reasoning.

The second test is to look for conflicting signs. Whereas one economist may point to decreased unemployment as a sign of economic upturn, another may conclude that there are fewer unemployed because the economy is so bad many workers have given up seeking jobs.

Unless a sign is infallible, most sign reasoning at best indicates the probability that a claim is true. For example, Figure 14.7 represents the argument about lower unemployment and the future of the economy. Based on the *grounds* that unemployment has declined, using the *warrant* that lower unemployment is a sign of economic recovery, based on the *backing*

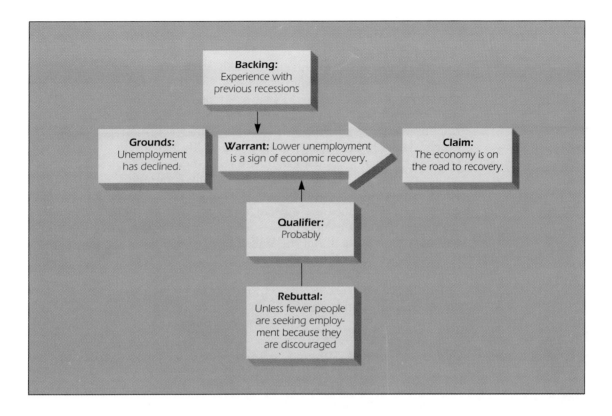

of experience with previous recessions, probably (*qualifier*) the *claim* is true that the economy is on the road to recovery, unless (*rebuttal*) fewer people are seeking employment because they are discouraged.

Mistaking Correlation for Cause The most common fallacy associated with sign reasoning is *mistaking correlation for cause*. A correlation simply means two things occur in conjunction with each other, without regard to their cause. How often have you heard someone claim that one event caused another, just because they occurred in tandem? Historically, when the stock market was on the rise, so were women's hemlines. Although one may be a "sign" of the other, it is ludicrous to assume the stock market caused the hemlines to go up or vice versa. Just because one event signifies another does not mean they are causally related. For example, a recent news report noted that there is a higher-than-normal incidence of heart disease among bald men. However, this does not prove that baldness causes heart disease or that wearing a toupee will reduce the risk of heart attack. While the two factors are correlated, the most likely explanation is that common underlying factors cause both baldness and heart disease.

FIGURE 14.7
Sign reasoning.

Authority Warrants

Sometimes the link between grounds and claim comes from the authoritativeness of the source of the grounds. An **authority warrant** is used in reasoning in which the claim is believed because of the authority of the source. Recall from Chapter 13 that many people respond almost unthinkingly to authority figures. This is not reasoning, but an unthinking response. Just because Tommy Lasorda drinks a certain diet shake, for example, does not mean it is either a safe or effective means to lose weight. On the other hand, when an argument relies on the expertise of a respected authority, that can be a valid reason for acting. For example, if your doctor tells you that you need to lose weight, you are likely to trust her judgment and at least *try* to shed the unwanted pounds. The key to an authoritative argument is that the person is truly an expert in the area of concern. Further, it is important that the authority is relying on correct information. If your doctor is given the wrong test results, no matter how knowledgeable or reliable she is, her conclusions are suspect.

Authority warrants are subject to tests of whether the authority is truly an expert and whether the authority has accurate information.

Questions to Ask When Evaluating Authority Warrants

- **Is the authority truly an expert in the area under discussion?**
- **Is the authority acting on reliable information?**

An example of an argument from an authority warrant is found in Figure 14.8. Based on the *grounds* that your doctor tells you to lose weight, using the *warrant* that you have confidence in the doctor's expertise, based on the *backing* of training in medical school and years of experience, almost certainly (*qualifier*) the *claim* is true that I should lose weight, unless (*rebuttal*) I can't afford a weight-loss plan and I am unable to lose weight on my own.

Halo Effect   One common fallacy associated with reasoning based on an authority warrant is called the *halo effect*. Just because you like or respect a person, you tend to believe whatever he or she says. You may have heard the term "dittoheads," used by fans of radio and TV host Rush Limbaugh. They call in to his show and say, "Mega dittos, Rush," meaning that whatever he says, they believe. However, Limbaugh has apparently misstated a number of "facts," according to a recent report by the media watchdog group, FAIR (Fairness and Accuracy in Reporting). For example, Limbaugh claimed that "if 4,000 votes . . . had gone the other way in Chicago— Richard Nixon would have been elected in 1960."[4] Yet FAIR points out that Kennedy won by a greater margin than all of Illinois' electoral votes, and

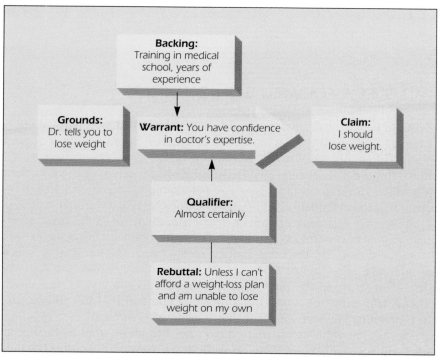

FIGURE 14.8
An argument using
an authoritative
warrant.

thus the results in Chicago could not have changed the outcome of the election. And FAIR cites Limbaugh as ignoring the overwhelming medical evidence to the contrary when he stated, "It has not been proven that nicotine is addictive."[5] Even dittoheads should check out the facts.

Ad Hominem   The reverse of the halo effect is called argument *ad hominem,* meaning an "argument against the person." This fallacy says a claim must be false because the person who said it is not credible, regardless of the argument itself. Ad hominem is often associated with name-calling. Name-calling occurs when a person or group of people are characterized by a term that is loaded with negative connotations. When a political candidate is characterized as a "bozo," "womanizer," or "wimp," these terms raise emotional feelings without providing rational grounds for rejecting the candidate. The use of negative terms for ethnic, religious, racial, and sexual groups is also a type of name-calling. Consider, for example, the use of terms such as "chick," "tomato," or "bimbo" to characterize a woman or terms such as "jock," "stud," or "hunk" to refer to a man. Sexist, racist, and bigoted language is an insidious form of name-calling that degrades entire groups of people. Just because you do not like someone or someone is called a derogatory name does not mean their arguments should be rejected out of hand. It is just as bad to reject everything Rush Limbaugh says as false as it is to assume everything he says is gospel.

FALLACIES ASSOCIATED WITH QUALIFIERS

Toulmin believes that arguers should qualify their claims. As pointed out in Chapter 13, a qualifier is an indication of the level of probability of a claim. Some arguments are virtually certain to be true, whereas others have a much lower degree of certainty. Depending on the nature of the argument, a qualifier can make a big difference. For example, in a criminal trial, the claim that the defendant is guilty must be true "beyond a reasonable doubt," a phrase that acts as the qualifier of the argument for guilt. Thus, a very high degree of certainty is required before a jury can convict someone of a criminal offense. On the other hand, in a civil case, the standard is "a preponderance of evidence." Thus, if it is more likely than not that the defendant wronged the plaintiff, the judgment should go to the plaintiff. That is why someone found not guilty in a criminal trial can still be sued in civil court. The level of proof that is required is different.

So, too, in your argumentation, you need to know what level of proof your audience will expect. Thus, as with virtually every other aspect of public speaking, the success of your reasoning depends on careful analysis of your audience. As a listener, you should also be clear about what level of proof you need before accepting a claim. Many of the fallacies of reasoning associated with qualifiers are a result of overstating or distorting the degree of certainty with which the arguer has supported his or her claim. Two common fallacies are the use of loaded language and hyperbole.

Loaded Language

Loaded language is language that has strong emotional connotations. Depending on the specific characteristics of your audience, what you might consider neutral language may in fact carry strong emotional connotations. The term "card carrying" was once associated with the phrase "card-carrying Communist." When George Bush accused Michael Dukakis of being a "card-carrying member of the ACLU," as he did in 1988, he was using loaded language for those who remembered the earlier association of "card carrying" with communism. Notice how Cassidy uses terms such as "anti-gun evangelism" and "gun prohibitionists" to characterize his opponents. Terms like evangelism and prohibition are "loaded" with connotations of extremism and closed-mindedness, thus overstating the claim against people who seek regulation, rather than outlawing, of guns.

Loaded language is a fallacy because it inflames passions rather than appealing to reason.

Hyperbole

Hyperbole is an exaggeration of a claim. Rather than properly qualifying or limiting the impact of a statement, the person engaged in hyperbole exaggerates the claim in question. For example, many weight-loss programs claim to provide a miracle discovery that melts the fat away. Anyone who has struggled with a diet knows there are no "miracles" to weight loss, no matter what the hype. Other examples of hyperbole include the use of such terms as "superstar," "greatest ever," and "mega-hit." It often seems as if it is not enough any more to be a star, to be great, or to have a mere hit. Hyperbole ends up cheapening the currency of our language, inflating claims and devaluing more moderate language.

FALLACIES ASSOCIATED WITH REBUTTALS

The rebuttal to an argument is an exception to or refutation of an argument. It too can be flawed. Fallacies of rebuttal can occur when a speaker misanalyzes an opponent's argument or sidesteps the other side of the issue completely.

Straw Person

The *straw person* fallacy occurs when someone attempts to refute a claim by misstating the argument being refuted. Rather than refuting the real argument, the other side constructs a person of straw, which is easy to knock down.

Sarah Brady favored a seven-day waiting period for the purchase of a handgun. J. Warren Cassidy's argument is based on defending "the right to keep and bear arms." But Brady never argued that there was no such right or that it should be abolished. She favored a regulation, not a "prohibition," of gun ownership. Thus, Cassidy's rebuttal attacks an argument that was never made. Be wary of rebuttals that seem too easy. It may be that the other side of the argument has been misstated just to make it easy to refute.

Ignoring the Issue

The fallacy of *ignoring the issue* occurs when the claim made by one side in an argument is ignored by the other. For example, imagine that you are speaking before a group about the effects of the depletion of the ozone layer on the environment. Skin-cancer death rates will increase, you argue. We need to change over to safer refrigerants in our cars. Suppose someone attempts to rebut your argument by saying that the government has grown too big and bureaucratic and that it is time to get rid of government waste. This rebuttal is simply not responsive to the argument you have posed. In short, the issue you have presented has been ignored, and the rebuttalist has shifted ground to another issue entirely.

THE NON SEQUITUR: AN ARGUMENT THAT DOES NOT FOLLOW

Up until now, we've looked at each component of an argument as a separate source of fallacies. Of course, you also have to look at the argument as a whole. Even if the grounds are true, the warrant believable, and so on, if the argument doesn't hang together logically, it is still fallacious. Thus, the final fallacy of reasoning we examine is the non sequitur.

A *non sequitur* is an argument that does not follow from its premises. In Toulmin's terms, there is no logical connection between the claim and the grounds and warrant used to support the claim. Consider the example of a person who called in this opinion to a local newspaper:

No wonder welfare is so popular

I'd like to thank the person who dropped the two little black lab-mix puppies off at the golf course some time in the week of Jan. 28. What irresponsible person caused others to try to find homes for these dogs? It's amazing people don't take responsibility for their actions and cause other people to. No wonder everybody's on welfare.[6]

Aside from stereotyping about people on welfare as irresponsible and hyperbolizing in claiming that "everybody's on welfare," this argument has absolutely no link between its grounds—the two dogs abandoned at the golf course—and its claim—this irresponsibility is symptomatic of the people on welfare.

We have discussed numerous fallacies in this chapter. To review them, see the box "Defects of Reasoning: The Fallacies" on page 444.

SUMMARY

Reasoning and critical thinking are important both in constructing good arguments and in listening critically to the arguments of others. Pseudo-reasoning involves arguments that may appear sound at first glance but ultimately contain a fallacy of reasoning. Argumentativeness is the trait of arguing for and against the positions taken on controversial claims. Verbal aggressiveness is the trait of attacking the self-concept of those with whom a person disagrees about controversial claims.

SPEAKING OF . . .

Defects of Reasoning: The Fallacies

ad hominem: The claim that something must be false because the person who said it is not credible, regardless of the argument itself.

arguing in a circle (begging the question): An argument that proves nothing because the claim to be proved is used as the grounds or warrant for the argument.

distorted evidence: Significant omissions or changes in the grounds of an argument that alter its original intent.

false analogy: The comparison of two different things that are not really comparable.

false dilemma: A generalization that implies there are only two choices when there are more than two.

hasty generalization: An argument that occurs when there are too few instances to support a generalization or the instances are unrepresentative of the generalization.

halo effect: The assumption that just because you like or respect a person, whatever he or she says must be true.

hyperbole: An exaggeration of a claim.

ignoring the issue: An argument made in refutation that ignores the claim made by the other side.

isolated examples: Nontypical or nonrepresentative examples that are used to prove a general claim.

loaded language: Language that has strong emotional connotations.

mistaking correlation for cause: The assumption that because one thing is the sign of another they are causally related.

misused statistics: Statistics that involve errors such as poor sampling, lack of significant differences, misuse of average, or misuse of percentages.

non sequitur: An argument that does not follow from its premises.

post hoc ergo propter hoc ("after the fact, therefore because of the fact"): The assumption that because one event preceded another, the first event must be the cause of the second event.

red herring (smoke screen): An irrelevant issue introduced into a controversy to divert attention from the real controversy.

slippery slope: The assumption that just because one event occurs, it will automatically lead to a series of undesirable events even though there is no relationship between the action and the projected events.

stereotyping: The assumption that what is considered to be true of a larger class is necessarily true of particular members of that class.

straw person: An argument made in refutation that misstates the argument being refuted. Rather than refuting the real argument, the other side constructs a person of straw, which is easy to knock down.

unsupported assertion: The absence of any argument at all.

Grounds for an argument consist of evidence supporting a claim, such as examples, facts, statistics, expert opinion, explanation, description, and narratives. There are a number of sources of fallacious grounds, including unsupported assertions, distorted evidence, isolated examples, and misused statistics.

Claims may be of fact, value, or policy. Examples of fallacies associated with claims are the red herring (or smoke screen) and arguing in a circle (begging the question), when a claim is used to prove itself.

Warrants link grounds and claims by means of generalization, comparison, cause, sign, and authority. Backing is support for the warrant and is especially important in cases in which the audience is either unfamiliar with the warrant or unconvinced of its truth. Each type of argument is subject to special tests of reasoning.

Sources of defective generalization warrants include hasty generalization, stereotyping, and false dilemmas. A common source of defective comparison warrants is the false analogy. Defective causation warrants may occur due to the post hoc ergo propter hoc and the slippery slope fallacies. A common source of defective sign warrants is mistaking correlation for cause. Common fallacies associated with authority warrants are the halo effect and the ad hominem fallacy.

Qualifiers are an indication of the level of probability of the claim. In using qualifiers, you should avoid fallacies such as loaded language and hyperbole. A rebuttal is an exception or refutation of an argument. A misguided rebuttal occurs when the argument refuted is not the real argument presented, but merely a straw person which is easy to knock down, or the issue is ignored. Finally, the non sequitur is an argument that does not follow from its premises.

Check Your Understanding: Exercises And Activities

1. Find a published argument, such as a letter to the editor, an advertisement, an editorial, or a political ad. Identify the claim being made and the grounds on which the claim is based. Is the warrant explicitly stated? If not, determine the implied warrant. What backing, if any, is offered for the warrant? Is the argument adequately qualified? Are there possible rebuttals to the argument?

2. Find an example of each of the following types of arguments in a publication: cause to effect, effect to cause, sign, comparison, establishing a generalization, applying a generalization, authority. Which of these arguments is the strongest, logically, and which is the weakest? Explain your answer in terms of the tests of reasoning outlined in this chapter.

3. Pick an advertisement from any print medium—for example, magazines, newspapers, or direct mail. In a brief paper, identify at least

three fallacies used in the advertisement. Define each fallacy in your own words. Cite the specific example of each fallacy from the ad, and explain why the example meets the definition. Finally, highlight the fallacies on a copy of the ad and attach the copy to your paper.

4. Analyze the arguments for and against gun control as presented by Sarah Brady in Chapter 13 and J. Warren Cassidy in this chapter. Which argument is logically the strongest? Which contains the most fallacies? Which do you find most persuasive?

Notes

1. Brooke Noel Moore and Richard Parker, *Critical Thinking,* 3rd ed. (Mountain View, Calif.: Mayfield, 1992), 411.

2. Dominic A. Infante, *Arguing Constructively* (Prospect Heights, Ill.: Waveland Press, 1988).

3. "Tell it to the ER," *Chico Enterprise Record,* 13 March 1992, 2A. Reprinted by permission.

4. "Facts and Fantasy," *Newsweek,* 11 July 1994, 6.

5. "Facts and Fantasy," 6.

6. "Tell it to the ER," *Chico Enterprise Record,* 16 February 1992, 2A. Reprinted by permission.

Answers to Uncritical Inference Test, "Self-Assessment" box, p. 424–425

1. ? Do you know that the "businessman" and the "owner" are one and the same?

2. ? Was there necessarily a robbery involved here? Perhaps the man was the rent collector—or the owner's son—they sometimes demand money.

3. F An easy one to keep up the test-taker's morale.

4. ? Was the owner a man?

5. ? May seem unlikely, but the story does not definitely preclude it.

6. T The story says that the owner opened the cash register.

7. ? We don't know who scooped up the contents of the cash register or that the man necessarily ran away.

8. ? The dependent clause is doubtful—the cash register may or may not have contained money.

9. ? Again, a robber?

10. ? Could the man merely have appeared at a door or a window without actually entering the store?

11. ? Stores generally keep lights on during the day.

12. ? Could not the man who appeared have been the owner?

13. F The story says that the man who appeared demanded money.

14. ? Are the businessman and the owner one and the same—or two different people? The same goes for the owner and the man who appeared.

15. ? "Dashed"? Could he not have "sped away" on roller skates or in a car? And do we know that he actually left the store? We don't even know that he entered it.

Emma Thompson's brief but eloquent thanks for her best-actress Oscar is a model for a gracious speech of acceptance.

15

Public Speaking
in Everyday Life

OBJECTIVES

After reading this chapter, you should be able to:

- Present a speech of introduction.
- Present or accept an award.
- Make a speech of commemoration.
- Make a speech to entertain.
- Be interviewed on television.

KEY CONCEPTS

eulogy   speech of introduction
speech of acceptance   speech of recognition
speech of commemoration   speech to entertain

You've been giving your attention to a turkey stuffed with sage; you are now about to consider a sage stuffed with turkey.
—William Maxwell Evarts (1818–1901), American statesman, speaking after a Thanksgiving dinner[1]

Syndicated newspaper columnist Anita Creamer has said in print what many people have no doubt thought. In response to the bumbling acceptance speeches of Academy Award winners Clint Eastwood and Al Pacino at the 1993 award ceremonies, Creamer wrote,

> Why are Americans so ill at ease in public . . . why is it so hard for us, as opposed to Europeans, to master the art of the gracious thank you speech?[2]

In making her point, Creamer went on to compare the acceptance speeches of Eastwood and Pacino with those of British actress Emma Thompson and Italian director Federico Fellini.

After being named best director, for example, Eastwood said, "This is pretty good. This is all right."[3] In contrast, Thompson's response to being named best supporting actress indicated to her audience that she had given serious thought in advance to how she would respond should she be named the winner. As she held the Oscar in her hand she said:

> Ladies and gentlemen, I really don't know how to thank the academy for this, but also for this view. It's overwhelming to see so many faces of people who have entertained me all my life. It takes my breath away.[4]

One explanation some have offered in defense of people such as Eastwood is humility. The reasoning behind the explanation is that a prepared speech of acceptance for an award tells the audience that you expected it. Thus, in the attempt to appear humble, a trait Americans admire, a speaker must respond off-the-cuff to an award or other symbol of recognition.

This explanation leaves a lot to be desired. Simply put, it is the obligation of potential honorees to show an audience that the honor justified conscious thought about what might be appropriately said. Emma Thompson's speech of acceptance said that she cared enough about the possibility of receiving the award to prepare an expression of genuine gratitude should she receive it. This attitude was again reflected in her acceptance speech at the 1996 Golden Globe awards, where she received an award for best screenplay for her adaptation of Jane Austen's *Sense and Sensibility*. In this instance, she assumed the persona of Jane Austen and presented a moving monologue in 19th-century prose that captivated her audience and millions viewing at home, while poking gentle fun at herself for purloining Austen's work.

This chapter focuses on the predictable and occasionally special situations in which you will be required to speak over the course of your everyday life. These situations include saying thank you when you've been singled out for recognition, introducing someone who is being honored or who is the principal speaker of the occasion, and speaking to commemorate an occasion of celebration or solemnity. The chapter then examines situations in which the degree of preparedness you have in regard to speaking is variable—for example, responding to the remarks of others, honoring a request to say a few words, and making a favorable impression on video. We also examine speeches specifically designed to entertain. Topics we cover include reframing your perspective about speaking in situations both everyday and special; guidelines you can use to organize your thoughts when required to speak without advance notice; speaking on special occasions; and speaking on TV.

REFRAMING: SPEAKING AS STORYTELLING

The late Senator Robert F. Kennedy was fond of paraphrasing Irish playwright George Bernard Shaw by saying, "Some people see things as they are and say: why? I dream things that never were and say: why not?"[5] This familiar quotation eloquently alludes to the importance of perspective in analyzing and responding to circumstance. This kind of behavior can be thought of in terms of reframing—revising your view of a situation or an event. Recall that the degree to which you are anxious about a speaking transaction depends on how you view it. Looking at a speech as a performance, for example, is likely to make you more anxious than looking at a speech as a natural but refined extension of your everyday communication skills.

One effective way to reframe your point of view about the kind of speaking this chapter describes is to think of it as a form of storytelling. Although you probably gave few "speeches" prior to taking this class, chances are good that you told innumerable stories. Good stories share a similar organizational sequence with good speeches. An involving story hooks an audience with its introduction, builds to a climax either humorous or dramatic, and concludes with a memorable resolution to the climax.

Rhetorical scholar Walter R. Fisher argues that storytelling is not only an effective way to involve an audience but also an effective way to share a message.[6] Former President Ronald Reagan frequently conveyed the point he was attempting to make through storytelling. Many pundits in the media, moreover, attribute much of his reputation as an effective communicator to his ability to weave an involving and convincing story.[7]

Storytelling needn't be long-winded nor overly complicated. To the contrary, many of the best stories are short and to the point. As we discussed in Chapter 7, Fisher believes effective stories or narratives share two common elements: *probability* and *fidelity.*

Probability

This property of storytelling is straightforward. Narrative probability is the internal coherence of the story. Coherence concerns the degree to which the structure of the story holds up in the eyes of an audience. Does the story make sense as told? Do the parts of the story hang together? Effective stories are logically consistent in structure, even if the content of the story requires that we suspend disbelief, as is the case with fairy tales and some science fiction.

Fidelity

This second property of effective storytelling concerns truthfulness. We are predisposed to believe stories whose message rings true with our own experience. Certainly this is true of juries when the prosecution and the defense weave their respective sides of the story in a criminal case. In his closing arguments in the O. J. Simpson trial, for example, Johnnie Cochran attempted to poke holes in the fidelity of the story that the prosecution told over the case of the trial. After the trial was over, many jurors told the press that the prosecution's case simply didn't ring true with their own experience. The prosecution failed to recognize that for many members of the jury, it was far from unthinkable that police could be motivated by racism or could plant evidence to win a case. Conversely, after the trial, many Americans found O. J. Simpson's attempts to explain his whereabouts on the night in question lacking in fidelity.

It can be helpful to approach a speech task such as thanking people or making an introduction as a form of storytelling. Audiences relate well to recognition speeches and the like when they are told as a story. Remember, though, that to be effective your speech and the story it tells must meet the tests of probability and fidelity.

IMPROMPTU SPEECHES: SPEAKING WITHOUT ADVANCE NOTICE

There will be times in your life when you will be asked to speak without specific, advance notice. Recall from Chapter 2 that such unrehearsed speeches are called impromptu. You'll be asked to make a toast or say a few words at a wedding, bar mitzvah, or christening. Or you'll be asked to defend or argue against the position of a colleague at work. Finally, you simply may be asked to explain yourself to a superior or agency to which you are accountable.

First Things First: Anticipate the Occasion

If you read Stephen J. Covey's book *The Seven Habits of Highly Effective People,* you'll learn that being unprepared isn't one of them.[8] Frankly, there are situations where the probability of your being asked to speak ranges from low to high. No one knows better than you the chances that you'll

be asked to say a few words at a social occasion or in a professional setting. Forewarned is forearmed. Thus, if there is even the slightest chance you'll be asked to speak, you should prepare in advance. Does this mean that you should write out a speech? Not really. What we are talking about here is anticipating what you might be asked to say based on the context in which you'll find yourself. This will, at the very least, enable you to mentally and visually rehearse your response. Should you not be asked to speak as you'd anticipated, you'll only be better prepared for the next time one of these occasions to speak pops up.

Making a toast at a wedding, bar mitzvah, or christening is a common form of impromptu speaking.

Guidelines for Impromptu Speaking

If you were to participate in impromptu speaking at a collegiate speech tournament, this is what would typically happen. You would be handed a slip of paper with three topics on it. The topics might be general and abstract, such as the quotation we cited from Robert F. Kennedy or an issue widely reported in the media. You would be given two minutes to prepare and five minutes to speak on the one topic you selected.

If this sounds frightening, then consider this: There may be times during your life when you don't even get two minutes to prepare, much less choose your topic from a choice of three. To assist you in adapting to such truly impromptu situations, we offer the following guidelines.

Get Organized   The thing that impresses people the most about people who speak effectively off-the-cuff is the appearance of organization. Whether you are responding to the query of an instructor or speaking to an issue being debated at work, the first thing you want to do is get organized. One of the easiest and most effective patterns for organizing an impromptu speech is to (1) introduce the point(s) you want to make, (2) expand on the point(s) you make, (3) and conclude with a statement that summarizes the point(s) made. This harks back to the "tell 'em what you're going to tell 'em, tell 'em, and then tell 'em what you told 'em" sequence introduced in Chapter 8. Consider a classroom example, in which the instructor asks, "What's your take on the effects of rap lyrics on violence?" One student responds:

> I have two points to make about the potential effects of rap on lyrics. First, the effects are exaggerated. Second, most people who think rap affects violence are clueless about modern music. So what I'm saying is they're making a mountain out of another molehill.

Notice in this example that the first sentence not only previews the points being made but also restates in modified form the question asked. The two points are made and then summarized in the final sentence. Compare this response with another hypothetical but not atypical one from a student:

> I don't know, I guess I disagree. It's just a bunch of people with nothin' better to do coming down on alternative music. They should get a life.

This second response is both disorganized and equivocal, bringing us to our second guideline.

Take a Position   Doonesbury cartoonist Gary Trudeau used a waffle as a symbol of President Bill Clinton. Few of us are favorably impressed with people who fail to take a stand, who equivocate even as they're trying to build a response to a query. When someone asks a speaker, "What's your opinion or your position?" we think the speaker is obligated to give it. On the other hand, if a speaker has not yet formulated a clear-cut opinion, an audience would much rather hear the person say, "I'm ambivalent" or "I'll need more information than I've been given," than hem and haw in response to such a query.

Use Powerful Language   Powerful language goes hand-in-hand with the first two guidelines. Organization is key to appearing powerful. We expect powerful people to not equivocate, to take a stand even if it is clearly one of neutrality. For example, sometimes a person may say simply, "That is re-

ally none of my business, it is for the people directly affected to decide for themselves." Recall that powerful language avoids the use of unnecessary qualifiers and long questions. Powerful people say such things as, "My opinion is firm" or "My experience leads me to the unequivocal belief." Powerful people do not say, "I could be wrong but I think" or "I believe it's okay, do you?" Impromptu speaking is tough enough without you undermining your authority with powerless language.

Hitchhike   It's sometimes effective to begin an impromptu message with what others already have said on the matter. This hitchhiking technique shows that you have been actively listening. It also acknowledges the contributions of others, even if you disagree with what they've said. For example, "Bill's point that this situation demands caution is well taken, but I must respectfully disagree for a couple of reasons." You also might say, "Let me summarize what's been said thus far, and then I'll add my two cents worth." Again, this kind of bridge tells your audience you are tuned in *and* organized.

Use Stories and Anecdotes   If you know a story or an anecdote that contains a lesson that is both relevant and straightforward, by all means use it as a basis for your impromptu speech. History is full of examples of stories and anecdotes about the famous and notorious. Organizational culture, moreover, often gives rise to stories about people and events that can be used to make one or more points in an impromptu speech. Some stories and anecdotes are so general they can be applied to almost any point you choose to make. The real power of Aesop's fables, for instance, is that each contains multiple lessons you can apply to life.

Invest in Reference Works   Impromptu speaking is a matter of when, not if. Thus, we recommend you purchase for your personal and permanent library at least two kinds of reference books. In addition to a standard book of quotations such as Bartlett's, look for one composed of contemporary quotes from well-known and widely recognized people. At the same time, invest in a book of anecdotes compiled from the lives of the famous and notorious. Then find and commit to memory quotes and anecdotes that can be applied generally to topics and issues you may be asked to speak about. You will find these kinds of references helpful when you're asked to speak at special occasions as well.

SPEAKING ON SPECIAL OCCASIONS

Some occasions at which we speak are, in fact, special. At such times your job will be to emphasize the special nature of the occasion in thought, word, and deed. Most of the time, you will be able to prepare and practice in advance of such situations. Other times, you may or may not be asked to "say a few words." The special occasions you can anticipate speaking at over the course of your life include: expressing thanks; introducing a speaker or honored guest; speaking in recognition of a person, group, or organization; making a commemorative speech; and speaking to entertain people.

Speech of Acceptance

A **speech of acceptance** is a speech expressing thanks for an award or honor. Let's go back to the 1993 Academy Award ceremonies and Emma Thompson's speech of acceptance. Recall that she said,

> Ladies and gentlemen, I really don't know how to thank the academy for this [holding the Oscar], but also for this view. It's overwhelming to see so many faces of people who have entertained me all my life. It takes my breath away.[9]

In connecting with her audience, Thompson combines the principles of reciprocity and liking to create a favorable impression. Not only does she thank the academy for the award, but for her view as well. In the process she tells members of the audience they have been giving something to her she can't repay: a life's worth of entertainment. Research shows that we have a tough time not liking people who like us, for example, people who sincerely flatter us. Thompson's thank-you speech, then, is a model you may want to follow in patterning your own. In the span of three sentences it lets you know that a good speech of acceptance (1) is brief, (2) is genuine, (3) reciprocates for the award or praise given, and (4) attempts to engender liking. This is not to say that all speeches of acceptance must be as brief as this speech. Thompson's thank you at the Golden Globe was much longer, yet did not exceed the patience of the audience.

Speech of Introduction

A **speech of introduction** is a speech that briefly sets the stage for an up-coming speaker. Speeches of introduction are designed to meet two objectives. The first is to enlist the audience's attention and interest. The second objective is to reinforce or induce audience perceptions of credibility. Perhaps the most widely seen speeches of introduction occur at political conventions. The party faithful are whipped into a frenzy as speaker after speaker builds up the enthusiasm for "the next president of the United States." Although you may never introduce the next president of the United States, it is likely that at some time you will be called on to introduce a speaker to an audience. Usually, the audience is favorably disposed toward the speaker or they wouldn't be there. However, sometimes a speaker is not well known and needs a buildup of credibility before the speech. In any case, a good way to look at a speech of introduction is to remember the three basic principles of introducing any speech: open with impact, connect with the audience, and focus on the upcoming presentation.

Open with Impact   Your first task as an introducer is to build enthusiasm for the main speaker. A lukewarm or trite introduction is worse than none at all. Thus, look for a way to capture the audience's attention immediately. Sometimes humor, a brief anecdote, or a moving story will fill the bill.

Connect with the Audience   Why should the audience listen to the speaker? What's in it for them? Just as you must connect with the audience in your own speeches, the same is true in a speech of introduction. What special qualifications does the speaker have? Why is the topic of special concern to the audience? Answer these questions in terms the audience can relate to if you want them to be motivated to listen. Focus on the speaker's competence and character. Even if a speaker's credibility is established, you should reinforce the perception by mentioning one or two examples that clearly emphasize competence and character. If the speaker's credibility has yet to be established, mention at least one thing that addresses the speaker's competence on the topic and one that addresses the speaker's good character.

Focus on the Upcoming Presentation   Finally, it is the introducer's task to focus the audience's attention on the upcoming presentation. Make sure you know the speaker's topic, and coordinate your introduction with his or her speech. Nothing is worse than preparing an audience to hear a speech on one topic only to have the speaker announce that the topic has been changed. There are also some general guidelines for a speech of introduction that you should follow.

Guidelines for a Speech of Introduction

- *Be brief.* The audience came to hear the speaker, not the introducer. A one- or two-minute introduction is sufficient for most speech situations. For a particularly lengthy or formal speech situation perhaps it should be longer. But in no case should your introduction exceed about 10 percent of the speaker's time (six minutes out of an hour, for example).

- *Don't steal the speaker's thunder.* While you want to prepare the audience for what is to come by focusing their attention on the topic, you should not discuss the substance of the speech topic. Again, the audience wants to hear the speaker's views on the topic, not yours. Your job is to create an appetite for the upcoming main course, not fill up the audience with hors d'oeuvres.

- *Work with the speaker in advance.* It is best to talk to the speaker or a representative about your role as introducer. Are there specific points to be stressed? Is there anything the speaker wants to avoid? Some speakers may even want to preview your introductory remarks or may provide written suggestions for you.

Speech of Recognition

The elements of a good speech of introduction apply to speeches of recognition. A **speech of recognition** is a speech presenting an award or honor to an individual. Open your recognition speech by discussing the importance of the occasion, the award being made, or the special contribution made by the honoree. Provide examples or testimony from those who know the honoree to illustrate his or her merit. Also, consider couching your speech in the form of a story about the person.

Connect with your audience. Give them a personal glimpse either from your own experience or from testimony of those who know the honoree. It is important for your audience to feel that the award is, in a sense, coming from them.

Focus on the honoree by name. Unless the name of the person is known in advance, it should be saved until the end of the recognition speech. Not only will this build suspense, audience members will start to guess at the honoree with each new bit of information you provide. Usually a recognition speech ends with something like, "And so it is my great pleasure to announce the winner of the lifetime achievement award, our own Taylor Smith!"

Speech of Commemoration

A **speech of commemoration** is a speech that calls attention to the stature of the person or people being honored, or emphasizes the significance of an occasion. There are several kinds of commemorative speeches. Some of these speeches focus on cause for celebration, for example, a national holiday or a fiftieth wedding anniversary. Remember it is the occasion or people who have given cause for celebration that should be the focus of your speech.

Another type of speech of commemoration is one given to memorialize a specific person (Martin Luther King, Jr.) or the people we associate with a special and solemn occasion (members of the armed forces on Memorial Day). Finally, a **eulogy** is a kind of commemorative speech about someone who has died that is usually given shortly after his or her death.

In many ways, a speech of commemoration is like an extended recognition speech. The honoree may even be present and asked to say a few words after the commemoration. Sometimes these speeches take a humorous form, such as a "roast." Although jokes and embarrassing incidents are recited, they are done in good fun and ultimately the honoree is praised for his or her accomplishments.

A speech of commemoration should, like any other speech, open with impact. Begin by calling attention to the stature of the person being honored or the occasion that necessitates the memorial.

Connect with the audience. What ties the audience and the person, people, and occasion together? A eulogy often recounts the deceased's common ties to the audience. Family and friends are usually present, and recounting memorable events from the life of the deceased helps everyone cope with their loss.

For the honoree, focus on the best that person has accomplished. For a retiree, it might be his or her accomplishments in the work force. For a public figure, it might be what he or she stood for. For a fallen hero, the heroic deeds that cost a life are a source of meaning.

The substance of a speech of commemoration is usually less structured than that of other speeches. Nevertheless, there should be a theme or an essential point that you want to share with the audience. For example, Ronald Reagan used the occasion of the *Challenger* disaster to reaffirm the nation's commitment to space exploration.

Close with impact. A verse of scripture might provide just the right note to close a eulogy. A familiar or inspirational line from a poem might be the right touch, as it was in Ronald Reagan's eulogy to the astronauts of the *Challenger*. The poem "High Flight" was familiar to Reagan from World War II and was included by speech writer Peggy Noonan over the objections of some staff members.[10]

Reagan's speech on the occasion of the explosion of the *Challenger* space shuttle was perhaps the most eloquent moment of his presidency.

IN THEIR OWN WORDS

Address to the Nation, January 28, 1986, by President Ronald Reagan

Ladies and gentlemen, I'd planned to speak to you tonight to report on the state of the Union, but the events of earlier today have led me to change those plans. Today is a day for mourning and remembering.

Nancy and I are pained to the core by the tragedy of the shuttle Challenger. *We know we share this pain with all of the people of our country. This is truly a national loss.*

Nineteen years ago, almost to the day, we lost three astronauts in a terrible accident on the ground. But we've never lost an astronaut in flight; we've never had a tragedy like this. And perhaps we've forgotten the courage it took for the crew of the shuttle; but they, the Challenger *Seven, were aware of the dangers, but overcame them and did their jobs brilliantly. We mourn seven heroes: Michael Smith, Dick Scobee, Judith Resnik, Ronald McNair, Ellison Onizuka, Gregory Jarvis, and Christa McAuliffe. We mourn their loss as a nation together.*

For the families of the seven, we cannot bear, as you do, the full impact of this tragedy. But we feel the loss, and we're thinking about you so very much. Your loved ones were daring and brave, and they had that special grace, that special spirit that says, "Give me a challenge and I'll meet it with joy." They had a hunger to explore the universe and discover its truths. They wished to serve, and they did. They served all of us.

We've grown used to wonders in this century. It's hard to dazzle us. But for 25 years the United States space program has been doing just that. We've grown used to the idea of space, and perhaps we forget that we've only just begun. We're still pioneers. They, the members of the Challenger *crew, were pioneers.*

And I want to say something to the schoolchildren of America who were watching the live coverage of the shuttle's take-off. I know it is hard to understand, but sometimes painful things like this happen. It's all part of the process of exploration and discovery. It's all part of taking a chance and expanding man's horizons. The future doesn't belong to the fainthearted; it belongs to the brave. The Challenger *crew was pulling us into the future, and we'll continue to follow them.*

I've always had great faith in and respect

Notice again how he uses the occasion of honoring the *Challenger* crew to reaffirm the nation's commitment to the exploration of space, while paying homage. (See the box "Address to the Nation, January 28, 1986, by President Ronald Reagan.")

Speeches to Entertain[11]

Sometimes known as after-dinner speaking because it often is given following a meal, a speech to entertain is more than just a string of jokes or a comedy monologue. A **speech to entertain** is speech that makes its *for our space program, and what happened today does nothing to diminish it. We don't hide our space program. We don't keep secrets and cover things up. We do it all up front and in public. That's the way freedom is, and we wouldn't change it for a minute.*

We'll continue our quest in space. There will be more shuttle flights and more shuttle crews and, yes, more volunteers, more civilians, more teachers in space. Nothing ends here; our hopes and our journeys continue.

I want to add that I wish I could talk to every man and woman who works for NASA or who worked on this mission and tell them: "Your dedication and professionalism have moved and impressed us for decades. And we know of your anguish. We share it."

There's a coincidence today. On this day 390 years ago, the great explorer Sir Francis Drake died aboard ship off the coast of Panama. In his lifetime the great frontiers were the oceans, and an historian later said, "He lived by the sea, died on it, and was buried in it." Well, today we can say of the Challenger *crew: Their dedication was, like Drake's, complete.*

The crew of the space shuttle

Challenger *honored us by the manner in which they lived their lives. We will never forget them, nor the last time we saw them, this morning, as they prepared for their journey and waved goodbye and "slipped the surly bonds of earth" to "touch the face of God."*

SOURCE: Reprinted from *Weekly Compilation of Presidential Documents,* Vol. 22, No. 5, February 3, 1986, 104–5.

point through the use of humor. Like all speeches, a speech to entertain should have a clear focus. Of course, many speeches contain humor as an element. What makes the speech to entertain different is that its primary purpose is to bring laughter to the audience, not to persuade or inform them, though that may occur along the way. A speech meant to entertain is ideally suited to the storytelling format of speaking. This type of speech also is every bit as taxing as persuasive or informative speaking.

Selecting a Topic   The first task is to select a topic for your speech. The best place to begin is with yourself. Have you had experiences that, at least looking back, were funny? A good topic needs to have the potential to develop into a full-blown speech, not just one or two good punch lines. It needs to be something your audience can relate to. Many of the funniest speeches are about the frustrations of everyday life. Avoid the temptation to adopt the latest *Saturday Night Live* routine. Work from your own experiences and from experiences shared by those in your audience.

Consider your audience's expectations for the speech. You probably don't want to repeat stories you know your audience has heard before. If you are speaking to a group of lawyers, you probably can count on them having heard every lawyer joke known to humankind. Pick something that can connect you, assuming you are not a lawyer, to them. For example, there are few people today who have not shared the frustrations of dealing with computers that seem to know just when to crash and make your life miserable.

You must, of course, be sensitive to an audience's diversity in developing and delivering a speech to entertain. We live in an era in which a racial or ethnic joke that would have been accepted a few years ago can end a career, or lead to the demise of a relationship as was the case with Whoopi Goldberg and Ted Danson. It wasn't that long ago, you may recall, that Danson, with Goldberg's approval, donned black face make-up to speak at a celebrity roast of Goldberg. The speech turned out to be an embarrassing disaster for both Danson and Goldberg, one we assume they would like all of us to permanently forget.

In developing the content of your speech to entertain, brainstorming is a useful technique. Recall from Chapter 2 that brainstorming involves a group of people getting together and rapidly firing off ideas. Someone keeps a list. No criticism or evaluation of the ideas is permitted—that comes later. The key to brainstorming is to hitchhike one idea on another. The wilder and crazier the ideas, at this point, the better. You can always tone them down later.

Once you have a list of ideas for jokes, write each one on a card or slip of paper. The next step is to sort them out and organize them into a speech.

Organization   A speech to entertain should resemble any other good speech in organization: Open with impact, connect with your audience, and provide a clear focus in your introduction. It is very important to capture your audience's attention almost immediately. Unless you are already a highly skilled and entertaining speaker, this is not the time for a three-minute story leading to one punch line. So, try to get a laugh in the first sentence or two. Sometimes just an outrageous statement will do this. The quotation at the beginning of this chapter is a good example of just such an opening.

Another example of an attention-getting opening came when Ed Rollins, former campaign manager for Ronald Reagan and briefly for Ross Perot, spoke at a university commencement. He began by announcing that he had graduated "summa cum lucky" from the university at which he was speaking. His comment immediately broke the ice by poking fun at the formal graduation ceremony in a self-deprecating way. It also provided an instant connection of the speaker with the audience, as he reminded them that he too had graduated from their university.

While it is important to focus your audience's attention on the topic of your speech, a preview of points is rare in an entertainment speech. Part of humor is surprise, and telegraphing your jokes in a preview will undermine the audience's surprise.

The body of your speech can be organized in a number of ways. A simple chronological or narrative form works well when telling a story or describing a series of events. A topical arrangement allows you to organize your speech around major topics.

In concluding a speech to entertain, you normally would not summarize your points. You would, however, want to close with impact or, as the old adage goes, "Leave 'em laughing."

Sources of Humor   What are some sources of humor? We hesitate to try to define what is funny. After all, everyone's sense of humor is different, and what is funny to one person will leave another completely stone-faced. Some people love David Letterman and hate Jay Leno, others the reverse, and some people enjoy them both.

Nevertheless, a few traditional sources of humor deserve mention:

- *Exaggeration.* Exaggeration is a well-tested source of humor. Wits from Mark Twain to Johnny Carson thrived on exaggeration. Every time Johnny's audience shouted back, "How hot was it?" they were asking for an exaggerated answer.

- *Incongruity.* Something that doesn't fit in seems funny. Woody Allen once wore tennis shoes with a tuxedo (semiformal attire?). We frequently poke fun at politicians whose words and deeds don't match. When the State of California was sending out IOUs instead of checks, Jay Leno commented that the latest Southern California earthquake wasn't really an earthquake, just Governor Pete Wilson bouncing more checks.

- *Attacking authority.* The attack on authority has been a staple of humor since anyone can remember. Will Rogers made fun of Congress, Jay Leno makes fun of politicians, and David Letterman makes fun of everybody, himself included!

- *Puns.* Use at your own risk!

- *Sarcasm.* Used with care, this can be a good source of humor (particularly when directed against sources of authority). But be careful you don't create sympathy for your victim. Sarcasm that is too edgy or biting can seem mean-spirited and bitter rather than funny.

- *Irony.* This is sometimes a powerful source of humor, which can also make a serious point. The fact that Ronald Reagan spent thousands of dollars of taxpayers' money to fly back to his ranch so that he could chop his own wood to save money on his heating bill is both funny and serious.

- *The rule of three.* Milton Berle once claimed that he could make an audience laugh at anything, if he preceded it with two funny jokes. Try it. Once you have people laughing, they often will continue to laugh even at a line that isn't funny.

- *Self-deprecating humor.* Often the safest humor is that directed at yourself. Not only do you avoid alienating anyone, you show that you are a regular person. When George Bush said he would "try to keep my charisma in check," he was acknowledging his own shortcomings and showing a strain of humility.

- *Delivery.* Humor depends on direct contact and immediacy with your audience. Thus, use of a manuscript or conspicuous notes will destroy the spontaneity of the experience. Even if you have memorized your speech, however, it is important that it sounds fresh and spontaneous.

  Use a lively and animated manner in presenting your speech. Timing in comedy is everything. Knowing when to pause, what word to punch, and the right tone of voice to use are not things you can learn from reading a book. Only by trying out your speech with friends and experimenting with different ways of delivering the same line can you tell what delivery is best.

Not everyone is comfortable with speaking to entertain. But done well and tastefully, it can be an enjoyable experience for both the speaker and the audience.

SPEAKING ON TELEVISION

Although you might not plan on being a television newscaster or celebrity, many people in ordinary life find themselves confronted with a television interview at some time or another. Not just business executives need to be able to handle a television interview, so do supervisors and line personnel who may be on the scene of a news-breaking event. Unless you expect to be on television and have been given a list of questions you will be asked in advance, speaking on TV is a lot like impromptu speaking. You want to appear organized, firm rather than indecisive, and use powerful language.

Speaking on TV also demands nonverbal immediacy behaviors, so you'll want to look back to Chapter 10 for a discussion of effective delivery tips.

One question that always arises when being interviewed on television is where to look. Do you look at the camera or at the interviewer or from one to the other? One suggestion comes from Dorothy Sarnoff, who provides communication training to corporate executives. She suggests: "Focus on the left eye of the interviewer, then the right eye—and back to the left. Not a windshield-wiper effect, but slowly so your own eyes don't look dead."[12] Some other suggestions for talking on television are included in the box "Chatting It Up on TV, by Paul Burnham Finney" on pages 466–467.

In conclusion, the best advice we can give is to be prepared and stick to your theme. Interviews are frequently videotaped and then edited for a sound bite. You want to make sure that whatever is left on the cutting-room floor, your essential message will reach the viewers.

One of the authors, Michael Scott, is shown here interviewing Al Roker on CNBC television.

SPEAKING OF . . .

Chatting It Up on TV, by Paul Burnham Finney

Many executives turn into TV regulars and routinely go out on cross-country tours to promote a new product or service. But few of the veterans take their camera assignments casually.

"Steal the show," says Mariana Field Hoppin, president of MFH Travel Marketing Ltd. and a longtime spokeswoman for Avis Europe. "When you walk into the studio, win over the camera crew and interviewer, and you've got them in the palm of your hands."

It's important to do that. "The public is taking the lazy way out—getting their information on the tube," as one corporate communications director puts it.

"Smart executives have to be prepared for surprises on the road," he goes on to say. When the Tylenol-tampering scare struck Johnson & Johnson, C.E.O. James E. Burke signed up for a crash course at the Executive Television Workshop before facing the public.

Screen test: Among the tips ETW feeds its corporate students:

- Get a good fix on the questions you'll be asked by contacting the TV or radio station. (Ask around if the direct approach doesn't work.)

- Tell your story, or somebody else will—and not always correctly.

- Memorize the basic points you want to make, and keep them uppermost in your mind.

- Stick to solid colors in dress—no loud patterns allowed. And wear contacts rather than glasses, if possible.

- Women: don't show up in a short skirt that rides above the knees.

SUMMARY

Public speaking is a fact of life. Over the course of yours, you can expect to speak on a number of predictable and sometimes special occasions. One way to approach these special speaking occasions is to treat them as opportunities for storytelling. Good stories are organized in similar fashion to speeches and are characterized by probability and fidelity.

Storytelling can be used effectively in a variety of types of speaking. One type is impromptu speaking, speeches given without advance preparation. Effective impromptu speeches demand clear organization, taking a stand, and using powerful language.

Other types of speeches that can benefit from storytelling include speeches of acceptance, speeches of introduction, speeches of recognition, speeches of commemoration, and speeches to entertain an audience.

- Park yourself in the front third of the chair. You'll look more alert and interested that way.
- Glance at 3-by-5 card notes during commercials or station breaks—never when on camera.
- Say it all in 45 seconds when answering an interviewer. "Short, clear answers," as TV commentator David Brinkley advises.
- Use anecdotes and "sparklers" to brighten your delivery.
- Don't repeat a negative statement— it only lends credence to it.

Digestible bits: "We stress the importance of establishing a conversational tone," says Executive Television Workshop marketing director Carol Heimann. "Executives get very techy in the way they talk. A reporter is only a conduit to the public. Break your explanations into digestible bits. Try to act as though you're in a living room, chatting with someone."

Ultimately, the impression you leave with your audience counts more than your words. Some 90% of what they remember is your "voice" and "nonverbal communications," according to studies. In short, body language matters as much as your thoughts.

"One of your biggest assets," says Heimann, "is a smile. It can change a million opinions. You can disarm your audience. If you're relaxed, you'll relax the people who are watching."

SOURCE: Article appeared first in *Newsweek's* 1990 Special Ad Section, "Management Digest." Reprinted by permission.

Although it once was a rarity, speaking on television is increasingly common. Rules for effective speaking on video include looking at the interviewer rather than the camera unless speaking directly to the camera and preparing in advance when possible for the questions you'll be asked.

Check Your Understanding: Exercises and Activities

1. Your best friend is getting married and you will be asked to say a few words at the wedding. Prepare your toast. Do the same thing for a wedding anniversary, a baptism, and a bar mitzvah or bat mitzvah.

2. Think of a special award for one of your classmates. Write a speech of recognition for presenting the award.

3. Track down several quotations and anecdotes that are general enough

to be used as an opening or a closing for a speech of acceptance or a speech of recognition. Three sources to which you can turn are:

Clifton Fadiman, ed., *The Little Brown Book of Anecdotes* (Boston: Little, Brown, 1985).

Edmund Fuller, ed., *2,500 Anecdotes for All Occasions* (New York: Avenel Books, 1980).

James B. Simpson, ed., *Simpson's Contemporary Quotations: The Most Notable Quotes Since 1950* (Boston: Houghton Mifflin, 1988).

4. A speech of nomination can either make or break the nominee's chances for being elected to office. Speeches of nomination are more common than you may think. Social clubs such as fraternities and sororities, business and professional associations such as the Soroptomists, Rotary, or local Bar are all examples. On a separate sheet of paper, list and explain what you think are the essential characteristics of a speech of nomination. Then see if you can find a published example of a speech of nomination that conforms to your criteria. Note conforming examples on a copy of the speech with a highlighter and share your analysis with classmates.

Notes

1. Edmund Fuller, ed. *2,500 Anecdotes for All Occasions* (New York: Avenel Books, 1980), 135.

2. Anita Creamer, "One More Word on the Oscars," *Sacramento Bee*, 3 April 1993, Scene, 1.

3. Creamer, "One More Word," 1.

4. Creamer, "One More Word," 1.

5. Theodore H. White, *The Making of the President 1968* (New York: Atheneum, 1969), 171. Shaw's original lines appear in his play *Back to Methuselah*, Part I, Act I. The Serpent in the Garden of Eden says to Eve, "You see things; and you say 'Why?' But I dream things that never were; and I say 'Why not?'" See George Bernard Shaw, *The Complete Plays of Bernard Shaw* (London: Odhams Press Limited, 1934), 857.

6. Walter R. Fisher, *Human Communication as Narration* (Columbia: University of South Carolina Press, 1987).

7. Peggy Noonan, *What I Saw at the Revolution: A Political Life in the Reagan Era* (New York: Random House, 1990).

8. Stephen J. Covey, *The Seven Habits of Highly Effective People* (New York: Fireside Books/Simon & Shuster, 1989).

9. Creamer, "One More Word," 1.

10. Noonan, *What I Saw at the Revolution,* 257–58.

11. Adapted from Jack Perella and Steven R. Brydon, "Speaking to Entertain," in *Intercollegiate Forensics: A Participants Handbook,* ed. T. C. Winebrenner, 42–46. ©1992 Northern California Forensics Association.

12. Article appeared first in *Newsweek's* 1990 Special Ad Section, "Management Digest," Paul Burnham Finney, "The Business of Communicating," 16.

APPENDIX A
Student Speeches

These student speeches were transcribed from videotape. Because speaking extemporaneously often leads to unintended errors or misspoken words, we have edited and corrected the transcripts for you to read.

This speech, prepared by Sally Garber, concerns avoiding the extremes of yo-yo dieting, advocating a healthy lifestyle with proper diet and nutrition, as well as healthy exercise. An outline of the speech appears in Chapter 2, page 39. If you have access to the videotape accompanying this book, you will find the speech in segment 3. As you read this speech, pay particular attention to the following:

- How effectively does the speaker gain her audience's attention and connect with their concerns? Could the speech have a stronger opening that would have greater impact?

- Notice how the speaker previews the points of her speech. Does the preview accurately reflect the content of the speech?

- Is the speech well signposted? That is, can you tell when one point is transitioning to the next?

- Evaluate the use of evidence in the speech. How convincing is her support for her claims about the need for nutrition and exercise in a weight-loss program?

- Is the speech adequately summarized at the end?

- Does the close of the speech make an impact that an audience is likely to remember?

Dieting and Physical Activity by Sally Garber

How many of you took a good look at yourself in the mirror this morning? Did you like what you saw? Statistics show that most Americans would say no. According to *University of California Berkeley Wellness Letter,* 1995, more than one third of American women and nearly one quarter of men are trying to lose weight at any given time. As a society we are not happy with our looks and are spending billions of dollars a year trying to achieve an ideal body. Yet the percentage of overweight Americans continues to increase. In this struggle lies the problem. Our methods behind our motives are destructive; dieting is destructive.

Today we will take a look at the issue of restrictive dieting, which is known as the restriction of calories to directly promote weight loss. We will explore some recent trends in dieting. We will explore why people turn to dieting, why dieting does not work, and why it is claimed unhealthy and destructive. After discussing the issue, I will give you some ideas on what you can do to achieve a healthy body without dieting.

Every day, Americans struggle with their weight, resulting in desperate attempts to be beautiful. "The obese now comprise one-third of the American population up from just one-quarter 15 years ago—with the trend cutting across race, age and gender. Overall, 58 million Americans are overweight, with adults weighing 8 pounds more on average than they did a decade ago," according to *Tufts University Diet and Nutrition Letter,* October 1994. So what can be done, one might ask? Well, it all depends on who you ask. Pro-dieters would simply say, "Go on a diet." Well, anyone who has struggled with weight loss can tell you that it's not that easy.

It sure sounds great, though, according to some recent diet ads for Slim Fast diet program—I can have a shake for lunch, a shake for breakfast, and a sensible dinner, and I'm on my way to a new me!

Anti-dieters will refute this in saying that this way of thinking is where problems arise. According to *Nutrition Today,* April 1993, "The treatments [for obesity] based on caloric restriction, or dieting, had only temporary effects. . . . [M]ost people treated with restrictive diets will regain their lost weight, "meaning diets are ineffective.

Is there a nondieting approach? How do we convince people that dieting is counterproductive to their goal of weight loss? Well, there is a nondieting approach and it works, but we must first examine why diets fail.

The best way to convince people that it works and that it is ultimately the healthiest way to achieve your goal is to simply give them the facts. So let's explore these facts. Why are people turning to diets, and why are their weight-loss attempts failing?

Since about the beginning of this century, Western civilization has placed extreme emphasis on being thin. This has resulted in discrimination against obese, who have come to be judged on their appearance rather than their character. This has led to unhappy, unloved people who feel that the only way to be happy is to lose weight. The tragedy for the obese occurs when the desperation to be thin is combined with the thought that diets are effective.

The continuing popularity of dieting can be explained by the emotional cycle which obese people seem to go through when struggling with weight loss. They begin by feeling fat and unloved. Wanting to be loved and happy, they feel that they must lose weight. Through many efforts they realize that their goals are unrealistic and eventually lose self-control, regaining any weight lost. This leaves them feeling like failures and further damaged; the cycle continues until something is done.

These beliefs that they fail because they lack willpower are rooted in the thought that they are failures. This is not only a falsehood, but it also promotes devastating, bad behavior.

At the beginning of a caloric restrictive diet, moods are elevated. Dieters feel good about themselves; they're motivated to get moving and exercise; weight is lost. This is where the misconception that diets work comes into play. The weight was lost, so the diet worked, right? Wrong? Soon after weight is lost the restriction of calories leads to uncontrollable cravings for high-fat foods. These cravings lead to binging and purging, starvation, and other extremely serious eating disorders. The resulting effect is exactly opposite of what the dieter intended to achieve. These facts have led many to believe that restrictive dieting has more negative than positive effects. So, let's explore the alternatives we have to achieve a healthier lifestyle and make better choices.

First, we must begin by knowing that successful weight control is a lifelong commitment, not a series of crash diets. To increase chances of success you must remember to set realistic goals that build on slow, steady success. "Gradual changes in diet and physical activity which build on success are expected to have more lasting lifestyle changes," states *Nutrition Today,* June 1995. Second, it is necessary to remember that eating should be a pleasurable experience. "[E]veryone should use eating as a positive opportunity to relax as they nourish themselves," states *Tufts University Diet and Nutrition Letter,* October, 1994. Along with enjoying your meals, wise food choices are equally important. We have seen that deprivation is not the answer—good healthy choices are. It is necessary to reduce daily fat intake in order to achieve a healthier body. Eating less fat will, one, reduce your risk for heart disease, chronic fatigue, and diabetes, as well as other major health problems. Second, eating less fat will increase your energy levels, motivating you to get moving, and to exercise, which brings me to our last requirement, exercise. That's right, you must move.

In order to achieve a healthy body, you must combine physical activity with a healthy eating plan. Weight loss will not happen overnight; and it will not happen depriving yourselves of your favorite foods; but it cannot happen until you exercise. Healthy weight loss can occur only when your muscles receive oxygen—you must breath, you must move. The smallest amount of activity proves beneficial. Begin by doing work in the yard or by taking a walk with a friend or pet, or taking the stairs instead of the elevator. "Periods as short as 8 to 10 minutes that total 30 minutes by the end of the day are adequate," according to *Nutrition Today,* June 1995.

The idea of "no pain, no gain," is dead. Low-impact exercise, something as simple as walking or riding your bike instead of driving to school, is the answer. But it must coincide with a healthy eating plan that includes choosing lots of fruits, vegetables, and grains, and definitely not deprivation.

There are no more excuses; given these guidelines, it is not impossible to reach your goal of weight loss. It is no secret that those who exercise and eat well regularly have more chance for survival, need less medical care, have more energy, and live life to the fullest. Believe it or not, living life to the fullest and achieving a healthy lifestyle can be an enjoyable process. It's not just about losing weight, it's a matter of choices. It's about feeling good about yourself. It's about leading a healthy balanced life. And it's about setting and reaching goals in all areas of your life.

So I leave you with this: enjoy your food, enjoy your exercise, but most importantly, enjoy your life. Thank you.

This speech, prepared by a former student, Deidra Dukes, concerns the problems created by secondhand tobacco smoke. An outline of the speech appears in Chapter 8, page 248, and if you have access to the videotape accompanying this book, you will find the speech in segment 12. As you read this speech, pay particular attention to the following:

- How does Deidra open and focus her speech?
- How does Deidra attempt to connect with her audience?
- What are the three main points she makes in this speech?
- How well does she summarize and close her speech?
- What purpose do you think Deidra had in presenting this speech? Was she seeking only to inform her audience or to persuade them as well?
- If you have access to the videotape, how would you compare the experience of reading this speech with seeing and hearing it?

The Right to Breathe by Deidra Dukes

How many of you have ever returned home from a night of innocent fun at your favorite club to find that your hair, skin, and clothes smelled as though you were a stand-in for the Marlboro Man?

As much as I enjoy going out to have a good time, I find myself doing less of both these days because I simply can't tolerate breathing other people's cigarette smoke.

Smoking in public places is an issue that's being debated across the country. On one side of the issue are people who feel that they should have the right to smoke wherever they want. On the other hand, I believe that smoking should be banned in public places.

To put it bluntly, people who smoke in public places are robbing us of the clean air we deserve to breathe. As former Surgeon General C. Everett Koop said: "The right of smokers to smoke ends where their behavior affects the health and well-being of others."

And, as if that weren't enough, *Newsweek* reported in June of 1990 that smokers may be killing us as well. For example, the same article cited a study demonstrating that as many as 50,000 of us may die this year due to secondhand smoke.

Put simply, that means there is not a single person in this room who is truly immune from the health dangers of smoking. Each time a smoker lights up in a restaurant, at a club, or in another public gathering, they are threatening our health.

Given this framework, I'd like to share three ideas with you that not only shed light on the problem, but also show why this health problem is something that we all need to deal with.

First, secondhand smoke contains harmful chemicals; second, it's a threat to public health; and third, it should be banned from public places.

First, let's consider the three harmful components of cigarette smoke:

First, there's carbon monoxide. Now this is the same substance that can cause death from automobile exhaust in a closed garage. Second, there's nicotine. Now nicotine is the addictive drug in cigarette smoke. And third, let's look at tar. It consists of 4,000 chemicals, 43 of which are known to cause cancer. And that's according to the Department of Health and Human Services.

These harmful substances don't just enter the smoker's lungs, and that brings me to my second point: Secondhand smoke is a health threat to the public.

According to the Environmental Protection Agency, secondhand smoke causes 3,800 lung cancer deaths each year. Dr. Stanton Glantz, a San Francisco heart researcher, has concluded that 30,000 to 40,000 heart disease deaths occur each year due to secondhand smoke. And overall, Dr. Glantz concludes that 50,000 deaths are attributable each year to second-hand smoke.

To put it another way, for every 8 people who will die this year from the direct effects of smoking, 1 person will die from secondhand smoke. Today alone, about 137 innocent bystanders will die from the effect of a smoker's actions.

We can't ignore this health problem any longer when a simple solution is available, which brings me to my third and final point: Smoking should be banned in public places.

Airlines have already banned smoking on all domestic flights of six hours or less. Workplaces also should be smoke-free. Many communities and companies already ban indoor smoking—this should be universally adopted. Finally, restaurants and public buildings should be smoke-free. Nonsmoking sections are often a joke, since there is no separate air-circulation system. The smoke keeps wafting right there at you anyway.

To summarize, today I have shared three main ideas with you: First, the chemicals in cigarette smoke make it a health hazard; second, secondhand smoke is a major cause of lung cancer and heart disease; third, banning smoking in public places would save thousands of lives a year.

If people choose to smoke, that's their business. But when they choose to ignore the dictates of common decency, forcing me to listen to their rattling coughs, or when I must breathe the foul consequence of their smoking, it becomes my problem and yours, too.

Smokers are constantly crying about their rights. Smoking in closed public spaces is not an issue of rights. It's an issue of health. And the last thing on the mind of the American Tobacco Industry when it spends millions of dollars lobbying is my health and yours.

This speech was delivered by Jonathan Studebaker, who is profiled in Chapter 2, page 29. If you have access to the videotape accompanying this text, you will find his speech in segment 12. In reading this speech, try to answer the following questions:

- How well does Jonathan open, focus, and connect with his audience?
- How does this speech of introduction differ from a more formal speech in terms of structure and use of supporting materials, such as evidence?
- Comment on Jonathan's use of rhetorical questions throughout his speech.
- What do you think is Jonathan's purpose in presenting this speech? In what ways is Jonathan using this opportunity to speak as an opinion leader on the issue of how we perceive persons with disabilities?
- If you have access to the videotape of this speech, compare the experience of seeing and hearing Jonathan with reading his speech.

Speech of Self-Introduction: Who Am I? by Jonathan Studebaker

Good morning!

Who am I? Why am I here? Seems like I've heard that before. For myself, I've been asked these and other questions. Two of them I'd like to answer for you today.

I've been asked, "Are you a midget? What do you have? What's your disability? Why are you small? But I'd really like people to ask me, "What do you like to do? What's your favorite color?" So what I'll try to do is answer both of these today.

I'm a nice guy. Don't worry, I won't bite. I like to do many things, except water ski. I've gone to school. I've gone to elementary school, high school, and I graduated from Cal State Chico.

A lot of people ask, "So why are you here?" Well, I'm here because I want to educate others. I've coached football at Chico State University. I was the kicking coach for three years. And out of those three years I had two kickers make first team all-conference. So how do you coach football? You do it by simply telling people what to do. Well, how do you do that? You do it by doing a lot of the things that we all do—by studying, by reading, by listening to others. And that's what I've done throughout my life, and that is what has made me who I am.

Like I said, I'm a nice person. I'm cheerful, I'm energetic. Okay, so I have a disability. I was born with osteogenesis imperfecta, a disease which causes my bones to be fragile. Have you ever accidentally dropped a glass on the floor? What happens? It breaks. Well, my bones kind of break like glass, which is why I tell people, when you carry me, treat me like your best crystal.

I'm happy about being who I am. I wouldn't change a thing. I've done a lot of things in my life. Like I said, I've coached football, I graduated from college, things that people wouldn't think a person with my condition would do.

So who am I? Well, I'm Jonathan Studebaker, Jonathan Peter Charles Studebaker. Why such a long name? Well, my middle name is Charles, which came later. And Charles is kind of a symbol of a lot of things. My dad used to call me chicken when I was younger. And then it evolved to chicken Charles, and now Charles. Now, some of you might be offended by being called chicken. But, you know what, it doesn't matter to me. I like being who I am. I've been put here to educate others, not by teaching others, but by just being myself.

Thank you.

This speech was presented by Jennie Rees, a student in a Chico State public speaking class in 1992. If you have access to the videotape accompanying this text, you will find the speech in segment 12. As you read this speech, attempt to answer the following questions:

- How effectively does Jennie open, focus, and connect her speech?

- Is the organizational pattern of the speech clear from the preview, and are the points clearly developed throughout the speech?

- Although this is a speech to inform, to what extend does Jennie also attempt to entertain her audience?

- Comment on Jennie's choice of topic. How well does it meet the criteria for topic choice discussed in the text?

- Jennie concludes her speech by singing a portion of the "Mickey Mouse Club" theme song. Does this seem to be a good way of closing her speech with impact?

- If you have access to the videotape, compare reading this speech with seeing and hearing it. To what extent do the visual aids in her speech enhance the presentation in comparison to reading the text? Compare the effectiveness of her use of humor in written and oral form. What is the difference between reading the words to her conclusion and actually hearing and seeing how she delivers them?

Informative Speech: Mickey: A Changing Image by Jennie Rees

"'Know thyself,' a wise old Greek once said. Know thyself. Now what does this mean, boys and girls? It means to be who you are. Don't try to be Sally or Johnny or Fred next door. Just be yourself. God gives to each of us a special talent. God wants some of us to be scientists, some of us doctors, and firemen, and even trapeze artists. And he gives us these special talents to become these things, provided we work to develop them. And we must work, boys and girls. So know thyself. Learn to understand your talents and then work to develop them. That is the only way to be truly happy."

These are the famous words from Jimmy Dodd. He was an adult Mouseketeer and appeared on the "Mickey Mouse Club" show in the 1950s. He called these words of advice his Doddisms.

Today I'm going to be talking about the animated life and character of Mickey Mouse from his first appearance in *Steamboat Willie* to how he impacts society today. We can all look back to our childhood years and remember one of the most celebrated fictitious animated characters of all time.

I'll tell you how, when, and who created the Mouse; his first films; the evolutionary changes in his character; and his place in society today.

Let's begin with how it all started and who's responsible for creating such a legend. His name is Mr. Walt Disney. He is the man behind the mouse. The idea to use a rodent as a cartoon character came to him on a train ride from New York to Los Angeles. He kept hearing the train saying, "chug-chug-chug-mouse, chug-chug-chug-mouse." And every time the whistle blew it would say "Mouuuuse," and that's where it all started.

His original name was to be Mortimer Mouse. But this didn't go over too well with his wife and the people of the studios. So, he finally decided on Mickey, and then he began to design him. They designed him using a circle for his head and oblong circles for his nose and snout. They also drew circles for his ears and drew them in such a way that they appeared to look the same any way Mickey turned his head. They gave him a pear-shaped body with pipe-stem legs, and stuffed them in big, oversized shoes, making him look like a little kid wearing his father's shoes. Then they began working on his first movie, and for the first time incorporated sound with animation.

Now that he has been born, let's take a look at how he became a movie star and took on the personality we all know and love. I'll start with the production of *Steamboat Willie* and move on to the changes in his character.

Steamboat Willie was Disney's first experimentation with his new-found character. After weeks of trying to find a voice for Mickey, and failing to do so, Walt Disney decided to use his own voice. *Steamboat Willie* was finished and released late in 1928. Needless to say, it was a huge success.

His next films that were to follow were *Wild Ways, Mad Dog,* and *The Klondike Kid.* And it was in these films that his gang was introduced. First there was Minnie, Mickey's love, then on to Pluto, Mickey's faithful dog, and later to come was Donald, a very ambitious duck, who usually ended up getting into a lot of trouble. And finally there was Goofy, Mickey's best friend. Well, there's been a lot of speculations as to what Goofy really is. If you can recall the scene in *Stand By Me,* when the boys are arguing about it around the fire, I don't think it was ever quite settled.

Now, on to Mickey's physical appearance, and the changes he has gone through, and how the public has viewed him.

Here we see him in 1928, and he is in black and white and is wearing no gloves. In 1931 they have changed his eyes and given him different shoes. In 1936 he's wearing different shoes again, and they have changed his eyes once more. In 1940 they changed his eyes once again and have taken away his tail. This was probably Mickey's most famous year, because this was the production of *Fantasia.* In 1941 he looks more of the same. And in 1947 they have given him eyebrows and brought back the tail after there was much controversy about people saying that he looked more like a human than mouse without a tail. In 1955 he looks more of the same, but you can tell he's changing with the times and the clothes he's wearing. And here he is today, more of a modern Mickey.

Time magazine described Mickey best in their December 27, 1954, issue, saying, "He was a skinny little squeaker, with match-stick legs, shoe-button eyes, and a long pointy nose."

We've all seen Mickey Mouse change throughout the years, and his popularity has made him a household name. Now in the 1990s we have seen the Mickey mania spread across the world. He's represented all over the world in theme parks, toys, memorabilia, and now a new chain of Disney stores that has opened. Disney has created the biggest and best theme parks in the whole world. The first Disneyland opened in Los Angeles in 1954 after years of hard work and expert planning. Walt Disney was quoted on his opening day. He said, "Disneyland will never be finished as long as there is imagination left in this world." Then came Disneyworld in Florida, another Disneyland in Tokyo, Japan, and a few years ago they opened Disney-MGM Studios in Florida. But one of the biggest celebrations in Disney history was the opening of EuroDisney in France in 1991. This opened many a door of opportunity for the Disney corporation to do their business in Europe. Mickey memorabilia is sold everywhere in everything from key chains to stuffed animals. And a chain of Disney stores opened eight years ago where genuine Mickey Mouse artifacts can be sold.

Let's look back on what we've learned today about our beloved rodent friend. We've learned that Mickey was invented by one of the most creative and imaginative people of our time, Mr. Walt Disney. His film debut in *Steamboat Willie* was the beginning of a very prosperous career and has made him the king of animated short film. He's gone from a steamboat captain to a sorcerer's apprentice, and along the way has made us laugh and earned a place in the hearts of millions of Americans. He's evolved physically each year resembling more of the times, and emotionally with his admiration for Minnie and his concern for his gang. Today the legend lives on in his films, theme parks, toys, and most of all, he is the universal object of innocence. So never forget this famous song: M-I-C—See you real soon. K-E-Y—Why, because we like you. M-O-U-S-E.

APPENDIX B
Public Speeches

This speech was delivered by Mary Fisher at the Republican National convention in Houston, Texas, on Wednesday, August 19, 1992. As founder of the Family AIDS Network, and a person who is HIV-positive, Fisher addressed a convention that was largely socially conservative about issues such as AIDS. As you read this speech, attempt to answer these questions:

- How well did Mary Fisher adapt to the rhetorical situation she faced as a speaker at the Republican National Convention?
- To what audience or audiences was this speech addressed?
- What do you see as Fisher's purpose or purposes in presenting this speech? What stages of opinion leadership do you see this speech addressing?
- How do you feel about the issue of AIDS after reading this speech? Have you changed your beliefs, attitudes, values, or behavioral intentions?

Remarks, August 19, 1992, by Mary Fisher[1]

Thank you. Thank you.

Less than three months ago at Platform Hearings in Salt Lake City, I asked the Republican Party to lift the shroud of silence which has been draped over the issue of HIV and AIDS. I have come tonight to bring our silence to an end. I bear a message of challenge, not self-congratulation. I want your attention, not your applause.

I would never have asked to be HIV-positive, but I believe that in all things there is a purpose; and I stand before you and before the nation gladly. The reality of AIDS is brutally clear. Two hundred thousand Americans are dead or dying. A million more are infected. Worldwide, 40 million, 60 million, or 100 million infections will be counted in the coming few years. But despite science and research, White House meetings,

---

[1]This text is from The Official Report of the Proceedings of the Thirty-Fifth Republican National Convention, published by the Republican National Committee.

and congressional hearings; despite good intentions and bold initiatives, campaign slogans and hopeful promises, it is—despite it all—the epidemic which is winning tonight.

In the context of an election year, I ask you, here in this great hall, or listening in the quiet of your home, to recognize that the AIDS virus is not a political creature. It does not care whether you are Democratic or Republican; it does not ask whether you are black or white, male or female, gay or straight, young or old. Tonight, I represent an AIDS community whose members have been reluctantly drafted from every segment of American society.

Though I am white and a mother, I am one with a black infant struggling with tubes in a Philadelphia hospital.

Though I am female and contracted this disease in marriage and enjoy the warm support of my family, I am one with the lonely gay man sheltering a flickering candle from the cold wind of his family's rejection.

This is not a distant threat. It is a present danger. The rate of infection is increasing fastest among women and children. Largely unknown a decade ago, AIDS is the third leading killer of young adult Americans today. But it won't be third for long, because unlike other diseases, this one travels. Adolescents don't give each other cancer or heart disease because they believe they are in love, but HIV is different; and we have helped it along. We have killed each other with our ignorance, our prejudice, and our silence.

We may take refuge in our stereotypes, but we cannot hide there long, because HIV asks only one thing of those it attacks. Are you human? And this is the right question. Are you human? Because people with HIV have not entered some alien state of being. They are human. They have not earned cruelty, and they do not deserve meanness. They don't benefit from being isolated or treated as outcasts. Each of them is exactly what God made—a person, not evil, deserving of our judgment; not victims, longing for our pity—people, ready for support and worthy of compassion. (Applause.)

My call to you, my Party, is to take a public stand, no less compassionate than that of the President and Mrs. Bush. They have embraced me and my family in memorable ways. In the place of judgment, they have shown affection. In difficult moments, they have raised our spirits. In the darkest hours, I have seen them reaching out not only to me, but also to my parents, armed with that stunning grief and special grace that comes only to parents who have themselves leaned too long over the bedside of a dying child.

With the president's leadership, much good has been done. Much of the good has gone unheralded, and as the president has insisted, much remains to be done. But we do the president's cause no good if we praise the American family but ignore a virus that destroys it. (Applause.)

We must be consistent if we are to be believed. We cannot love justice and ignore prejudice, love our children and fear to teach them. Whatever our role as parent or policymaker, we must act as eloquently as we speak—else we have no integrity.

My call to the nation is a plea for awareness. If you believe you are safe, you are in danger. Because I was not hemophiliac, I was not at risk. Because I was not gay, I was not at risk. Because I did not inject drugs, I was not at risk.

My father has devoted much of his lifetime to guarding against another holocaust. He is part of the generation who heard Pastor Nemoeller come out of the Nazi death camps to say, "They came after the Jews and I was not a Jew, so, I did not protest. They came after the trade unionists, and I was not a trade unionist, so, I did not protest. Then they came after the Roman Catholics, and I was not a Roman Catholic, so, I did not protest. Then they came after me, and there was no one left to protest." (Applause.)

The lesson history teaches is this: If you believe you are safe, you are at risk. If you do not see this killer stalking your children, look again. There is no family or community, no race or religion, no place left in America that is safe. Until we genuinely embrace this message, we are a nation at risk. Tonight, HIV marches resolutely to AIDS in more than a million American homes. Littering its pathway with the bodies of the young men, young women, young parents, and young children. One of those families is mine. If it is true that HIV inevitably turns to AIDS, then my children will inevitably turn to orphans.

My family has been a rock of support. My 84-year-old father, who has pursued the healing of nations, will not accept the premise that he cannot heal his daughter. My mother refuses to be broken. She still calls at midnight to tell wonderful jokes that make me laugh. Sisters and friends, and my brother Phillip, whose birthday is today, all have helped carry me over the hardest places. I am blessed, richly and deeply blessed, to have such a family. (Applause.)

But not all of you have been so blessed. You are HIV-positive, but dare not say it. You have lost loved ones, but you dare not whisper the word AIDS—you weep silently. You grieve alone. I have a message for you. It is not you who should feel shame. It is we, we who tolerate ignorance and practice prejudice, we who have taught you to fear. We must lift our shroud of silence, making it safe for you to reach out for compassion. It is our task to seek safety for our children, not in quiet denial but in effective action.

Some day our children will be grown. My son Max, now 4, will take the measure of his mother; my son Zachary, now 2, will sort through his memories. I may not be here to hear their judgments, but I know already what I hope they are. I want my children to know that their mother was not a victim. She was a messenger. I do not want them to think, as I once did, that courage is the absence of fear. I want them to know that courage is the strength to act wisely when we are most afraid. I want them to have the courage to step forward when called by their nation or their party and give leadership, no matter what the personal cost. I ask no more of you than I ask of myself or my children. To the millions of you who are grieving, who are frightened, who have suffered the ravages of AIDS firsthand—have courage and you will find support. To the millions who are strong, I issue the plea—set aside prejudice and politics to make room for compassion and sound policy. (Applause.)

To my children, I make this pledge: "I will not give in, Zachary, because I draw my courage from you. Your silly giggle gives me hope; your gentle prayers give me strength; and you, my child, give me reason to say to America, 'You are at risk.' And I will not rest, Max, until I have done all I can to make your world safe. I will seek a place where intimacy is not the prelude to suffering. I will not hurry to leave you, my children, but when I go, I pray that you will not suffer shame on my account." To all within the sound of my voice, I appeal: "Learn with me the lessons of history and of grace, so my children will not be afraid to say the word AIDS when I am gone. Then, their children and yours may not need to whisper it at all." God bless the children, God bless us all, and good night.

This speech was delivered by President William Jefferson Clinton on November 27, 1995, as he spoke from the Oval Office to announce that he was committing troops to the peace-keeping mission in Bosnia. As you read this speech, ask yourself:

- What was the rhetorical situation faced by Clinton? Does he adequately explain his goals and the urgency of sending troops to meet them? Does he adapt to an audience of Americans for whom Bosnia was a remote and unfamiliar place? Did the fact that he had not himself served in the military constitute a constraint for him in sending U.S. troops into harm's way?

- Consider the language used in the speech. Do his descriptions of the situation in Bosnia bring the suffering of the Bosnian people to life for American audiences?

- Apply the tests of critical thinking to your reading of this speech. What claims does Clinton make, and how well does he back them up with evidence? Are there fallacies that you find in his argument? If you were to speak in opposition to his policy, what points would you make in refutation?

President's Statement on Bosnian Peace-Keeping Mission, November 27, 1995, by William Jefferson Clinton[2]

Good evening. Last week, the warring factions in Bosnia reached a peace agreement, as a result of our efforts in Dayton, Ohio, and the support of our European and Russian partners. Tonight, I want to speak with you about implementing the Bosnian peace agreement, and why our values and interests as Americans require that we participate.

Let me say at the outset, America's role will not be about fighting a war. It will be about helping the people of Bosnia to secure their own peace agreement. Our mission will be limited, focused and under the command of an American general.

In fulfilling this mission, we will have the chance to help stop the killing of innocent civilians, especially children; and at the same time, to bring stability to Central Europe, a region of the world that is vital to our national interests. It is the right thing to do.

From our birth, America has always been more than just a place. America has embodied an idea that has become the ideal for billions of people throughout the world. Our founders said it best: America is about life, liberty, and the pursuit of happiness.

In this century especially, America has done more than simply stand for these ideals. We have acted on them and sacrificed for them. Our people fought two world wars so that freedom could triumph over tyranny. After World War I, we pulled back from the world, leaving a vacuum that was filled by the forces of hatred. After World War II, we continued to lead the world. We made the commitments that kept the peace, that helped to spread democracy, that created unparalleled prosperity, and that brought victory in the Cold War.

Today, because of our dedication, America's ideals—liberty, democracy and peace—are more and more the aspirations of people everywhere in the world. It is the power of our ideas, even more than our size, our wealth and our military might, that makes America a uniquely trusted nation.

With the Cold War over, some people now question the need for our continued active leadership in the world. They believe that, much like after World War I, America can now step back from the responsibilities of leadership. They argue that to be secure we need only to keep our own borders safe and that the time has come now to leave to others the hard work of leadership beyond our borders. I strongly disagree.

[2]This transcript was obtained electronically from The White House, Office of the Press Secretary, November 27, 1995 [http://docs.whitehouse.gov/white-house-publications/1995/11/1995-11-27-presidents-statement-on-bosnian-peace-keeping-mission.text].

As the Cold War gives way to the global village, our leadership is needed more than ever because problems that start beyond our borders can quickly become problems within them. We're all vulnerable to the organized forces of intolerance and destruction; terrorism; ethnic, religious and regional rivalries; the spread of organized crime and weapons of mass destruction and drug trafficking. Just as surely as fascism and communism, these forces also threaten freedom and democracy, peace and prosperity. And they, too, demand American leadership.

But nowhere has the argument for our leadership been more clearly justified than in the struggle to stop or prevent war and civil violence. From Iraq to Haiti, from South Africa to Korea, from the Middle East to Northern Island, we have stood up for peace and freedom because it's in our interest to do so and because it is the right thing to do.

Now, that doesn't mean we can solve every problem. My duty as president is to match the demands for American leadership to our strategic interest and to our ability to make a difference. America cannot and must not be the world's policeman. We cannot stop all war for all time; but we can stop some wars. We cannot save all women and all children; but we can save many of them. We can't do everything; but we must do what we can.

There are times and places where our leadership can mean the difference between peace and war, and where we can defend our fundamental values as a people and serve our most basic, strategic interests. My fellow Americans, in this new era there are still times when America and America alone can and should make the difference for peace.

The terrible war in Bosnia is such a case. Nowhere today is the need for American leadership more stark or more immediate than in Bosnia. For nearly four years a terrible war has torn Bosnia apart. Horrors we prayed had been banished from Europe forever have been seared into our minds again. Skeletal prisoners caged behind barbed-wire fences; women and girls raped as a tool of war; defenseless men and boys shot down into mass graves, evoking visions of World War II concentration camps; and endless lines of refugees marching toward a future of despair.

When I took office, some were urging immediate intervention in the conflict. I decided that American ground troops should not fight a war in Bosnia because the United States could not force peace on Bosnia's warring ethnic groups, the Serbs, Croats, and Muslims. Instead, America has worked with our European allies in searching for peace, stopping the war from spreading, and easing the suffering of the Bosnian people.

We imposed tough economic sanctions on Serbia. We used our air power to conduct the longest humanitarian airlift in history, and to enforce a no-fly zone that took the war out of the skies. We helped to make peace between two of the three warring parties, the Muslims and the Croats. But as the months of war turned into years, it became clear that Europe alone could not end the conflict.

This summer, Bosnian Serb shelling once again turned Bosnia's playgrounds and marketplaces into killing fields. In response, the United States led NATO's heavy and continuous air strikes, many of them flown by skilled and brave American pilots. Those air strikes, together with the renewed determination of our European partners and the Bosnian and Croat gains on the battlefield, convinced the Serbs, finally, to start thinking about making peace.

At the same time, the United States initiated an intensive diplomatic effort that forged a Bosnia-wide cease-fire and got the parties to agree to the basic principles of peace. Three dedicated American diplomats—Bob Frazier, Joe Kruzel and Nelson Drew—lost their lives in that effort. Tonight we remember their sacrifice and that of their families. And we will never forget their exceptional service to our nation.

Finally, just three weeks ago, the Muslims, Croats and Serbs came to Dayton, Ohio, in America's heartland, to negotiate a settlement. There, exhausted by war, they made a commitment to peace. They agreed to put down their guns; to preserve Bosnia as a single state; to investigate and prosecute war criminals; to protect the human rights of all citizens; to try to build a peaceful, democratic future. And they asked for America's help as they implement this peace agreement.

America has a responsibility to answer that request, to help to turn this moment of hope into an enduring reality. To do that, troops from our country and around the world would go into Bosnia to give them the confidence and support they need to implement their peace plan. I refuse to send American troops to fight a war in Bosnia, but I believe we must help to secure the Bosnian peace.

I want you to know tonight what is at stake, exactly what our troops will be asked to accomplish, and why we must carry out our responsibility to help implement the peace agreement. Implementing the agreement in Bosnia can end the terrible suffering of the people—the warfare, the mass executions, the ethnic cleansing, the campaigns of rape and terror. Let us never forget a quarter of a million men, women and children have been shelled, shot and tortured to death. Two million people, half of the population, were forced from their homes and into a miserable life as refugees. And these faceless numbers hide millions of real personal tragedies. For each of the war's victims was a mother or daughter, a father or son, a brother or sister.

Now the war is over. American leadership created the chance to build a peace and stop the suffering. Securing peace in Bosnia will also help to build a free and stable Europe. Bosnia lies at the very heart of Europe, next-door to many of its fragile new democracies and some of our closest allies. Generations of Americans have understood that Europe's freedom and Europe's stability is vital to our own national security. That's why we fought two wars in Europe. That's why we launched the Marshall Plan to restore Europe. That's why we created NATO and waged the Cold War.

And that's why we must help the nations of Europe to end their worst nightmare since World War II, now.

The only force capable of getting this job done is NATO, the powerful, military alliance of democracies that has guaranteed our security for half a century now. And as NATO's leader and the primary broker of the peace agreement, the United States must be an essential part of the mission. If we're not there, NATO will not be there. The peace will collapse. The war will reignite. The slaughter of innocents will begin again. A conflict that already has claimed so many victims could spread like poison throughout the region, eat away at Europe's stability and erode our partnership with our European allies.

And America's commitment to leadership will be questioned if we refuse to participate in implementing a peace agreement we brokered right here in the United States, especially since the Presidents of Bosnia, Croatia and Serbia all asked us to participate and all pledged their best efforts to the security of our troops.

When America's partnerships are weak and our leadership is in doubt, it undermines our ability to secure our interests and to convince others to work with us. If we do maintain our partnerships and our leadership, we need not act alone. As we saw in the Gulf War and in Haiti, many other nations who share our goals will also share our burdens. But when America does not lead, the consequences can be very grave, not only for others, but eventually for us as well.

As I speak to you, NATO is completing its planning for IFOR, an international force for peace in Bosnia of about 60,000 troops. Already, more than 25 other nations, including our major NATO allies, have pledged to take part. They will contribute about two-thirds of the total implementation force, some 40,000 troops. The United States would contribute the rest, about 20,000 soldiers.

Later this week, the final NATO plan will be submitted to me for review and approval. Let me make clear what I expect it to include, and what it must include, for me to give final approval to the participation of our Armed Forces.

First, the mission will be precisely defined with clear, realistic goals that can be achieved in a definite period of time. Our troops will make sure that each side withdraws its forces behind the front lines and keeps them there. They will maintain the cease-fire to prevent the war from accidentally starting again. These efforts, in turn, will help to create a secure environment, so that the people of Bosnia can return to their homes, vote in free elections and begin to rebuild their lives. Our Joint Chiefs of Staff have concluded that this mission should and will take about one year.

Second, the risks to our troops will be minimized. American troops will take their orders from the American general who commands NATO. They will be heavily armed and thoroughly trained. By making an overwhelming show of force, they will lessen the need to use force. But unlike the U.N. forces, they will have the authority to respond immediately, and the training and the equipment to respond with overwhelming force to any threat to their own safety or any violations of the military provisions of the peace agreement.

If the NATO plan meets with my approval I will immediately send it to Congress and request its support. I will also authorize the participation of a small number of American troops in a NATO advance mission that will lay the groundwork for IFOR, starting sometime next week. They will establish headquarters and set up the sophisticated communication systems that must be in place before NATO can send in its troops, tanks and trucks to Bosnia.

The implementation force itself would begin deploying in Bosnia in the days following the formal signature of the peace agreement in mid-December. The international community will help to implement arms control provisions of the agreement so that future hostilities are less likely and armaments are limited, while the world community, the United States and others, will also make sure that the Bosnian Federation has the means to defend itself once IFOR withdraws. IFOR will not be a part of this effort.

Civilian agencies from around the world will begin a separate program of humanitarian relief and reconstruction, principally paid for by our European allies and other interested countries. This effort is also absolutely essential to making the peace endure.

It will bring the people of Bosnia the food, shelter, clothing and medicine so many have been denied for so long. It will help them to rebuild— to rebuild their roads and schools, their power plants and hospitals, their factories and shops. It will reunite children with their parents and families with their homes. It will allow the Bosnians freely to choose their own leaders. It will give all the people of Bosnia a much greater stake in peace than war, so that peace takes on a life and a logic of its own.

In Bosnia we can and will succeed because our mission is clear and limited, and our troops are strong and very well-prepared. But, my fellow Americans, no deployment of American troops is risk-free, and this one may well involve casualties. There may be accidents in the field, or incidents with people who have not given up their hatred. I will take every measure possible to minimize these risks, but we must be prepared for that possibility.

As President my most difficult duty is to put the men and women who volunteer to serve our nation in harm's way when our interests and values demand it. I assume full responsibility for any harm that may come to them. But anyone contemplating any action that would endanger our troops should know this: America protects its own. Anyone— anyone—who takes on our troops will suffer the consequences. We will fight fire with fire—and then some.

After so much bloodshed and loss, after so many outrageous acts of inhuman brutality, it will take an extraordinary effort of will for the people of Bosnia to pull themselves from their past and start building a future of peace. But with our leadership and the commitment of our allies, the people of Bosnia can have the chance to decide their future in peace. They have a chance to remind the world that just a few short years ago the mosques and churches of Sarajevo were a shining symbol of multiethnic tolerance; that Bosnia once found unity in its diversity. Indeed, the cemetery in the center of the city was just a few short years ago a magnificent stadium which hosted the Olympics, our universal symbol of peace and harmony. Bosnia can be that kind of place again. We must not turn our backs on Bosnia now.

And so I ask all Americans, and I ask every member of Congress, Democrat and Republican alike, to make the choice for peace. In the choice between peace and war, America must choose peace.

My fellow Americans, I ask you to think just for a moment about this century that is drawing to a close and the new one that will soon begin. Because previous generations of Americans stood up for freedom and because we continue to do so, the American people are more secure and more prosperous. And all around the world, more people than ever before live in freedom. More people than ever before are treated with dignity. More people than ever before can hope to build a better life. That is what America's leadership is all about.

We know that these are the blessings of freedom. And America has always been freedom's greatest champion. If we continue to do everything we can to share these blessings with people around the world, if we continue to be leaders for peace, then the next century can be the greatest time our nation has ever known.

A few weeks ago, I was privileged to spend some time with His Holiness, Pope John Paul II, when he came to America. At the very end of our meeting, the Pope looked at me and said, "I have lived through most of this century. I remember that it began with a war in Sarajevo. Mr. President, you must not let it end with a war in Sarajevo."

In Bosnia, this terrible war has challenged our interests and troubled our souls. Thankfully, we can do something about it. I say again, our mission will be clear, limited and achievable. The people of Bosnia, our NATO allies, and people all around the world are now looking to America for leadership. So let us lead. That is our responsibility as Americans.

Goodnight and God bless America.

Glossary

abstract A summary of an article or a report.

active listening Listening that involves conscious and responsive participation in the communication transaction.

ad hominem The claim that something must be false because the person who said it is not credible, regardless of the argument itself.

anxiety Feelings of fear and uncertainty usually accompanied by physical symptoms such as butterflies in the stomach, perspiring, and unsteadiness.

appreciative listening Listening that involves obtaining sensory stimulation or enjoyment from others.

arguing in a circle (begging the question) An argument that proves nothing because the claim to be proved is used as the grounds or warrant for the argument.

argumentativeness The trait of arguing for and against the positions taken on controversial claims.

attitude A learned predisposition to respond in a consistently favorable or unfavorable manner with respect to a given object.

audience The individuals who share and listen to a public speech.

audience diversity The cultural, demographic, and individual characteristics that differ among audience members.

audio aids Presentational aids that use sound only, such as tape recordings.

audiovisual aids Presentational aids that combine sound and sight, such as films, videotapes, filmstrips, and slide/tape presentations.

authority warrant Reasoning in which the claim is believed because of the authority of the source.

backing Support for the warrant.

bar chart A chart that uses bars or columns to represent various quantities.

behavior The skill component of learning; the ability to do something with the knowledge acquired.

behavioral intention A person's subjective belief that he or she will engage in a specific behavior.

belief An assertion about the properties or characteristics of an object.

Boolean operators Terms, such as *and, or,* and *not,* used to narrow or broaden a computerized search of two or more related terms.

brainstorming A creative process used for generating a large number of ideas.

canons of rhetoric Classic laws of invention, arrangement, style, delivery, and memory, refined by the Romans.

categorical imperative Immanuel Kant's ethical principle that one should act only in a way that one would will to be a universal law.

categorical pattern A pattern of organization based on natural divisions in the subject matter.

causal pattern A pattern of organization that moves from cause to effect or from effect to cause.

causal warrant An argument that claims a cause will produce or has produced an effect.

CD-ROM Compact disc–read only memory, used for storage and retrieval of data.

channel The physical medium through which communication occurs.

chat lines Real-time discussions with other computer users on topics of common interest.

claim A conclusion that persuasive speakers want their audience to reach as a result of their speech.

cognition The purely mental component of learning.

comparison (analogy) warrant A statement that two cases that are similar in some known respects are also similar in some unknown respects.

compatibility The perception that a message is consistent with existing belief systems.

competence-enhancing language Words that emphasize rather than undermine audience perceptions of your competence.

comprehensibility The perception that a message is not too difficult or complex to understand.

comprehension The act of understanding what has been communicated.

comprehensive listening Listening that is targeted at understanding.

connotative meanings The subjective meanings of words, often with a strong emotional, personal, and subjective component.

constraint A limitation on one's choices in a rhetorical situation.

constructive self-talk The use of positive coping statements instead of negative self-talk.

content (of messages) The essential meaning of what a speaker wants to convey.

context Information that surrounds an event and contributes to the meaning of that event.

coping skills Mental and physical techniques used to control arousal and anxiety in the course of speaking in public.

credibility The degree to which your audience trusts and believes in you.

critical listening Listening for the purpose of making reasoned judgment about speakers and the credibility of their messages.

critical thinking The process of making sound inferences based on accurate evidence and valid reasoning.

cross cue-checking Gauging what a person says verbally against the nonverbal behaviors that make up metacommunication.

cultural diversity Differences among people in terms of language, beliefs, and customs.

cultural relativism The notion that the criteria for ethical behavior in one culture should not necessarily be applied to other cultures.

culture A learned system of language, beliefs, and customs with which specific people identify.

decoding The process by which a code is translated back into ideas.

deficiency needs Basic human needs, which must be satisfied before higher-order needs can be met. They include needs for food, water, air, physical safety, belongingness and love, and self-esteem and social-esteem.

delivery The nonverbal behaviors by which a speaker conveys his or her message to an audience.

demographic diversity Differences among people in terms of demographics.

demographics Basic and vital data regarding any population.

denotative meanings Those meanings of words generally agreed on and which are found in the dictionary.

description A word picture of something.

discriminative listening Listening that distinguishes auditory and/or visual stimuli.

distorted evidence Significant omissions or changes in the grounds of an argument that alter its original intent.

elaboration likelihood model A model of persuasion designed to explain why audience members will use an elaborated thinking process in some situations and not in others.

e-mail Electronic mail; a message sent electronically from one computer, over the network, to one or more other computers.

emblem Nonverbal behavior that can be directly translated into words and phrases and may replace them.

encoding The process by which ideas are translated into a code that can be understood by the receivers.

environment Our physical surroundings as we speak and the physical distance separating us from our audience.

ethical relativism The philosophy based on the belief that there are no universal ethical principles.

ethics A system of principles of right and wrong that govern human conduct.

ethos The combination of competence and character of a speaker.

eulogy A kind of commemorative speech about someone who has died that is usually given shortly after his or her death.

example A specific instance that represents some larger class.

expert opinion A quotation from someone with special credentials in the subject matter.

explanation An account, an interpretation, or a meaning given to something.

extemporaneous delivery A mode of presentation that combines careful preparation with spontaneous speaking. The speaker generally uses brief notes rather than a full manuscript or an outline.

extended narrative A pattern of organization in which the entire body of the speech is the telling of a story.

fact Something that is verifiable as true.

fallacy An argument in which the reasons advanced for a claim fail to warrant the acceptance of that claim.

false analogy The comparison of two different things that are not really comparable.

false dilemma A generalization that implies there are only two choices when there are more than two.

feedback Audience member responses, both verbal and nonverbal, to a speaker.

first-order data Evidence based on personal experience.

flip charts A series of drawings, charts, or graphs, usually attached at the top by a binding and supported on an easel.

flow chart A chart that uses boxes and arrows to represent the relationship of steps in a process.

formal outline A detailed outline used in speech preparation, but not, in most cases, in actual presentation.

ganas A desire to succeed regardless of the odds against it.

generalization warrant A statement that either establishes a general rule or principle or applies an established rule or principle to a specific case.

general purpose The primary function of a speech. The three commonly agreed upon general purposes are to inform, to persuade, and to entertain.

good reasons Statements, based on moral principles, offered in support of propositions concerning what we should believe or how we should act.

goodwill   The perception by the audience that a speaker cares about their needs and concerns.

grounds   Evidence a speaker offers in support of a claim.

growth needs   Higher-order human needs, which can be satisfied only after deficiency needs have been met. They include self-actualization (the process of fully realizing one's potential), knowledge and understanding, and aesthetic needs.

halo effect   The assumption that just because you like or respect a person, whatever he or she says must be true.

hasty generalization   An argument that occurs when there are too few instances to support a generalization or the instances are unrepresentative of the generalization.

hyperbole   An exaggeration of a claim.

ignoring the issue   An argument made in refutation that ignores the claim made by the other side.

illustrators   Nonverbal behaviors that accompany speech and "show" what is being talked about.

impromptu delivery   A spontaneous, unrehearsed mode of presenting a speech.

inclusive language   Language that helps people believe that they not only have a stake in matters of societal importance but also have power in this regard.

incremental goals   Those steps you must complete to accomplish your long-term goal.

index   A listing of sources of information, usually in journals and magazines, alphabetically by topic.

inference   The process of moving from ground, via a warrant, to a claim.

informative speaking   The process by which an audience gains new information from a speaker.

interaction   An exchange of messages between two or more people that has clear-cut steps with a beginning and an end.

Internet   A collection of computer networks connecting computers around the world.

invention   The creative process by which the substance of a speech is generated.

isolated examples   Nontypical or nonrepresentative examples that are used to prove a general claim.

key term   A word or phrase used in library catalogs and indexes to identify a subject.

language intensity   The degree to which words and phrases deviate from neutral.

learning   The acquisition of new information.

linear   Moving in one direction, from cause to effect.

line graph   A graph in which numerical data are shown as a series of points connected by a line; often used to show changes over time.

linguistic relativity hypothesis   The idea that what we perceive is limited by the language in which we think and speak.

listening   The process of receiving, attending to, and assigning meaning to aural as well as visual and tactile stimuli.

loaded language   Language that has strong emotional connotations.

logos   The proof a speaker offers to an audience through the words of his or her message.

long-term goals   Those ends that you can hope to achieve only over an extended period of time.

main points   The key ideas that support the thesis of a speech.

manuscript delivery A mode of presentation that involves writing out the speech completely and reading it to the audience.

marginalizing language Language that diminishes people's importance and makes them appear to be less powerful, less significant, and less worthwhile than they are.

memorized delivery A mode of presentation in which the speech is written out and committed to memory before being presented to the audience without the use of notes.

message The meaning produced by communicators.

meta-communication The message about the message; generally conveyed nonverbally.

mistaking correlation for cause The assumption that because one thing is the sign of another they are causally related.

misused statistics Statistics that involve errors such as poor sampling, lack of significant differences, misuse of average, or misuse of percentages.

Monroe's motivated sequence A five-step organizational scheme, developed by speech professor Alan Monroe, including (1) attention, (2) need, (3) satisfaction, (4) visualization, and (5) action.

narrative fidelity The degree to which a narrative rings true to a real-life experience.

narrative probability The internal coherence or believability of a narrative.

narratives Extended stories that are fully developed, with characters, scene, action, and plot.

negative self-talk A self-defeating pattern of intrapersonal communication, including self-criticizing, self-pressuring, and catastrophizing statements.

non-sequitur An argument that does not follow from its premises.

nonverbal behavior A wordless system of communicating that also is continuous, uses multiple channels simultaneously, and is spontaneous.

novelty The quality of being new and stimulating.

observability The degree to which information can be seen.

online catalog A computerized listing of library holdings.

online service A commercially available way to connect to the Internet.

opinion leader A person who influences others to adopt innovative ideas, products, or processes.

organizational chart A chart that represents the structure of an organization, using boxes and lines to convey hierarchy and lines of authority.

overhead transparency A plastic sheet that can be drawn on or used in a photocopier to produce an image to be projected on a screen for an audience to see.

pathos The emotional states in an audience that a speaker can arouse and use to achieve persuasive goals.

perception The process by which we give meaning to our experiences.

physiological arousal The physical changes that occur when a person is aroused, such as increased pulse, greater alertness, and more energy.

pie chart A circular chart that divides a whole into several parts, each represented by a slice of the circle proportional to its share of the whole.

pinpoint concentration Listening that focuses on specific details.

plagiarism Stealing the ideas of others and presenting them as your own.

post hoc ergo propter hoc ("after the fact, therefore because of the fact") The assumption that because one event preceded another, the first event must be the cause of the second event.

presentational aids Visual, audio, and audiovisual devices can add an important dimension to a speech.

preview A forecast of the main points of a speech.

proactive delivery Delivery in which the speaker takes the initiative and anticipates and controls for as many variables as possible, rather than merely reacting to them.

problem-solution pattern A pattern of organization that analyzes a problem in terms of (1) harm, (2) significance, and (3) cause, and proposes a solution that is (1) described, (2) feasible, and (3) advantageous.

pseudoreasoning An argument that appears sound at first glance but contains a fallacy of reasoning that renders it unsound.

qualifier An indication of the level of probability.

rebuttal An exception to or a refutation of an argument.

red herring (smoke screen) An irrelevant issue introduced into a controversy to divert attention from the real controversy.

refutational pattern A pattern of organization that involves (1) stating the argument to be refuted, (2) stating the objection to the argument, (3) proving the objection to the argument, and (4) summarizing the impact of the refutation.

regulators Gestures that influence the amount and type of feedback received from the audience.

relational component (of messages) The collective impact of the verbal and nonverbal components of a message as it is conveyed.

relative advantage The perception that a message is beneficial.

research The process of gathering supporting materials for a speech.

retention The act of storing what was communicated in either short- or long-term memory.

rhetorical question A question that the audience isn't expected to answer out loud.

rhetorical situation A natural context of persons, events, objects, relations, and an exigence (goal) which strongly invites utterance.

second-order data Evidence based on expert testimony.

selective attention The fact that we make a conscious choice to focus on some people and some messages, rather than others.

selective perception The tendency to ascribe meaning to a message that corresponds to our predispositions.

self-adapting behaviors Distracting touching behaviors that speakers engage in unconsciously.

self-talk (sometimes referred to as intrapersonal communication) Communicating silently to oneself.

sensorial involvement A process that involves listening with all the senses, not simply the sense of hearing.

sexist language Language that stereotypes gender roles, such as *housewife* and *fireman*.

short-term goals Those ends you can accomplish in the near future.

signposts Transitional statements that bridge your main points.

sign warrant Reasoning in which the presence of an observed phenomenon is used to indicate the presence of an unobserved phenomenon.

simultaneity The quality of occurring at the same time.

situational ethics The philosophy that there are overriding ethical maxims, but that sometimes it is necessary to set them aside in particular situations to fulfill a higher law or principle.

slippery slope The assumption that just because one event occurs, it will automatically lead to a series of undesirable events, even though there is no relationship between the action and the projected events.

source credibility The audience's perception of the believability of the speaker.

sources and receivers Speakers and audience members.

spatial pattern A pattern of organization based on physical space or geography.

speaker's notes Brief notes with key words, usually written on cards, used when you are presenting a speech.

specific purpose The goal or objective you hope to achieve in speaking to a particular audience.

speech anxiety Feelings of discomfort that people experience in the course of speaking in public.

speech transaction The simultaneous exchange that occurs between public speakers and their audience.

speech of acceptance A speech expressing thanks for an award or honor.

speech of commemoration A speech that calls attention to the stature of the person or people being honored, or emphasizes the significance of an occasion.

speech to entertain A speech that makes its point through the use of humor.

speech of introduction A speech that briefly sets the stage for an upcoming speaker.

speech of recognition A speech presenting an award or honor to an individual.

statistics Numerical data, such as percentages, ratios, and averages, that are presented in a meaningful way.

stereotyping The assumption that what is considered to be true of a larger class is necessarily true of particular members of that class.

straw person An argument made in refutation that misstates the argument being refuted. Rather than refuting the real argument the other side constructs a person of straw, which is easy to knock down.

subpoint An idea that supports a main point.

supporting point An idea that supports a subpoint.

symbol Something that stands for or suggests something else by reason of relationship or association.

therapeutic listening Listening that helps someone talk through a problem.

thesis statement A statement that focuses your audience's attention on the central point of your speech.

third-order data Evidence based on facts and statistics.

time pattern A pattern of organization based on chronology or a sequence of events.

totalizing language Language that defines a people exclusively on the basis of a single attribute, such as race, ethnicity, biological sex, or ability.

transaction Simultaneous exchange of messages between two or more people.

trialability The opportunity to experiment with an idea, a product, or a practice without penalty.

trustworthiness The perception by the audience that they can rely on a speaker's word.

usenet groups Electronic "newsletter" to which subscribers can contribute.

universalism The philosophy that there are ethical standards that apply to all situations regardless of the individual, group, or culture.

unsupported assertion The absence of any argument at all.

utilitarianism The philosophy based on the principle that the aim of any action should be to provide the greatest amount of happiness for the greatest number of people.

values   More general than attitudes, enduring beliefs that hold that some ways of behaving and some goals are preferable to others.

verbal aggressiveness   The trait of attacking the self-concept of those with whom a person disagrees about controversial claims.

verbal immediacy   The use of language that promotes the perception of closeness between speaker and audience.

verbal qualifiers   Words and phrases that erode the impact of what you say in a speech.

visual aids   Presentational aids that convey a message visually.

warrant   The connection between grounds and claim.

web browser   A program that allows the user to search for and reach World Wide Web sites from his or her own computer.

wide-band concentration   Listening that focuses on patterns rather than details.

World Wide Web   A collection of thousands of sites called "home pages" available on the Internet.

zone of interaction   The area in which speakers can easily make eye contact with audience members.

Index

Credits